INTERNATIONAL LAW ON THE LEFT

Against expectations that the turn away from state socialism would initiate a turn away from Marxist thought, recent years have seen a resurgence of interest in Marxism and its reassessment by a new generation of theorists. This book pursues that interest with specific reference to international law. It presents a sustained and ground-breaking exploration of the pertinence of Marxist ideas, concepts and analytical practices for international legal enquiry from a range of angles. Essays consider the relationship between Marxism and critical approaches to international law, the legacy of Soviet international legal theory, the bearing of Marxism for the analysis of international trade law and human rights, and the significance for international legal enquiry of such Marxist concepts as the commodity, praxis and exploitation.

SUSAN MARKS is Professor of Public International Law at the School of Law, King's College London.

INTERNATIONAL LAW ON THE LEFT

Re-examining Marxist Legacies

Editor
SUSAN MARKS

CAMBRIDGE
UNIVERSITY PRESS

CAMBRIDGE UNIVERSITY PRESS
Cambridge, New York, Melbourne, Madrid, Cape Town, Singapore,
São Paulo, Delhi, Dubai, Tokyo

Cambridge University Press
The Edinburgh Building, Cambridge CB2 8RU, UK

Published in the United States of America by Cambridge University Press, New York

www.cambridge.org
Information on this title: www.cambridge.org/9780521882552

© Cambridge University Press 2008

This publication is in copyright. Subject to statutory exception
and to the provisions of relevant collective licensing agreements,
no reproduction of any part may take place without the written
permission of Cambridge University Press.

First published 2008

A catalogue record for this publication is available from the British Library

ISBN 978-0-521-88255-2 Hardback

Transferred to digital printing 2010

Cambridge University Press has no responsibility for the persistence or
accuracy of URLs for external or third-party internet websites referred to in
this publication, and does not guarantee that any content on such websites is,
or will remain, accurate or appropriate. Information regarding prices, travel
timetables and other factual information given in this work are correct at
the time of first printing but Cambridge University Press does not guarantee
the accuracy of such information thereafter.

CONTENTS

Contributors   *page* vii
Acknowledgements   x

Introduction   1

1 What should international lawyers learn from Karl Marx?   30
MARTTI KOSKENNIEMI

2 An outline of a Marxist course on public international law   53
B. S. CHIMNI

3 The commodity-form theory of international law   92
CHINA MIÉVILLE

4 Positivism versus self-determination: the contradictions of Soviet international law   133
BILL BOWRING

5 Marxism and international law: perspectives for the American (twenty-first) century?   169
ANTHONY CARTY

6 Toward a radical political economy critique of transnational economic law   199
A. CLAIRE CUTLER

7 Marxian insights for the human rights project   220
BRAD R. ROTH

8 Marxian embraces (and de-couplings) in Upendra Baxi's human rights scholarship: a case study   252
OBIORA CHINEDU OKAFOR

9 Exploitation as an international legal concept   281
SUSAN MARKS

Index   309

CONTRIBUTORS

BILL BOWRING is a practising barrister and Professor of Law at Birkbeck College, University of London. He has many publications on topics of international law, human rights and Russian law, in which he frequently acts as a court expert. He founded and is Chair of the European Human Rights Advocacy Centre (EHRAC), which is assisting with over 1,000 cases against Russia, Georgia and Latvia at the European Court of Human Rights. He is a long-time activist and former Treasurer of the International Association of Demcratic Lawyers, and is President of the European Association of Lawyers for Democracy and Human Rights. He speaks fluent Russian and has travelled to Russia and other countries of the former USSR and Central and Eastern Europe for international organisations on a regular basis. His first visit to Russia was in 1983, when Andropov was General Secretary of the CPSU.

ANTHONY CARTY is Professor of Public Law at the University of Aberdeen. He has had a long interest in so-called Third World problems and produced *International Law and Development* (Ashgate) in 1993. He ran a development law programme for government lawyers in the English-speaking Caribbean, funded by the EU and the US government. He has published joint projects with Dutch and French international lawyers interested in development. He has just published *Philosophy of International Law* (Edinburgh University Press). At Aberdeen he has set up an LL.M (taught master's course) in International Law and Globalisation.

DR. B. S. CHIMNI is Professor of International Law in the School of International Studies, Jawaharlal Nehru University, New Delhi. He has been a Visiting Professor at the International Center for Comparative Law and Politics, Tokyo University, a Fulbright Visiting Scholar at Harvard Law School, and a Visiting Fellow at Max Planck Institute for Comparative and Public International Law, Heidelberg. He has published three books and numerous articles on a range of subjects of international law. He is a General Editor of the *Asian Yearbook of International Law*. His central research interest is to elaborate in association with a group of likeminded scholars a critical Third World approach to international law.

DR. A. CLAIRE CUTLER is Professor of International Law and Relations in the Political Science Department at the University of Victoria, Victoria, British Columbia, Canada. She teaches International Law, International Organization, International Relations Theory, Critical Globalization Studies and Histories of the States System and Global Capitalism. Her publications include *Private Power and Global Authority: Transnational Merchant Law in the Global Political Economy* (Cambridge University Press, 2003) and *Private Authority and International Affairs* (State University of New York Press, 1999).

MARTTI KOSKENNIEMI is Academy Professor with the Academy of Finland. He is also Professor of International Law at the University of Helsinki and Hauser Global Professor of Law at New York University School of Law. He has been a member of the UN International Law Commission (2002–06) and Judge at the Administrative Tribunal of the Asian Development Bank (1997–2002). In the 1980s and early 1990s, he was First Secretary and Counsellor for Legal Affairs at the Ministry for Foreign Affairs of Finland. His main works are *From Apology to Utopia. The Structure of International Legal Argument* (Cambridge University Press, reissue with a new epilogue, 2005) and *The Gentle Civilizer of Nations. The Rise and Fall of International Law 1870–1960* (Cambridge University Press, 2001). Professor Koskenniemi's research interests focus on the theory and history of international law.

SUSAN MARKS is Professor of Public International Law at King's College London. She is the author of *The Riddle of All Constitutions* (Cambridge University Press, 2000) and (with Andrew Clapham) *International Human Rights Lexicon* (Cambridge University Press, 2005).

CHINA MIÉVILLE is a novelist and writer on international law and politics. He is an honorary research fellow at Birkbeck, University of London, School of Law, and is on the editorial board of the journal *Historical Materialism*. His non-fiction includes *Between Equal Rights: A Marxist Theory of International Law* (Brill, 2005; Haymarket, 2006).

OBIORA CHINEDU OKAFOR is an Associate Professor at the Osgoode Hall Law School; Faculty Member at the Centre for Refugee Studies; and Faculty Associate at the Harriet Tubman Institute for the Study of the African Diaspora, York University, Toronto, Canada. He holds a Ph.D and an LL.M from the University of British Columbia, Vancouver, Canada; and an LL.M and LL.B (Honours) from the University of Nigeria. He recently served as a Canada-US Fulbright Scholar at the Massachusetts Institute of Technology, USA, and has previously served as SSRC-MacArthur Foundation Fellow on Peace and Security in a Changing World.

BRAD R. ROTH is Associate Professor of Political Science and Law at Wayne State University, where he teaches courses at the undergraduate, graduate, and professional levels in international law, human rights and political theory. He is the author of *Governmental Illegitimacy in International Law* (Clarendon Press, 1999), winner of the 1999 Certificate of Merit from the American Society of International Law as 'best work in a specialized area', and the co-editor (with Gregory H. Fox) of *Democratic Governance and International Law* (Cambridge University Press, 2000). In over two dozen journal articles, book chapters and commentaries, he has explored questions of sovereignty, human rights, constitutionalism, and democracy.

ACKNOWLEDGEMENTS

The idea of producing a volume along these lines goes back quite a long way, to a small symposium on the theme of 'Marxism and International Law' held in The Hague in September 2003 and organised by Miklós Redner and myself under the auspices of the *Leiden Journal of International Law*. The symposium was itself Miklós Redner's idea, and I thank him for that crucial contribution to this book. Five of the essays here – by Anthony Carty, B. S. Chimni, Martti Koskenniemi, China Miéville and Brad Roth – are revisions or reprints of papers that have appeared in the *Leiden Journal of International Law* ((2004) vol. 17, issues 1 and 2), and I give thanks, too, to the editors of that journal for permission to include them here. I am immensely grateful to Govert Coppens for research assistance in connection with the preparation of the manuscript, and to Matthew Craven, Daniel Joyce and Nigel Parke for help in elaborating my own contributions. Finally, appreciation of editorial support is something routinely expressed, but it has to be said that Finola O'Sullivan at Cambridge University Press really has been exceptionally patient and supportive in this case.

INTRODUCTION

This book is concerned with the contemporary relevance of Marxism for the study of international law. As a general theme of theoretical investigation, this question of the 'contemporary relevance of Marxism' has become in recent years a staple of the social sciences and humanities. Against expectations that the turn away from state socialism would likewise initiate a turn away from Marxist thought, the trend has been rather the reverse. From one perspective, this is a strange paradox of our era of unrivalled capitalism. From another, it is a perfectly logical state of affairs, inasmuch as Karl Marx and his interpreters have produced some of the most sustained and penetrating analysis we have of capitalism as an economic system with globalising tendencies. Either way, the collapse of Eastern bloc communism clearly released the grip of orthodox Marxism as an unchallengeable body of doctrine, and created an opening for fresh consideration of Marxist texts by a new generation of readers. At the same time, the emergence in the succeeding decade of an oppositional politics that goes under the banner of 'anti-capitalism' added renewed impetus to the familiar Marxist enquiry into the character, limits and transformation of the capitalist mode of production.

Any effort to take stock of what Marxism has to offer today must reckon with a tradition that ranges across an immense array of disciplines, preoccupations and debates, and is at once distinctive and persistently plural. This plurality is not just a matter of multiple and contending positions within the tradition, but also of complex connections with other bodies of thinking. For all its important departures, Marxism remains connected to the ideas against which it developed. Marx's own reference points came mainly from classical German philosophy (especially Hegel and his followers) and classical economics (Adam Smith, David Ricardo, Thomas Malthus and others). Working in the shadow of the Industrial Revolution, his outlook on capitalist modernity was also informed by the political struggles and cultural orientations of Victorian England. Together with his writings, the various alternative currents of twentieth-century

Marxism (and perhaps especially the Western Marxism of Lukács, Gramsci, Benjamin, Adorno and Horkheimer) have left a rich legacy of concepts, insights and analytical practices. As a route into the discussion of how Marxism can contribute, and has contributed, to the specific field of international legal scholarship, let us begin by recalling something of this inheritance.

1. Some Marxist legacies

1.1. Materialism

To engage with Marxism is, above all, to engage with the idea that history is to be understood in materialist terms. In the text known as *Preface to a Critique of Political Economy* Marx gives an often-quoted account of what this entails.

> [L]egal relations as well as forms of the state are to be grasped neither from themselves nor from the so-called general development of the human mind, but rather have their roots in the material conditions of life.[1]

In his account, the material conditions of life are in turn to be grasped with reference to an historically specific mode of production, and to the relations of production associated with that mode:

> The sum total of these relations of production constitutes the economic structure of society, the real foundation, on which rises a legal and political superstructure and to which correspond definite forms of social consciousness.[2]

In consequence, '[i]t is not the consciousness of men that determines their being, but, on the contrary, their social being that determines their consciousness'.[3]

That these passages have inspired some very reductive forms of analysis is well known, but most contemporary theorists hold to a far more subtle reading, in which the relation between the determining base and the determined superstructure is posed as a question, rather than an explanatory theory. Thus, Fredric Jameson writes of 'base-and-superstructure not as a fully-fledged theory in its own right, but as the name for a problem, whose solution is always a unique, ad hoc invention'.[4] From this perspective,

---

[1] Reprinted in D. McLellan (ed.), *Karl Marx: Selected Writings*, 2nd edn (Oxford: Oxford University Press, 2000), p. 424, at p. 425.
[2] *Ibid.* [3] *Ibid.*
[4] F. Jameson, *Late Marxism* (London and New York: Verso, 1990), p. 46.

the materialist vision of history does not imply any particular relation between economic structure on the one hand and prevailing ideas and institutions on the other, but it does imply that, whatever the relation may be in a specific context, it is key to an understanding of social realities and possibilities, and hence needs to be investigated. At the centre of discussions about the analytical priority of material conditions is the complex idea of 'determination'. As Raymond Williams explains, the root sense of the verb 'to determine' is 'to set limits'.[5] Keeping this sense in mind, Williams proposes that determination involves the 'setting of limits' – which in practice also includes the positive 'exertion of pressures'.[6] What crucially distinguishes this understanding from an understanding of determination as the operation of predictable laws is that here the limits and pressures – the conditions set by the material base – are not seen as 'external' to human will and action, such that our only option is to accommodate to them and 'guide [our] actions accordingly'. Rather, they are seen as historical inheritances that are the 'result of human actions in the material world' and hence 'accessible' and revisable.[7]

The idea that history is to be understood in materialist terms has many implications. Where the study of international law is concerned, one implication that merits particular emphasis is that it points up the inadequacy of 'idealist' forms of analysis. The term 'idealist' has a special meaning in this context, quite different from its everyday sense: it refers to the tendency to contemplate the world in a manner that implicitly overstates the autonomous power of ideas. In *The German Ideology*, Marx and Engels criticise their philosophical contemporaries for challenging received tenets of German philosophy, yet failing to 'inquire into the connection between German philosophy and German reality, into the connection between their criticism and their own material surroundings'.[8] Without investigation of those connections, there could be no understanding of what accounted for the problems, and hence no understanding of what would be required to bring about change. The temptations of idealism remain strong, and no less in international legal scholarship than in other fields of academic endeavour. However, Marxism delivers here a reminder of the need not to take international legal ideas and interpretations at face value, but instead to delve deeper and ask about the material conditions of their emergence and deployment. What was it that

---

[5] R. Williams, *Marxism and Literature* (Oxford: Oxford University Press, 1977), p. 85.
[6] *Ibid.*, pp. 85, 87.   [7] *Ibid.*, p. 85.
[8] K. Marx, *Early Political Writings*, J. O'Malley, ed. and trans. (Cambridge: Cambridge University Press, 1994), p. 123.

made it possible for those particular ideas and interpretations to develop and become useful? In Williams's terms, what limits and pressures were in play?

1.2. Capitalism

I have highlighted the Marxist insight that the material conditions of life have a determining role in relation to forms of consciousness and social arrangements, including those associated with international law. I have also indicated that, in this account, the material conditions of life are seen as referable to an historically specific mode of production and to the relations of production concomitant with that mode. Marx, of course, was particularly interested in the capitalist mode of production and in its distinctive productive relations, characterised by a division between the capitalist class and the working class, according to ownership or non-ownership of the means of production. For all the very considerable changes affecting capitalism since Marx's time, and for all its diversity within the contemporary world, the consolidation of capitalism as a global system means that, today, any investigation of the material conditions of life must likewise concern itself with capitalism and with class. In the context of international legal scholarship, this is significant because 'capitalism' is a word rarely pronounced in writing about international law. Marxism puts onto the agenda questions that, under the influence of liberal traditions, have generally been set aside. These include questions about the limits set, and pressures exerted, by forces within the world economy in a given context. They also include questions about particular features of capitalist production, exchange and accumulation. Thus, for example, Marxism calls for a deeper and more wide-ranging investigation than hitherto of such phenomena as exploitation, immiseration, alienation and commodification, and of the ways in which these phenomena shape and are themselves shaped by international law.

What then of class? The relation between class and other axes of social division, such as gender, race and sexuality, is a familiar debate of recent decades. Most analysts agree that the relative neglect of social divisions other than class in classical Marxism is a major (if symptomatic) omission. In the study of international law this awareness is exemplified in an influential and growing body of scholarship in the mode of feminist analysis. Where positions differ is with regard to the place of class. Some analysts doubt its pertinence in a world where relationship to the means of production appears less telling than wealth, prestige and more generally 'cultural capital'; many more doubt the structural pre-eminence of class in the analysis of social life. Marx was famously terse about class as a category, and it remains the case that, at the level of social 'existence' or ontology, the category eludes specification. On one view, however, 'the "truth" of the concept of class . . . lies rather in the operations to which it gives rise': class analysis 'is able to absorb and refract' the various other hierarchies which history has thrown up.[9] By this is not meant that class subordination is more serious or more troubling than subordination on other grounds. Rather, the claim is that class realises itself and becomes embodied through gender, race, sexuality, etc., so that asymmetries indexed to those categories take on a distinctively capitalist slant.

I mentioned above the phenomenon of commodification. Discussion of this takes inspiration from Marx's concept of the 'fetishism of commodities', elaborated in *Capital*.[10] Starting from the observation that the 'wealth of societies in which the capitalist mode of production prevails appears as an "immense collection of commodities"', Marx proposes that the commodity is capitalism's 'elementary form'.[11] What is distinctive about a commodity is that it exists not for its own sake, but for the sake of being exchanged. Though a product of human labour, an outcome of a social relation (between the buyer of the labour (the capitalist) and the seller of it (the worker)), and an element in a productive process, the commodity assumes the character of an autonomous, objective thing. For Marx this is an aspect of the 'alienation' associated with capitalism – workers are alienated from the products of their own labour, and hence from themselves, and indeed from authentic humanity. The fetishism of commodities inheres in the transmutation whereby 'the definite social relation between men . . . assumes . . . for them, the fantastic form of a relation between things'.[12] Drawing on ideas of his time about 'primitive' religious practice and the use of fetishes, he proposes that commodities are 'fetishised' insofar as 'products of the human brain [come to] appear as autonomous figures endowed with a life of their own, which enter into relations with each other and with the human race'.[13] At a general level,

---

[9] F. Jameson, 'Actually Existing Marxism', in S. Makdisi, C. Casarino and R. E. Karl (eds.), *Marxism Beyond Marxism* (New York and London: Routledge, 1996), p. 14 at pp. 40, 42.
[10] See K. Marx, *Capital*, Vol. 1 (London: Penguin, 1976), pp. 163 ff.
[11] *Ibid.*, p. 125. (Marx is quoting himself here.)   [12] *Ibid.*, p. 165.   [13] *Ibid.*

Marx is showing here that, as further explained by later theorists, 'capitalism is secretly possessed by a series of pre-modern forms' – and not just as residues of what came before, but as 'effects' of modernity itself.[14] More specifically, he is signalling the way in which, in capitalist society, the market comes to dominate life. Social artefacts begin to escape human control, and appear as extra-social facts.

In the 1920s Georg Lukács returned to this idea, giving it a label only occasionally used by Marx: reification.[15] Through reification the world comes to seem a collection of discrete things, disconnected from one another and alien to us. Ceasing to recognise our social environment as the outcome of human endeavour, we begin to see it as fixed and unchangeable, an object of contemplation rather than a domain of action. Marx observes that, while the 'fetish character [of the commodity-form] is still relatively easy to penetrate', not all of the reified categories of economic theory are so readily accessible; defetishisation may take considerable imaginative effort.[16] At the same time, as he implies, and as Lukács makes explicit, 'the problem of commodities' is not only a problem relating to economic categories; it is 'the central structural problem of capitalist society in all its aspects'.[17] In Lukács's memorable phrase, capitalism creates a 'second nature',[18] scarcely less self-evident, solid and enveloping than the first one. It follows that the critique of reification must be equally pervasive. For those interested in international law, this critique begins with the category 'international law' itself, and with the tendency to speak of it as a set of rules, a thing, rather than a social (and especially interpretative) process. Such a critique then also takes in the various concepts and categories in which international law trades: among very many others, 'sovereignty', 'states', 'treaty bodies', 'barriers to trade', 'the environment', 'the United Kingdom', 'the Universal Declaration of Human Rights' – all of them artefacts that come to appear as facts, and social relations that are apt to assume the 'fantastic' form of autonomous objects. What is fascinating about the concept of reification is that, of course, reification too is an objectified category. Thus, Timothy Bewes remarks that this is

---

[14] P. Osborne, *How To Read Marx* (London: Granta, 2005), pp. 16–17. (Of the many available introductions to Marx's writings, this book is, in my view, the best.) For one important later elaboration of this idea, see M. Horkheimer and T. Adorno, *Dialectic of Enlightenment* (New York: Continuum, 1994).
[15] G. Lukács, *History and Class Consciousness* (London: Merlin Press, 1974), p. 83 ff.
[16] *Capital, Vol. 1* (London: Penguin, 1976), p. 176.
[17] Lukács, *History and Class Consciousness*, p. 83.
[18] *Ibid.*, p. 86.

a peculiarly 'self-reflective' form of critique;[19] it constantly curves back on itself. But if we cannot *overcome* reified consciousness, the point here is that we can and must prise it open to demystify the transmutations involved.

1.3. Ideology

Marx's concept of commodity fetishism was elaborated in connection with his readings in classical economics, and his critique of the failure of even that discipline's 'best representatives, Adam Smith and Ricardo' to escape what he saw as the bourgeois tendency to treat historically specific forms as 'self-evident and nature-imposed' essences.[20] However, this was by no means Marx's first consideration of the 'necessary illusions' of capitalism.[21] In earlier work, when engaged in debates about Left Hegelian philosophy, he had also explored the mystificatory processes whereby social reality reproduces itself. Then, though, the key concept was ideology. The term 'ideology' is today used in many different senses. We use it as a synonym for dogma. We use it to refer to the world-view or framework of beliefs and values of a particular social group or historical epoch. We use it in discussions of political traditions – the 'ideologies' of liberalism, socialism, fascism, and so on. Marx also used the term in more than one sense, but mostly what he had in mind was the role of ideas and rhetorical processes in the legitimation of ruling power. In *The German Ideology*, Marx and Engels explain how the ruling class:

> is obliged, even if only to achieve its aims, to represent its interests as the common interests of all members of society; that is to say, in terms of ideas, to give its thoughts the form of universality, to present them as the only reasonable ones, the only ones universally valid.[22]

Elsewhere in the same text, the authors refer, in a similar vein, to the way historically contingent doctrine relating to the organisation of public power is 'pronounced to be an "eternal law"'.[23] These processes whereby

---

[19] T. Bewes, *Reification, or The Anxiety of Late Capitalism* (London and New York: Verso, 2002), p. 96. The 'anxiety of late capitalism' in Bewes's title refers to his idea that the critique of reification is 'always troubled by a vein of anxiety concerning the susceptibility of the concept itself to the reifying process'. See p. 93.
[20] *Capital, Vol. 1*, p. 174, n. 34 and p. 175 respectively.
[21] The concept is Lukács's. See Lukács, *History and Class Consciousness*, p. 92.
[22] Marx, *Early Political Writings*, p. 146.   [23] *Ibid.*, p. 145.

particular interests are made instead to appear universal, historically contingent arrangements take on the aspect of eternal laws, and political outcomes come to seem the only reasonable possibilities, exemplify for Marx operations of ideology.

Theorists of ideology draw two distinctions which are useful in grasping the specificity of this Marxian account.[24] One is a distinction between neutral and critical conceptions of ideology. The notions of ideology as world-view and political tradition are examples of neutral conceptions. By contrast, the Marxian conception of ideology is critical; to point to ideology in Marx's sense is to imply the need for criticism and change. The second distinction is between conceptions of ideology that have epistemological concerns – concerns about truth and falsity – and conceptions that have political or ethical concerns. After Marx's death, Engels developed a notion of ideology as 'false consciousness'. In his words:

> [i]deology is a process accomplished by the so-called thinker consciously, it is true, but with a false consciousness. The real motive forces impelling him remain unknown to him . . . Hence he imagines false or seeming motive forces.[25]

This identification of ideology with false consciousness has, of course, been extremely influential, and it is an obvious instance of a conception of ideology with epistemological concerns. However, the Marxian conception is different. Where the focus is on legitimation processes of the kind described above (universalisation, eternalisation, rationalisation), the problem with ideology is not that it involves error, but that it sustains privilege. To be sure, mystification is in play, but the ideas nurtured are not simple mistakes or inaccuracies; they are as much part of the prevailing reality as is the privilege they serve to sustain. Informing this conception of ideology, then, is a political concern about the function of ideas in social life.[26]

---

[24] See esp. R. Geuss, *The Idea of a Critical Theory* (Cambridge: Cambridge University Press, 1981); J. Thompson, *Ideology and Modern Culture* (Oxford: Blackwell, 1990); and T. Eagleton, *Ideology* (London and New York: Verso, 1991).

[25] Letter from Engels to Mehring (1893), quoted in D. McLellan, *Ideology*, 2nd edn (Buckingham: Open University Press, 1995), p. 16.

[26] Among many later reconceptualisations of this 'political' account of ideology, the work of Louis Althusser has been especially prominent. For Althusser, the study of ideology is concerned with the practices, rituals and institutions through which social subjectivity is produced and social cohesion ensured. See, e.g., L. Althusser, 'Ideology and Ideological State Apparatuses (Notes Towards an Investigation)', in S. Žižek (ed.), *Mapping Ideology* (London and New York: Verso, 1994), p. 100.

In the 1930s and 1940s, Max Horkheimer, Theodor Adorno and other members of the Frankfurt School placed the critique of ideology at the centre of the project they called critical theory. By 'critique' they meant a distinctive form of criticism, premised on the idea that meanings are never fully stable, but always in some sense strain at their own limitations, and point beyond themselves. As Adorno explains, it is in the nature of concepts that '[d]issatisfaction with their own conceptuality is part of their meaning'.[27] In the work of Adorno and his colleagues, ideology is criticised for the sake of drawing out these dissatisfactions. That is to say, it is not criticised in order to dismiss or negate it, but rather (to speak again with Adorno) to make it 'mean beyond itself'.[28] What does this entail? On the one hand, the critique of ideology is a matter of calling upon actuality to live up to its claims. Terry Eagleton expresses this engagingly:

> Marxism takes with the utmost seriousness bourgeois society's talk of freedom, justice and equality, and enquires with *faux* naivety why it is that these grandiloquent ideals can somehow never enter upon material existence.[29]

On the other hand, the critique of ideology is also a matter of exposing how actuality works to block the realisation of its claims. (Eagleton's enquiry may involve *faux* naivety insofar as systemic obstacles are part of materialist analysis, but it necessarily involves some element of genuine naivety as well, insofar as ideological obstacles are, by definition, never fully transparent.)

In the case of international law, this sets an agenda that includes the themes on which Marx and Engels touch in *The German Ideology*. How does that which appears universal conceal particular interests? How does that which seems eternal entrench historical inequities? And how does that which purports to be rational function as an argument against redistributive claims? At the same time, the critique of ideology also sets an agenda that goes further, and invites consideration of *all* the rhetorical and other symbolic manoeuvres through which ruling power mobilises meaning to legitimate itself. For this, it is important to remain open and alert to the shifting and often very subtle and surprising articulations of meaning with power. Particularly inspiring in that regard is the work of Slavoj Žižek. Žižek has made it his business to track the cunning of latecapitalist reason, and to follow the twists and turns through which ideology keeps ahead of its critics today. From him we can take the important

---

[27] T. Adorno, *Negative Dialectics* (London: Routledge, 1973), p. 12.
[28] *Ibid.* (quoting Emil Lask). [29] Eagleton, *Ideology*, p. 172.

insight that '[w]hen some procedure is denounced as "ideological *par excellence*", one can be sure that its inversion is no less ideological'.[30] If ideology critique directs attention to the processes by which historically specific conditions may be made to seem universal, eternal and rational, sometimes too, then, its task is the reverse. Sometimes what is needed is precisely to bring out the universal resonance of what passes for local preference, the 'hidden necessity in what appears as mere contingency',[31] and the rational explanation for what is depicted as the tragic eruption of unfathomable political passions.

1.4. Imperialism

According to Frantz Fanon, ideology found its limits in European colonial government. 'In the capitalist countries', he remarks, 'a multitude of moral teachers, counsellors and "bewilderers" separate the exploited from those in power'. In the colonial countries, by contrast, 'the policeman and the soldier, by their immediate presence and their frequent and direct action, maintain contact with the native and advise him by means of rifle-butts and napalm not to budge'.[32] Marx's writings about colonialism are relatively few, and mostly take the form of popular publications.[33] The 'language of pure force'[34] of which Fanon writes is not very prominent in these texts. Marx was certainly aware of the 'blood and dirt, ... misery and degradation' of colonial subjugation, but he thought it was just the same blood and dirt, misery and degradation as that inflicted by the bourgeoisie on the proletariat in Europe.[35] He also thought its purpose in this context was 'progress', and spoke of the 'Asiatic mode of production' in terms of its stagnancy, deficiency and need for 'regeneration'.[36] By contrast, the distinctive violence of capitalist imperialism is central to the later work of Rosa Luxemburg.

In *The Accumulation of Capital*, Luxemburg discusses the expansionist logics of capitalism and the dynamics of its worldwide spread.

---

[30] S. Žižek, 'Introduction', in Žižek (ed.), *Mapping Ideology*, p. 1, at p. 4.
[31] *Ibid*. On this point, see further below.
[32] F. Fanon, *The Wretched of the Earth*, C. Farrington, trans. (London: Penguin, 1967), p. 29.
[33] See esp. Marx's journalism on India for the New York Daily Tribune, available at: www.marxists.org/archive/marx/works /subject/newspapers/new-york-tribune.htm.
[34] Fanon, *The Wretched*, p. 29.
[35] 'The Future Result of British Rule in India', *New York Daily Tribune*, 8 August 1853. (The dispatch itself is dated 22 July 1853.) Available at: www.marxists.org/archive/marx/works/1853/07/22.htm.
[36] *Ibid*.

In penetrating pre-capitalist societies (or, as she calls them, 'natural' economies), competition will not work, for there is no pre-existing market in which to compete. There is 'no demand, or very little, for foreign goods, and also, as a rule, no surplus production, or at least no urgent need to dispose of surplus products... A natural economy thus confronts the requirements of capitalism at every turn with rigid barriers'.[37] Against this background, if capitalism is to expand into new terrain, it has to force its way in and break up what is already there. 'Capitalism must therefore always and everywhere fight a battle of annihilation against every historical form of natural economy that it encounters.'[38] She explains that this annihilation is literal: '[e]ach new colonial expansion is accompanied, as a matter of course, by a relentless battle of capital against the social and economic ties of the natives, who are also forcibly robbed of their means of production and labour power'.[39] From those natives' perspective, as she writes, 'it is a matter of life or death: for them there can be no other attitude than opposition and fight to the finish – complete exhaustion and extinction'.[40] In this regard, she refers to the tendency towards 'growing militarism' that is associated with the processes of capital accumulation. For Luxemburg, then, '[f]orce is the only solution open to capital; the accumulation of capital, seen as an historical process, employs force as a permanent weapon, not only at its genesis, but further on down to the present day'.[41]

Luxemburg's study was first published in 1913. It was followed a few years later by what was to become the canonical Marxist text on imperialism, Lenin's *Imperialism – the Highest Stage of Capitalism*.[42] This work is subtitled 'A Popular Outline' and, according to Lenin's later Preface to the French and German editions, his aim was to present 'a *general picture* of the world capitalist system in its international relationships at the beginning of the twentieth century – on the eve of the first world imperialist war'.[43] Commentators emphasise the text's character as a pamphlet, with little in-depth or original analysis.[44] Nonetheless, it is instructive in bringing

---

[37] R. Luxemburg, *The Accumulation of Capital* (London: Routledge, 2003), p. 349. For her reply to her critics, see also R. Luxemburg, *The Accumulation of Capital: An Anti-Critique* (New York: Monthly Review Press, 1973).
[38] Luxemburg, *The Accumulation of Capital*, p. 349.   [39] *Ibid.*, p. 350.
[40] *Ibid.*, p. 351.   [41] *Ibid.*
[42] V. I. Lenin, *Imperialism – the Highest Stage of Capitalism* (New York: International Publishers, 1939).
[43] *Ibid.*, p. 9.
[44] See, e.g., A. Brewer, *Marxist Theories of Imperialism*, 2nd edn (London and New York: Routledge, 1990), p. 116. (This book provides an excellent overview of Marxist perspectives on imperialism, and the discussion here draws heavily on it.)

out the point that imperialism needs to be understood in relation to the development of capitalism, rather than simply as a policy of particular states. In Lenin's account, imperialism corresponds to a particular 'stage' in the development of capitalism. According to his periodisation, this was the monopoly stage, during which capital become concentrated in 'monopolistic' holdings by banks and financiers, and large corporations emerged, bringing with them a new network of relations between proprietors, managers and shareholders. Marxist theories of imperialism elaborated in the second half of the twentieth century maintained this focus on capitalist dynamics, but, in examining the worldwide development of capitalism, their terms of reference shifted. In post-colonial conditions, the discussion was of the production of 'under-development', the division between 'core' and 'periphery' (and, in some accounts, 'semi-periphery'), the reduction of the periphery to a state of 'dependence', the emergence of 'neo-colonialism', and the processes of 'unequal development'.[45] More recent scholarship paints a somewhat more complicated picture of colonial and post-colonial relations, and also investigates cultural and other dimensions of imperialism that were not part of the analysis in development economics. In doing so, however, it leaves in place the basic insight that imperialism and capitalism belong together.

From these writings we can take at least three important points which are relevant to international legal debates in the sphere of human rights and international development, as to all investigations of poverty on a global scale. First, 'under-development' is not simply given, but produced. Thus, for example, as Mike Davis shows in *Late Victorian Holocausts*, mass starvation is not a token of backwardness, but a modern phenomenon, linked to the integration of non-European societies into the system of global capitalism.[46] In the case of the events with which Davis is concerned in that book – the successive famines of the late nineteenth century that devastated much of what is now known as the Third World – nature certainly played a part. The famines corresponded to a series of exceptionally severe occurrences of the climatic disturbance known as 'El Niño'. At the same time, however, incorporation into global commodity markets and subjection to colonial economic priorities had destroyed

---

[45] See esp. A. G. Frank, *Capitalism and Undevelopment in Latin America*, rev. edn (New York: Monthly Review Press, 1969); S. Amin, *Unequal Development* (New York: Monthly Review Press, 1976); and I. Wallerstein, *The Capitalist World Economy* (Cambridge: Cambridge University Press, 1979).
[46] M. Davis, *Late Victorian Holocausts: El Niño Famines and the Making of the Third World* (London and New York: Verso, 2001).

pre-existing arrangements for food security – through local storage, interregional assistance, and in some places, centralised strategic planning – and left local populations mortally exposed. Secondly, the production of 'under-development' is not simply spontaneous. As Luxemburg explains, it entails the use of coercive force. To refer again to Davis's study of the late nineteenth-century El Niño famines and of the context in which they could produce such catastrophic consequences, the 'looms of India and China were defeated not so much by market competition as they were forcibly dismantled by war, invasion, opium and a Lancashire-imposed system of one-way tariffs'.[47] What was, and is, at stake is 'redistributive class struggle'.[48] Finally, just as the production of 'under-development' is not a spontaneous phenomenon, nor is it an anonymous phenomenon. Bertolt Brecht once famously quipped that 'famines do not simply occur; they are organised by the grain trade'. Brecht reminds us here that hunger is not simply an objective fact of the world, but a policy option and an outcome of decisions taken by particular people in particular contexts. Whether one has in mind acute shortages, as he does, or more chronic forms of undernourishment, and whether scrutiny is needed of the grain trade or of other institutions, some people make it happen that others are deprived of the means of subsistence.

1.5. Totality

The critique of imperialism directs attention to the global dimensions of capitalism. In the *Communist Manifesto*, Marx and Engels write of how the 'bourgeoisie cannot exist without continually revolutionising the instruments of production . . .'.[49] Capitalism is characterised by perpetual motion and continual expansion. 'Large-scale industry has established a world market, for which the discovery of America prepared the way.'[50] Through the exploitation of this market, 'we have a universal commerce, a universal dependence of nations on one another'. And, 'as in the production of material things, so also with intellectual production. The intellectual creations of individual nations become common currency.' In consequence, '[n]ational partiality and narrowness become more and

---

[47] *Ibid*, p. 295.
[48] *Ibid*., p. 20 (quoting A. Rangasami, '"Failure of Exchange Entitlements" Theory of Famine: A Response', *Economic and Political Weekly*, 12 October 1985, p. 178).
[49] K. Marx, *Later Political Writings*, T. Carver, ed. and trans. (Cambridge: Cambridge University Press, 1996), p. 1, at p. 4.
[50] *Ibid*., p. 3.

more impossible, and from the many national and local literatures a world literature arises'.[51] Marx and Engels highlight the integrative nature of these processes. 'Through rapid improvement in the instruments of production, through limitless ease of communication, the bourgeoisie drags all nations, even the most primitive ones, into civilisation.' It 'forces all nations to adopt the bourgeois mode of production or go under ... In a phrase, it creates a world in its own image'.[52] Quite clearly, Marx and Engels could not have imagined the transformations of capitalist modernity in our own time, and globalisation has turned out to be, and perhaps always was, a much more complex phenomenon than is described in these passages. With economic interdependence has come deepened dependency; with greater openness has come appeal to national interest; with cultural exchange and the enlargement of horizons has come parochialism; and with homogenisation has come the renewed assertion of difference.

What remains illuminating in this account, however, is its emphasis on the expansive, integrative nature of capitalism, and on the globalising tendencies which compel us to consider the entire world as a dynamic whole. The idea that the world must be grasped as a totality is a distinctive theme of Marxist theorising. While this idea is understood in a range of different ways, one important set of connotations emerges from the work of Lukács, Adorno and, more recently, Fredric Jameson, Michael Hardt and Kathi Weeks. I mentioned earlier Lukács's claim that reification – the fetishism of commodities – is the defining experience of life in capitalist society. As he explains it, 'the whole life of society is ... fragmented into the isolated acts of commodity exchange' between atomised and objectified people.[53] Thus the world comes to appear a collection of discrete objects, the connections between which remain for the most part invisible. Lukács uses the terms 'atomisation', 'fragmentation', 'isolation', 'self-estrangement', 'alienation', 'abstraction', 'commodification' and, as indicated, 'reification', to describe this situation and, in contrast, proposes that the key to emancipatory change lies in undoing these processes and confronting the 'problem of totality'.[54] Discussing the later meditations on this problem by Adorno, Jameson observes that totality is today a 'copiously stigmatized idea'.[55] It seems to suggest a totalising concept, grand narrative, or indeed totalitarian scheme. But these elisions are too hasty. The concept of totality is not used here to refer to the possibility of explaining everything, still less to the desirability of subsuming

[51] *Ibid.*, p. 5.   [52] *Ibid.*   [53] Lukács, *History and Class Consciousness*, p. 91.
[54] *Ibid.*, p. 151 (emphasis omitted).   [55] Jameson, *Late Marxism*, p. 26.

everything under the order of a single ruling idea. Rather, it is used to refer to the actuality that phenomena in the world are interrelated, and hence can only properly be understood when viewed as elements within larger social systems, including the system of global capitalism.

Hardt and Weeks point out that in this account totality is less a metaphysical concept than an epistemological proposition with methodological implications. In their words, it:

> function[s] as a prescription to strive constantly to relate and connect, to situate and interpret each object or phenomenon in the context of those social and historical forces that shape and enable it, and ultimately with respect to the entire set of its conditions of possibilities.[56]

Where international law is concerned, the concept of totality highlights the need for a complex kind of analysis that connects international legal norms with the wider processes through which their interpretation is shaped and enabled. It urges us to approach things relationally, rather than in isolation, and to pay attention to the larger social forces that create the conditions in which international legal ideas and concepts emerge, develop and get deployed. In doing so, it also reminds us of the value of engagement with a plurality of different literatures, and conversely points up the dangers of confinement within disciplinary boundaries. At the same time, the concept of totality brings into focus something else, already hinted at in various ways in this discussion. International legal scholars are today quite attentive to the 'false necessity'[57] that treats social reality as naturally arising, rather than historically constructed. That men and women make their own history, and can therefore change it, is the premise, and sometimes part of the explicit argument, of much of the most influential writing on international law. But *how* can they change it? What tends to receive less attention is the insight, expressed in Marx's celebrated statement in *The Eighteenth Brumaire of Louis Bonaparte*, that history is not made in conditions that are freely chosen, but rather 'in present circumstances, given and inherited'.[58] The systemic logics which affect present circumstances, and hence future possibilities, are not generally part of the analysis. As a result, a kind of 'false contingency' is left unchallenged, according to which injustices appear random, accidental

---

[56] M. Hardt and K. Weeks, 'Introduction', in M. Hardt and K. Weeks (eds.), *The Jameson Reader* (Oxford: Blackwell, 2000), p. 1 at p. 22.
[57] The phrase is Roberto Unger's. See R. Unger, *False Necessity*, rev. edn (London and New York: Verso, 2004).
[58] Marx, *Later Political Writings*, p. 31, at p. 32.

and arbitrary. With the concept of totality comes an invitation to challenge that false contingency.

2. Our re-examination

Karl Marx wrote, then, about many things that have implications for the study of international law. I have recalled a few of them; many more are recalled in the remainder of this volume. But international law was not part of his project, and he did not himself advert to those implications. That was, and is, left to later scholars. Is this something we should still be interested in today? The suggestion by some in the international legal field that Marxism is 'out-dated, oversimplified and wrong'[59] may have relevance to debates about the 'orthodox' Marxism of the Second and Third Internationals, but it cannot begin to capture the resources of the Marxist tradition as a whole.[60] With the demise of state socialism, it is that larger set of resources, notable rather for its richness, complexity and engagement with questions of vital and enduring importance, on which attention currently focuses. In the chapters that follow, we explore the bearing of Marxism for the study of international law from a variety of angles. As will become apparent, the essays have – for all their differences of focus, standpoint, analysis and style – at least five features in common.

First, each gives priority to the perspective of those who (to borrow a phrase from Robert Cox) 'cannot be content with things as they are'.[61] Whether through explicit reference to 'subaltern classes', 'subordinate groups' and 'oppressed classes' or by implication, the orientation is always towards those seeking emancipatory change. Second, and connectedly, each proceeds from relative scepticism about the claims of universality, and is attentive to the ways in which universality works ideologically to conceal particular interests. At the same time, the contributors are no

---

[59] T. Hale and A.-M. Slaughter, 'Hardt and Negri's "Multitude": the worst of both worlds', *openDemocracy*, 26 May 2005, available at: www.opendemocracy.net/globalization-vision_reflections/marx_2549.jsp ('*Multitude* mixes Marxism with postmodern pastiche that produces, in some places, the worst of both worlds. Marxism may be out-dated, oversimplified, and wrong, but it is at least clear.').

[60] Even as an assessment of orthodox Marxism, however, this is far too dismissive. See, e.g., B. Bowring, 'Positivism versus self-determination: the contradictions of Soviet international law', in this volume. See also S. Žižek, *Revolution at the Gates: Žižek on Lenin, the 1917 Writings*, 2nd edn (London: Verso, 2004), Introduction and Afterword.

[61] R. Cox, 'Democracy in Hard Times: Economic Globalization and the Limits to Liberal Democracy', in A. McGrew (ed.), *The Transformation of Democracy?* (Cambridge: Polity Press, 1997), p. 49, at p. 70.

moral relativists, and criticise universality not to dismiss it, but rather to invite consideration of its limits and unrealised potentials. Third, each treats international law as enmeshed with global forces. The interconnections are seen to be complex. Just as international law is shaped by those forces, so too, the contributors show, it shapes them. Fourth, each understands law as fruitfully brought within the same analytical optics that Marxism has used for other social phenomena. In a number of the essays, this is pursued through the idea that international law can be analysed in the same way as is the commodity.

Finally, while the contributors take up a diversity of positions with respect to Marxism, each engages with it in a manner quite different from the style of orthodox debates. Speaking of his own intellectual trajectory, Raymond Williams once observed that, when he first encountered Marxism in the 1940s and 1950s, the classic question asked in a debate about someone's work was: 'are his ideas Marxist or not?'[62] He noted that this kind of question had persisted in some quarters down to the 1970s, when he was writing this. But, he went on:

> now that I knew more of the history of Marxism, and of the variety of selective and alternative traditions within it, I could at last get free of the model ... of fixed and known Marxist positions, which in general had only to be applied ...

And '[o]nce the central body of thinking was itself seen as active, developing, unfinished, and persistently contentious, many of the questions were open again'. Thus, he explained, 'I have come to see more and more clearly its [Marxism's] radical differences from other bodies of thinking, but at the same time its complex connections with them, and its many unresolved problems'.[63] Each of the contributors approaches the discussion in the spirit with which Williams identifies here.

Martti Koskenniemi addresses the question: 'what should international lawyers learn from Karl Marx?' His essay suggests a three-fold answer. To begin with, Koskenniemi recalls Marx's dissatisfaction with the limits of Feuerbach's critique of religion: Feuerbach criticised religious self-estrangement, but failed to see that this was only a symptom of a much more pervasive phenomenon. The state and bourgeois humanism (today reflected in human rights) are also theologies, albeit secularised ones. Koskenniemi discusses the way these two theologies seem to clash, and

---

[62] Williams is speaking here of argument about the work of Christopher Caudwell: R. Williams, *Marxism and Literature* (Oxford: Oxford University Press, 1977), p. 3.
[63] *Ibid.*, pp. 3–4.

then come into alignment. Secular modernity adopts the religion of statehood, but then corrects it through the religion of human rights. Thus, the state and human rights are locked into one another, and together locked into what Koskenniemi refers to as the 'prison-house of modern political theology'. This, then, is the first thing international lawyers should learn from Marx. In considering how we might break out of this prison-house without lapsing into another political theology, Koskenniemi goes on to discuss the relationship between Marxian dialectics – the method of analysis and argument which Marx developed through a reorientation of Hegel's ideas – and deconstruction.

Deconstruction is a practice and concept that has been very important for Koskenniemi's work, and he examines here its relation to Marxian dialectics. In his account, 'deconstruction performs the work of dialectics by showing the radical instability of forms of representing society'. On the other hand, dialectics, for its part, shows that legal indeterminacy and the various dichotomies around which law revolves are not dead-ends, but can be used 'as frameworks for historical explanation'. This, according to Koskenniemi, is the second thing lawyers should learn from Marx. Central to Marx's historical explanation is the distinction between real and false universalism, and between truly human and merely political emancipation. How, Koskenniemi asks, are we to conceive real universality and truly human emancipation today? In his contention, Marx's work points to a vision of universality as 'universal violation'. By this, Koskenniemi means a violation that touches no-one in particular, but everyone in general. The universality here arises not from any harmony of interests, but from the unity that can come from a shared sense of violation. Koskenniemi illustrates this with reference to protests against the Iraq War. With this notion of universal violation in mind, he proposes that the third thing international lawyers should learn from Marx is that international law's emancipatory promise may be best understood in terms of its capacity to serve as an 'instrument through which particular grievances may be articulated as universal ones and in this way . . . [to] construct a sense of universal humanity through the act of invoking it'.

B. S. Chimni takes theoretical reflection on the bearing of Marxism for the study of international law into the crucial context of international legal education. His essay has the form of an outline of a Marxist course on public international law. Encompassed within his course are the familiar topics of the sources of international law, the relationship between international law and municipal law, state jurisdiction, international economic law, international environmental law, international human rights law, international law of state responsibility, and international law and the use of force. For each topic Chimni shows what an alternative account, informed by Marxist insights, might begin to look like. In introducing his outline course, he also makes some general observations about the limits of received pedagogy. In Chimni's assessment, mainstream accounts of international law are characterised by four features. First, they are rooted in an epistemology and metholodogy that foster formal and abstract concepts and doctrines. Second, the history of international law is related as a narrative of progress, and contemporary international law is portrayed as inherently progressive. Third, international law is seen as a system of rules that can be objectively known and applied. Interpretation is not seen as an activity that engages power. Finally, there is a failure to recognise structural constraints in the international system which limit the pursuit of the common good through international law.

Chimni has long been at the forefront of efforts to re-examine and theorise international law from a Marxist perspective.[64] As he characterises it, the project is to elaborate and identify 'an ensemble of methods, practices and understandings that go to empower the subaltern classes'. By 'subaltern classes', he intends 'all oppressed and marginal groups in society', whether on the basis of class or on the basis of some other social division. Against this background, he calls attention to four features that distinguish what he refers to as 'critical Marxist international law scholarship'. First, it historicises international law and its doctrines, and analyses them in terms of the groups, classes and states that have the greatest role in directing outcomes and reaping benefits. Second, it highlights the existence and nature of structural constraints that limit the extent to which international law can serve as an instrument of social transformation. Third, it underlines the indeterminacy of all international legal processes, but also their susceptibility to strategic deployment in ways that can contribute to the welfare of the subaltern classes. Finally, it challenges tendencies to universalise the perspective of those from powerful countries, and encourages the creation of a more inclusive scholarly community. Overall, as is made clear in the essay's conclusion, Chimni seeks to present international law in a manner that will inspire critical alertness to its limitations, but also imaginative engagement with its unrealised possibilities.

China Miéville's essay introduces the 'commodity-form theory' of international law, elaborated in more detail in his book, *Between Equal*

---

[64] See esp. his path-breaking book, B. S. Chimni, *International Law and World Order: A Critique of Contemporary Approaches* (New Delhi: Sage, 1993).

Rights.[65] Though only published in 2005, the book has already been very influential, not least for the other contributors to this volume. Miéville's theory draws on and reformulates the work in the 1920s of Russian jurist E. B. Pashukanis. Pashukanis was an immensely important legal scholar. His *General Theory of Law and Marxism*, denounced by Vyshinksy and burnt in the 1930s, is widely considered one of the key texts of Marxist legal theory.[66] He is also among the very few in this period who wrote specifically on international law, producing for the *Encyclopaedia of State and Law* an entry on the subject, which, though brief, constitutes a similarly pivotal contribution to international legal theory.[67] What most interests Miéville in these writings is Pashukanis's account of law as a distinctive form in capitalist conditions, comparable to the commodity. In this account, the legal subject is seen as homologous to the commodity owner, and legal relations are seen as homologous to commodity exchange. This applies equally to international law. As Pashukanis explains, '[s]overeign states co-exist and are counterposed to one another in exactly the same way as are individual property owners with equal rights'. In the international legal system 'the necessary conditions for the execution of exchange, i.e. equivalent exchange between private owners, are the conditions for legal interaction between states'.[68]

Miéville adopts this account, but pushes it further in one very significant respect. Whereas Pashukanis considered that commodity exchange carried the implication that property disputes can and will be resolved peacefully, Miéville contends that, on the contrary, the possibility of coercive force is always implicit in commodity relations. In this regard, Miéville recalls Marx's observation in *Capital* that the conditions for equivalent exchange between property owners (which, as Pashukanis maintains in the passage quoted above, are also the conditions for legal interaction between states) include within them the ultimate resort to force: '[b]etween equal rights, force decides'.[69] What of the fact that there is no system of organised international coercion, no superordinate authority standing over

---

[65] C. Miéville, *Between Equal Rights: A Marxist Theory of International Law* (Leiden: Brill, 2005).

[66] E. B. Pashukanis, *Law and Marxism: A General Theory*, C. Arthur, ed., B. Einhorn, trans. (London: Pluto Press, 1978).

[67] This is reprinted as an Appendix to Miéville, *Between Equal Rights*, p. 321. It also appears in E. B. Pashukanis, *Selected Writings on Marxism and Law*, P. Beirne and R. Sharlet, eds., P. Maggs, trans. (London: Academic Press, 1980), p. 168.

[68] Appendix to Miéville, *Between Equal Rights*, p. 329. See, alternatively, Pashukanis, *Selected Writings on Marxism and Law*, p. 176.

[69] *Capital*, Vol. 1, p. 344.

sovereign states? Highlighting Pashukanis's insight that superordinate authority is contingent to the legal form, Miéville proposes that the lack of superordinate authority does not (as has long been debated) deprive international law of its character as law; on the contrary, it actually makes international law an exemplary case of the law form. But the lack of superordinate authority does mean that the 'force' which 'decides' is force by sovereign states themselves, 'self-help'. Turning from the form of law to its content, Miéville shows how this is determined by the struggle for control over resources, which necessarily spills over into political violence. In his assessment, then, 'imperialism is embedded in the very structures of which international law is an expression and a moment'. It follows, for him, that there can be 'no prospect of any systematic progressive political project or emancipatory dynamic coming of international law'.

Bill Bowring also takes up themes from Russian international legal theory, during both the Bolshevik period and the later Soviet period. While Soviet international legal theory is often dismissed today as a narrow, formalist and hyper-positivist body of writing, with no vision of international justice going beyond the contractual arrangements of states, Bowring shows how things appear different when we focus on the Soviet contribution with regard to the right of self-determination. A host of suggestive contradictions then come into view between the positivism of Soviet legal textbooks on the one hand, and the traditions and practice of Marxism-Leninism on the other. Bowring considers the writings of Lenin and Stalin on self-determination and the 'national question', and also discusses the early twentieth-century debates about national and regional autonomy in the context of the break-up of the Tsarist empire. Against this background, he also examines the work of Pashukanis, engaging in debate with Miéville over Pashukanis's emphasis on law as a form. For Bowring, this emphasis led Pashukanis to isolate law from its content, and left no space in his work for engagement with the right of self-determination.

Turning to later writings, Bowring examines the work of a number of Soviet international legal scholars, of whom the best known outside the USSR was perhaps G. I. Tunkin. Bowring also highlights Soviet practice with regard to self-determination after World War II, arguing that the USSR played an instrumental role in securing the recognition of self-determination as a right that would support the independence of colonised peoples. Inasmuch as Soviet support for Third World peoples continued in the post-colonial period, he maintains that this was not simply a matter of 'Soviet propaganda', but a reflection of the 'logic of the new international law', developed in part through the efforts of the USSR. At the same time, Bowring calls attention to the contradictions and hypocrisies of this time, discussing in the last section of his essay the invasion of Czechoslovakia and the Vietnam war. In the contradictory character of the Soviet approach to self-determination lies, for Bowring, its compromised history, but also its enduring significance. He concludes that Bolshevik and Soviet international legal theory made an important contribution to the emergence of self-determination as an international legal entitlement, and that self-determination for its part made an important contribution to the development of Soviet international legal theory, serving as a counterpart or shadow-double to the positivist tendencies on which critical attention has mostly concentrated.

Anthony Carty is interested in contemporary debates about globalisation. His discussion focuses in particular on the very influential intervention in these debates by Michael Hardt and Antonio Negri, with the publication in 2000 of their book *Empire*.[70] Hardt and Negri argue in this book that developments of the later twentieth century brought about a reconfiguration of sovereignty. As they explain, 'sovereignty has taken a new form, composed of a series of national and supranational organisms united under a single logic of rule'.[71] They call this new global form of sovereignty 'Empire'. Although this term is obviously chosen to suggest continuities with earlier imperialism, Hardt and Negri emphasise the distinctiveness of the contemporary conjuncture: 'In contrast to imperialism, Empire establishes no territorial center of power and does not rely on fixed boundaries or barriers.'[72] In particular, the 'United States does not, and indeed no nation-state can today, form the center of an imperialist project'.[73] Carty considers this account unpersuasive, or at any rate unhelpful.

In the first place, he contends that it is characterised by 'hopeless awe' of the great industrial and financial powers. This induces resignation and passivity. Second, inasmuch as Hardt and Negri depict 'Empire' in terms of the emergence of a new 'biopolitical' paradigm of power, in which power is embraced and activated in the daily lives of those ruled, and social life hence regulated (as the authors put it) 'from its interior',[74] Carty maintains that, again, this closes the space for resistance. Third, he takes issue with Hardt and Negri's explanatory claims. In his words:

---

[70] M. Hardt and A. Negri, *Empire* (Cambridge, MA: Harvard University Press, 2000). See also their later *Multitude* (New York: Penguin, 2004).
[71] *Ibid.*, p. xii.   [72] *Ibid.*   [73] *Ibid.*, pp. xiii–xiv (emphasis omitted).   [74] *Ibid.*, p. 23.

[m]aybe there are perfectly obvious and feasible responses to the ills of the global economy that states cannot implement because these responses are resisted by other, more powerful states whose own interests argue against them.

Finally, against the authors' insistence that no nation-state can today form the centre of an imperialist project, Carty asserts the imperial role of the United States in contemporary geopolitics. Relating this to US engagements with international law, he maintains that 'Marxist analyses of the impact of the international economy on the general structure of international law remain the most convincing for the present'.

Claire Cutler investigates globalisation from a different angle, focusing on international trade law. At the outset she calls attention to two aspects of the contemporary trade regime. First, it is a regime of transnational, as distinct from merely international, law. Liberalisation is pursued well beyond border controls, reordering state competences within national boundaries. Second, it is an exclusionary regime that works to legitimate the legal subjectivity of corporate entities, even as it delegitimates the legal subjectivity of other non-state collectivities. With these aspects in mind, Cutler's point of departure is the need for a 'radical political economy critique' of international trade law. In elaborating her critique, she begins with colonial history, highlighting the way colonial relations developed into economic relations that were justified not simply by the right to dispossess, but by the right and even duty to produce capital.[75] This identification of capital accumulation with human nature and purpose constitutes – Cutler proposes – the 'single most important historical and analytical link between the classical imperialism of the past and the "new imperialism" of the present'. It also 'takes us to the heart of the intersection between international trade law and empire'. For Cutler, market ideology confers on international law the character of a form of 'natural law', constitutionalised through trade disciplines that 'reach deep inside states to govern matters once regarded as proper subjects of domestic public policy and national social regulation'.

To illustrate her discussion, Cutler refers to the General Agreement on Trade in Services (GATS), adopted in the outcome of the Uruguay Round of GATT negotiations to extend the regime so as to include trade in services. Under this treaty, states are invited to undertake commitments to liberalise trade in services by removing barriers to cross-border activity

---

[75] Cutler draws here on the work of Ellen Meiksins Wood. See E. Wood, *Empire of Capital* (London and New York: Verso, 2003).

of various kinds. For this purpose 'service' could include, and has included, the provision of water supply and the maintenance of educational institutions. Drawing on Marx's analysis of the commodity, Cutler discusses the ways in which the GATS commodifies these spheres of governmental responsibility. What were once public goods become commodities, offered for sale to householders and students who are now consumers, within a public arena which is now a market. Cutler also connects this with the commodity form of law, echoing some of the points made by Miéville in this regard. Under the GATS, she writes, 'the commodity form of law operates to fetishise services', and to abstract social regulation from its diverse contexts and dimensions. In challenging these developments, Cutler attaches importance to the dialectical nature of law, and evokes a 'praxis conception of transnational economic law [which] directs attention to the human dimension of law-making and the realisation that just as people make laws, so too they can modify or change them'.

Brad Roth's essay is concerned with human rights. In 1982 Steven Lukes posed the question: 'Can a Marxist believe in human rights?'.[76] His answer was 'no'; 'Marxists who do so can only . . . be revisionists who have discarded or abandoned . . . central tenets of the Marxist canon which are incompatible with such a belief'.[77] Roth's enquiry is different. He asks: 'Can Marxian political thought make a positive contribution to the contemporary project of international human rights advocacy?'. His answer to this question is 'yes'. An important text in this context is Marx's *On the Jewish Question*, written in 1843.[78] Emphasising the distinction mentioned earlier between political emancipation and human emancipation, Marx there criticises the human rights that had been proclaimed in the preceding half-century in French and North American constitutions as instruments of purely political emancipation. As he declares:

> [n]one of the so-called human rights . . . goes beyond the egoistic man, beyond man as member of civil society, namely withdrawn into his private interests and his private will, separated from the community.[79]

In these constitutions, 'society appears to be a context external to the individuals, and a restriction of their original independence. The one tie that holds them together is natural necessity, need and private interest, the conservation of their property and their egoistic person'.[80] At a time when the human rights movement occupies a central place in emancipatory

---

[76] S. Lukes, 'Can a Marxist Believe in Human Rights', (1982) 1 *Praxis International* 334.
[77] *Ibid.*, 344.   [78] Marx, *Early Political Writings*, p. 28.   [79] *Ibid.*, p. 46.   [80] *Ibid.*

politics, Roth argues that these and other Marxian insights can be used to bring out the limitations of human rights practice, rather than to repudiate it.

Roth considers that the contribution of Marxian thought is to be located at two principal levels. First, Marxian analysis can call into question the universality of human rights. As he explains, '[l]egality, rights and democracy all trade on promises that, in a class-divided society, they must necessarily betray'. Inasmuch as they operate to reaffirm and reinforce the prevailing dynamics of economy and society, this opens up a contradiction between the values they espouse and the conditions which those dynamics impose on subordinated classes. It follows that the 'class struggle will ... be played out as contestation over the essential meanings of these concepts'. In the case of human rights, the meaning of universality in the context of class division is a key aspect of this. Second, Roth highlights the value of Marxian analysis as a challenge to what he terms the 'neutralist' ethos that informs human rights. By this, he intends the liberal postulate of neutrality with respect to the good, its notion of human beings as fundamentally choosers of their own ends. In contrast, as he describes it, the Marxian project of social transformation invests in perfectionism; that is to say, it presupposes that there exists a better and more authentic way to live than that which is available in capitalist conditions. Roth shows how, when set against the foil of this approach, neutralism begins to appear problematic. Under the guise of neutrality, liberalism serves simply to 'reaffirm and to reinforce an existing way of life'. For Roth, then, the significance of Marxian thought for human rights is not as a replacement for liberal theorising, but as an immanent critique of it.

Obiora Okafor is also interested in the relationship between Marxian thought and human rights. At the same time, he is interested in the relationship between Marxism and the movement known as 'Third World Approaches to International Law' (TWAIL). TWAIL began as a self-conscious grouping of international legal scholars in the late 1990s. However, the movement traces its origins much further back, to the writing on international law that emerged in connection with the rise of Third World nationalism in the 1950s, 60s and 70s, and indeed to earlier decades and centuries of anti-colonial struggle. Okafor is himself, along with Chimni, a key figure within this movement, and in this essay he examines the scholarship of another prominent theorist associated with it, Upendra Baxi. Much TWAIL scholarship has been concerned with highlighting the ways in which colonialism can be shown to be a legal construct, and international law a colonial construct, and with bringing out the 'afterlives' of this interrelation. In *The Future of Human Rights*, Baxi extends the enquiry to point up the emergence of what he considers a new paradigm of 'trade-related market-friendly human rights'.[81] It is on this work that Okafor primarily focuses, using it to explore the intersection of Marxism and 'Third Worldism' in international law.

In Okafor's account, Baxi's Marxian influences are evident in three main features of his scholarship. The first is Baxi's focus on the 'subaltern classes'. As indicated, this is also the central category in Chimni's work. The second feature concerns Baxi's substantive analysis of late twentieth- and early twenty-first-century developments in the field of human rights, against the background of an increasingly extensive and intensive regime of international trade law. Informing the claim that a new paradigm of 'trade-related market-friendly human rights' has emerged is an attentiveness to exploitation. Baxi wants us to see that this paradigm serves to legitimate the exploitation of the subaltern classes by various formations of global capital. The final feature has to do with Baxi's approach to human rights activism, his relative scepticism about 'elite' or professional activism and his valorisation of 'self-conscious mass struggle'. In calling attention to these features, Okafor also highlights some of the ways in which Baxi's work diverges from particular variants of Marxism. Overall, his theme is the 'complicated and sophisticated relationship of Baxi's TWAIL human rights scholarship to Marxian thought'.

My own essay revolves around the Marxist concept of 'exploitation', just touched upon. I take as my starting point the observation that, for all the talk in international law about discrimination, injustice, exclusion, violence, indignity and abuse, there is very little discussion of exploitation. For all the talk about victims, perpetrators and vulnerable groups, there is not much reference to beneficiaries. Marxism has a rich account to offer of exploitation, beginning with Marx's account of the production of surplus-value in *Capital*, and encompassing later debates. However, very little of this is reflected in international law. Insofar as exploitation does feature in international legal materials, the focus is primarily on human trafficking and child labour. While these are clearly very serious forms of exploitation, they by no means exhaust the meaning of exploitation in contemporary conditions. In exploring why exploitation as an international legal issue maps only inadequately onto the much more pervasive phenomenon described by Marx and later analysts, I examine what I refer to as the 'ideology of mutuality'. I take this to be reflected in expert

---

[81] U. Baxi, *The Future of Human Rights* (Oxford: Oxford University Press, 2002).

discourses, everyday talk and unspoken 'common sense' in which the focus is on mutual gain. I propose that the ideology of mutuality has become central to the legitimating ideology of capitalism today, obscuring the ways in which the privilege of some is related to the deprivation of others. And if mutuality has become central to the legitimating ideology of capitalism, then so too, I argue, exploitation must become central to the critique of that ideology.

3. 'On the left'

In September 1999 the BBC held an online poll to discover the 'greatest thinker of the millennium'. Votes were received from across the world, and the result was a 'top ten' that included Kant, Descartes, Darwin, Aquinas, Einstein and Newton. But by a clear margin, it was Karl Marx who emerged as the voters' choice.[82] The outcome was reaffirmed in 2005 by another BBC poll, this time for the 'greatest philosopher of all time'. Marx again won, and no less decisively.[83] Reactions to these polls were unsurprisingly mixed. Some applauded the results, claiming them as a testament to the enduring strength of socialism and an illustration of the hostility that exists towards capitalist society even amongst sections of the middle class.[84] Others deplored what they took rather to illustrate the blindness of those sections of the middle class, and their continuing failure to reckon with the catastrophe that was twentieth-century state socialism.[85] A third group also expressed criticism, but for a different reason. The 'Marx' who had won these polls, they said, was a Marx 'cleansed of his revolutionary, anti-capitalist ideas', a 'shadow Marx'. Since '[a]t every possible turn [in the accompanying BBC debates] Marx's political project was ignored, marginalized or misrepresented', on this view Marx may have won, but Marxism certainly lost.[86]

A similar concern about the depoliticisation of Marxism has also been voiced in connection with academic writings about Marx and Marxism. Commenting on Jacques Derrida's work on the 'spectres of Marx' and the 'New International',[87] Terry Eagleton contends that Derrida 'wants to

---

[82] See http://news.bbc.co.uk/hi/english/static/events/millennium/ sep/winner.stm.
[83] This poll was organised by the BBC Radio Four programme 'In Our Time'. See www.bbc.co.uk/radio4/history/inourtime/ greatest philosopher vote result.shtml.
[84] See, e.g., www.socialistparty.org.uk/2005/402/index. html?id=np9b.htm.
[85] See, e.g., S. Sebag Montefiore, 'Marx The Monster', *Daily Mail*, 14 July 2005.
[86] D. Murray and M. Neocleous, 'Marx comes first again, and loses', (2005) 134 *Radical Philosophy* 59 at 59, 60.
[87] J. Derrida, *Specters of Marx* (New York and London: Routledge, 1994), pp. 85–6.

exploit Marxism as critique, dissent . . . but is far less willing to engage with its positivity'.[88] According to Eagleton, Derrida mistakes Marxism for 'a vaguely leftish commitment to the underdog'; what he wants, 'in effect, is a Marxism without Marxism'.[89] While some would dispute that assessment of Derrida's perspective, Eagleton makes an important general point here, with implications for this book. 'Re-examining Marxist legacies' in connection with the study of 'international law on the left' is all very well, but we need to be careful not to treat Marxism as though it were a synonym for generic left thought. For their critics, the BBC's 'greatest thinker' and 'greatest philosopher' contests illustrate how this may happen. 'It was Marx as a cultural icon, rather than Marx as a communist, that people were voting for', these analysts remark. 'The vote for Marx was thus another way of "branding" the self, a left*ish* self which can only associate with Marx once an alternative Marx has taken over – a Marx falsely associated with things that many on the left value but which are in fact not part of Marxism at all.'[90]

In a number of the essays in this book, as well as earlier in this Introduction, the concept of commodification, rooted in Marx's account of the fetishism of commodities, is evoked. Here we are reminded that Marxism itself has no immunity to this process. In the twenty-first century it too is a commodity – a brand in the marketplace of affiliations. But before we rush to conclude that the old questions of authenticity and revisionism that so preoccupied orthodox Marxists are once again being raised by these critics of 'Marxism without Marxism', we should be clear about the precise nature of their complaint. The concern is certainly not with the idea of Marxism as an historical product, to be reappropriated and rethought in ever-changing circumstances. Nor is it with the idea of Marxism as a cultural practice, with relevance to everyday life, personal identity, and the experience of relating to a tradition. Rather, the concern is with the idea of Marxism as an apolitical concept. What worries these critics is the evacuation of its political content, the abstraction of Marxism from its significance as a political project, and the resulting loss of its capacity to mobilise political action and all that that entails: 'organization, apparatuses and reasonably well formulated doctrines and programmes.'[91]

One of Marx's best known aphorisms is his eleventh thesis on Feuerbach: the 'philosophers have only *interpreted* the world in different

---

[88] T. Eagleton, 'Marxism without Marxism' in M. Sprinkler (ed.), *Ghostly Demarcations* (London and New York: Verso, 1999), p. 82, at p. 86.
[89] Ibid., pp. 86–7.   [90] Murray and Neocleous, 'Marx comes first again', 60.
[91] Eagleton, 'Marxism without Marxism', p. 86.

ways; the point is to *change* it'.[92] In typically insightful and provocative (and also characteristically Marxian) fashion, Slavoj Žižek proposes that we might now do better to turn this proposition around, and maintain the reverse. 'The first task today', he writes, 'is precisely *not* to succumb to the temptation to act, to directly intervene and change things (which then inevitably ends in a cul-de-sac of debilitating impossibility: "what can one do against global capital?")'.[93] Instead, Žižek contends, 'the task is to question the hegemonic ideological coordinates' within which action – any action – can occur.[94] The essays in this book belong with the questioning of hegemonic ideological coordinates. But it is important not to lose sight of the point of this endeavour, which is to open up those coordinates and locate footholds for transformative change.

[92] Marx, *Early Political Writings*, p. 118.
[93] S. Žižek, 'Have Michael Hardt and Antonio Negri Written the *Communist Manifesto* for the Twenty-First Century?', (2001) 13(3/4) *Rethinking Marxism* 190 at 194.
[94] *Ibid.*

1

What should international lawyers learn from Karl Marx?

MARTTI KOSKENNIEMI

1. Introduction

Many claim, or at least suspect, that international law is in a crisis. For some, informal globalisation and the Iraqi war have demonstrated international law's increasing marginality in international life, the growing pattern of violation of its key provisions interpreted as proof of its irrelevancy.[1] For others, the crisis emerges from endogenous origins, from international law's having become yet another aspect of a bureaucratic system of bargaining at Western-dominated international institutions by an 'international *Hofmafia*'.[2] While both criticisms have a bite, my interest is drawn directly by neither. Instead, I want to examine the inside of the profession where the crisis sometimes appears as a sense of the loss of international law's emancipatory promise, a creeping scepticism about whether there ever was any such project to begin with.

I have elsewhere told the story of international law's emergence as part of liberal modernity in the latter half of the nineteenth century.[3] That it has been a part of 'modernity' has meant that it has been animated by a progressive and universalistic spirit, firm confidence in the ability of liberal political institutions to transform the world into a democratic and

[1] Whether these facts are celebrated or regretted depends today, of course, on one's standpoint in regard to the merits of American unilateralism. Jürgen Habermas has made the point that 'the Bush regime has through its moral phrases relegated *ad acta* the 220-year-old Kantian project of the legalisation of international relations', interview with Eduardo Mendieta, published as 'Wege aus der Weltunordnung' (2004) *Blätter für deutsche und internationale Politik*, translation by Martti Koskenniemi.

[2] This latter criticism is sharpest in the works of Philip Allott. For the expression in the text, see his 'International Law and the International Hofmafia. Towards a sociology of international diplomacy', in P. Allott, *The Health of Nations. Society and Law beyond the State* (Cambridge: Cambridge University Press, 2003), pp. 380–98.

[3] M. Koskenniemi, *The Gentle Civilizer of Nations. The Rise and Fall of International Law 1870–1960* (Cambridge: Cambridge University Press, 2001).

30

rule-governed Kantian *Völkerstaat*. My sense, however, is that like many other aspects of modernity, the profession of international law has in recent years been bogged down in fruitless and repetitive forms of thinking about the international world; bureaucratic étatism on the one hand, imperial or nostalgic humanism on the other. It has become increasingly difficult for international lawyers to find a meaningful place in the international world that would resonate with the expectations of progress and enlightenment that characterised the profession's heroic period.

To assist international lawyers in grappling with this sense of existential crisis, I wish to draw attention to three aspects of the teaching of Karl Marx. First, I shall provide a rapid sketch of the nature of the Marxian critical project to the extent that it seems relevant as an extension of international law's original effort to transform the international world. Second, I shall examine the relationship between Marxian thinking and certain critical analyses of international law, including the one in which I have been engaged for more than a decade. And, last, I shall try to sketch an understanding of the role of international law as an element of international justice that would reach beyond the false universalisms offered by the equally unappealing alternatives of bureaucratic institutionalism and morally based empire.

I am not writing this as a Marxist. Marx would not have spoken about justice or injustice – except as a strategic concession, even then with the greatest reluctance.[4] 'Justice', Engels once wrote, was a 'social phlogiston'. For the cool eye of Marx, the language of justice obstructed reliable analysis of social relations. For him, notions such as 'justice' and of course 'international law' – had he given it a second's thought, which he never did – were part of the problem, not of its resolution. But I am writing this as an international lawyer to other international lawyers who are, I assume, as concerned as I am about the state of their craft. I am not asking 'what did Marx really say?', or 'what would be the Marxian analysis of the international world today?' These are good questions, but not the ones I am interested in. I am using Marx in an instrumental and heretic fashion, in order to assist in a project that can scarcely be called Marxian in any traditional sense.

International law will not bring about world revolution. Perhaps no such revolution is possible, or necessary. But it might support just causes in the international world and become an object of progressive political

---

[4] For a useful discussion, see S. Lukes, *Marxism and Morality* (Oxford: Oxford University Press, 1985), pp. 48–70.

commitment.[5] This, however, requires perceiving it as an aspect of something larger, some general approach to the problems of the international social world. If it is possible at all to redeem international law's transforming promise, and to make its adherents think more sharply and act more efficiently, this will require positioning it in a historical continuum that recognises its being part of modernity and of a critique of modernity simultaneously. 'All significant concepts of the modern theory of the state are secularised theological conceptions', Carl Schmitt once wrote, pointing to one of modernity's ambivalent aspects.[6] This ambivalence characterises major concepts of international law, too, sovereignty and human rights above all: they provide the lineaments of a stable political order only on the basis of a *faith* that resolves interpretative controversies and fills normative vacuums by a matrix that situates this activity within a larger vision. That by itself is no problem. The problem is a *loss of faith* in the profession in any such matrix or vision, identified sharply within national law in the last sentence of Roberto Unger's manifesto for critical legal studies twenty years ago:

> When we came, they were like a priesthood that had lost their faith and kept their jobs. They stood in tedious embarrassment before cold altars. But we turned away from those altars and found the mind's opportunity in the heart's revenge.[7]

2. The nature of the critical project

The year 1843 was a key year in the life of Karl Marx. He was dismissed from his position as the responsible editor of the *Rheinische Zeitung* where his articles had grown increasingly radical and hostile against the Prussian Government. In April he got married, spent the summer in Kreutznach compiling the first five of his famous notebooks and, in November, moved to Paris. He threw himself into an intensive study of the French social philosophers and deepened his reflections on the materialist theses

---

[5] For extensive analysis of international law's past oscillation between periods or renewal and stagnation, consensus and anxious disputation, and a call for reactivating the profession as a 'voice, viewpoint and a whole bunch of people pursuing projects with and against one another', see D. Kennedy, 'When Renewal Repeats. Thinking Against the Box' (2000) 32 *New York Journal of International Law and Politics* 335 at 466.

[6] C. Schmitt, *Political Theology. Four Chapters on the Concept of Sovereignty*, Georg Schwab trans. (Cambridge, MA: MIT Press 1985), p. 36.

[7] R. Unger, *The Critical Legal Studies Movement* (Cambridge, MA: Harvard University Press, 1986), p. 119.

that had been put forward by Ludwig Feuerbach that same year in his *Preliminary Theses on the Reformation of Philosophy*. These developments led Marx to break with his left-Hegelian friends. Using the method he had learned from Hegel he commenced the project of turning the latter's idealism on its head in two writings that he began that year, *Contribution to the Critique of Hegel's Philosophy of Right* and *On the Jewish Question*.[8]

The left-Hegelian radicals had been engaged in a fundamental critique of religion. Now Marx decided that this critique, while right in principle, did not go far enough. Religion had already become a pre-modern relic. The important task was instead to develop that critique into an attack on aspects of modernity itself. The key question was: why had the French Revolution failed? Answering it required an attack on the politics of liberal republicanism as it emerged from the restoration. These politics, Marx claimed, had remained imprisoned within what remained a religious pattern of thinking. It was thus necessary to attack that pattern itself – the 'idealism' it manifested – so as to produce an effective critique of liberal modernity. The writings of 1843–44 extend the critique of religion in two directions: into a critique of the bourgeois state on the one hand, and into a critique of bourgeois humanism on the other.

2.1. Against the bourgeois state

Hegel had secularised Christianity into the ethical life (*Sittlichkeit*) that he saw embodied in the family, civil society and the state. Family and civil society represented 'morality' and 'abstract right', neither of which could stand alone in the process that would lead human society – Hegel's 'Spirit' – to freedom. The pure subjectivity of morality and the abstract personhood of the legal subject in civil society needed to come together – and to be transcended – in the political life of the state that made concrete and universal what without it would remain only abstract and particular.[9]

From Feuerbach, Marx learned that to say that social phenomena were produced by the 'Spirit' of an 'age' was mere tautological abstraction.

---

[8] K. Marx, 'On the Jewish Question' in K. Marx, *Early Political Writings* Joseph O'Malley, (ed.) (Cambridge: Cambridge University Press, 1994), p. 28; and 'A Contribution to the Critique of Hegel's Philosophy of Right: Introduction', *ibid.*, p. 57.

[9] See G. W. F. Hegel, *Philosophy of Right* S. W. Dyde (trans.) (Amherst: Prometheus Books, 1996 [1821/1896]), pp. 248–74 (paras 260–71). For a very useful recent discussion of the passage from 'abstract right' to the (concrete) ethical life (and universal freedom) in the State, see P. Franco, *Hegel's Philosophy of Freedom* (New Haven: Yale University Press, 2000).

What existed were historical events and qualities. To say that they were the effect of a German '*Geist*' or the 'spirit of the Revolution' was to pin empty labels on concrete human acts and patterns of action. History was not produced by such abstractions but by human individuals acting within material conditions that enabled such events to take place.[10] By 1843, such theses had been widely used so as to discredit religion: '*man makes religion*, religion does not make man'.[11] Now this argument was to be transposed to the social realm.

For Hegel, the place of God as the Absolute had been taken over by the state, standing over family and civil society. This was what made Hegel *the* philosopher of secular modernity in the first place. Marx saw this transposition as sheer pre-modern mysticism. Only the family and civil society were real contexts of human action. The state was only a hypothesised reflection of some activities in which concrete individuals had been engaged within those two realms. 'So long as this is not recognised, Marx reasoned, humanity's genuine universal existence, its collective communal being, will be dissipated in the false universality of the political state.'[12] Where pre-modern religion set God above human society, liberal modernity (as articulated by Hegel) did the same with the personified the state, thus creating the condition for human society's self-alienation. When Marx now famously turned Hegel on his head, this meant he overturned the state vs. civil society relationship in the same way as the critique of religion had transformed the relation between God and human society.

So much for the religious mysticism underlying the bourgeois state. Later on, Marx and his followers elaborated on the instrumental uses of the state for upholding the class relations in civil society. But the famous thesis of the withering away of the state after the end of human prehistory remained an intrinsic part of Marx's view of history. Here Marxian thought is joined by much non-Marxian historical sociology, including the sociology of interdependence that has been a firm aspect of the ideology behind international law through the twentieth century. Today, international lawyers may point to aspects of globalisation that seem

---

[10] See further I. Berlin, *Karl Marx: His Life and Environment*, 4th edn (Oxford: Oxford University Press 1978), pp. 57–8.

[11] Marx, 'A Contribution', p. 57.

[12] W. Breckman, *Marx, the Young Hegelians and the Origins of Radical Social Theory* (Cambridge: Cambridge University Press 1999), p. 285.

to advance the cosmopolitan promise in Kant's famous 1795 essay.[13] However, few of them think that this also commits them to support the policies of the World Bank or the World Trade Organization, humanitarian intervention or the fight against terrorism. So the question is: how to distinguish between commitment to universalism and the policies of powerful international actors constantly invoking the universal so as to justify their particular agendas. To make a distinction between real and false universalism, transformative promise and institutional realisation, international lawyers could learn not only the Marxian critique of the state but the critique of the political theology that sustains it.

2.2. Against liberal humanism

The state was not the only object of reified mysticism. The liberal humanism that was the practical opponent of the Prussian state and claimed to bear the heritage of the revolution was, too, building pre-scientific dogma. Making this point was the gist of that other key text from 1843, *On the Jewish Question*, drafted in response to the suggestion by Marx's former ideological fellow traveller, Bruno Bauer, that Jewish emancipation could take place only by the emancipation of Jews from religion altogether. Like other left liberals, Bauer saw freedom in modern society in terms of secular political liberty and equality of the citizen. Emancipation would mean full enjoyment of human rights within a non-confessional public order of the state.

For Marx such merely 'political' emancipation, was not enough. Instead, a real 'human emancipation' would reach beyond religion and the state (itself founded on religious thinking), so as to grasp at the human relations that constituted the reality of civil society. To redeem the actuality of human beings and their relationships with each other, the abstract person developed by liberal humanism had to be set aside just as the critique of religion had done to God. The state and human rights related to each other in liberal modernity like God and theology had done in pre-modern societies, alienating, as Marx would say, human beings from themselves and blinding them to the reality of their condition in bourgeois society.

---

[13] I. Kant, 'Perpetual Peace: A Philosophical Sketch' in Kant, *Political Writings*, Hans Reiss (ed.), (Cambridge: Cambridge University Press, 2nd edn, 1991), p. 93.

In Hegel, the view of universal human rights as transcendental conditions of *Sittlichkeit* is vulnerable to the critique of morality as pure subjectivity. The individual is detached from the conditions in which individuality is produced. For Marx, political emancipation through human rights enjoyed by the abstract individual was, again, political theology at work, the presentation as transcendentally given of something that was socially produced.[14] It was only an apparent paradox that the atheistic, democratic state fulfils Christianity's separation of the individual from humanity: 'Political democracy is Christian in that in it man – not merely one man but every man – has value as a *sovereign* being, the highest being . . .'[15] No wonder, Marx thought, a fully secular state such as the United States was compatible with a flourishing religious civil society.[16]

The *droits de l'homme* are yet another political theology: yet another personification of something transcendental over human species-nature.[17] But the abstract individual is in truth the individual of bourgeois society and the rights of this individual are, Marx famously argued, rights:

> of egoistic man, of the man who is separated from other men and from the community . . . This is the freedom of man as a monad isolated and withdrawn into himself.[18]

Moreover, how human rights function in society is conditioned by the specific form of liberal modernity – namely the separation of the public from the private, state from civil society. Into this separation is injected a particular anthropology: '[I]t is not man as citizen but man as bourgeois who is taken to be the *real* and *true* human being.'[19] The initial freedom at the level of civil society ensures that only abstract individuals meet each other:

---

[14] See also M. Koskenniemi, 'The Effect of Rights on Political Culture', in P. Alston (ed.), *The EU and Human Rights* (Oxford: Oxford University Press, 1999), p. 99.

[15] Marx, 'On the Jewish Question', p. 41.

[16] *Ibid.*, p. 33. Marx's critique of political theology is twofold, or contradictory: on the one hand, theological questions are reduced into secular ones, on the other hand, secular phenomena (e.g. bourgeois democracy) are interpreted as Christian theology. For Marx, ultimately, any non-socialising notion of the individual personhood was theological, and as such, 'synonymous with heteronomy and alienation': Breckman, *Marx, the Young Hegelians*, pp. 295 and 297.

[17] For the process through which the human individual emerges to take the place of God in secular society, and 'human rights' is instituted as a theology of an agnostic modernity, see L. Ferry, *L'Homme-dieu ou le Sens de la vie* (Paris: Grasset, 1996) p. 109 ff.

[18] Marx, 'On the Jewish Question', pp. 44, 45. [19] *Ibid.*, p. 46.

> [T]he human right of freedom is not based on the connection of man with man, but much more on the separation of man from man. It is the *right* of this separation, the right of the individual who is *limited*, enclosed within himself.[20]

The practical application of this in the sphere of civil society is the right of private property. Every other right serves this purpose: equality is the right of everyone to be considered a self-possessed monad ('individual') while the right to security is to be secure in such possession.

This famous critique highlights the way the abstract individuality presumed by human rights is imposed over the concrete relations of civil society so that forms of factual subordination (capitalist/worker, man/woman) are made miraculously to appear like equality (citizen/citizen). That this critique is valid independently of whether the state is a monarchy or a republic separates it from the thinking of liberal reformists. Human rights are about perpetuating bourgeois civil society through the distribution of rights to individuals by the political state, not seen in terms of distribution, however, but as merely giving effect to something that exists 'naturally', beyond the realm of political contestation. And this, Marx delights to point out, is where the practice of bourgeois politics comes into conflict with its theory. As Robespierre already stated, 'freedom of the press should not be permitted when it compromises public freedom'. 'Freedom' and 'human rights' are completely conditioned by the needs of political life and turn into instruments of terror when they conflict with it: 'the end appears as the means and the means as the end'.[21]

This relationship between the bourgeois state and human rights can be viewed as two theologies first clashing, then merging into each other through the affirmation of state authority. On the one hand, secular modernity avoids chaos by adopting the single religion of statehood within which social conflict is redescribed as political – that is, religious – conflict. On the other hand, the danger this poses to civil society is countered by the postulation of human rights, presumed to exist naturally, as a set of transcendental limits to political power – yet applied by the same authorities whose power they should limit.[22] The totalitarian state of the twentieth

---

[20] *Ibid.*, p. 45. [21] Quoted *ibid.*, p. 47.
[22] The liberal theory of rights proposed by John Rawls or Ronald Dworkin, for instance, is premised on the functional idea of rights as limits to politics. Being 'outside' politics, they become absolute and non-negotiable, however and can, as Michael J. Perry has pointed out, be only transcendentally grounded. Human rights, as he puts it, are 'ineliminably religious'. M. J. Perry, *The Idea of Human Rights. Four Inquiries* (Oxford: Oxford University Press, 1998), pp. 11–41.

century is counter-reformation in a modernistic garb. Within it, the rights and freedoms of members of civil society are worshipped through all-encompassing legislation that regulates the permissible uses of their freedom to the smallest detail. This seems necessary as the gifts both of faith and of freedom cannot coexist in real individuals. As Dostoyevsky's Grand Inquisitor famously told his prisoner:

> Why is the weak soul to blame for being unable to receive gifts so terrible? Surely you did not come here only to the chosen and for the chosen? But if so, then there is a mystery here and we cannot understand it. And if it is a mystery, then we, too, were entitled to preach mystery and to teach them that it is neither the free verdict of their hearts nor love that matters but the mystery which they must obey blindly, even against their conscience. So we have done. We have corrected your great work and have based it on *miracle, mystery, and authority*. And men rejoiced that they were once more led like sheep and that the terrible gift which had brought them so much suffering had at last been lifted from their hearts.[23]

Human rights cannot trump the power of the inquisitor, as jurisdiction over what those rights are, and how conflicts over them should be resolved, belongs to him.[24] So this is the difficulty. Human rights must either be accepted as faith, or then given over to the state. But the faith of weak (liberal) souls is thin, and so the inquisitor will have final authority; what that religion says, when it counts, is conclusively determined by him. The state and human rights are locked into each other to form the realm of politics against which stands civil society as the enjoyment of bourgeois freedoms by autonomous monads: bureaucracy here, class rule there.

This is the prison-house of modern political theology that Marx sought to break. To break it, and not to resort to yet another theology, required that one start from what is, and not from what should be. This required dialectical thinking.

3. Dialectical thinking: how Marx connects with the indeterminacy of the law?

The state/civil society opposition was, for Marx, the defining moment of political modernity. But the important general point was that to define

---

[23] F. Dostoyevsky, *The Brothers Karamazov* (London: Penguin, 1982) p. 301.
[24] I have discussed this paradox in detail in M. Koskenniemi, 'The Effect of Rights on Political Culture'.

something by reference to an opposition was the starting point of a properly *historical* view of that something – in this case of human society. An opposition was not an abstract 'problem' that had to be resolved by reason, as bourgeois politics always suggested. Instead, it was to be taken seriously, that is dialectically, as the source through which historical development would proceed by the 'negation of the negation', that is by the resolution of conflicts not by synthesis into some tranquil (bourgeois) normality but through moments of challenge, collapse and construction.[25]

Stated formally, dialectics would show how any social reality would consist of an inherent tension between its opposite elements. The secondary element (e.g. civil society, working class) would put to question the major element (state, bourgeois rule) so that it would eventually collapse. In postmodernity, however, (pure) materialist dialectics enters itself into a dialectical relationship with the processes of symbolic representation of society that take place through the practices whereby social agents seek to control the meanings of shared symbols. Political struggle will then be understood as waged also on the meaning of legal symbols – words such as 'sovereignty', 'democracy', 'human rights', *'jus cogens'* or 'terrorism', for example. Where dialectics shows the historical contingency of the social, 'deconstruction' points to the radical indeterminacy (or 'undecidability') of the symbolic and redescribes social conflict in terms of (political) conflict over what social symbols should mean – whose action they should support, whose action they should condemn. This is why it seems right to say that deconstruction performs the work of dialectics by showing the radical instability of forms of representing society. In this way it 'would be either inconceivable or irrelevant if it were not related to the spirit of the tradition of a certain Marxism'.[26]

Such a perspective would enable international lawyers to interpret the dichotomies of international law in light of the historical tensions in the international world – for instance, the relationship between the public realm of state diplomacy on the one hand, and that of the international civil society on the other. But the important move would be not merely to notice this opposition (after all, it is the dominant focus of mainstream analyses) *but to analyse it deconstructively*, that is, by

---

[25] Here again was a crucial difference between Marx and social revolutionaries such as Proudhon, for instance, for whom it would suffice to suspend what was 'bad' so as to bring about that which in society was 'good'. See J. Ellul, *La pensée marxiste. Cours professé à l'Institut d'études politiques de Bordeaux de 1947 à 1979* (Paris: Table Ronde, 2003), pp. 77–8.
[26] E. Laclau, 'The Time is Out of Joint', in E. Laclau, *Emancipation(s)* (London: Verso, 1996), p. 66.

including in the analysis not only the critique of diplomacy by actors in civil society (negation) but also the challenge of legitimacy to the self-promoted representatives of civil society that calls for organisation in the image of accountability structures that define formal statehood (negation of negation). This would mean a description of the setting in which 'public diplomacy' conflicts with 'civil society' as indeterminate: neither side possesses a final truth, each depends on aspects of its counterpart. This would make the moment of *decision* visible: no choice within such a setting can be fully determined by a pre-existing structure (because, after all, the structures flow into each other). Deconstruction becomes a pragmatism:[27] if a decision is necessarily ungrounded in existing structure, then the way it affects actual individuals now is highlighted while any supposed long-term benefits appear increasingly dubious.

A dialectical-deconstructive analysis of the challenges to public diplomacy by globalisation critics and social movements would accept that the tension between the public and the private encompassed within it is not going to go away through successive transformations but that each novel configuration of forces would always already contain a critique of its achieved hierarchies and thus the seeds of their eventual collapse.[28] Had Marx analysed communism deconstructively (which he was not in a position to do, as he was seeking to bring it about), he could not have failed to envisage the foreseeable historical role of non-submissive groups within that configuration whose activity was to lead to the eventual collapse of its totalising ambition.

3.1. Dialectics and deconstruction in law

International lawyers are familiar with how legal thought is locked into what seem like irresolvable dichotomies and paradoxes. Posing ourselves the question as to why a putative norm should be binding, we receive two responses. Either something is binding as an effect of a subject's will or command, or it is binding independently of that will, because it is just that the standard should be so. Much of what international lawyers have to say about the sources of the law captures this dualism. But though the setting of the problem seems to demand a firm decision

---

[27] This is the theme of the series of small essays by Simon Critchley, Jacques Derrida, Ernesto Laclau and Richard Rorty in C. Mouffe (ed), *Deconstruction and Pragmatism* (London: Routledge, 1996).

[28] See also M. Koskenniemi, 'Hierarchy in International Law: A Sketch' (1997) 8 *European Journal of International Law* 566.

one way or another, neither seems fully able to trump its contrary. The 'justice' of an agnostic (liberal) society can only be what its members have 'consented' to – while why 'consent' should have such force, and where its limits lie ('you cannot consent to genocide') must be received from some non-consensual principle of 'justice'. For modernity's secular religion, the emptiness of '*jus cogens*' or 'obligations *erga omnes*' is not an unfortunate temporary weakness but an absolutely central aspect of its constant putting into question of its own normativity in a terrain of radical political indeterminacy and social contingency.

When, again, we seek to answer the question about legal authority (sovereignty) in regard to a piece of territory or a group of people, we look both into what it is that history has produced ('effectiveness'), as well as what ideas of just government might tell us ('legitimacy'). Much of the law on territory and jurisdiction captures this opposition – though none of it is able to explain exhaustively why 'effectiveness' should trump 'legitimacy' (after all, *ex injuria jus non oritur*) or vice-versa (after all, 'rights cannot be presumed to exist merely because it might seem desirable that they should'[29]). Neither is able to override the other because their opposition is part of the discursive world in which they belong – which they, in fact, create. Notions such as effectiveness and legitimacy (like consent and justice) interact dialectically: effectiveness creates legitimacy while legitimacy singles out the types of *effectivités* that have normative value (in contrast to those that are merely *contra legem*).[30] Paradox and self-reference become the postmodern description of what in a Marxian view would be a properly historical dialectic.[31] Each points to the way political intervention, that is, definite decision, is needed to achieve consequences in the lives of human beings.

Such structural dichotomies reflect the contradictory ways in which modern society sees itself. Voluntarist and naturalist theories of agreement, and historical and rational views of authority, mirror formidable oppositions between fact and value, individual and society. It is never just that there are two alternative institutional projects from which to

---

[29] International Court of Justice, South-West Africa Case (2nd phase), Reports 1966, p. 48.
[30] For an example of this dialectic in terms of the opposition between and mutual interpenetration of 'title' and '*effectivités*', see International Court of Justice, Cameroon-Nigeria Land and Maritime Boundary (Bakassi Peninsula) Case, Reports 2002.
[31] Such paradox and self-reference are central to the kind of understanding of society expounded in N. Luhmann, *Die Wissenschaft der Gesellschaft* (Frankfurt: Suhkamp, 1992). For a useful application of Luhmannian analysis in international law, see A. Fischer-Lescano, 'Die Emergenz der Globalverfassung' (2003) 63 *Zeitschrift für ausländisches öffentliches Recht und Völkerrecht* 717.

choose, or two solutions for every legal problem, but that the proposed solutions, while cancelling each other out, also rely for their identity and force on each other. None can rid itself of its rival because it also needs the latter's support.[32] A command view of legal obligation has point only if we assume that 'will' overrides 'justice'. Indeed, that is what liberal voluntarism is supposed to do. And yet, when or whose commands should have that kind of force can be defended only by a theory of justice – while what the content of such a theory is, can be demonstrated only by reference to what someone wills: the permissibility of reservations to treaties is determined by the 'object and purpose test', while what the 'object and purpose' of a treaty is, is exhaustively determined by what it is that the parties have willed as such.

Discussed in this way, the law's constitutive oppositions seem irresolvable and legal reason appears condemned to the eternal recurrence of the same: voluntarists engage with solidarists, positivists with naturalists, formalists with non-formalists. And so on.[33] But though none of the positions can claim priority on logical grounds, every legal regime still always appears as a *particular arrangement* of the opposites. Although at the level of abstract reason, there is no closure, at the level of concrete history, there is always some configuration of forces, some hierarchical arrangement. And how to reach that level of concreteness requires going beyond political theology. What is it that makes one term dominate the other here, in this case, between these contestants? And why would such domination justify *this* particular distribution of social costs and benefits?

3.2. International relations: an excursus

Parallel considerations give a novel perspective to what it means that thinking about international relations continues to be trapped in a juxtaposition of 'realism' and 'idealism' as alternative frameworks for understanding the international world: each defers to the other without being able to grasp (self-reflectively) the historical role of its momentary predominance over its opposite. This may seem evident when applied to classical idealist views of international history, seen as a function of great

---

[32] See further M. Koskenniemi, 'The Politics of International Law' (1990) 1 *European Journal of International Law* 4.

[33] This is what I have described in *From Apology to Utopia. The Structure of International Legal Argument* (Helsinki: Lakimiesliiton kustannus, 1989).

ideas, cultures or successions of epochal *Geiste*. But perhaps more relevant is to note that even as 'realism' describes international politics as struggle for power by states to realise interests, it moves in one second from the account of the Peloponnesian wars by Thucydides around the year 400 BC to a discussion of the relations between Italian city-states in the fourteenth and fifteenth centuries, to the peace of Utrecht in 1713 and to the Cold War. What is the force of a theory that freezes two and half millennia into a single, unchanging pattern?[34]

A critique of political theology would show realism emptied of content by its privileging the political state over the 'structural configuration of forces' that in civil society create the conditions of official diplomacy. Such an analysis would focus on the social and economic relations of each period as the proper context for understanding its diplomacy: is there a need for the functional differentiation of a political realm distinct from the economic, for example in order to resolve problems of co-ordination in the reproduction of particular types of social relations?[35] This, however, means setting aside the distinction between the internal and the international that founds the disciplinary tradition of 'international relations' that, to paraphrase Marx, 'hangs like a nightmare over the minds of the living'.

Now it is true that the development of liberal epistemology has undermined this type of realism, downgrading it to a style of populistic commentary on current affairs.[36] 'Reality' is today seen as constructed by frameworks involving normative preferences.[37] The normative turn in international relations studies in the 1990s is paralleled by the turn to ethics in international politics. Struggle of power becomes a 'clash of civilisations' or a function of some inherent tension within a multicultural system. Recent studies suggest that transformations in the international world result from 'changes in metavalues', predominant among which is the 'moral purpose of the state'. Under this view, normative change is crucial: Protestantism created the Westphalian system; anti-colonial ideas

---

[34] Reliance on a single, unchanging notion of 'human nature' is regularly identified as a weak spot and a hidden idealism in such classical realists as Morgenthau or Niebuhr, for example.

[35] Such a critique and alternative construction is made in J. Rosenberg, *The Empire of Civil Society* (London: Verso, 1994).

[36] See typically, R. D. Kaplan, *Warrior Politics. Why Leadership Demands a Pagan Ethos* (New York: Vintage, 2002).

[37] For a useful review and critique, see M. Zehfuss, *Constructivism in International Relations* (Cambridge: Cambridge University Press, 2002).

brought about decolonisation.[38] As in all idealism, the conditions of the emergence or decline of such ideas remain shrouded in mystery.

The juxtaposition of realism and idealism remains undecidable. Both appear as political theologies engaged in a shouting match over whether human nature is bad or good, whose God is strongest. Dialectics would understand this undecidability as inscribed in the liberal world-view itself. It would seek to explain the predominance of one over another at any particular moment from the hegemonic role it plays in upholding or challenging some particular configuration of forces.[39] The rise and fall of realism, for instance, could be connected with the transformation and dissolution of a Cold War consciousness. Against this, the new normative orientations might be seen in terms of a new struggle between an unmediated foreign policy moralism advocated by a single superpower and an anti-imperial formalism insisting on mediation through law and international institutions.[40]

Dialectics would understand the realism/idealism opposition as a clash of political theologies, each manifesting what could be called a logic of *identity*, a pattern of thought that reduces social phenomena to a mechanical series of single truths each of which appears final and authentic – perhaps human nature, perhaps the good – whose repetition forms the passing of social time. For dialectics, as for deconstruction, there is no such nature or good that would be independent from history, conceived as struggle between articulations emerging from opposing social forces: time is prior to meaning. Every identity is constructed by *decisions* that employ existing structures without being reducible to them. This is why each identity also carries within itself its own negation. '*Chaque époque rêve la suivante*', Walter Benjamin once wrote. The move in thinking from a logic of identity for which the dichotomies of law are fatal, into dialectics that uses the dichotomies as frameworks for historical explanation is what lawyers should learn from Marx – just as they should today accept the indeterminacy of each such framework, that is, unlearn the essentialism through which Marxism and subsequent realisms thought about them.

---

[38] D. Philpott, *Revolutions in Sovereignty. How Ideas Shaped Modern International Relations* (Princeton: Princeton University Press, 2001).

[39] I have discussed the hegemonic aspect of normative debate in international politics in M. Koskenniemi, 'International Law and Hegemony. A Reconfiguration' (2004) 17 *Cambridge Review of International Affairs* 197.

[40] This is how the US/Europe controversy is seen e.g. by Jürgen Habermas, above n. 1.

3.3. Beyond dichotomies?

This would mean analysing the play of legal dichotomies, too, not in terms of an abstract logic of concepts but as a series of articulations of positions in concrete, historically situated political struggles. Legal concepts would then be seen not as carriers of fixed meanings but as surfaces or, to follow Ernesto Laclau, floating signifiers, on which social conflict would become visible, receive meaning and shape.[41] The irreducibly *political* character of law would not then cancel out law's legal character. It would merely point to the inevitable moment of choice in legal practice in favour of one contested meaning against another.

For example, the dichotomy of consent and justice could be seen as one field of articulation of social relations. One aspect is predominant, the other a latent modification. In vulgar capitalism, as in much of international law, consent is understood to structure the market (diplomacy), while justice steps in as an occasional corrective. The corrective involves, however, a denial or a negation of the *raison d'être* of the predominant term with which it stands in tension. In a historical sense, the two act dialectically: social struggle is expressed in the way the secondary term challenges and finally overtakes the prominent one, overturning their relationship. The market of hunters-gatherers collapses into a system of public distribution in accordance with tribal decision: the emergence of common ownership in primitive society. Critique of tribal authority and distribution of labour will lead into class society and private property, a system that would again be collapsed into common property in socialism.

The point is not whether this particular account of history is correct but that it provides one example of how conceptual oppositions express the dialectics of social struggle. The logic of identity in standard realism and idealism is profoundly conservative in its search for that which is always already known: balance of power, humanitarian ideals. By contrast, dialectics grasps the world as history for which change and *practice* are central. Instead of some structure endlessly repeating itself, everything depends on decisions to maintain or challenge it. It is the dynamism of *practice* – where 'the subject changes the object by understanding it'[42] – and not the internal forms of diplomacy or the market that accounts for change. The two are linked by political practice that now becomes

---

[41] See especially Laclau, *Emancipation(s)*.
[42] L. Kolakowski, *Main Currents of Marxism 1: The Founders* (Oxford: Oxford University Press, 1978), p. 144.

the focus of what is simultaneously an explanatory and an emancipatory interest.[43]

A Marxian analysis would not take the distinction between public diplomacy and private economic relations for granted, ahistorically given. The privileging of the former by the reformist international lawyer would only appear as an international equivalent of advocating 'merely political emancipation'. It would leave intact the relations of domination in civil society by assuming that they organise themselves automatically. But an international law that would only focus on limiting what states do, and that celebrates the spontaneous realm of civil society is profoundly ideological. It would buttress a limited public realm of sovereign equality with occasional intervention, and an unlimited, imperial structure of economic domination. A dialectical approach, by contrast, would focus on the fragility of each, by pointing to the fundamental nature of their mutual criticisms: republicanism as a negation of capitalism; cosmopolitan democracy as a *negation* of public diplomacy. A demonstration of the conceptual indeterminacy of the public/private distinction would break its ideological, passivity-inducing power. Transformative action would seem not only possible but perhaps the only justifiable choice.

So I conclude that present reality does give the appearance of harmony – that is what by definition 'present reality' always does. But dialectical thought reveals the hidden contradiction, the unconscious desire, the dangerous supplement, and makes room for political decision. Dialectics, as Jacques Ellul notes, is intrinsically critical.[44] It sees its object as a contradictory process, a movement of which the observer is a part. And one has to insist that apart from encompassing such oppositions as those of civil society and state, base and superstructure, it also includes the dichotomy between materialism and idealism. Today, dialectical imagination fuses with deconstruction to include also Marxian and other structuralist thought within its compass. After all, it may be that agents in civil society are able to identify their interests or even themselves as 'agents'

---

[43] In Marxian theory, 'practice' is an epistemological category: the validity of a view of society is measured by the type of practice it produces. The indissociable nature of theory and practice accounts for some of the optimistic romanticism of early left politics. Through notions such as 'objective interests' and 'self-reflection', it remains central to later critical theory. For a very accessible introduction, see R. Geuss, *The Idea of a Critical Theory: Habermas and the Frankfurt School* (Cambridge: Cambridge University Press, 1981), especially pp. 45–95.

[44] Ellul, *La pensée marxiste*, p. 71.

only by reference to liberal-republican and democratic ideas of law and state. Democracy surely is a process that has itself as its (impossible) objective. The process of representation may become the source of the identity of that which is represented.[45]

Thus, for example, the unresolved tension in Marxian thinking between self-determination and internationalism can finally be seen not as a theoretical failure but an openness to what can be attained through praxis.[46] Many have pointed out the interdependence of these two opposing notions. For Marxian thought they present not a problem to be resolved, but a *horizon of political possibility*. Whether one would prefer action within a national or an international frame remains then a pure issue of situated reason, of addressing the consequences of alternative choices, and not a derivation from some abstract and unhistorical either/or theory. Against Rosa Luxemburg, Lenin was right. Only the historical situation can tell; only praxis may achieve. But what is that 'situation' today?

4. Civil society and universalism

Following Feuerbach, Marx set against the abstract – and thus false – universality of liberal rights the concrete universality of human beings as species-beings but, unlike the former, interpreted this as their *social being*. Political theologies had created personified abstractions such as 'the state', 'the individual', 'the monarch', the 'nation', or 'private property'. Sovereignty and private property, for instance, were structually analogous: the state enjoyed sovereignty in the same way as the abstract individual enjoyed private property.[47] These were to be countered by concrete notions. The human being as a social species-being was one that would enjoy property as shared by the species.

The redemption of civil society against the state by new social movements is today a routine aspect of transformative debates that take up the left-Hegelian themes of which Marx was profoundly critical.[48] The call is for political emancipation in order to rid the international world of the distorting structures of statehood against which civil society is portrayed as an authentic realm of human spontaneity. Yet there is a danger that the critiques of the state – as much a part of international law as statehood

---

[45] See further, E. Laclau, 'Power and Representation', in Laclau, *Emancipation(s)*, pp. 98–9.
[46] See R. Miliband, *Marxism and Politics* (Oxford: Oxford University Press, 1977), pp. 98–105.
[47] Breckman, *Marx, the Young Hegelians*, p. 289.
[48] See B. Rajagopal, *International Law from Below: Development, Social Movements and Third World Resistance* (Cambridge: Cambridge University Press, 2003).

itself – collapse into an uncritical endorsement of informal social power. Something that is said to exist 'naturally' is celebrated because that is what it appears to be. The claims against the state have force, as they are made as claims of *authenticity* (the indigenous way of life, the real wishes of the proletariat, the unaffected state of the environment, the universal aspirations of women and so on). The 'real' now truly becomes 'rational' in the reactionary Hegelian sense, and the 'movement' another transcendental (religious) condition for politics that cannot be touched by politics.

All this is pre-modern nostalgia. Marx would have had none of it. If he did privilege civil society against the state, this never promised that the life of the human species-being recognising itself as such would be a state of pre-political harmony. The harmony of interests – the organic solidarity that Durkheim saw binding together the factory owner and the shoemaker – was a bourgeois notion that merely veiled the domination of the weak by the strong. Globalisation is that too, the informal empire of economic forces no longer obstructed by 'irrational' boundaries. Though Marx was not free from occasionally lapsing into the Utopian assumption that communism would unite the objectives of the individual and the community, the more important point is that, in the transition, social conflict would not vanish but its resolution would no longer be achieved by automatically supporting the ruling class.

For international lawyers, it has always been the point of the states-system to constrain the claims of authenticity propagated in the global market of ideas. Nothing has undermined the need for a republican realm beyond this market that may judge such claims. But the Marxian critique of 'merely political emancipation' has shown that, although this may be necessary in the work for a just society, it is far from sufficient. In order to reach towards 'human emancipation', a notion of universal humanity – or 'universality' *tout court* – is needed that goes beyond the representational structures of political states. But what is there, outside statehood, that might be able to represent 'humanity' and thus provide the perspective of international progress and enlightenment?

When Marx wrote of the 'positive possibility of German emancipation', he conceived this through his theory of civil society's division into classes and by extrapolating the proletariat as the universal class. When economics dictates that civil society in conditions of modernity will organise itself as a class society, dialectics persuades us that this is also what will undo it. Capitalist modernity itself contributes to the formation of one particular class, 'a class with *radical* chains', as Marx explained:

a class in civil society that is not of civil society, an estate that is the dissolution of all estates, a sphere of society having a universal character because of its universal suffering and claiming no *particular right* because no *particular wrong* but *unqualified wrong* is perpetrated on it.[49]

This class – the proletariat – would not just continue the old antagonisms. For it 'can only redeem itself through the *total redemption of humanity*'.[50] Here, for Marx, was the privileged particular that transcended its own particularity and became a representative of the whole.

Now the experience of class struggle and real socialism has made it impossible to take in full seriousness the view of the proletariat as a universal class and proletarian revolution as human emancipation. Marx's economic reductionism remained blind to the significance of divisions emerging in the political and cultural realms of civil society – indeed, he himself remained, as noted by Jean Cohen, imprisoned by a 'fetishistic logic'.[51] Instead, more recent left-liberal theory has focused on human rights as the representative of that which is universal. But, as we have seen, human rights are a theology of the bourgeois state whose citizens are obsessed by their weakness and, fearful of 'evil', ever ready to turn whatever powers into the hands of a bureaucratic theocracy.[52] So how to conceive that which is universal in a genuine, and not a 'false', sense?

*****

In June 2006, perhaps five miles inland from the centre of the city of Recife, Brazil, on a pink concrete wall, I saw a text in Portuguese that read 'No to the war of Bush'. Why was it there? The inhabitants of Recife were in no way touched by the military activities of a handful of Western countries in the Middle East. Indeed, the inhabitants of this suburban quarter of a major South American city seemed to have a number of other things to be concerned over – massive and endemic poverty, enormous differences of economic wealth, domestic violence, and so on. And they are concerned about these facts, as demonstrated by the election of Luiz Inácio ('Lula') da Silva as the country's first left President. And still, not only that one

---

[49] Marx, 'Contribution to a Critique', p. 69.   [50] *Ibid.*
[51] J. Cohen, *Class and Civil Society. The Limits of Marxian Critical Theory* (Oxford: Martin Robertson, 1982), p. 188.
[52] This is also the gist of the ('communist') critique of the ethics of human rights in A. Badiou, *Ethics. An Essay on the Understanding of Evil* (London: Verso, 2001), pp. 8–17 and *passim*.

concrete wall, but countless pieces of graffiti all over the city condemned the war waged by 'Bush' in no uncertain terms and often not just as 'wrong' but as 'illegal'. Nor is this phenomenon any Brazilian idiosyncrasy. In the city of Helsinki, where I live, in my street on the lamp-post nearest to the door to my flat was a sticker that declared the war against Iraq 'illegal'. And in Geneva, where I was attending the UN International Law Commission the week after leaving Recife, there was an enormous demonstration to protest against the meeting of the 'G8'. A large number of the protesters carried slogans that condemned the Iraqi war in uncompromising terms: the war and the ensuing occupation were 'illegal'. Nor is this only my experience. The protests against the (then) planned Iraqi war that took place on 15 February 2003 gathered on the streets of the world more people than any other event since the end of World War II.

The point of this story is that the protest against 'Bush's war' has nothing bureaucratic and routine about it. It focuses on a single fact and event, and condemns that event often as not merely 'wrong', but 'illegal'. This highlights that the war in Iraq is not only another brick in the wall of globalisation. It is a singular scandal that cannot be explained away as a geographical or a 'Third World' problem, or a problem about communism, or capitalism, or 'market', the 'Washington consensus' or even 'American imperialism'. It may be all of these, but there is something more in this scandal. That fact is that the war is so patently and arrogantly 'illegal' that even its proponents never really cared to make a serious defence of it in terms of its lawfulness but were contented with half-hearted, manipulative generalities about the suspicion of the existence of weapons of mass destruction, of Iraq's links with al-Qaeda, 'pre-emptive self-defence' and so on – justifications in which it is today difficult to see anything beyond cynicism.[53]

The scandal lies in the mockery that the war has sought to make of the desire for a world of justice and equality. It is a paradox that while diplomats and academics now often declare central aspects of international law 'dead', or at least in a severe crisis, there has never in the past half-century been such widespread invocation of international law as there is today. This is significant.

The events in Iraq raise the theme of the universal being conceived not in terms of a blueprint or a positive programme, or in terms of identity politics or sectarian interests but, as Marx conceived it, as a *universal*

---

[53] For discussion, see T. M. Franck, 'What Happens Now? The United Nations after Iraq' (2003) 97 *American Journal of International Law* 607.

violation. The political struggles in Recife, Geneva or Helsinki are different. The claims that are raised at these locations emerge from different experiences. But though the global trade regime, environmental degradation and the occupation of Iraq may have different victims and follow different paths of rationality, they are not hermetically isolated from each other. They form a pattern, a hierarchy, and a particular configuration of forces. As the criticism of the Iraqi war was made in terms of its illegality, a grievance was being articulated that through that articulation was being lifted from the realm of what is particular to that which is universal.

That the war was condemned as a 'violation of international law' or an attack on the 'rights' of Iraqi civilians is to appeal to something beyond particular interest, privileges or charity enjoyed or claimed by someone. Such an invocation appeals to something that concerns every member of a projected (legal) community, a violation that touches no-one in particular but *everyone in general*. It makes the point that the coalition actions are not an affair between the Iraqis and the Americans (nor indeed did they implicate only Bush and Saddam), but that everyone has a stake in them because the violation is universal. 'I do not condemn this action because it is against my interests or preferences. I condemn it because it is objectively wrong, *a violation not against me but against everyone.*'

The proletarian revolution that unites all is a myth. But like Georges Sorel's 'general strike', myths – for instance, myths of the 'nation' – act as reference points against which individuals see themselves as something larger than particular identities with idiosyncratic preferences.[54] In the conditions of complex modernity, a sense of universality cannot be created out of objective interests (of the proletariat) or historical missions (of nations). Difference is irreducible to such stories. But those that are different may be united by what they experience as a violation that is directed at no-one in particular but at everyone in general. This is where international lawyers, learning from Marx, could see international law's emancipatory promise. International law may act precisely as an instrument through which particular grievances may be articulated as universal ones and, in this way, like myth, construct a sense of universal humanity through the act of invoking it. From such a perspective, the project of

---

[54] See further, E. Laclau and C. Mouffe, *Hegemony and Socialist Strategy. Towards a Radical Democratic Politics*, 2nd edn (London: Verso, 2001), pp. 36–42 (on Sorel) and *passim* (for 'articulation' as central to the – hegemonic – effort to occupy the position of the general).

universal justice appears as a horizon at the intersection of a public realm of states regulated by international law and the civil society reaching beyond sectarian interests. That this intersection appears only occasionally, and even then in connection with events of exceptional magnitude, even scandal, is an aspect of the difficulty that any fundamental challenge to the iron laws of power must imply.

2

An outline of a Marxist course on public international law

B. S. CHIMNI

1. Introduction

1.1. The difficulties in telling an alternative story

There is today an urgent need to offer to students of international law critical alternative texts exploring the nature, character and subject matter of international law. Alternative stories have to be told, for growing international legal regulation is translating into injustice for the subaltern classes in both the Third and First Worlds.[1] But introducing critical alternative texts is not an easy task, given the dominance of mainstream international law scholarship (MILS) in the world of international law. MILS may be defined as an ensemble of methods, practices and understandings in relation to the identification, interpretation and enforcement of international law.[2] This ensemble of methods, practices and understandings comprises a number of features. Four may be mentioned in order to bring out its distinctive nature. First, broadly speaking, MILS is parasitic on an epistemology of law that dictates the fragmentation of social sciences in relation to the creation, interpretation and implementation of international law. It advances a distinctive international law methodology which tells us which practices count in the world of international law and which do not. Such a methodology, going by the name of positivism, excludes a range of social and political practices as falling outside the domain of

---

[1] The term 'subaltern class' is being used in this chapter to include all oppressed and marginal groups in society. It therefore includes exploitation and oppression based on class, gender, race and caste. But since 'subaltern class' is not simply a cultural formation, but a historical category, this exploitation and oppression is to be located in the matrix of both property relations and lived histories.

[2] On the difficulties of making the characterisations of 'mainstream' and 'marginal' approaches in international law, see R. Müllerson, *Ordering Anarchy: International Law in International Society* (Leiden: Martinus Nijhof, 2000), p. 49.

international law. MILS therefore ends up offering formal/abstract definitions of international law and its doctrines. Second, MILS writes the history of international law as a narrative of progress.[3] In this view, whatever may have been the sins of international law in the past it is an instrument of common good today. There is also the embedded belief that every increase in international legal regulation is necessarily a step towards establishing a just world order. Therefore, more international law is always better, since it is a move towards establishing the rule of law in international relations. Third, there is the understanding that international law is a system of rules that can be objectively known, interpreted and applied. Interpretative disputes and their outcome are never seen as a function of power but simply a result of unclear texts that are a product of compromises arrived at during the course of international negotiations. Fourth, the practitioners of MILS do not recognise that there are structural constraints in the international system that greatly limit the pursuit of common good through international law. It is not as if MILS is naïve. It often takes the factors of power and interest into account in explaining the international legal process and its outcomes.[4] However, what MILS does not recognise is that there are deep structures that entrench rules and systems of belief which sustain the domination of subaltern states and peoples. These features lead MILS to the sanguine conclusion that 'today, principled criticisms of international law as such, of its contents and general orientation, can be heard only rarely'.[5] To put it differently, the strategy adopted by MILS to exclude critical alternative narratives is either to deny their existence through subsuming them under its own banner or to represent them as deviant scholarship unworthy of engagement. Thereafter, the space of critical dissent is occupied by mild reformists pretending to be radical oppositionists.[6] What is worse, some alternative narratives that position themselves as critical alternatives can be even more accommodating of power than MILS. The New Haven School is a good example of an interdisciplinary approach that presents itself as sharply critical of MILS (and is in many respects) but is even less willing to speak truth to power.[7] It is,

---

[3] A. Orford, 'Embodying Internationalism: The Making of International Lawyers' (1998) 19 *Australian Yearbook of International Law* 1 at 16.
[4] But see M. Byers, *Custom, Power and the Power of Rules: International Relations and Customary International Law* (Cambridge: Cambridge University Press, 2000), p. 214.
[5] C. Tomuschat, 'International Law: Ensuring the Survival of Mankind on the Eve of the New Century' (1999) 281 *Recueil des Cours* 9 at 39.
[6] D. Kennedy, 'When Renewal Repeats: Thinking Against the Box' (2000) 32 *New York University of International Law and Politics* 335 at 372.
[7] For a detailed critique of the New Haven approach, see B. S. Chimni, *International Law and World Order: A Critique of Contemporary Approaches* (New Delhi: Sage, 1993), ch. 3.

in other words, not enough to offer critical or interdisciplinary alternative texts. Such texts can be complicit with power in a different way. What is necessary is an ensemble of methods, practices and understandings that go to empower the subaltern classes.

The present paper uses the insights of Marxism to outline such a critical alternative text in the form of a general course on contemporary international law (CIL). This story has been told before, but, as we all know, in the service of 'actually existing socialism'. Its demise has opened up the possibility of a critical retelling, a retelling which is not dogmatic in any way and is fully conscious of the enormous human costs of 'actually existing socialism'. The story is retold in the belief that Marxism as critique has not exhausted itself (albeit without attributing any foundational role for Marxist critical reflection), despite its failure to articulate the normative basis for creating a just society. The reason for choosing the genre of 'a course on public international law' is that it is not enough to critique CIL at a structural level, inter alia, through linking its evolution to developments in the capitalist world economy. It must be followed up by a more detailed and integral exposition of the doctrines and rules of CIL as carriers of dominant interests and discourse. For we believe that it is the textbook on CIL that is the most influential vehicle in disseminating the MILS world-view, especially in the Third World. Textbooks condense and assemble a mass of materials on different topics/areas of international law in a systematic and coherent manner to impart knowledge to students of international law. Unless alternative textbooks do the same in a more persuasive and illuminating way, deploying a different ensemble of methods, practices and understandings, the MILS textbooks will retain their influence despite the most acute critiques of aspects of CIL and MILS.[8] The word 'outline' in the title indicates the extremely modest aim of this chapter. It does no more than offer some glimpses into what is possible. It is not exhaustive either in terms of the subjects considered or in the analysis of those that are included.

1.2. What is distinctive about our text?

It will perhaps be helpful, to begin with, to state in a schematic fashion some of the distinctive features of critical Marxist international law scholarship (CMILS). First, in contrast to the formal definitions of international

---

[8] From a feminist standpoint, an attempt has been made in H. Charlesworth and C. Chinkin, *The Boundaries of International Law: A Feminist Analysis* (Manchester: Manchester University Press, 2000).

law and its doctrines offered by MILS, CMILS advances more meaningful definitions that distinguish the character of international law and its doctrines in different historical phases and identifies the groups/classes/states that are the principal movers and beneficiaries. CMILS contends that, while MILS does use the categories of interest and power in analysing CIL, the manner in which these categories are deployed deprives them of critical edge. Thus, MILS works with the empty concept of 'national interest', excluding the possibility of discovering particular group or class interests that determine its content. Likewise, the concept of power is mostly identified with its more overt and discrete manifestations rather than being understood as a force that continuously informs the creation, interpretation and enforcement of international law.

Second, CMILS, in contrast to MILS, identifies the structural constraints on the democratic transformation of CIL. It posits both external and internal constraints (and their linkages) that stop CIL from becoming an instrument of social transformation. At the external level, CMILS recognises, *inter alia*, that at least since the sixteenth century, when an incipient capitalist world economy began to take shape, its structure has constrained the democratisation of international law. Internally, the problem principally lies with the frozen and power-driven doctrine of sources of international law. CMILS instead seeks to embed deliberative democracy in the law-making process, for it allows the notion of ethical compromise to come into play in the creation of international law. Ethical compromise (i.e., compromise that leads to the realisation of generalisable interests), in contrast to a compromise informed by power (i.e., compromise that actualises particular interests), helps to promote the interests of the subaltern classes.[9] From this perspective, CMILS seeks, *inter alia*, changes in the law of treaties and celebrates 'soft law' texts that represent the outcome of communicative action.

Third, CMILS underlines the element of indeterminacy, which characterises all international law interpretation of texts and facts. While it eschews the radical indeterminacy of the New Haven School (which uses this understanding to justify its subjective perceptions of particular texts and events), it reveals the problems with the mainstream transparency/objectivity thesis. In other words, CMILS aspires to occupy the middle ground between complete objectivity and radical indeterminacy

---

[9] B. S. Chimni, 'Discourse Ethics and International Negotiations' (mimeo). See generally J. Habermas, *Moral Consciousness and Communicative Action* (Cambridge, MA: MIT Press, 1990); J. Habermas, *Theory of Communicative Action*, 2 vols. (Boston: Beacon Press, 1987), vol. I.

to create space for interpretative rules and strategies that contribute to the welfare of the subaltern classes.

Fourth, in contrast to MILS, CMILS takes cognisance of dissenting voices, in particular critical Third World approaches to international law (TWAIL). It is disturbed by the incestuous debate carried out between American and European mainstream scholars and the tendency to universalise it as *the* discourse of international law. CMILS refuses to believe that the only way to bring about the democratisation of CIL is by embracing the 'tools' of MILS.[10] Instead, it supports protocols of scholarship which engender inclusion of international law outsiders, whether in the First or Third Worlds. This is a matter of importance, for in many ways international law is what international lawyers say it is.

In sum, CMILS provides a more coherent and meaningful story of international law than does MILS. It uses the insights of historical materialism to explain better the changes visiting the doctrines and rules of international law, by linking them to extra-textual realities. It eschews, however, determinism of any kind, albeit without embracing the opposite trap of enumerating endless variables that shape society (whether domestic or international) so that CIL appears a product of sheer chance. CMILS is, in other words, interdisciplinary in a different way. CMILS, by avoiding the trap of legal nihilism, also hopes to suggest ways of dealing with unjust laws.

2. The state, the capitalist world economy and international law

The state is at the centre of the universe of international law. It is, even today, the principal 'subject' of international law. The definition that international law offers of its central actor is, however, a formal one. It is confined to indicating the criteria of statehood. There is the inevitable reference in MILS to the 'best known formulation of the basic criteria of statehood' laid down in Article 1 of the 1933 Montevideo Convention on Rights and Duties of States.[11] It states:

> The State as a person of international law should possess the following qualifications: (a) a permanent population; (b) a defined territory; (c) government; and (d) capacity to enter into relations with other States.

---

[10] Feminist international lawyers had to confront this critique from MILS. See Orford, 'Embodying Internationalism' 25–6.

[11] J. Crawford, *The Creation of Statehood in International Law* (Oxford: Clarendon Press, 1979), p. 36.

The formal definition excludes from view the fact that the state is a function and form of social relations.[12] It therefore fails to record that the modern state emerged in response to certain fundamental social transformations (representing the transition from feudalism to capitalism) that visited sixteenth- and seventeenth-century Europe. 'The state only *fully* becomes', as Pashukanis noted, 'the subject of international law *as the bourgeois state.*'[13] More significantly, this bourgeois state, from the very beginning, co-existed with the colonial state in an evolving capitalist world economy, indelibly marking the body of international law.[14] Since MILS does not perceive the state as an integral part of the capitalist world economy, it fails to appreciate that its structure does not allow all states to develop simultaneously but instead spawns uneven development between states. There is, in other words, no recognition that this 'uneven development is not a residue or an impurity . . . *it is the constitutive form* of the reproduction of the CMP [capitalist mode of production]'.[15] To put it differently, MILS rejects the understanding that capitalism can only be imperialist.

The colonial state remained an object of international law until it recovered its independence in the middle of the twentieth century. The arrival of 'newly independent states' meant that the bourgeois states now co-existed not only with 'socialist' states (in the post-October Revolution phase) but also with non-capitalist states in much of the decolonised world. On the other hand, the survival, expansion and development of the capitalist world economy demanded that the bourgeois democratic state (the best shell for capitalism) be established as the universal form of state. The collapse of 'actually existing socialism' facilitated this. A range of laws and practices have been deployed by advanced capitalist states to universalise the bourgeois state. To take just one example, on 16 December 1991 the European Community adopted 'Guidelines on the Recognition of New States in Eastern Europe and in the Soviet Union'.[16] The guidelines

---

[12] For a very basic introduction to relevant Marxist sociology, see Chimni, *International Law and World Order*, pp. 213–20.

[13] E. Pashukanis, *Selected Writings on Marxism and Law*, P. Bierne and R. Sharlet (eds.) (London: Academic Press, 1980), p. 174 (emphasis added).

[14] A. Anghie, 'Francisco de Vitoria and the Colonial Origins of International Law' (1996) 5 *Social and Legal Studies* 321.

[15] N. Poulantzas, *Classes in Contemporary Capitalism* (London: Verso, 1978), p. 49 (emphasis added).

[16] Letter from the Representatives of Belgium, France and the United Kingdom of Great Britain and Northern Ireland to the United Nations Addressed to the President of the Security Council, UNSC Doc. S/23293 of 17 December 1991, Annex II. The text of the Guidelines has been reprinted in (1992) 31 *International Legal Materials* 1486–7.

laid down the criteria that must be satisfied before recognition could be granted to a new state. These included, *inter alia*, commitment 'to the rule of law, democracy and human rights', key words for describing a bourgeois democratic state. This attempt to ensure that the bourgeois state form be embraced by all newcomers has been reinforced by the emerging norm of a 'right to democratic governance'.[17] Thus, not merely the recognition of new states but also the recognition of governments has become the concern of international law in a bid to make the bourgeois state the universal form of state.[18] What MILS does not appreciate is that the norm of democratic governance can subsume a wide spectrum of social formations, leading to 'a flattening out of the variegated global conditions within which democratizing projects are embedded'.[19] There is therefore little understanding of the fact that the creation of a bourgeois democratic state under mismatched social conditions transforms the concerned society into a dependent and dominated social formation with the principal function of facilitating the presence and operation of transnational capital:[20]

> A dependent and dominated social formation and state is one whose specific economic, political and ideological structure is constituted by asymmetrical relationships with the dominant social formations and states which enjoy a position of power over it.[21]

The form and content of dependence and dominance change according to the different phases of the evolution of the capitalist world economy. The last two decades (the era of accelerated globalisation) have seen a substantial redefinition of the relationship of dependent and dominated states with dominant social formations and states. It has witnessed the direct inscribing of international laws in dependent and dominated states, facilitating greater imperialist domination. A network of international laws that extend and deepen the reign of global capitalism by further limiting

---

[17] T. M. Franck, 'The Emerging Right to Democratic Governance' (1992) 86 *American Journal of International Law* 46.
[18] For the distinction between recognition of states and recognition of governments, see Crawford, *The Creation of Statehood*, pp. 27–9.
[19] H. Smith, 'Why Is There No International Democratic Theory?', in H. Smith (ed.), *Democracy and International Relations: Critical Theories/Problematic Practices* (Hampshire: Palgrave Macmillan, 2000), p. 1 at 4.
[20] J. Grugel, 'State and Business in Neo-liberal Democracies in Latin America', in Smith (ed.), *Democracy and International Relations*, p. 125; S. Marks, *The Riddle of All Constitutions* (Oxford: Oxford University Press, 2000).
[21] Poulantzas, *Classes in Contemporary Capitalism*, pp. 43–4.

the autonomy of the dependent and dominant state has been adopted.[22] In key areas of sovereign economic, social and political life, the dependent and dominated state cannot take independent decisions, since it has ceded its powers to international law and institutions. On the other hand, the prescription of 'democratic governance' offers advanced capitalist states a pretext for intervening against forces that do not further their economic and geostrategic interests, as long as it can be established that those forces are in violation of liberal-democratic norms.[23] Among other things, it is my contention below that, in view of these developments, spelled out in greater detail later, the character of CIL is in the era of globalisation metamorphosing from a bourgeois democratic international law to a bourgeois imperial international law.[24]

3. The character of contemporary international law

The character of CIL is not, it is important to clarify, shaped merely by the developments in the capitalist world economy. That assertion would represent crude economic determinism. It is shaped by a range of factors including: (i) the dominant understanding of the history of international law; (ii) the cohesiveness and strength of the class that occupies centre stage at the global level at a particular historical conjuncture; (iii) the nature and logic of the states system; (iv) the role of non-state actors, including international institutions and civil society organisations; (v) the strength of domestic and international resistance movements; and (vi) the internal dialectic of international law. Each of these factors may play a decisive role, depending on the subject, arena and political conjuncture of law-making.

---

[22] B. S. Chimni, 'Third World Approaches to International Law: A Manifesto', in A. Anghie et al. (eds.), *The Third World and International Order: Law, Politics and Globalization* (Leiden: Brill, 2003), pp. 51 ff.; B. S. Chimni, 'Marxism and International Law: A Contemporary Analysis', *Economic and Political Weekly*, 6 February 1999, p. 337.

[23] B. R. Roth, *Government Illegitimacy in International Law* (Oxford: Oxford University Press, 1999), p. 426.

[24] The different historical phases of modern international law may be classified as follows: 1600–1760: old colonialism; 1760–1875: new colonialism; 1875–1945: imperialism; 1945–1980 imperialism (neo-colonialism); and 1980–: imperialism (globalisation). For a brief analysis of the first four phases, see Chimni, *International Law and World Order*, pp. 223–36. For a review of developments in the current phase of globalisation, see Chimni, 'Third World Approaches'. Bourgeois imperial international law is to be distinguished from bourgeois imperialist international law of the period 1875–1945. The former characterisation seeks to capture the essence of international law in the current period of accelerated globalisation dating from the early 1980s.

The origin of CIL, as already noted, is inextricably bound up with colonialism. Colonisation meant the erasure of the personality of the colonised state. It was in this period that the doctrines and rules of CIL were shaped, as a way of responding to and justifying colonialism. Be it the law relating to acquisition of territory, the rules of recognition, or the law of state responsibility, it was dictated by the necessity of consolidating and sustaining colonial rule. The decolonisation process saw the arrival of 'newly independent states' and the relative democratisation of international law through the universalisation of the principle of sovereign equality of states. Attempts at a more substantive democratisation of international relations were resisted by the former colonial masters. MILS followed suit in the literature of international law. The colonial foundations of international law were easily acknowledged in a world that was officially decolonised. However, the continuing critique of CIL was seen as illegitimate. MILS refused to accept the argument that the more substantive democratic transformation of world economic and political laws and institutions is controlled by certain global social forces through, *inter alia*, a network of laws, doctrines, and interpretative devices. Thus, the moment of confession of the relationship between colonialism and international law was deployed by MILS to legitimise CIL by distancing it from its origins. The subjects of oppression were now seen as occupying the same place as the perpetrators. The uncomfortable fact that formal equality in law translated into dependence and domination in the real world was quickly passed over; as Marx pithily observed: 'Between equal rights force decides.'[25] What emerged by the 1970s may, however, be characterised as bourgeois democratic international law, since structural dependence in this period permitted post-colonial states considerable autonomy in the formulation and implementation of internal social and economic policies.

From the last two decades on, the character of CIL has been in the course of being transformed from bourgeois democratic to bourgeois imperial international law by changes in the world economic and political situation which have led to the ascendance of the transnational fractions of the capitalist class in advanced capitalist countries. This class acts in collaboration with the now ascendant transnational fractions in the Third World.[26] The emerging transnational capitalist class (TCC) 'is comprised of the owners

---

[25] K. Marx, *Capital*, 3 vols. (New York: Vintage, 1977), vol. I, p. 225.
[26] On the emergence of a transnational capitalist class, see W. I. Robinson and J. Harris, 'Towards a Global Ruling Class? Globalization and the Transnational Capitalist Class' (2000) 64 *Science and Society* 11. A '*fraction* denotes segments within classes determined by their relation to social production and the class as a whole', at 23.

of transnational capital, that is, the group that owns the leading worldwide means of production as embodied principally in the transnational corporations and private financial institutions'.[27] The TCC seeks to establish international laws and institutions that facilitate the globalisation of production and finance through the internationalisation of property rights and limiting the autonomy of the dependent and dominated states. This objective is being achieved, as noted earlier, through adopting relevant international laws (in areas of foreign investment, trade and finance) and transferring sovereign powers from states to international institutions. The World Trade Organization (WTO) and the international financial institutions are the key players here, albeit accompanied by a range of other social and environmental institutions. The international institutions, it is perhaps important to stress, do not possess their own power but *'express and crystallize class powers'*.[28] The class powers that are being crystallised and expressed today are those of an emerging TCC that exercises the most influence in the global arena.

We must, however, hasten to add that the existence of a sovereign state system ensures that CIL does not represent a direct translation of the interests of the TCC. The fragmentation of states at the international level ensures this. While a dominant class (the TCC) has emerged at the global level (through a complex coalescing process), and a global state is in the process of being created, the TCC has today still to contend with the demands of the logic of the states system.[29] There is therefore a need to factor in the autonomy of the state (however constrained) when it enters the domain of international relations.[30] State autonomy is a function of a range of social and cultural factors, including perceptions of national security and the imperative of 'free and fair elections'. It is the factor of state autonomy, which, inter alia, explains the differences between the United States and EU states in various international fora. It also explains why there has to be a degree of responsiveness, even by dependent and dominated states, to the concerns and aspirations of its peoples. Therefore, all negotiations leading to the adoption of international law texts are not, despite the collaboration of the TCC across global space, sham

---

[27] Ibid., 22.
[28] Poulantzas, *Classes in Contemporary Capitalism*, p. 70 (emphasis added).
[29] On the emergence of the global state, see B. S. Chimni, 'International Institutions Today: An Imperial Global State in the Making' (2004) 15 *European Journal of International Law* 1.
[30] See generally, A. Linklater, *Beyond Realism and Marxism: Critical Theory and International Relations* (London: Macmillan, 1990).

negotiations. There is a complex process (among other things regulated by international law) through which dominant interests are mediated to yield solutions that have legitimacy in the eyes of the population over which each government presides. Therefore compromises have to be reached, especially when there is organised resistance by the subaltern classes to certain policy outcomes. But the emergent compromises do not necessarily represent ethical compromises and thereby a setback to the dominant classes. In any case, the role of the advanced capitalist states in the international system is not only to defend the narrow corporate interests of the TCC but to create and sustain a normative system that facilitates and legitimises the functioning of the world capitalist system.[31] This requires holding out the illusion that the success of capitalism means the welfare of the subaltern classes and concessions have to be made to support it.

Powerful states have also to get to grips today with non-state entities that are coming to play an important role in the law-making process. These non-state entities range from sub-national authorities to international institutions to non-governmental organisations (NGOs). Of course, the significance of the role of non-state entities varies with the subject matter and the extent of organisation in the field, so that there are, for instance, NGOs and NGOs. They are, like states, also informed by the north-south divide. This allows northern NGOs, in particular business NGOs (for example, the International Chamber of Commerce), to play a critical role in the international law-making process. Likewise, the networking of sub-national authorities allows them to shape the law literally outside the democratic process. It has meant that the dependent and dominated state is being hollowed not only through measures from above but also through networking from below. There are also, of course, dissenting civil society organisations (leading and combining old and new social movements), which provide some kind of – even if ineffective – counterweight. Their resistance has in recent years drawn increasing attention to the inequities that inform contemporary international law and institutions and have often to be taken into account.

But despite the constraints of the states system, the need to ensure the survival of formal democracies and the presence of dissenting social movements and so on, the extant nature of the capitalist world economy

---

[31] A. Gramsci, *Selections from the Prison Notebooks* (London: Lawrence & Wishart, 1971), pp. 181–2; Marx, *Capital*, vol. I, chs. XXVI–XXXIII. The fact also explains the recent differences between the United States and some key EU states; it reflects, *inter alia*, different strategies of exploitation and dominance.

ensures that, overall (as opposed to under particular rules and regimes), the interests of the TCC and powerful states prevail and are codified. CIL may, therefore, in general terms, be defined as a system of principles and norms arrived at primarily between states, and secondarily through a network of non-state and sub-national entities, embodying particular international class interests, that are enforced by a range of means, increasingly international institutions. More specifically, CIL is today in transition from being bourgeois democratic in character to a bourgeois imperialist international law that increasingly codifies the interests of an emerging TCC at the expense of interests of the subaltern classes and substantive global democracy. The principal features of bourgeois imperialist international law are that it greatly limits the autonomy of the dependent and dominated state through, *inter alia*, relocating sovereign powers from states to international institutions, it facilitates and safeguards the free mobility of capital, in particular international finance capital, it creates and protects international property rights without imposing corresponding duties on the rightholders, and it legitimises greater use of force through introducing new doctrines to protect the emerging globalised system of production and finance and the accompanying geo-politics.[32] These features, among other things, reflect a process of international law that severely constrains the ability of dependent and dominated states and subaltern classes to have their aspirations codified in international law. The characterisation of CIL, as bourgeois imperialist does not, however, mean that it therefore offers no advantage to the dependent and dominated states and the subaltern classes in the international system.

CIL is not simply a mask for class rule. While we would not go so far as Thompson as to contend that the institution of law is an 'unqualified human good', he is right in noting that the view of 'structural reductionism' 'overlooks . . . the immense capital of human struggle . . . inherited in the forms and traditions of the law'.[33] In the context of CIL, mention need only be made of the struggle of colonised peoples, in particular the sacrifices of the subaltern classes, to overthrow colonial rule and thereby democratise international law. Their continuing struggle has also shaped the content of international law in many ways. Furthermore, as Thompson stresses:

---

[32] In these regards see the discussion below.
[33] E. P. Thompson, 'Whigs and Hunters', in M. D. A. Freeman, *Lloyd's Introduction to Jurisprudence* (Stevens Publishing, 1985) p. 1057.

[T]he essential precondition for the effectiveness of law, in its function as ideology, is that it shall display an independence from gross manipulation and shall seem to be just. It cannot be seen to be so without upholding its own logic and criteria of equity; indeed, on occasion by actually *being* just.[34]

Even powerful states, therefore, often have to be respectful of the rule of law in the international system. The need to sustain the integrity of the system in turn opens up spaces that can be used to advance the cause of the subaltern classes. But the relative independence of international law does not mean that it does not incorporate and codify class interests, as Thompson concedes.[35] Thus, it is only at the point that Thompson calls law 'an unqualified human good' that it becomes problematic.[36] Certainly, the *idea* of the rule of law is not an empty one, and it possesses substantive independence from class interests. But, equally, the idea of the rule of law lends itself to manipulation and control by class interests. The limits of the rule of law in international relations are today defined by the extent to which it safeguards the interests of the TCC and the powerful states that articulate it. Since a complete mismatch between the rules of international law and the interests and practices of powerful states is rare, violation is not a frequent event. However, when there is a mismatch in periods of rapid development (as in the past two decades), either the rules themselves are transformed (e.g., the WTO rules) or these are violated (e.g., the rules relating to the use of force). International law, to reiterate, does possess relative independence but is constrained by the interests of the dominant actors and classes.

The implications of these developments and reflections on different aspects of international law form the subject of the rest of the article. The idea will not be to deal in detail with the various topics of international law; the aim of the article is to show, in contrast to MILS, the relationship between concepts, texts, and extra-textual developments.

4. Sources of international law

Most textbooks begin their exposition of CIL with a discussion of 'sources of international law'. MILS distinguishes between 'sources' and 'ultimate sources' of international law, and excludes the latter from

---

[34] *Ibid.*, p. 1056 (emphasis in original). [35] *Ibid.*
[36] H. Collins, *Marxism and Law* (Oxford: Clarendon Press, 1982), p. 144.

consideration.[37] This refusal to engage with extra-textual reality means, *inter alia*, that MILS does not have a serious theory of social change to explain its formal definition of international law. CMILS, on the other hand, marries international political economy to a historical sociology to explain systematically the basis of transformation of international law norms by reference to evolving social structures, forces and classes that constitute the world economy and the states system, even as it does not deny that international legal rules are also constitutive of social practices. To put it differently, CMILS is better positioned to clarify the meaning and implications of the formal sources of international law. These are most authoritatively stated in Article 38(1) of the Statute of the International Court of Justice (ICJ). We, however, merely look at the two principal sources of international law identified there, namely treaties and customary international law, and also touch on the phenomenon of 'soft law'.

4.1. Treaties

MILS, as is its wont, offers a formal definition of treaties. It usually refers the reader to Article 2(1)(a) of the Vienna Convention on the Law of Treaties 1969, which defines a treaty as 'an international agreement concluded between States in written form and governed by international law, whether embodied in a single legal instrument or in two or more related instruments, and whatever its particular designation'.[38] There is little indication in this abstract definition of the social relationships encapsulated in a treaty. Contrast this with the definitions offered by the Soviet scholars Korovin and Pashukanis: 'Every international agreement is the *expression of an established social order*, with a *certain balance of collective interests*';[39] 'A treaty obligation is nothing other than *a special form of the concretization of economic and political relationships.*'[40] These definitions, through drawing in extra-textual reality, offer greater insight into the meaning of a treaty than the formal definition offered by MILS. They refer us to both the fact of an established (capitalist) social order and to

---

[37] M. Shaw, *International Law* (Cambridge: Cambridge University Press, 1997), p. 55; P. Malanczuk, *Akehurst's Modern Introduction to International Law* (Oxford: Routledge, 1997), p. 35.

[38] The treaty entered into force on 27 January 1980. For the text of the Convention, see (1969) 8 *International Legal Materials* 679.

[39] E. A. Korovin, 'Soviet Treaties and International Law' (1928) 22 *American Journal of International Law* 753 at 763 (emphasis added).

[40] Pashukanis, *Selected Writings on Marxism and Law*, p. 181 (emphasis added).

its concretisation as economic and political rules embodying a certain balance of collective (class) interests.

A treaty is arrived at in the matrix of the already existing rules of the 'treaty game' that clarify what is permissible and what is objectionable in the course of negotiating and adopting international agreements. These rules, codified in the 'treaty of treaties', namely the Vienna Convention on the Law of Treaties 1969, favour powerful participants in the treaty-making process. First, the Vienna Convention does not require anything more than formal adherence to the rules of deliberative democracy. Thus it does not prevent the quiet coercion of states – a fact that tends to be overlooked by MILS.[41] In other words, as Brilmayer points out, 'arguments based on consent are deceptively simple' as explanation for the binding nature of agreements.[42] Their 'theoretical power lies in the suggestion that perhaps nothing really needs to be justified'.[43] But, as is evident to any observer of international negotiations, 'bargaining frequently takes place in a world of uneven resources and opportunity costs'.[44] It provides the soil in which quiet coercion flourishes. Second, there is the question of who is consenting: the state or the people who constitute it? MILS does not address this issue, for the norm of the 'right to democratic governance' does not require participatory democracy to be institutionalised. In the circumstances, the treaty often conceals the interests of certain social classes, even as MILS pretends that it embodies agreed compromises of different 'national interests'. While it is admittedly difficult to capture the class dimension of treaties in the language of international law when it comes to the law-making process,[45] there is no reason why MILS cannot

---

[41] In the words of Klein, 'in view of the rather restrictive definition of "coercion" in the classical law of treaties (as embodied in Art. 52 of the 1969 Vienna Convention), powerful states would still seem to enjoy a reasonably large freedom to press their claims': P. Klein, 'The Effects of US Predominance on the Elaboration of Treaty Regimes and on the Evolution of the Law of Treaties', in M. Byers and G. Nolte (eds.), *United States Hegemony and the Foundations of International Law* (Cambridge: Cambridge University Press, 2003), p. 363, at p. 368.

[42] L. Brilmayer, *American Hegemony: Political Morality in a One-Superpower World* (New Haven: Yale University Press, 1996), p. 75.

[43] Ibid.   [44] Ibid., p. 72.

[45] On the other hand, however, as Benvenisti emphasises, 'international law must recognize that governments are agents of only a part of the communities they purport to represent at the international negotiating table'. E. Benvenisti, 'Domestic Politics and International Resources: What Role for International Law?', in M. Byers (ed.), *The Role of Law in International Politics: Essays in International Relations and International Law* (Oxford: Oxford University Press, 2000), p. 114. For a critique of the state as a unitary actor from a legal–constitutional perspective, see U. Kischel, 'The State as a Non-unitary Actor: The Role of the Judicial Branch in International Negotiations' (2001) 39 *Archiv des Völkerrechts* 268.

concern itself with the exclusion of some subjects of interest to subaltern classes from the treaty-making process,[46] address the issue of the absence of substantive democracy in consenting states, and endorse the idea of transnational state responsibility (a matter to which we return later), in order to advance the cause of marginal and oppressed groups.[47]

It has been aptly observed that 'treaties and treaty-like instruments at the close of the twentieth century have become much too important to the functioning of international society to remain or to become the property of any one discipline or sub-discipline'.[48] For there is in the era of globalisation no aspect of international relations, which is not regulated by international treaty law. It therefore calls for more sophisticated approaches to treaties than is being offered by MILS. According to Johnston, a 'substantial change in the treatment of treaties on the part of legal discipline must be premised . . . *on the basis of functional – not formal – logic* . . .'.[49] The functionalist view he proposes 'stresses the relevance of considerations inherent in the context within which the issue or problem occurs, so that legal norms are kept in balance with institutional and political realities'.[50] We also share the understanding that it is:

> useful to *distinguish three kinds of consent*, varying with the instrument and the circumstances of its negotiation: consent to be juridically accountable in a court of law, consent to be held operationally answerable in the diplomatic arena, and *consent to be morally bound in the eyes of progressive public opinion.*[51]

CMILS understands the last as a call for the evaluation and recasting of a treaty in the light of its impact on certain groups in social life, namely the working class, women, peasants and the landless, children, indigenous peoples, and so on. CMILS, however, goes beyond the functionalist approach to advance a comprehensive strategy that furthers the interests of the subaltern classes, without entirely undermining a rule-oriented approach. The following elements, among others, constitute such a strategy.

First, CMILS calls for the further codification of the rules of deliberative democracy. The Vienna Convention on the Law of Treaties needs to be amended to include provisions that proscribe the use of all forms of

---

[46] Charlesworth and Chinkin, *The Boundaries of International Law*, p. 123.
[47] See section 10, below.
[48] D. M. Johnston, *Consent and Commitment in the World Community: The Classification and Analysis of International Instruments* (Ardsley: Transnational Publishers, 1997), p. 57.
[49] *Ibid.*, p. 49 (emphasis added).   [50] *Ibid.*, p. 58.   [51] *Ibid.*, p. 276 (emphasis added).

OUTLINE OF A MARXIST COURSE 69

coercion (for example, economic and diplomatic coercion) in international negotiations.[52] CMILS would also, to further deliberative democracy, call for the greater representation of subaltern classes in the negotiation teams sent by states.

Second, CMILS would like to introduce a form of peoples-based social impact assessment system. In support of such a process CMILS would require, inter alia, that treaties be negotiated and ratified with the consultation and consent of the elected representatives of the people. While this move may still not prevent consent to treaties that are not in the interests of subaltern classes, it would help render the process more transparent and amenable to dissent and political mobilisation.

Third, when it comes to treaty implementation, CMILS would prescribe a set of legal tools that would offer dependent and dominated states flexibility to implement its obligations in a manner that safeguards the interests of the subaltern classes. Thus, for example, in the context of the WTO, CMILS would argue for a greater deference to national interpretations and implementation of rules rather than a uniform mode insisted on by the WTO Dispute Settlement Body (DSB). For the national deference principle translates into greater autonomy to states at a time when it is being subverted through a network of international agreements.[53] It would allow the subaltern classes to put pressure on the state to adopt interpretations that safeguard their interests.

Fourth, CMILS would call for the clarification and development of customary international law rules of interpretation in order to reveal, and thereafter limit, the influence of power in the interpretative exercise. Following Wittgenstein, CMILS believes that since the meaning of a word lies in its use in the language, there is no such thing as determinacy/indeterminacy outside the world of social practices.[54] Consequently, what should be problematised are social (class) practices and not the abstract concept of meaning. Such problematisation would help focus on the social (class) roots of interpretation. Thereafter, there is a need to develop and use 'interstitial norms' that recognise the social (class) roots of conflicting interpretations (as manifested, *inter alia*, in resistance to particular interpretations) and reach closure after taking cognisance of

[52] See Chimni, 'Discourse Ethics and International Negotiations'. The grounds for the invalidity of a treaty listed in Part V of the Vienna Convention presently include error, fraud, corruption or coercion of a representative of a state and coercion of a state by the threat or use of force.
[53] B. S. Chimni, 'India and the Ongoing Review of the WTO Dispute Settlement System: A Perspective', *Economic and Political Weekly*, 30 January 1999, pp. 264–7.
[54] For details, see Chimni, *International Law and World Order*, ch. 3.

the social consequences of both.[55] The interstitial norms could be legal (principle of good faith) or moral (equity in settling conflicting claims).[56]

Fifth, CMILS would re-examine and highlight the *rebus sic stantibus* or material change in circumstances doctrine and make it integral to the concept of a balanced and just treaty, albeit in its consensual form.[57] This is in contrast to MILS, which contends that 'in modern times it is agreed that the rule applies *only in the most exceptional circumstances*, otherwise it could be used as an excuse to evade all sorts of inconvenient obligations'.[58] This view overlooks the fact that dependent and dominated states can only turn to the *rebus sic stantibus* doctrine for addressing the problem of unjust treaties. Of course, in the final analysis, the invocation of the clause would hinge both on the social consequences of obeying a rule and on the collective resistance to it by affected peoples. In this context, international human rights law is of obvious relevance, and CMILS suggests that it should be increasingly drawn on to support the invocation of the *rebus sic stantibus* doctrine.

4.2. Customary international law

For a practice to be designated a custom, it must constitute 'evidence of a general practice accepted as law'. From a CMILS standpoint, the significant question is why certain norms are designated or evolve as norms of customary international law and others do not. It is not very different from the question as to what the process is which gives rise to a rule of customary international law.[59] But the response to the question cannot simply be to uncover the class interests involved, for this would be to ignore the whole realm of international relations in which the state acts as an actor with a certain independent set of interests, as well as to fail to take into account the role of specific historical conjunctures (World War II, the Cold War, and so on). In other words, each norm of customary

---

[55] According to Lowe, 'interstitial norms': 'have no independent normative charge of their own. They do not instruct persons subject to the legal system to do or abstain from doing anything, or confer powers, in the way primary norms do. They direct the manner in which competing or conflicting norms that do have their own normativity should interact in practice.' V. Lowe, 'The Politics of Law-making: Are the Method and Character of Norm Creation Changing?', in Byers (ed.), *The Role of Law*, p. 207 at p. 216.
[56] A. Bagchi, 'Compulsory Licensing and the Duty of Good Faith in TRIPS' (2003) 55 *Stanford Law Review* 1529.
[57] See Art. 62 of the Vienna Convention on the Law of Treaties.
[58] Malanczuk, *Akehurst's Modern Introduction*, p. 144 (emphasis added).
[59] Byers, *Custom, Power*, p. 205.

international law would have to be analysed separately to determine the range of factors that go to constitute it.

However, while the formation of a customary international law norm is a complex process, it is a 'source' which closely manifests the will of powerful states. Indeed, it is accepted wisdom that the weight of some actors will matter more in the formation of customary international law. As Shaw puts it, the process 'is democratic in that all states may share in the formulation of new rules, though the precept that some are more equal than others in this process is not without a grain of truth'.[60] This inequality also assumes another form: 'for a custom to be accepted and recognized *it must have the concurrence of the major powers in that particular field*', generally the usual suspects, namely powerful states.[61] This weighing of the practices and interpretations of the advanced capitalist states reveals the bourgeois character of international law. In the colonial era the entire law of state responsibility with respect to the rights of aliens was developed through customary international law to justify imperialist practices. Thus it does not require much imagination to argue that the principle of prompt, adequate, and effective compensation was designated as a principle of customary international law to protect the property rights of foreign capital as against the rights of subaltern peoples. The postcolonial era has been no different. Norms of customary international law have been engendered that are against the interests of dependent and dominated states, for example the norm of humanitarian intervention.

However, not all norms of customary international law are necessarily against the interests of subaltern states. For 'the influence of powerful States on customary law-making is not always decisive, because the "power of rules" [or what we call the "relative independence" of rules] sometimes affects what they are able to accomplish, when they seek to develop, maintain or change rules of customary international law'.[62] For if it were always to be decisive, it would both destabilise and delegitimise the international legal system.[63] But what is equally true is that states and classes without power cannot even collectively utter the magic words 'customary international law'. Thus the dependent and dominated states

---

[60] Shaw, *International Law*, p. 58; Byers, *Custom, Power*, p. 205.
[61] Shaw, *International Law*, p. 63 (emphasis added).
[62] Byers, *Custom, Power*, p. 206. See also S. Toope, 'Powerful but Unpersuasive? The Role of the United States in the Evolution of Customary International Law', in Byers and Nolte (eds.), *United States Hegemony*, p. 287.
[63] Toope, 'Powerful but Unpersuasive?', 62.

failed to have any norm of the new international economic order (NIEO) designated as a norm of customary international law or, to take a different example, the principle of burden-sharing as a part of customary international refugee law.[64] For the acceptance of such norms calls forth an interpretative exercise that vests power in those very states (and MILS ideologues) on which obligations are to be imposed through the norm of customary international law. The satisfaction of the element of *opinio juris* depends to a great extent on their pronouncements. Furthermore, there is the persistent objector exit clause which powerful states can use to prevent the application of a customary norm inimical to their interests.[65] To put it differently, the content of customary international law, in contrast to treaty law, offers a more flexible mode of law-making and is therefore more easily attuned to class interests.

4.3. Soft law

While treaties and customary international law can never become instruments of change for subaltern states and classes, new sources (resolutions of international organisations or texts adopted in the non-governmental world) are banished to the realm of 'soft law'. For, according to MILS, '"soft law" is not law'.[66] This result is achieved by embracing a positivist conception of law that is on the one hand de-linked from underlying social relations and, on the other hand, obsessed with (pseudo-) clarity of obligations and the availability of (unreflective) sanctions. The real anxiety is that to accept new democratic sources would mean the radical restructuring of the international system to the disadvantage of the international capitalist class. To put it differently, while 'soft law' reflects generalisable interests, hard law in a bourgeois world order embodies particular interests.

Unsurprisingly, the ideals of deliberative democracy and distributive justice that inform much 'soft law' are confined to political processes within nation-states, allowing imperialism to escape transnational state responsibility. These ideals, despite growing global integration, have even

---

[64] See B. S. Chimni, *International Refugee Law: A Reader* (New Delhi: Sage, 2000), pp. 146–52.
[65] One state alone, even if it is as powerful as the United States today, may not be able to influence the process of the formation of customary international law. In the present-day world a single state cannot redefine the rules of the game without undermining the legitimacy of the international (capitalist) system. That is why even the United States is compelled to heed the views and concerns of other advanced capitalist countries. See Toope, 'Powerful but Unpersuasive', pp. 308–13.
[66] Shaw, *International Law*, p. 92.

less relevance in the emerging bourgeois imperial international law. In brief, notwithstanding the fact that 'soft law' is most often the product of communicative action and power (and not as suggested by MILS the 'tyranny of the majority'), it remains marginal to the operation of the international legal system. Not merely class issues meet this fate. Gender concerns are treated in the same way. As Charlesworth and Chinkin point out, gender issues 'suffer a double marginalization in terms of traditional international law-making: they are seen as "soft" issues of human rights and are developed through "soft" modalities of law-making that allow states to appear to accept such principles while minimizing their legal commitments'.[67]

5. The relationship between international law and municipal law: growing integration

Two standard theories are used to explore the nature of the international legal system through determining the relationship between municipal law and international law, namely the monist and dualist theories. The dualist view 'assumes that international law and municipal law are two separate legal systems which exist independently of each other. The central question then is whether one system is superior to the other.'[68] The monist doctrine, on the other hand, 'has a unitary conception of the "law" and understands both international law and municipal law as forming part of one and the same legal order'.[69] The conceptual debate between the two schools has yielded few significant insights.[70] For the relationship between municipal law and international law is validated or transformed not at the level of theoretical construct but in the realm of life, be it internal or international life. In a significant way 'the dualism – monism distinction reflects the degree of openness of a domestic society as a whole and particularly its constitutional (legal) subsystem to the outside world'.[71] The distinction, in other words, depends on the intensity and depth of interstate relations or – which is the same thing – the development of the capitalist world economy. Its deepening integration in the era of accelerated globalisation compels advanced capitalist states increasingly to impose its will on dependent and dominated states. Therefore, in many areas of

---

[67] Charlesworth and Chinkin, *Boundaries of International Law*, p. 66.
[68] Malanczuk, *Akehurst's Modern Introduction*, p. 63.   [69] Ibid.
[70] I. Brownlie, *Principles of Public International Law* (Oxford: Oxford University Press, 1999), p. 55.
[71] Müllerson, *Ordering Anarchy*, p. 172.

international life the monist theory is coming to prevail. As Müllerson notes, 'in some areas the distinction between international and domestic [law] is *completely disappearing*'.[72]

Of course, the openness of domestic society is not necessarily a choice exercised by subaltern states, but is in many cases a product of quiet coercion by dominant states and international institutions that they control. In the face of an expropriating monism that does not translate into justice, adhering to a dualist approach may serve a progressive purpose. It could help retain maximum autonomy for the dependent and dominated state in the interpretation and implementation of uniform global standards. Since in states adhering to the dualist approach international obligations have to be incorporated into municipal law, it would give greater flexibility in the implementation of international obligations. Thus, as argued above, the application of a national deference principle in implementing WTO obligations would create space for implementing legislation which safeguards, albeit within defined limits, the interests of subaltern classes without the state being seen to be in violation of its international obligations. The autonomy that the national deference principle provides is the reason why the United States incorporated it (*vide* Art. 17.6) into the WTO Anti-Dumping Agreement. Of course, it is the class character of the state following the dualist approach, and the strength of resistance movements, which would determine the extent to which and the context in which subordination to international law will be spurned and a national deference approach adopted, where it does not bring commensurate benefits to subaltern classes.[73]

6. The jurisdiction of states

If the relationship of municipal law to international law is determined on the stage of global capitalism, so is the nature and extent of jurisdiction exercised by states. Historically, the jurisdiction exercised by a state under international law has been primarily related to its territory. It is the area for which laws can be prescribed and in which they can be enforced. However, the territorial principle was never absolute, as testified to by the nationality and protective principles of jurisdiction. But what MILS is silent about is the fact that, in the colonial era, the metropolitan powers went far beyond

---

[72] *Ibid.*, at pp. 17, 178 (emphasis added).
[73] Thus, while on the whole the dependence of Third World states today translates into unequal integration into the international system, it is important to recognise that it is not integration per se but its character that is problematic.

the nationality or protective principles to exercise near-complete extraterritorial jurisdiction in colonised territories, either through capitulation treaties or territorial control. Then came the decolonisation process. The story of international law since then has been the effort by imperial powers to recover the loss of jurisdiction through legitimising postcolonial forms of extraterritorial jurisdiction. This trend has been accentuated by growing global integration. The essence of contemporary developments, then, is the creation of a jurisdictional field that: (i) seeks to limit the jurisdictional competence of the postcolonial state by constituting the bourgeois state as the normal state, to the advantage of the TCC; (ii) attempts to turn all geographical spaces into productive spaces through appropriate jurisdictional mechanisms; (iii) embeds a set of jurisdictional competences that simultaneously allows the advanced capitalist states to exercise extraterritorial jurisdiction and to use the territorial foundations of the law to shield the TCC and imperial state functionaries from advocates of transnational justice; and (iv) facilitates a dispute settlement regime that meets the needs of the transnational corporate world to establish a private justice system. The developments that support the first three elements of this thesis are touched on below. The aspect related to the privatisation of jurisdiction is briefly noted in the next section.

First, a distinction between acts *jure imperii* and *jure gestionis* has been adopted by advanced capitalist states in order to extend jurisdiction over the commercial acts of third states. This separation of sovereign from commercial functions allows the consolidation of the power of the capitalist class in the sphere of production and the constituting of the bourgeois state as the universal state. The separation is today an integral part of the law of state immunity.[74]

Second, there is the expansion of jurisdiction of states over new geographical spaces. This development reflects the capitalist drive to subjugate and transform all space into productive space. It led, for instance, the 1982 Law of the Sea Convention to extend the jurisdiction of states (12-mile territorial waters, a 24-mile contiguous zone, a 200-mile exclusive economic zone) as well as establish rules relating to the exploration and exploitation of seabed beyond national jurisdiction. In the latter context, the idea of a common heritage of mankind was advanced to create

---

[74] The fact that today even China, despite protestations, more or less accepts the principle of restrictive immunity reveals the extent to which the bourgeois state has become the normal sovereign state. G. Wang, 'Sovereignty in Global Economic Integration: A Chinese Perspective', in S. Yee and W. Tieya (eds.), *International Law in the Post-Cold War World: Essays in Memory of Li Haopei* (Oxford: Routledge, 2001), p. 357.

what can be called planetary jurisdiction. But the concept was stood on its head and the private exploitation of the seabed minerals through large consortiums was permitted by establishing a parallel system of exploration and exploitation. This led to the legitimisation of international property rights as against common property rights as the matrix for the exercise of jurisdictional rights in new geographical spaces.

Third, there is the increasing incidence of the exercise of unilateral extraterritorial jurisdiction by advanced capitalist countries, in particular the United States.[75] It is justified, *inter alia*, by reference to the protective and effects doctrines. This expansion in extraterritorial jurisdiction is a function of both market and power.[76] The greater integration of the world market compels imperial states to attempt to control external situations and events that have consequences for domestic corporations and citizens.[77] To this end power is used, among other things, to universalise the national laws of imperial states. Several ways have been used, by the United States for example, to achieve this objective. Two may be mentioned to illustrate the point. The use of the certification mechanism is one. As Krisch notes, 'the extensive use of the certification mechanism provides a tool for the United States to create law for other States and to monitor its observance, while the United States itself remains unbound and unmonitored'.[78] Second, there is a move to 'substantivism' in the US courts, a term used to describe 'a choice-of-law methodology whose goal is to select the better law in any given case'.[79] While democratic on the face of it, 'substantivism' means 'the potential over-application of US law, and the potential for process-related unfairness in the resolution of economic conflicts'.[80]

---

[75] A good example of it is the Helms-Burton Act 1996. For the text, see (1996) 35 *International Legal Materials* 357. The impression that European states do not exercise extraterritorial jurisdiction is erroneous. See Brownlie, *Principles of Public International Law*, pp. 311–12, n. 70.

[76] It is perhaps true that 'the adoption of an extra territorial rule or decision is not always contrary to international law, it is only contrary to international law when it does not have a reasonable link with the State enacting such a rule or making such a decision'. B. Stern, 'How to Regulate Globalization?', in Byers (ed.), *The Role of Law*, p. 247 at p. 257 (emphasis in original). But in the era of globalisation, a 'reasonable link' is not always difficult to establish for imperial states, especially when it is backed by power: H. L. Buxbaum, 'Conflict of Economic Laws: From Sovereignty to Substance' (2002) 42 *Virginia Journal of International Law* 932.

[77] As Krisch puts it in the context of the internet: 'Through dominance of the markets, US law is spread globally': N. Krisch, 'More Equal than the Rest? Hierarchy, Equality and US Predominance in International Law', in Byers and Nolte (eds.), *United States Hegemony*, p. 135 at p. 164.

[78] *Ibid.*, p. 161.   [79] Buxbaum, 'Conflict of Economic Laws' 957.   [80] *Ibid.*, 966.

It also acts 'as a lever of forcing convergence . . . outside the political process that generally structures the harmonization movement'.[81] This is already happening in the field of banking, securities regulation, civil aviation, cyber law and other fields.[82] In other words, a bourgeois imperial international law is being entrenched in several spheres of international law through the unilateral move to harmonise.

Fourth, extraterritorial jurisdiction has assumed a multilateral form. Thus, for example, the WTO, besides exercising compulsory jurisdiction over disputes arising from texts that constitute the WTO regime, also permits a member state, in certain circumstances, to make extraterritorial prescriptions. Such is, for instance, the case with national laws dealing with the relationship of trade and environment. Subject to the precondition of carrying out good faith dialogue with the other state(s) to arrive at a bilateral or multilateral solution to the environmental 'problem' in question, unilateral measures are deemed legitimate.[83] This is the substance of the decision of the WTO Appellate body in the *United States – Import Prohibition of Certain Shrimp and Shrimp Products: Recourse to Article 21.5 of the DSU by Malaysia* case.[84]

Fifth, there is the denial of what may be termed 'justice jurisdiction' by the courts of advanced capitalist states when confronted with the phenomena of 'mass torts' committed by transnational capital in the poor world. At the very moment that globalisation unites the world, and extraterritorial jurisdiction is exercised by advanced capitalist states, its courts have sought to create 'new national frontiers of responsibility for the conduct of global capital'.[85] As Baxi notes, 'the jurisprudence of jurisdiction is also the history of construction and creation and annihilation of spaces of justice'.[86] Doctrines such as *forum non conveniens* have been used 'maximally [to] deny foreign mass disaster plaintiffs their day in their chosen

---

[81] *Ibid.*, 972.
[82] J. Braithwaite and P. Drahos, *Global Business Regulation* (Cambridge: Cambridge University Press, 2000), pp. 475–7.
[83] But, as Stern notes, 'the fact that the enforcement is territorial does not conceal or erase the fact that the prescription is extraterritorial, and thus the entire law remains illegal'. Stern, 'How to Regulate Globalization?', p. 258.
[84] For the text of the decision see WT/DS58/AB/RW, 22 October 2001: Report of the Appellate Body. For a comment, see B. S. Chimni, 'WTO and Environment: The Legitimization of Unilateral Trade Sanctions' *Economic and Political Weekly*, 12–18 January 2002, p. 133.
[85] U. Baxi, 'Mass Torts, Multinational Enterprise Liability and Private International Law' (1999) 276 *Recueil des Cours* 297 at 312.
[86] *Ibid.* at 343; H. Zhenjie, '*Forum Non Conveniens*: An Unjustified Doctrine' (2001) 48 *Netherlands International Law Review* 143 at 159–62.

forum'.[87] The Bhopal case, in which a US court applied this doctrine, is just one instance of this jurisprudence of injustice.

Sixth, there is the evolving realm of universal jurisdiction in the domain of international crimes.[88] It extends the jurisdictional autonomy of all states, albeit in directions that may promote justice in the world, with the state acting as a surrogate for the international community.[89] But there is a troubling downside in an imperial world. The exercise of universal jurisdiction can, even its advocates admit:

> produce conflicts of jurisdiction between states that have the potential to threaten world order, subject individuals to abuses of judicial processes, human rights violations, politically motivated harassment, and denial of justice. In addition, *there is the danger that universal jurisdiction may be perceived as hegemonistic jurisdiction exercised mainly by some Western powers against persons from developing nations.*[90]

7. International economic law

The growing integration of the capitalist world economy in the era of globalisation has meant rapid developments in international investment and trade laws entrenching international property rights, ensuring the mobility of industrial, service and finance capital, and undermining the autonomy of the dependent and dominated states, with grave consequences for the social and economic rights of subaltern classes. Reference may be made to certain key developments that inform the emergence of bourgeois imperial international law.

First, at the initiative of the imperial states, several international treaties have been adopted on the subject of foreign investment. These include bilateral investment protection treaties (BITs), the Agreement establishing the Multilateral Investment Guarantee Agency (MIGA), the Agreement on Trade Related Intellectual Property Rights (TRIPS), the Agreement on Trade Related Investment Measures (TRIMS), and the General Agreement on Trade in Services (GATS). The essence of these international legal developments is to confer on TNCs a bundle of rights that range from ease of entry and establishment, the proscription of performance

---

[87] Baxi, 'Mass Torts', 352; Zhenjie, 'Forum Non Conveniens', 86.
[88] C. M. Bassiouni, 'Universal Jurisdiction for International Crimes: Historical Perspectives and Contemporary Practice' (2001) 42 *Virginia Journal of International Law* 82.
[89] *Ibid.*, 96.   [90] *Ibid.*, 154–5 (emphasis added).

requirements, the strong protection of intellectual property rights, generous rules of compensation in the event of nationalisation or expropriation and insurance against non-economic risks to the free choice of settlement of disputes in order to avoid problematic national laws and fora. The subject of trade and investment is also included in the WTO Doha Round of trade negotiations. It may add to this bundle of rights. On the other hand, few duties are imposed on the TNCs vis-à-vis host states and peoples.

Second, international trade law has expanded greatly through the adoption of the General Agreement on Tariffs and Trade (GATT) Final Act of the Uruguay Round of Trade Negotiations ('Final Act') which, *inter alia*, established the WTO. GATT incorporates the basic principles of 'free trade'. These include the most-favoured-nation and national treatment principles. There are also rules that govern the use of quantitative restrictions, subsidies, anti-dumping duties, customs unions and emergency measures. The essence of the principles of free trade that have been elaborated in the GATT/WTO regimes is to pry open the markets of the dependent and dominated economies without giving sufficient access to competitive products from these countries to the markets of advanced capitalist states. The agreements that constitute the Final Act go beyond the statement of basic principles to regulate a whole range of non-trade areas, such as intellectual property rights (IPRs), investment measures and services. More areas are the subject of the Doha Round of trade negotiations, namely trade and the environment, competition policy, and so on. Implied in the regulation of non-trade areas is the transfer of sovereign power to the WTO. While through this process the GATT/WTO regimes encourage the free mobility of goods, capital and services, little has been done to increase the mobility of labour, revealing the bias of CIL vis-à-vis the subaltern classes. Indeed, during the very period in which barriers to the movement of goods, capital and services are being brought down, the advanced capitalist states are raising the barriers to the movement of labour. While the multilateral spirit of the GATT/WTO regime is not to be scoffed at, any overall assessment of the operations of GATT/WTO regimes can only conclude that they are not to the advantage of the subaltern classes in the Third World. It may also be noted in this context that the principle of special and differential treatment has been considerably watered down.

Third, an international monetary law has evolved to constrain the dependent and dominated economies from breaking free and implementing autonomous economic and financial policies. This international monetary law is essentially the creation of the international financial institutions. The essence of international monetary law is the imposition of conditionalities, which ensure that a neo-liberal agenda suited to the interests of TCC is implemented.[91] One result has been the privatisation of public assets and, perhaps even more significantly, a capital-account liberalisation culture that has allowed hyper-mobile finance to run roughshod over subaltern states to the benefit of TCC. The 1997 East Asian crisis was a manifestation of this loss of monetary sovereignty and control that severely affected the living standards of the subaltern classes.

Fourth, there has evolved over the last few decades 'the notion of *lex mercatoria*', which 'enables private power to be exercised in the making of international commercial law'.[92] First, of course, private entities are playing, through various organisational fronts (for example, the International Chamber of Commerce), a role both in adopting international law standards and in influencing inter-state negotiations to enhance the interests of the TCC. The state is no longer the only participant in the international law-making process, although it remains the principal actor. The globalisation process is breaking the historical unity of law and state and creating 'a multitude of decentered law-making processes in various sectors of civil society, independently of nation-states'.[93] Second, a separate world of international commercial arbitration has been created to resolve business disputes. Earlier, 'forum-selection clauses were deemed invalid as attempts to oust the forum court of its jurisdiction, and choice-of-law clauses were deemed invalid as inconsistent with the absolute right of a sovereign to apply its law to persons and conduct within its territory'.[94] In contrast, at present party autonomy 'has been interpreted expansively'.[95] Party autonomy allows a private entity to choose the jurisdiction and law it likes. Thus what is essentially a system of private justice has been established through the international commercial arbitration movement in the name of facilitating international trade and business. What is more, this world of international commercial arbitration is controlled by a club

---

[91] 'The extension of the normative force of international standards by the device of conditionality is an important characteristic of contemporary international law.' Lowe, 'Politics of Law-Making', p. 212.

[92] M. Sornarajah, 'Globalization and International Law: The Law as an Instrument of Hegemonic Power', 76 (on file with the author).

[93] G. Teubner, 'Foreword: Legal Regimes of Global Non-state Actors', in G. Teubner (ed.), *Global Law Without a State* (Brookfield: Dartmouth, 1997), p. xiii.

[94] Buxbaum, 'Conflict of Economic Laws', 938.   [95] *Ibid.*, 939.

of arbitrators 'who make law that is favorable to the large commercial conglomerates that straddle the world'.[96]

8. International environmental law

International environmental law is another area in which the interests of imperialism are coming to prevail. CIL and MILS have in this case, too, failed to confront the differing perspectives of the First and Third Worlds, or the global ruling and subaltern classes, as the central debate regarding the conceptual foundation of international environmental law.[97] First, according to Mickelson, while advanced capitalist states and MILS do present 'an historical context for international environmental law', it is a truncated historical context that does not include the ravages of colonialism.[98] A full historical account would take cognisance of the manner in which nature was appropriated by the colonial powers to stabilise and expand capitalism within the world economy. In the colonial period, Third World spaces were treated as *terra nullius* for the exploitation of natural resources unconstrained by any international law of sustainable development. But this historical relationship between the expansion and accumulation of capital and environmental degradation is left unconsidered, conveniently erasing Third World histories.

Second, advanced capitalist states and MILS gloss over the possibility that the world has already been transformed into a zero-sum game for development. Yet no distinction is made between the basic human needs of the subaltern classes and consumerism. The focus on the idea of intergenerational equity subtly de-emphasises the fact, even as it does not deny it, that without intragenerational equity we will not be able to achieve equity among generations. It means that the principle of common but differentiated responsibility, the central principle of international environmental law from the perspective of subaltern states and classes, does not receive the content it would have done had historical responsibility been taken seriously. There is thus the unfulfilled potential of legal instruments, be this the bio-diversity convention or the climate change convention.

Third, contradictory legal principles have been adopted in different international agreements to the detriment of the overall goal of environmental protection and to the benefit of TCC. Thus, for example,

---

[96] Sornarajah, 'Globalization and International Law'.
[97] K. Mickelson, 'South–North, International Law, and International Lawyers' (2000) 11 *Yearbook of International Environmental Law* 52 at 53.
[98] Ibid., 56.

while several environmental law agreements talk of the need to transfer environment-friendly technology to the Third World, the WTO Agreement on TRIPS establishes a hard patent regime that limits such a possibility by making this technology more expensive. In other words, the goal of sustainable development is subject to the protection of international property rights. The reason is that the TCC has come to exercise great influence on international environmental negotiations. As one acute observer of these negotiations has noted, 'corporations influence almost every negotiation on the environment that has taken place under the auspices of the UN'.[99]

Fourth, as has already been alluded to, courts of advanced capitalist states and MILS do not take seriously the violation of environmental standards in subaltern states by transnational capital, even when it involves the gross violation of the human rights of the subaltern classes.[100] The *locus classicus* here is the Bhopal disaster case. In 1984 a leak of methyl isocyanite gas from a pesticide plant in Bhopal, India, owned by the US corporation Union Carbide, resulted in thousands of deaths and the exposure of an estimated 500,000 individuals to the gas, resulting in chronic illnesses, including depression of the immune response. The Indian government, representing the plaintiffs, failed in its attempt to sue in the United States, thanks to the *forum non conveniens* doctrine, and following much-delayed litigation the case was settled in India for a paltry $470 million.[101]

9. International human rights law

The discourse of human rights is today omnipresent. States, irrespective of the class(es) in power, seek to present themselves as the embodiment of international human rights. The reasons are that the universalisation of the bourgeois state necessitates that the free and equal individual be placed at the centre of that universe; that it is the necessary condition for the creation of global markets and a global system of production; and that the language of human rights helps entrench the private rights of individuals and corporations. As Evans puts it:

---

[99] A. Aggarwal *et al.* (eds.), *Poles Apart* (New Delhi: Centre for Science and Environment, 2001), p. 382.
[100] For some of the cases that have captured public attention in recent years, see M. Anderson, 'Transnational Corporations and Environmental Damage: Is Tort Law the Answer?' (2002) 41 *Washburn Law Journal* 399 at 405–6.
[101] See generally Baxi, 'Mass Torts'.

in the current period, legitimate human rights can be defined only as that set of rights that require government abstention from acts that violate the individual's freedom to innovate and to invest time, capital, and resources in processes of production and exchange.[102]

But, to be sure, it is not my argument that the language of rights is not empowering for subaltern classes. The language of rights can shield against arbitrary state action, a matter of supreme importance to resistance movements. However, it is equally the case that, despite the enormous expansion in human rights law and institutions in the past few decades, both the international (north–south) and internal divides have increased and the welfare state is on the retreat.

Right, as Marx observed, 'can never be higher than the economic structure of society and its cultural development conditioned thereby'.[103] Since the bourgeois state with the free and equal individual at its centre is superimposed on dependent and dominated societies, it is difficult to deliver on the promise of the realisation of social and economic rights. It explains the continuing reluctance of the United States to ratify, and thereby give greater legitimacy to, the International Covenant on Economic, Social and Cultural Rights (ICESCR). What the imperial world fears is the universalisation of alienation to which ICESCR draws attention, namely the absence of control over conditions of work and its product. It dreads the implications of the insurrectionary fact that, for the subaltern classes, 'life itself appears only as a *means to life*' with the accompanying 'loss of ... self'.[104] It is conscious of the fact that the universalisation of alienation is, among other things, a function of neocolonial policies and laws which violate the economic, social and cultural rights of the nationals of dependent and dominated states. Thus, for example, the WTO, the International Monetary Fund (IMF) and the World Bank are promoting a neo-liberal agenda at the initiative or behest of the advanced capitalist states on the ground that it would promote human welfare. However, despite growing evidence that the structural adjustment programmes of the IMF–World Bank combine and the rules of the WTO have a negative impact on the rights of subaltern classes, there has been no attempt to rethink these policies. The UN Human Rights Commission even passed a

---

[102] T. Evans, 'Citizenship and Human Rights in the Age of Globalization' (2000) 25 *Alternatives* 415 at 416.

[103] K. Marx and F. Engels, *Selected Works*, 3 vols. (Moscow: Progress Publishers, 1970), vol. III, p. 19.

[104] K. Marx, *Economic and Philosophic Manuscripts of 1844* (Moscow: Progress Publishers, 1959), p. 73 (emphasis added).

resolution that calls for ensuring that international economic agreements help actualise human rights.[105] But notwithstanding this resolution, the United Nations itself is busy placing its faith in the neo-liberal agenda. This becomes clear from, among other things, its global compact initiative and the bid to create neo-liberal post-conflict states through relying on the IMF–World Bank combine.[106] In brief, developments in international human rights law need to be given meaning today in the matrix of an imperial global dispensation. This places limits on the realisation of human rights, that is, without substantial transformation of the societies that are its subjects. It also explains why, for example, victims of human rights violations 'have to clear more hurdles and accept more limited access to remedies than the owners of intellectual property'.[107] In the circumstances, framing all issues and strategies in the language of rights distracts from their realisation.[108]

10. The international law of state responsibility

On the other hand, however, the international law of state responsibility excludes answerability for the policies of imperialism. The law of state responsibility was historically designed to protect the rights of aliens in the era of colonialism, in particular property rights. It is no accident that it evolved inextricably linked with the law relating to the nationalisation and expropriation of alien property. While today the law of state responsibility 'is in the main dealing with a set of principles concerned with second-order issues, in other words the procedural', a number of textbooks still deal with the law along with the rights of aliens.[109] The first Special Rapporteur of the International Law Commission (ILC), F. V. Garcia Amador, who submitted six reports on the subject between 1956 and 1966, did the same.[110] It was only later that the focus shifted to 'the framework or matrix of rules of responsibility, identifying whether there has been a

---

[105] UN Doc. E/CN.4/Sub.2/2000/7, 17 August 2000, Commission on Human Rights: Subcommission on the Promotion and Protection of Human Rights, Fifty-second Session: Intellectual Property Rights and Human Rights.
[106] B. S. Chimni, 'Refugees and Post-Conflict Reconstruction: A Critical Perspective', in E. Newman and A. Schnabel (eds.), *Recovering from Civil Conflict: Reconciliation, Peace and Development* (Oxford: Routledge, 2002), p. 163 at p. 166–7.
[107] T. Collingsworth, 'The Key Human Rights Challenge: Developing Enforcement Mechanisms' (2002) 15 *Harvard Human Rights Journal* 183 at 203.
[108] D. Kennedy, 'The International Human Rights Movement: Part of the Problem?' (2002) 15 *Harvard Human Rights Journal* 101 at 108.
[109] Shaw, *International Law*, p. 541.
[110] J. Crawford, *The International Law Commission's Articles on State Responsibility* (Cambridge: Cambridge University Press, 2002), p. 1.

breach by a State and what were its consequences'.[111] The Commentary on the ILC's Draft Articles on Responsibility of States for Internationally Wrongful Acts states:

> The articles do not attempt to define the content of the international obligations breach of which gives rise to responsibility. This is the function of the primary rules, whose codification would involve restating most of substantive international law, customary or conventional.[112]

This de-coupling of the procedural from substantive rules is a significant step towards erasing the historical link between the protection of alien property rights and the law of state responsibility, thereby allowing it to occupy an apparently neutral field, with the result that the injustice of an obligation (as manifested in resistance of subaltern classes and the violation of their human rights) is not a defence against its violation.[113] Thus, the formalism of the principle of sovereign equality that informs the law of treaties is matched by the formalism of the law of state responsibility. Each returns to the other to legitimate itself; the law of state responsibility returns all questions relating to the negotiations, interpretation, and content of the treaty back to the law of treaties:

> It is a matter of the law of treaties to determine whether a State is a party to a valid treaty, whether the treaty is in force for that State and with respect to which provisions, and how the treaty is to be interpreted.[114]

The double manoeuvre renders victims of international law invisible and without remedy.[115] This has not, of course, prevented MILS from including rules relating to countermeasures in the ILC's Draft Articles on State Responsibility, which favours, as has been pointed out by Nepal, Switzerland and Greece in the Sixth Committee, powerful states (and classes) and undermines the prestige of the international legal order.[116]

---

[111] *Ibid.*, p. 2.   [112] *Ibid.*, p. 74.
[113] None of the recognised 'circumstances precluding wrongfulness', including the defence of 'necessity', covers the case.
[114] Crawford, *International Law Commission's Articles*, p. 75.
[115] To put it differently, positivism 'allow[s] international lawyers to avoid recourse to controversial moral judgements'. Brilmayer, *American Hegemony*, p. 98.
[116] W. Czaplinski, 'UN Codification of Law of State Responsibility' (2003) 41 *Archiv des Völkerrechts* 76. Earlier, too, some governments, such as those of Cuba, India and Mexico, had suggested the 'deletion of the Chapter on countermeasures altogether'. Crawford, *International Law Commission's Articles*, p. 48. 'On the other hand, USA declared that the regulation proposed is too restrictive and in fact constituted an important limitation upon the right to apply countermeasures, the Draft should be re-thought and better elaborated in this respect': Czaplinski, 'UN Codification', 76.

On the other hand, the 'solidarity measures' included (termed by Art. 48 of the ILC Draft as 'invocation of responsibility by a State other than an injured State') exclude from scope state responsibility for transnational harm. It conceives some situations (best termed 'international harm') as calling for solidarity measures, thereby normalising and legitimising transnational harm. In contrast, what CMILS proposes is, first, opposition to the idea of countermeasures in the absence of fair institutional procedures. Second, it would argue the case for a regime of transnational responsibility of states for transnational harm.[117] CIL should make each state responsible not only to its own citizens but also to the citizens of other states, that is when its acts result in the human rights violations of citizens of other states. Unless some form of transnational state responsibility is institutionalised it is difficult to see how subaltern classes can access justice. CIL, as Gibney points out:

> has already codified certain kinds of transnational duties, but this codification has occurred in the context of the enforcement of human rights violations committed in or by 'other' countries. What is missing is an interpretation of the duties states take on when they assist and allow offending governments to operate – and in doing so become offending states themselves.[118]

Or, for that matter, prescribe policies (either themselves or through international institutions) that result in human rights violations in other states but are generally attributed (*vide* the principle of state consent) to the state of which the persons are nationals whose rights have been violated. Transnational state responsibility has, of course, to go hand in hand with transnational corporate responsibility and transnational institutional responsibility (left out of the ILC's Draft Articles). This three-pronged approach is necessary to democratise the emerging bourgeois imperial international law.

---

[117] 'Transnational harm refers to injury which the state, or non-state actors, or forms of social organization do to the members of other societies. The revolution in transnational harm is . . . the result of the globalization of capitalist relations of production and exchange.' A. Linklater, 'Towards a Critical Historical Sociology of Transnational Harm', in S. Hobden and J. M. Hobson (eds.), *Historical Sociology of International Relations* (Cambridge: Cambridge University Press, 2002), p. 162 at p. 170.

[118] M. Gibney, 'Transnational State Responsibility for Violations of Human Rights' (1999) 12 *Harvard Human Rights Journal* 267 at 295.

11. International law and the use of force

Laski wrote that:

> as long as the effective purpose of the state, internally regarded, is to protect the principles of capitalism, so long, in its external aspect, will it require to retain the use of war as an instrument of national policy . . . capitalism and a world-order are incompatible; war is rooted in the capitalist system in our experience of its necessary functioning.[119]

To put it differently, 'imperialism is, in general, a striving towards violence and reaction'.[120] Force thus has a class content and is used to further the interests of the international capitalist class. The subaltern classes are its victims in a triple sense. First, the decision to go to war is taken without consultation with them. Second, it is from these classes that combatants are largely recruited and sacrificed. Third, they inhabit an unprotected and immobile universe where related non-combatants (women and children) invariably become victims of conflict.

Force assumes different forms in different eras. In the colonial phase of imperialism, the unapologetic and open use of coercion was deemed legitimate. The postcolonial phase itself can be divided into two phases: the Cold War and globalisation phases. During the Cold War there was a broad consensus over the UN Charter obligation not to resort to the threat or use of force against the political independence and territorial integrity of states (Art. 2(4)) unless it was in self-defence (Art. 51) or authorised by the UN Security Council (under Chapter VII). The Charter framework has now slowly begun to unravel. The era of accelerated globalisation has seen attempts to redefine the norms relating to the use of force in order to realise the current interests of imperialism: the doctrine of pre-emptive attack is one outcome. To be sure, it is not 'the dogmatism of international law' that accounts for the new thinking on the question of use of force;[121] sufficient interpretative flexibility was always available to justify the threat or use of force by powerful states as long as some procedural constraints were respected. Today, however, the foremost imperial state, the United States, in the absence of a global countervailing power, seeks to change the rules of the game in a bid to legitimise total global domination. The military role of the imperial state is, among other things, crucial to the overseas

---

[119] H. J. Laski, *The State in Theory and Practice* (London: George Allen & Unwin, 1935), p. 229.
[120] V. I. Lenin, *Selected Works*, 3 vols. (Moscow: Progress Publishers, 1975), vol. I, p. 702.
[121] J. Habermas, 'The Fall of the Monument-I', *The Hindu*, 5 June 2003.

expansion of transnational capital. Towards this end, the United States has established over 100 military bases in the world and has repositioned NATO. On the other hand, it is not willing to pay heed to global protests (as in the war on Iraq) or to international humanitarian law (IHL) (e.g., the Gulf War, Kosovo and Iraq). However, given the fact that the Charter law is a 'powerful constituent element of peace',[122] and the consensus that was in place for decades, and also the fear of the consequences of unravelling the Charter framework and undermining IHL, differences are likely to arise (as they have) among imperial states from time to time on the need to reject it.

There is much greater unity among these states when it comes to the doctrine of humanitarian intervention, the understanding, of course, being that it will be selectively enforced. It reflects the successful ideological deployment of the contemporary discourse of human rights opportunistically to present the global capitalist crisis as a local crisis and to legitimise killing with kindness. The doctrine of humanitarian intervention therefore has the support of MILS and also of much of public opinion in the imperialist world. It will now combine with the ongoing 'war against terror' to produce a lethal legitimacy for violence against subaltern states and peoples.[123] In terms of international law, humanitarian intervention outside the UN Charter framework is clearly unlawful. In the *Case Concerning Military and Paramilitary Activities in and against Nicaragua* (*Nicaragua v. United States of America*), the ICJ had directly considered the relationship between human rights and the violation of the principle of the use of force by the United States and concluded that 'while the United States might form its own appraisal of the situation as to the respect of human rights in Nicaragua, the use of force could not be the appropriate method to monitor or ensure such respect'.[124] It may also be recalled that the authoritative 1970 Friendly Relations Declaration does not make an exception in favour of humanitarian intervention.

---

[122] H. Lauterpacht, *The Function of Law in the International Community* (Oxford: Clarendon Press, 1933), p. 437. According to Lauterpacht, 'peace is pre-eminently a legal postulate', at p. 438.

[123] Note in this respect the shift from 'weapons of mass destruction' to 'regime change' as justification for the war against Iraq. See generally T. J. Farer, 'Humanitarian Intervention before and after 9/11: Legality and Legitimacy', in J. L. Holzgrefe and R. O. Keohane (eds.), *Humanitarian Intervention: Ethical, Legal, and Political Dilemmas* (Cambridge: Cambridge University Press, 2003), p. 53 at pp. 80–9.

[124] [1986] ICJ Rep. 392, at para. 268.

It is often argued that there has evolved a customary international law norm that permits armed unilateral humanitarian intervention. But this view has been persuasively contested by others. After a review of the principal authorities and state practice on the subject, Brownlie has concluded:

> Whilst in theory customary law could develop in such a way as to legitimize action by way of humanitarian intervention, the proponents of a change in the customary law have a burden of proof of a new consensus among States which could not be discharged on the evidence available.[125]

Thus there is no rule of international law that permits unilateral armed humanitarian intervention. But such a contention is met with the slogan that humanitarian intervention may be illegal but moral. In short, the doctrine of humanitarian intervention, along with the doctrine of pre-emptive attack, has been invented as an integral part of an emerging bourgeois imperial international law in a bid to establish global political domination.

12. Looking ahead

In 1935 Laski wrote that 'the high road to an effective international order lies through the reconstruction of the class-relations of modern society'.[126] A year later, Dutt observed that 'conflict between enlarged world productive forces against the existing social and political forms is the crux of world politics'.[127] Both these observations retain their validity even today, albeit the vision of what has to replace the existing world order has undergone transformation. The old socialist model has lost much of its attraction after the collapse of 'actually existing socialism' and growing evidence of the violation of the civil and political rights of socialist citizens. On the other hand, the global capitalist system continues to reproduce development and underdevelopment in a single movement in the international system. It is the cause of the massive violation of the rights of peoples the world over. Yet there is no third model that has caught the imagination of the subaltern classes. But those who are the subjects of oppression are not waiting for an alternative to be fully articulated. They are willing to muddle through history, for it is a struggle for survival with dignity. There is

---

[125] I. Brownlie, 'Kosovo Crisis Inquiry: Memorandum on the International Law Aspects' (2000) 49 *International and Comparative Law Quarterly* 878 at 904.
[126] Laski, *The State in Theory and Practice*, p. 254.
[127] R. P. Dutt, *World Politics 1918–1936* (London: Gollancz, 1936), p. 23.

thus the hope that the growing protests in the north and the south against an unequal globalisation process will invent the new model as it brings about changes in the existing global capitalist dispensation. At the very least, these resistance movements, if they gather strength and unity, can reform several key sites of the system and make the world a better place to live in.

What role should international lawyers play in this struggle? Given the crucial role that MILS has played in codifying and legitimising dominance it would be naïve to expect its proponents suddenly to appreciate the protests of the old and new social movements and join them as organic intellectuals in an attempt to reform the existing rules of the game. It underlines the significance of critical scholarship. But critical scholarship, unfortunately, is a divided house. The Third-Worlders, the Marxists, the feminists, the new approaches are unable to come together to contest MILS. The reasons are more fundamental than the simple lack of co-ordination. There are profound differences in their vision of the future and about what can be done to get from here to there. But this should not preclude collective critical reflection and thinking on MILS. Fragmented efforts at critiquing MILS are unlikely to dent it seriously. The results of the efforts of New Approaches to International Law (NAIL), Third World approaches to international law (TWAIL) and feminist approaches to international law (FtAIL) have already made a difference. It would make a bigger difference if they were to come together without in any way merging their identities to produce, *inter alia*, alternative critical texts.

For those who believe that critique must be followed by reconstruction, the challenge is to use CIL and institutions to the advantage of the subaltern classes. The Austro-Marxist Karl Renner believed that legal institutions of capitalist society could play an effective role in its transformation to a socialist society. As Bottomore has pointed out, Renner was 'occupying a place precisely between Bolshevism and reformism'.[128] While Renner perhaps went too far in his belief that 'capital as the object of property, though *de jure* private, has in fact ceased altogether to be private', or that law is an 'empty frame', or that 'the development of law works out what is reasonable', there is no gainsaying that legal nihilism is not

---

[128] T. Bottomore and P. Goode (eds.), *Austro-Marxism* (London: Clarendon Press, 1978), p. 44.

the appropriate counter.[129] What is called for is a creative and imaginative use of existing international laws and institutions to further the interests of the 'wretched of the earth', even as we underline its class character. International lawyers cannot pretend to do more.

[129] K. Renner, 'The Institutions of Private Law and Its Social Functions', in Freeman, *Lloyd's Introduction to Jurisprudence*, p. 1071.

3

The commodity-form theory of international law

CHINA MIÉVILLE

1. The necessity of (Marxist) theory

1.1. The blight of managerialism

International law has notoriously and accurately been described as a 'wasteland' for theory.[1] Of course, the tsunami of managerialist writing[2] is informed by theories of law, international law and the world, but mostly unexamined and the more ideological for that. In this context the rise of what has been called the 'New Stream' of radical international law scholarship has been of immeasurable importance, with its project to 'dislodge the discipline... from its stagnation... and rejuvenate the field as an arena of meaningful intellectual inquiry'.[3]

'The New Stream... stands as part of a broader movement in contemporary legal theory commonly known as Critical Legal Studies (CLS) or critical jurisprudence.'[4] The CLS movement is united in its critical

---

[1] B. S. Chimni, *International Law and World Order* (New Delhi: Sage, 1993), p. 15.
[2] It is estimated that 80,000 books on international law had been published by 1967, and that currently 700 books and 3,000 articles on international law are published annually (P. Malanczuk, *Akehurst's Modern Introduction to International Law*, 7th revd edn (Oxford: Routledge, 1997), p. 8).
[3] D. Kennedy, 'A New Stream of International Legal Scholarship' (1988) 7 *Wisconsin International Law Journal* 1 at 6. Useful introductions to and overviews of the New Stream include N. Purvis, 'Critical Legal Studies in Public International Law' (1991) 32 *Harvard International Law Journal* 81; A. Carty, 'Critical International Law: Recent Trends in the Theory of International Law' (1991) 2 *European Journal of International Law* 66; H. Charlesworth, 'Subversive Trends in the Jurisprudence of International Law' (1992) 86 *American Society for International Law Procedings* 125; D. Cass, 'Navigating the Newstream: Recent Critical Scholarship in International Law' (1996) 65 *Nordic Journal of International Law* 341; W. Aceves, 'Critical Jurisprudence and International Legal Scholarship: A Study of Equitable Distribution' (2001) 39 *Columbia Journal of Transnational Law* 299 at 309–24. D. Kennedy and C. Tennant, 'New Approaches to International Law: A Bibliography' (1994) 35 *Harvard International Law Journal* 417 contains a comprehensive list of critical international legal sources up to 1994.
[4] Purvis, 'Critical Legal Studies', 89.

attitude to mainstream legal theory and has drawn on eclectic bodies of thought to pursue this. This has led to a problem: despite its powerful critical tools, the New Stream has sometimes been left with a poverty of systematic theory. '[I]t is a movement in search of a theory, but at the same time it is a movement which has not agreed that such a theory is either possible or desirable.'[5]

The New Stream and CLS's influences include:

> normative philosophy, critical theory, structuralism, anthropology, prepositional logic, literature, sociology, politics and psychiatry... Legal Realism, New Left anarchism, Sartrean existentialism, neo-progressive historiography, liberal sociology, radical social theory and empirical social science[6]

along with the now ubiquitous postmodern social and linguistic theory, in both Foucauldian and Derridean variants. The coagulation of these into an often rather nebulous 'critical theory' can obscure the real philosophical differences between various of these strands,[7] and lead to a sometimes internally contradictory body of thought.[8]

The desire to systematise radical theory, and to do so from a Marxist perspective, does not imply a theoretical closed-mindedness or intellectual sectarianism. My own Marxist studies in international law, for example, have been fundamentally informed by certain postmodern approaches, in particular, that of Martti Koskenniemi.

---

[5] A. Hunt, 'The Critique of Law: What is Legal About Critical Legal Theory?', in P. Fitzpatrick and A. Hunt (eds.), *Critical Legal Studies* (Oxford: Blackwell, 1987), p. 5.

[6] Purvis, 'Critical Legal Studies', 88–9.

[7] Many authors point out the instability of the movement, given these contradictory influences. See P. Fitzpatrick and A. Hunt, 'Critical Legal Studies: Introduction' in Fitzpatrick and Hunt, *Critical Legal Studies*, p. 2; Purvis, 'Critical Legal Studies', 124.

[8] For example, M. Koskenniemi, *From Apology to Utopia: The Structure of International Legal Argument* (Helsinki: Finnish Lawyers Publishing Company, 1989), p. 475, cites Derrida to the effect that interpretation will only ever offer up more words, each of which are as unstable as their fellows, ultimately maintaining a situation of radical indeterminacy in legal discourse (and discourse in general). However, this 'Derridean' sense of indeterminacy is not the same indeterminacy that Koskenniemi has outlined elsewhere in his book. That was a product of the peculiar nature of the modern international system, the unstable, contradictory vacillation between sovereignty and world order. Koskenniemi mis-sells his own analysis when he equates it with Derrida's linguistic essentialism. As Alcantara puts it, '[e]ven in *disregard* of verbal indeterminacies, Koskenniemi explains, law as a system would still be indeterminate'. This is '[m]ore significant' than the 'indeterminacy of legal texts': O. Alcantara, 'Ideology, Historiography and International Legal Theory' (1996) IX(25) *International Journal for the Semiotics of Law* 39 at 67, 66) (emphasis in original).

1.2. The insights of indeterminacy

Koskenniemi systematises the observation that the fundamental categories of international law move in contradictory directions: as Myres McDougal puts it, they are 'pair[s] of opposing concepts'.[9] Koskenniemi famously shows how the fundamental categories of international law can be used to argue absolutely contradictory positions, with 'descending' arguments by reference to international law's 'Utopian' pole of concern for 'world society', or 'ascending' ones derived from its 'Apologist' pole, for which individual state rights are fundamental:

> The two patterns – or sets of arguments – are both exhaustive and mutually exclusive ... The result ... is an incoherent argument which constantly shifts between the opposing positions while remaining open to challenge from the opposite argument.[10]

The conclusion is that, as Purvis puts it, international legal doctrines are 'entirely reversible'.[11] Take, say, the controversial question of reprisals activity in international law. The mainstream opinion is that reprisals are illegal.[12] The 1964 UN Security Council resolution condemning a British reprisal against Harib Fortress in Yemen, stated that the council '[c]ondemns reprisals as incompatible with the purposes and principles of the United Nations'.[13] This recourse to the 'purposes and principles' of the UN represents a 'descending' normative argument against unfettered state retaliation. In response to this, proponents of the legality of reprisals point to Article 51 of the UN Charter, allowing the use of force in self-defence. Some reprisals, they say, are the 'functional equivalents' of self-defence, and should be legal as such.[14] This is to counter the descending argument with an ascending one, based on the central importance of state sovereignty.

---

[9] M. McDougal, (1954) *American Society of International Law, Proceedings* 120.
[10] Koskenniemi, *From Apology to Utopia*, pp. 41–2.
[11] Purvis, 'Critical Legal Studies', 113.
[12] See, for example, I. Brownlie, *International Law and the Use of Force by States* (Oxford: Oxford University Press, 1963), p. 281; G. Schwarzenberger, *Manual of International Law*, 3rd edn (London: Stevens, 1952), p. 82; D. Bowett, *Self-Defence in International Law* (Manchester: Manchester University Press, 1958), pp. 13–14. (Bowett here states the majority view. His own position is ambivalent.)
[13] Cited in R. Falk, 'The Beirut Raid and the International Law of Retaliation' (1969) 63 *American Journal of International Law* 415 at 429 (emphasis in original).
[14] Y. Dinstein, *War, Aggression and Self-Defence*, 2nd edn (Cambridge: Cambridge University Press, 1994), p. 216; R. Tucker, 'Reprisals and Self-Defense: The Customary Law' (1972) 66 *American Journal of International Law* 586, *passim*.

However, any such ascending argument contains its own counter-position. By definition, reprisals are illegal incursions against another state's sovereignty, and, if sovereignty is the basis of obligation and authority, it is hard to see how that sovereignty can legally be disrupted. This is the ascending version of the argument that reprisals are illegal. The counter to this is to be found in the descending justifications for reprisals activity, according to which reprisals can 'advance the purposes of the United Nations'.[15]

There is something in the structure of the argument that allows both sides to make plausible, logical claims based on fundamental legitimating concepts of international law. It is this indeterminate process of legal argument that Koskenniemi outlines. For Koskenniemi, and the CLS perspective, these contradictions are reflections of contradictions in liberalism itself – 'a system of thought ... beset by internal *contradiction* ... and by systematic *repression* of the presence of those contradictions'.[16]

1.3. The limits of idealism

One of the limitations of the New Stream approach is in its implicit theory of the social world, an idealist constructivism. Alcantara makes this clear when he talks about 'how the inherited myths, concepts and models of human thought shape the manner in which we view external phenomena'.[17] This is to depict international law as a kind of constraining myth inherited from the past: in Purvis's construction, '[i]nternational law's weaknesses are in some sense irrelevant; self-validation sanctions the international-law myth'.[18]

The structures of everyday life that surround us – such as international law – are deemed the accretions of ideas. Ideas progress here by autopoeisis. This is a radically idealist philosophy, privileging abstract concepts over the specific historical context in which certain ideas take hold, and how. There is no theory in Koskenniemi, for example, of precisely *why* the edifice of international law should be thrown up as part of liberalism.

---

[15] E. Colbert, *Retaliation in International Law* (New York: King's Crown Press, 1948), pp. 203–4. The same argument is advanced in B. Levenfeld, 'Israel's Counter-Fedayeen Tactics in Lebanon' (1982) 21 *Columbia Journal of Transnational Law* 1 at 35.
[16] M. Kelman, *A Guide to Critical Legal Studies* (Cambridge, MA: Harvard University Press, 1987), p. 3 (emphasis in original). See Koskenniemi, *From Apology to Utopia*, p. 52.
[17] Alcantara, 'Ideology, Historiography', 72.   [18] Purvis, 'Critical Legal Studies', 112–13.

1.4. The Marxist response

For the underlying political-economic dynamics that the contradictory edifice of liberalism might be expressing we can turn to Marx. In *Capital*, he briefly shows how the social relations of general commodity production are the foundation for liberalism and its contradictions.

> It is ... the direct relationship of the owners of the conditions of production to the immediate producers ... in which we find the innermost secret, the hidden basis of the entire social edifice, and hence also the political form of the relationship of *sovereignty and dependence*, in short, the specific form of the state in each case.[19]

At the level of individuals, as Marx suggests, the ascending and descending arguments are mediated by the state. However, this is not the case internationally, when the units are states themselves: in this instance, the relationship is still one of sovereignty and dependence, but it is no longer contained by an overarching power.

For Koskenniemi, liberalism underpins international law because of the constant application of the 'domestic analogy' by liberal writers, because without an overarching power 'the structuring power of liberal ideas in international law' was so strong – and again, there is no real historical context underpinning the claim.[20] Building on Marx's suggestive comments, however, we can get beyond idealism and see that the logic of modern inter-state relations is defined by the same logic that regulates individuals in capitalism, because since the system's birth – and in the underlying precepts of international law – states, like individuals, interact as property owners. This can be seen in early modern writings. 'Grotius... transferred the notion of liberty-as-property to the state in international affairs, viewing the character of state boundaries as that of a private estate.'[21]

This kind of historical-materialist analysis – an attempt to explain why certain ideas and structures come to the fore in certain political-economic contexts – is often misunderstood and denounced by CLS scholars as a

---

[19] K. Marx, *Capital*, Vol. 3 (New York: Vintage, 1981), p. 927 (emphasis added).
[20] Koskenniemi, *From Apology to Utopia*, p. 72, and more generally at pp. 68–73.
[21] P. Gowan, *The Global Gamble: Washington's Faustian Bid for Global Dominance* (London: Verso, 1999), p. 145. See H. Grotius, *The Freedom of the Seas* (Union, NJ: Lawbook Exchange, 2001), at p. 29: 'the jurist [Ulpian] is speaking of private estates and of public law, but in speaking here of the territory of peoples and of private law the same reasoning applies, because from the point of view of the whole human race peoples are treated as individuals' – insofar, evidently, as those individuals are owners of estates.

bogeyman of crudity. Thus Purvis, in passing, dismisses the 'deterministic Marxist dialectic between an economic base and its ideological superstructure'.[22] Alcantara excoriates how '[t]he realm of pure human thought and idea is relegated by the Marxist to a state of jejune non-effectuality'.[23]

Among the many responses to this trite canard, Engels himself makes it quite clear that 'if somebody twists this [materialist conception of history] into saying that the economic factor is the *only* determining one, he transforms that proposition into a meaningless, abstract, absurd phrase', and that ideas and 'systems of dogma also exercise their influence upon the course of historical struggles and in many cases determine their form in particular'. Materialism inheres in the fact that 'the *ultimately* determining factor in history is the production and reproduction in real life'.[24]

The CLS alternative – some un- or under-theorised constructivism – leaves us no way of understanding the systematic structural constraints and dynamics operating on actually existing international law, and why it should take the form it does. For all their devastating and persuasive analysis of the failures and contradictions of liberalism and international law, they offer no theory of the specificity of the legal form itself.

1.5. The black box of the legal form

This is not, of course, unique to CLS theorists: a failure to conceptualise the legal form underpins the traditional definition of international law. The notion that it is a 'body of rules' implies a contingency to the specific 'law-ness' of those rules, as Hedley Bull perspicaciously points out.[25] HLA Hart crystallises the lacuna over the legal form in his claim that the analogy between international and municipal law 'is one of content not of form'[26] – the content here being the shared normative obligation contained in both sets of 'social rules'. If the legal form is not shared between international

---

[22] Purvis, 'Critical Legal Studies', 99.   [23] Alcantara, 'Ideology, Historiography', 42.
[24] K. Marx and F. Engels *Selected Works* (Oxford: Blackwell, 1970), vol. III, p. 487 (emphasis in original).
[25] H. Bull, *The Anarchical Society* (London: Macmillan, 1977), p. 122. See also his restatement of the argument in pragmatic terms, which nonetheless leaves the essential 'law-ness' untheorised – a lacuna dismissed as 'theoretical difficulties'. 'If the rights and duties asserted under these rules [of international law] were believed to have the status merely of morality or of etiquette, this whole corpus of activity [of statesmen, legal advisors, international assemblies] could not exist. The fact that these rules are believed to have the status of law, whatever theoretical difficulties it might involve, makes possible a corpus of international activity that plays an important part in the working of international society.' (p. 130).
[26] H. L. A. Hart, *The Concept of Law* (Oxford: Clarendon Press, 1961), p. 231.

and municipal law, then there is nothing *legal* inhering in both beyond the fact that they are called law.

This implicit theory of law's contingency is quite unsatisfactory. There is surely something specifically 'legal' about international law, and its historical emergence is part of a process of historical transformation. The universalisation of international law is predicated on the legal form. An international legal theory must open up the black box at the centre of international law. The fundamental unit of analysis must be that legal form itself.

2. Marxism(s)

2.1. *The specificity of Marxism*

Classical Marxism is, above all, a rigorously materialist theory, according to which ideas, concepts and bodies of theory must be made sense of within a particular material context. Concomitant with that:

1. it is a total theory, in which social reality is not a discombobulated morass of ontologically distinct phenomena, but an interrelated, conflictual, complex totality;
2. it is a dynamic theory, for which a dialectical understanding of the contradictory dynamics within social totality is necessary to understand changes in that totality;
3. it is a theory in which modes of production and productive relations, the specific and conflictual contexts of political economy in history, are key to the understanding of social reality (including international law); and
4. it is a theory for which class as a category, and the conflict between classes – between those with differential access to and control over the productive resources – are key.

What follows is an attempt to outline a Marxist theory of international law, which is able to supersede the limitations of earlier Marxist and 'mainstream' theories. At the same time, I will attempt to show how this theory might build on the indispensable insights of some of the New Stream writers, while constructing materialist foundations to put these insights on a firmer base. To do this, I build on the astonishing work of the Bolshevik legal theorist Yevgeny Pashukanis, and attempt to apply and extrapolate his groundbreaking methodology and insights to the field of international law.

2.2. 'Official' Marxism

One group of theories which can quickly be dispensed with are the 'official' theories of international law of the erstwhile Soviet Bloc. After 1928–30, when the era of more open theoretical debate was suppressed and theory became nothing but a tool for the exigencies of official policy,[27] the 'debates' in the USSR tended to revolve around the extent to which a new and separate sphere of 'socialist international law' existed.[28]

Tunkin and other Soviet writers offered slightly modified variants of mainstream international legal theory,[29] with the addition of this peculiar and untheorised addendum. This was devoid of theoretical rigour, and was asserted less because it explained anything than because 'it was unacceptable to Soviet scholars to even contemplate for a moment that the relationship between socialist countries and the outside world was regulated by bourgeois international law'.[30] Official Soviet 'Marxism' added nothing new or helpful to international legal theory.

---

[27] A second and even more crushing period of theoretical stagnation was ushered in in 1939. '[T]he imposition of A. J. Vyshinskii's legal concept on the scholarly community at the meeting of the Institute of State and Law of the Soviet Academy in 1939 meant a full stop to (and practically a deadly reprisal against) any sign of further innovation' (C. Varga, 'Introduction', in C. Varga (ed.), *Marxian Legal Theory* (New York: New York University Press, 1993), p. xv).

[28] This crude, tendentious and apologetic theory, expounded to serve the perceived needs of foreign policy, raises the question of what kind of political-economic dynamics were at work in these states, though this question – what kind of societies and formulations were the Stalinist states? – ranges well beyond the scope of this chapter. My own research has led me to identify with that body of theory which holds that the dynamic of competitive accumulation in the USSR and its satellites (originally a competition with the west over the means of destruction – military hardware – as well as means of production – the heavy industry needed to produce them) subordinated the inchoate movement toward grass-roots democracy and workers' control of the state, and that therefore far from being 'socialist' or even a 'degenerate workers' state', the USSR can best be described, certainly after 1928, as 'bureaucratic state capitalism', whatever its propaganda claimed. See among many expositions of this theory especially T. Cliff, *State Capitalism in Russia*, (1948 available at www.marxists.org/archive/cliff/works/1955/statecap/intro.htm) and A. Callinicos, *Trotskyism* (Buckingham: Open University Press, 1990), section 5.1.

[29] G. Tunkin, 'International Law in the International System' (1975) IV *Recueil des Cours* 3; G. Tunkin, *International Law: A Textbook* (Moscow: Progress Publishers, 1986). For the history of this theory, including its early exposition by Korovin, see V. Kubálková and A. Cruickshank, *Marxism and International Relations* (Oxford: Oxford University Press, 1989), pp. 160–7, and more generally on Soviet international legal theory at pp. 158–92.

[30] Chimni, *International Law and World Order*, p. 247.

2.3. Alternative Marxisms

In 1983, Maureen Cain demanded 'nothing less than ... a political economy of international law'.[31] Since then, debates about globalisation and the relation between states and international markets has forced questions of international regulation onto the agenda and some historical materialists have drawn attention to specific trans/international legal issues arising from considerations of the 'international state'.[32] However, this work has so far been somewhat tentative. It is true that a new generation of writers, such as Claire Cutler, is beginning to pick up this theoretical baton,[33] but there is a dearth of Marxist or historical-materialist writing on international law.

Sol Picciotto is one of the few Marxists to have taken seriously the injunction to formulate a theory of the changing nature of international law, but with the exception of an invaluable short essay on international law *tout court*,[34] his impressive work has tended to focus on the immediate interrelation between international regulation and economic neoliberalism.[35] His work, with its analysis of the role of state-sponsored international legislation in bleeding 'stateness' across national boundaries, has been a powerful antidote to the widespread and simplistic assertion that globalisation is eroding the nation-state. However, without any analysis of the intrinsic limits of international law, he vacillates between arguing that international regulation is desirable for increasing democracy (a politically progressive move) and for 'underpin[ning] the security and confidence on which markets depend'[36] – hardly a self-explanatory good for a Marxist writer. Essentially, in the absence of an articulated theory

---

[31] M. Cain, 'Introduction: Towards an Understanding of the International State' (1983) 11 *International Journal of the Sociology of Law* 1 at 2.

[32] Most importantly, in 1983, issue 11 of the *International Journal of the Sociology of Law* was a special issue devoted to this issue.

[33] See, for example, C. Cutler, 'Globalization and the Rule of Law: Reconstituting Property, Capital and the State', paper delivered at 'Now More than Ever: Historical Materialism and Globalisation' Workshop at Warwick University (1999); and C. Cutler, 'Critical reflections on the Westphalian assumptions of international law and organization: a crisis of legitimacy' (2001) 27 *Review of International Studies* 133.

[34] S. Picciotto, 'International Law: The Legitimation of Power in World Affairs', in P. Ireland and P. Laleng (eds.), *The Critical Lawyers' Handbook 2* (1997), p. 13.

[35] See, for example, S. Picciotto, 'Jurisdictional Conflicts, International Law and the International State System' (1983) 11 *International Journal for the Sociology of Law* 11; S. Picciotto, 'The Control of Transnational Capital and the Democratisation of the International State' (1988) 15 *Journal of Law and Society*, 58.

[36] S. Picciotto, 'Globalisation, Liberalisation, Regulation', paper presented at conference on globalisation at Sussex University (1998), p. 13.

of the parameters of the legal form, it is unclear to what extent Picciotto sees international law as a force for social transformation.[37]

There has been one book-length exposition of international law from a Marxist perspective. B. S. Chimni's trailblazing work[38] is indispensable for any serious student of international law and of Marxism. Chimni's periodisation of the epochs of international law, his attention to history and imperialism, and his critique of traditional theories all repay careful attention. Despite his sophistication, however, Chimni's theory is still predicated on rules as the fundamental particles of international law, explicitly opposing the indeterminacy thesis.

> If rules are assigned no significant place within the legal system ... the result can only be free competition between different ideological interepretations ... This state of affairs is guaranteed to ensure the collapse of the international legal system. In so far as its formal presence is yet retained it cannot but become an instrument of oppression in the hands of the more powerful states. It is important, therefore, to uphold the central place of rules within the international legal system.[39]

Elsewhere, Chimni is clear on the limitations of international law for an emancipatory project: the realm of law, he says, is 'not the arena from which the struggle for radical changes could be launched'[40] and that 'international law is class law'.[41] However, based in part on his belief in the 'relative autonomy that the legal sphere enjoys',[42] Chimni expresses cautious optimism about the progressive potential of international law.[43] At the very least he sees the application of 'legal rules' as contributing to stability,[44] and – as the above quote makes clear – as a brake on the instrumentalisation of law in the hands of the powerful states.

Contra Chimni, I have argued (after Koskenniemi *et al.*) that the 'free competition' between interpretations he describes does not ensure the destruction of the international legal system but is in fact a constitutive feature of that system. Chimni, too, has no theory of the legal form, so the fundamental specifics of law itself are contingent, and the limits or otherwise of law's supposed 'progressive' 'emancipatory' project are unclear.

---

[37] *Ibid.*, p. 11–14. [38] Chimni, *International Law and World Order*. [39] *Ibid.*, p. 103.
[40] *Ibid.*, p. 208. [41] *Ibid.*, p. 102. [42] *Ibid.*, p. 143. [43] *Ibid.*, p. 205.
[44] *Ibid.*, p. 205.

2.4. Law as ideology

Some Marxists (and others) have seen law as 'an ideological fiction, imposed on a social reality to which it has no correspondence by some organ of centralised authority'.[45] This view finds 'the origins of law in ideology, in the "heads of people", rather than in real, socioeconomic interactions or the material relationships of people'.[46]

Of course, it would be absurd to counterclaim that law does not have an ideological function. One modulation of this ideology can easily be seen, for example, in the enormous surge in publishing on human rights in international law. This often articulates a vision of 'rights' that:

1. derives from bourgeois 'first-generation' rights ('negative rights which protect the individual from arbitrary state action and are associated with Western liberal democracies')[47] and thereby tacitly takes bourgeois capitalism for granted;[48]
2. updates the notion of the civilising mission of the West by producing what Orford calls a 'heroic narrative' in which the West 'is associated with attributes including freedom, creativity, authority, civilization, power, democracy, sovereignty and wealth',[49] and is the only agent capable of injecting them into a Third World cast as a passive object; and
3. by showing that the attempt to support 'human rights' involves international action, implies that human rights problems are intrinsically foreign, and that there are no abuses at home: 'Many Americans thus believe and perpetuate the quaint fiction that human rights problems exist only in places that must be reached by crossing large bodies of saltwater.'[50]

---

[45] B. Fine, 'Law and Class', in B. Fine *et al.* (eds.), *Capitalism and the Rule of Law* (London: Hutchinson, 1979), p. 36.
[46] R. Sharlet, P. Maggs and P. Beirne, 'P. I. Stuchka and Soviet Law', in P. Beirne (ed.), *Revolution in Law* (Armonk, NY: Sharpe, 1990), p. 51.
[47] P. Cheah, 'Posit(ion)ing Human Rights in the Current Global Conjuncture' (1997) 9 *Public Culture* 233 at 235.
[48] This is expressed, in arid Althusserian form, in J. Lenoble, 'The Implicit Ideology of Human Rights and its Legal Expression' (1986) 8 *Liverpool Law Review* 153.
[49] A. Orford, 'Muscular Humanitarianism: Reading the Narratives of the New Interventionism' (1999) 10 *European Journal of International Law* 679 at 687.
[50] J. Donnelly, 'Human Rights in the New World Order' (1992) 9 *World Policy Journal* 249 at 254–65.

Ideology critique can thus be of great importance in international law scholarship, as Susan Marks has argued.[51] However, there are serious limitations in focusing exclusively on law as ideology. Shirley Scott, for all the insights in her discussion of international law as ideology,[52] is, like so many of the New Stream writers, idealist, seeing the power of international law inhering in its 'ideas', which 'do seem to constitute a form of power'.[53]

One is left with no sense of why this 'idea' of international law should have arisen at a certain time and political-economic context. Ideology here is a posited structuring category rather than an expression of an underlying logic. The weakness of Scott's idealism is visible in her failure to contextualise historical change, most starkly in her depiction of decolonisation, in which the self-activity of those at the sharp end of colonialism is ignored for a claim simply that there was a 'rejection of the ideology of colonialism', seemingly out of the blue.[54]

Again, at heart the limitations of the critique of law as ideology lie in the failure to theorise the legal form. Pashukanis did not deny that law can have an ideological function – he saw there to be 'no argument about this'[55] – but he disputed that that is all, or even primarily or most interestingly what there is to it.

> Having established the ideological nature of particular concepts in no way exempts us from the obligation of seeking their objective reality, in other words the reality which exists in the outside world, that is, external, and not merely subjective reality.[56]

Actually existing law is manifestly not 'merely' ideological, but impinges on and regulates everyday life at all levels. As Pashukanis points out, the afterlife exists 'in some person's minds', as does the state. But:

> [u]nlike the afterlife, Pashukanis observes, the concepts of law and state reflect not only a particular ideology but the objective reality of the court system, the police and the military, the administrative and fiscal

---

[51] S. Marks, 'Big Brother is Bleeping Us – With the Message that Ideology Doesn't Matter' (2001) 12 *European Journal of International Law* 109.
[52] S. Scott, 'International Law as Ideology: Theorizing the Relationship between International Law and International Politics' (1994) 5 *European Journal of International Law* 313.
[53] *Ibid.*, 317.   [54] *Ibid.*, 317.
[55] E. Pashukanis, *Law and Marxism: A General Theory* (London: Ink Links, 1978), p. 74.
[56] *Ibid.*, p. 75.

organizations of the state, and so forth ... Legal concepts are embodied in various forms of regulations demanding compliance rather than mere belief.[57]

Scott's claims that 'the power of international law can only be the power of the idea of international law'[58] is insufficient. The power of international law is also, of course, the armed might of powerful states enforcing their interpretation of legal rules with cluster bombs and gunships. International law's power is emphatically not only the power of ideas, it is the power of violent coercion, as will become clear.

2.5. Law as iniquitous content

An alternative conception of law, much-favoured by Marxists of Pashukanis's time, was the 'sociological' theory of law, which 'treat[ed] law as the product of conflict of interest, as the manifestation of state coercion'.[59]

This position is essentially positivist, in that law is seen as the will of the state. Enforcement – coercion – is definitional to this theory. Of course, for Marxists like Stuchka or Plekhanov, the state was not a neutral body but an organ of ruling class control, which was why '[m]any Marxists assumed that by simply adding in the element of class struggle to ... [positivist] theories, they would attain a genuinely materialist, Marxist theory of law'.[60]

In the international law sphere, one can see as an example of this 'content-oriented' Marxism, Chimni's discussion of international law's 'class basis'.

> From the Marxist perspective it is this resort to principles, policies and other standards which facilitates the continuous development of the law on a class basis. For they manifest ... the ethical-political hegemony of the ruling classes. And if international law is class law, as it is ... then after peculiar features of the international context have been accommodated this understanding holds good for it as well.[61]

Here, the class nature of international law derives from 'principles' and 'policies': in other words, it is the content of particular legal rulings, as laid out and enforced by 'ruling classes', that makes law a class weapon,

---

[57] S. Von Arx, 'An Examination of E. B. Pashukanis's *General Theory of Law and Marxism*' PhD thesis, State University of New York, (1997), p. 35.
[58] Scott, 'International Law as Ideology', 317. [59] Pashukanis, *Law and Marxism*, p. 53.
[60] Ibid., p. 53.   [61] Chimni, *International Law and World Order*, p. 102.

rather than anything in the structure of international law. Chimni sees the progressive counterpoint to this tendency as manifest in 'rules'.

Compared to the 'high-sounding phrases about the "eternal idea of law"', Pashukanis was clear that this kind of left positivism was a source of 'particular satisfaction'.[62] However, it remained a source of 'disappointment' to him, because it 'exclude[d] the legal form as such from ... [the] field of observation'.[63] As has been argued above, this kind of theory is unable to explain the specific *legalness* of law:

> [A] sociological approach which looks to the economic and political interests behind specific legal and penal measures appears as a significant advance over ... formalism. But here again there is a disappointment. For exclusive attention is directed towards the class interests served or the economic functions performed by one or other measure of law or punishment; in other words, exclusive to the question of content. Why these interests or functions should have been served by the *legal* form of regulation or by *penal* repression remains a question unaddressed ...
>
> This exclusive focus on the content of law leaves the social and historical character of its form unexamined ...[64]

3. The commodity-form theory of law

3.1. *The General Theory of Law and Marxism*

Pashukanis's reputation was won with his book, *The General Theory of Law and Marxism* (GTLM),[65] published in 1924. Pashukanis saw his book as only the starting point for Marxist jurisprudence. He described it as a 'sketch', as 'a first draft of a Marxist critique of the fundamental juridical concepts'.[66] The fundamental thrust of the theory that Pashukanis

---

[62] Pashukanis, *Law and Marxism*, p. 53.   [63] *Ibid.*, p. 53.
[64] Fine, 'Law and Class', pp. 34–5.
[65] Peter Maggs's translation of the first edition is printed in P. Beirne and R. Sharlet, *Pashukanis: Selected Writings on Marxism and Law* (London: Academic Press, 1980), pp. 40–131. *The General Theory of Law and Marxism* ran to a second edition in 1926. This second edition, though without substantial revisions, 'was a corrected and supplemented edition', which, for example, expanded on the 'underdeveloped topic' of the state (Beirne and Sharlet, *Pashukanis*, p. 38). This second edition also included a useful and theoretically interesting foreword (Pashukanis, *Law and Marxism*, pp. 37–45). The second edition is available in English translated by Barbara Einhorn from the German translation of 1929 (*Ibid.*). I refer to both these English editions of the *General Theory* (the first English translation, in J. Hazard (ed.), *Soviet Legal Philosophy* (Cambridge, MA: Harvard University Press, 1951), pp. 111–225, is not well translated, with eccentric renderings of Marxist terminology: commodity fetishism becomes 'goods fetishism' for example).
[66] Pashukanis, *Law and Marxism*, p. 36.

outlined was an 'attempt to approximate the legal form to the commodity form'.[67]

'The basic thesis' of the commodity exchange or commodity-form theory of law, Pashukanis claimed, 'namely that the legal subject of juridical theories is very closely related to the commodity owner, did not, after Marx, require any further substantiation'.[68] This is modest to the point of coy. Not only are the wisps of jurisprudence throughout Marx's oeuvre far from systematic, but Pashukanis claims far more than the vague 'close relation' between the commodity owner and the legal subject. He argues that the logic of the commodity form is the logic of the legal form. Chris Arthur puts it very well:

> Pashukanis argues that *the juridical element in the regulation of human conduct enters where the isolation and opposition of interests begins*. He goes on to tie this closely to the emergence of the commodity form in mediating material exchanges. His basic materialist strategy is to correlate commodity exchange with the time at which man becomes seen as a legal personality – the bearer of rights (as opposed to customary privileges). Furthermore, this is explicable in terms of the conceptual linkages which obtain between the sphere of commodity exchange and the form of law. The nature of the legal superstructure is a fitting one for this mode of production. For production to be carried on as production of commodities, suitable ways of conceiving social relations, and the relations of men to their products, have to be found, and are found in the form of law . . .
>
> As the product of labour takes on the commodity form and becomes a bearer of value, people acquire the quality of legal subjects with rights . . .
>
> For Pashukanis, legal forms regulate relationships between autonomous subjects – it is the subject that is the 'cell-form' of the legal system . . . [T]he basic element in legal regulation is contestation – two sides defending their rights. In deliberately paradoxical fashion he says that historically law starts from a law-suit.[69]

Pashukanis argues that for exchange to be exchange, each commodity must be the private property of its owner, given in return for the commodity owned by the other. Each agent in the exchange must be an owner of private property, and formally equal to the other agent(s). Otherwise, what occurred would not be commodity exchange. In the opposition and equality of the legal subjects, whether the exchange is peaceable or not, contestation is implied and is at the heart of the legal form. Where there is the potentiality of disputation between two sovereign, formally

---

[67] *Ibid.*, p. 38.   [68] *Ibid.*, p. 39.   [69] Introduction to *ibid.*, pp. 13–15 (emphasis in original).

equal individuals implied by commodity exchange a specific form of social regulation is necessary. It must formalise the method of settlement of any such dispute without diminishing either party's sovereignty or equality. That form is law, which is abstract, based on the equality of its subjects and pervasive in capitalism.

Pashukanis relates the necessary, actually existing, materially effective legal form with the system of wider social relations. He takes his starting point from Marx. 'In as much as the wealth of capitalist society appears as "an immense collection of commodities", so this society itself appears as an endless chain of legal relations.'[70] Nor is this appearance illusory.

> The exchange of commodities assumes an atomised economy . . . The legal relationship between subjects is only the other side of the relation between the products of labour which have become commodities. The legal relationship is the primary cell of the legal tissue through which law accomplishes its only real movement. In contrast, law as a totality of norms is no more than a lifeless abstraction.[71]

It is the focus on law as a real regulatory force which explains why the legal norm – the rule – cannot be the basis of the legal form. The legal form is the form of a particular kind of relationship. Rules can only be derived from that relationship. They are secondary, and in fundamental jurisprudential terms, their specific content is contingent.

> In material reality a relationship has primacy over a norm. If not a single debtor repaid a debt, then the corresponding rule would have to be regarded as actually non-existent and if we wanted nevertheless to affirm its existence we would have to fetishize this norm in some way.[72]

According to the alternative, norm-driven position, in the words of one of its adherents:

> [i]t is not because creditors generally demand repayment of a debt that the right to make such a demand exists, but, on the contrary, the creditors make this claim because the norm exists; the law is not defined by abstraction from observed cases, but derives from a rule posited by someone.[73]

However, this leaves unanswered why some such 'posited' rules should be generalised and not others, and the norm-driven paradigm cannot

---

[70] Pashukanis, *Law and Marxism*, p. 85. The quotation is from K. Marx, *Capital*, vol. 1 (New York: Vintage, 1976), p. 125.
[71] Pashukanis, in Beirne and Sharlet, *Pashukanis*, p. 62. [72] *Ibid.*, p. 63.
[73] Shershenevich, quoted in Pashukanis, *Law and Marxism*, p. 86.

explain why one apparently 'valid' law is effective and another is not. For Pashukanis, given that the subject for analysis is actually existing law, that law inheres inasmuch as it regulates social behaviour.[74]

In locating the legal form in the 'economic' relationships of commodity exchange, rather than the superstructure of political power, as suggested by the norm-derivation theory, Pashukanis locates 'the moment of dispute' as at the basis of the legal form.[75] 'The law differentiates itself from the social relations of production in the resolution of disputes, in particular through the medium of the lawsuit.'[76]

This is the basis of Pashukanis's assertion that private law, rather than public law, is the 'fundamental, primary level of law'.[77] The rest of the legal superstructure can be seen as essentially derived from this. The concept of public law, for example:

> can only be developed through its workings, in which it is continually repulsed by private law, so much that it attempts to define itself as the antithesis of private law, to which it returns, however, as to its centre of gravity.[78]

A complex legal system regulating all levels of social life can be thrown up which appears to differentiate itself sharply from private law, but it ultimately derives from the clash of private interests. The legal form is that form which regulates the legal relationship: dispute is central, because without dispute there would be no need of regulation. The legal subject is part of this legal relationship, as '[e]very legal relation is a relation between subjects. The subject is the atom of legal theory, its simplest, irreducible element.'[79]

The juridical relation exists in the interface between humans' relations with their commodities and concomitant relations with each other. This, Pashukanis takes from Marx.

> In order that these objects may enter into relation with each other as commodities, their guardians must place themselves in relation to one another as person whose will resides in those objects, and must behave in such a way that each does not appropriate the commodity of the other, and alienate his own, except through an act to which both parties consent. The guardians must therefore recognise each other as owners of private property. This juridical relation, whose form is the contract, whether as part of a developed legal system or not, is a relation between two wills which mirrors

---

[74] Pashukanis, *Law and Marxism*, p. 88. [75] *Ibid.*, p. 93.
[76] Von Arx, 'An Examination', p. 48. [77] Pashukanis, *Law and Marxism*, p. 103.
[78] *Ibid.*, p. 106. [79] *Ibid.*, p. 109.

the economic relation. The content of this juridical relation ... is itself determined by the economic relation.[80]

The importance of this passage to Pashukanis can hardly be overstressed. 'By asserting that exchange requires mutual recognition of private property rights, Marx clearly acknowledges that the legal relation between subjects is *intrinsic* to the value relation.'[81] The legal subject is defined by virtue of possessing various abstract rights – '[t]he isolated, abstract, impersonal legal subject... cannot be identified with the specific attributes or roles of any particular social actor'.[82] This formal equality of distinct and different individuals is an exact homology with the equalisation of qualitatively different commodities in commodity exchange, through the medium of abstract labour (the stuff of value). Thus with the generalising of legal relations, '[l]egal fetishism complements commodity fetishism'.[83]

The historical generalisation of 'equal rights' is the generalisation of the abstract legal subject, 'an abstract owner of commodities raised to the heavens'.[84] This is why contract is so vital to Pashukanis's theory of law. Legal subjects relate to each other through contract, which is the formalisation of mutual recognition of equal subjects. Without a contract, Pashukanis writes, 'the concepts of subject and of will only exist, in the legal sense, as lifeless abstractions. These concepts first come to life in the contract.'[85]

The history of international law is beyond the bounds of this essay, but it should be clear that Pashukanis's categories become germane to international law with the early rise of capitalism, at a time when states, categorised as the owners of their own territories, consolidated their power in a context of increasing international interaction and conflict.

The seventeenth and eighteenth centuries saw the massive expansion of international trade, and this trade was central to the structure of the most powerful European states. It is during this period that the categories concomitant on that trade – the legal forms – begin to universalise. This was the birth of true international law. As trade became global, and definitional to the sovereign states, the international order could not but become an international legal order.

Often considered the epoch of the Absolutist state, this was even more the epoch of the Mercantilist state. Mercantilism was crucial for the consolidation of the sovereign state (absolutist or otherwise), and was a vital part of a transition to a capitalist world economy. The 'shifting

---

[80] Marx, *Capital*, vol. 1, p. 178.   [81] Von Arx, 'An Examination', p. 66 (emphasis added.)
[82] *Ibid.*, p. 69.   [83] Pashukanis, *Law and Marxism*, p. 117.   [84] *Ibid.*, p. 121.
[85] *Ibid.*, p. 121.

combination of tendencies' which characterised different mercantilist theories varied with political context: what they were all geared towards, however, was 'the increase of national power'.[86] 'The core of mercantilism is the strengthening of the State in material resources; it is the economic side of nationalism.'[87] This underlying conception was intrinsically international.

From their initial position in 'the pores' of society, commodity relations generalised, both between individuals and between states, and the abstracted, reified relations that follow – including law – generalised also.

3.2. From form to content

3.2.1. The excesses of state derivation

As we have seen, Pashukanis himself was concerned to stress the importance of not fetishising the politics, the content of law as the source of class inequality. Focusing on the legal form, he stressed that:

> the fundamental juridical categories cited above are not dependent on the concrete content of its legal norms, in the sense that they retain their meaning irrespective of any change in this concrete material content.[88]

However, this does not mean that the analysis of the content of law is unimportant – only that it must proceed on the right basis. Though Pashukanis's is a theory of the legal form, it does not follow that it is a theory inimical to examinations of particular legal contents.[89] Even one of his critics observes that '[t]he theoretical achievement of Pashukanis ... has been to steer a course between the fetishism of form and the fetishism of content'.[90] What is missing, however, is a systematically outlined relation between form and content.

Domestically, the state has a monopoly on authoritative legal interpretation, and internationally the states are the very subjects whose

[86] P. J. Thomas, *Mercantilism and the East India Trade* (London: P. S. King & Son, 1926), p. 3.
[87] *Ibid.*, p. 3. The theory of mercantilism as at core about state-building was seminally expressed by Schmoller in 1884 (reprinted G. Schmoller, *The Mercantile System and its Historical Significance: Illustrated Chiefly from Prussian History* (New York and London: Macmillan, 1967)). The most influential modern reformulation of Schmollerian ideas is Heckscher's monumental 1932 work (reprinted E. Heckscher, *Mercantilism* (London: Routledge, 1994)). For a harsh critique of Heckscher, see D. C. Coleman, 'Eli Heckscher and the Idea of Mercantilism', in D. C. Coleman (ed.), *Revisions in Mercantilism* (London: Methuen, 1969).
[88] Pashukanis, *Law and Marxism*, p. 47.
[89] As implied, for example, in R. Warrington, 'Standing Pashukanis on his Head' (1984) 12 *Capital and Class* 102.
[90] Fine, 'Law and Class', p. 34.

interpretations are key to coercively actualising specific contents of the legal form. An understanding of the state is therefore important to theorising politics and coercion in law. It is sometimes claimed, by the school known as the 'capital logic' or 'state derivation' school, that as part of his theory of law, Pashukanis 'derived' – theorised the necessity for and existence of – the bourgeois state.

> The principal concern of the so-called 'capital logic' school is to derive the *form* of the capitalist state from the nature of capital and/or to establish those *functional prerequisites* of accumulation whose satisfaction must be mediated through state activity.[91]

Pashukanis's status as a progenitor of this school is widely accepted,[92] as supposedly he 'tried to derive the specific historical form of bourgeois law *and its associated state* from the essential qualities of commodity circulation under capitalism'.[93] The starting point for many of the state-derivationists is Pashukanis's formulation of the question:

> [W]hy does class rule not remain what it is, the factual subjugation of one section of the population by the other? Why does it assume the form of official state rule, or – which is the same thing – why does the machinery of state coercion not come into being as the private machinery of the ruling class; why does it detach itself from the ruling class and take on the form of an impersonal apparatus of public power, separate from society?[94]

The argument goes that Pashukanis derived the bourgeois state, with its apparent neutrality, its abstract nature, its irreducibility to a set of particularistic interests, from the necessities of generalised commodification. In Jessop's summary:

> Pashukanis tried to derive the form of the bourgeois state as an impersonal apparatus of public power distinct from the private sphere of civil society. He argued that the legal form of the *Rechtsstaat* (or constitutional state based on the rule of law) characteristic of bourgeois societies is required by the nature of market relations among free, equal individuals. These must

---

[91] B. Jessop, *State Theory* (Cambridge: Polity, 1990), p. 52 (emphasis in original).
[92] Von Arx, 'An Examination', p. 6. 'The "capital logic" school in Germany is perhaps most directly indebted to Pashukanis's work.' For essential overviews, see J. Holloway and S. Picciotto (eds.), *State and Capital: A Marxist Debate* (London: Edward Arnold, 1978); S. Clarke (ed.), *The State Debate* (London: Macmillan, 1991).
[93] Jessop, *State Theory*, p. 52 (emphasis added). See also J. Holloway and S. Picciotto, 'Introduction: Towards a Materialist Theory of the State', in Holloway and Picciotto, *State and Capital*, p. 18: 'Pashukanis ... was concerned to derive the form of law and the closely related form of the state from the nature of capitalist commodity production.'
[94] Pashukanis, *Law and Marxism*, p. 139.

be mediated, supervised and guaranteed by an abstract collective subject endowed with the authority to enforce rights in the interests of all parties to legal transactions.[95]

There is no doubt that Pashukanis, at various points, does seem to imply this. There is also no doubt that much of the 'derivationist' theory is fascinating and extremely theoretically fecund.[96] However, Pashukanis's theory of law and his theory of the state are, in fact, extricable. Most of the claims made in his chapter on 'Law and the State'[97] are historical and more or less contingent. For example:

> thanks to its new role as guarantor of the peace indispensable to the exchange transaction, feudal authority took on a hue which had hitherto been alien to it: it went *public.*[98]

This, and other similar claims,[99] are historical and suggestive, not statements about the logical necessity or the derivation of the bourgeois state form.

And nor were they intended to be. At the very heart of his supposed derivation, after he has asked the 'classical question'[100] as to why class dominance takes on the form of an impersonal mechanism, Pashukanis insists that what must be explained is how the abstract bourgeois state '*could*', not 'did' or 'must', arise.[101] He is demanding a sufficient, not a necessary, theory of the bourgeois state.

When Pashukanis does make stronger claims for the derivation, attempting logically and systematically to derive the necessity for an abstract state, a third force, to act as guarantor of legal relations, he bases his theory on a false premise. 'Coercion', he writes, 'as the imperative addressed by one person to another, and backed up by force, contradicts the fundamental precondition for dealings between the owners of

---

[95] Jessop, *State Theory*, p. 53.
[96] Particularly the essays in Holloway and Picciotto, *State and Capital*, esp. J. Hirsch, 'The State Apparatus and Social Reproduction: Elements of a Theory of the Bourgeois State'; B. Blanke, U. Jürgens and H. Kastendiek, 'On the Current Marxist Discussion on the Analysis of Form and Function of the Bourgeois State'; and C. von Braunmühl 'On the Analysis of the Bourgeois Nation State within the World Market Context'.
[97] Pashukanis, *Law and Marxism*, pp. 134–50.   [98] *Ibid.*, p. 136 (emphasis in original).
[99] See, for example, *ibid.*, p. 136 on 'the "modern" state', and p. 138.
[100] Blanke, Jürgens and Kastendiek, 'On the Current Marxist Discussion', p. 121.
[101] See Pashukanis, *Law and Marxism*, pp. 139–40. See also his crucially revealing footnote – Beirne and Sharlet, *Pashukanis*, fn 47 at p. 130 – in which he states that the 'authority standing above classes' – the state – can be banished or banish itself at times of 'intensified revolutionary struggle'.

commodities.'[102] This is absolutely untrue, and is a characteristic slip – sometimes, Pashukanis's excessive formalism lead him to neglect the 'succulence' of dialectical contradictions inherent in seemingly stable categories.

Contrary to some of Pashukanis's claims, disputation and contestation is implied in the very form of the commodity, in the fact that its private ownership implies the exclusion of others. Violence – coercion – is at the heart of the commodity form. For a commodity meaningfully to be 'mine-not-yours' – which is, after all, central to the fact that it is a commodity that will be exchanged – some forceful capabilities must be implied. If there were nothing to defend its 'mine-ness', there would be nothing to stop it becoming 'yours'. Coercion is implicit.

> If the category of contract, a joint act of will founded on mutual recognition, is considered to be the original modus of law, then it is clearly a form that cannot exist without constraint.[103]

In other words, and contrary to Pashukanis's claim, coercion backed up by force is implied in a generalised form and 'addressed by one person to another' – i.e. by all owners of commodities to all other owners of commodities. In the realisation that violence is integral to commodity exchange, 'politics' – coercive force, violence – is brought closer, but its specific form – here the bourgeois state – can be seen to be not so fundamental, and certainly not 'necessary'.

It is worth noting that some of the most interesting of the state-derivationist theorists acknowledge that Pashukanis's theory, while crucially asserting the necessity of coercion and politics, does not imply the bourgeois state form:

> These arguments [Pashukanis's focus on the freedom and equality of the subjects of exchange] lead ... to the category of the *form of law* and to the necessity of a force to guarantee the law, a force which we will call *extra-economic (coercive) force*. By this we mean not so much the organised apparatus (or an instrument) but essentially only a basic function which can be derived on the conceptual level of form analysis. With that we have by no means arrived at 'the state', but at different forms of social relations, namely economic and political relations, which are peculiar to the bourgeois mode of production.[104]

---

[102] *Ibid.*, p. 143.
[103] Blanke, Jürgens and Kastendiek, 'On the Current Marxist Discussion', p. 123.
[104] *Ibid.*, p. 121 (emphasis in original).

3.2.2. The contingency of superordinate authority and the 'law-ness' of international law

Pashukanis's theory does imply coercion and politics, but does not imply the necessity of a particular form of organisation of that coercion. We can go further: for Pashukanis at his systematic and theoretical best, the state as an abstract arbiter, in fact any overarching public authority, is radically contingent to the legal form itself, and it is this which makes Pashukanis such a vital theorist for international law.

He makes clear time and again that the lack of a sovereign does not make international law any less 'law'. Pashukanis does not deny the need for coercion, but is clear that superordinate and abstract coercion, while it does 'inject stability' and is functional to capitalism, is contingent to the legal form itself:

> It is obvious that the idea of external coercion, both in its idea and organization, constitutes an essential aspect of the legal form. When no coercive mechanism has been organised, and it is not found within the jurisdiction of a special apparatus which stands above the parties, it appears in the form of so-called 'inter-dependence'. The principle of inter-dependence, under the conditions of balance of power, represents the single, and it can be said, the most unstable basis of international law.[105]

Similarly, in his excellent and neglected essay on international law, Pashukanis excoriates bourgeois jurisprudence for the amount of ink spilt on the question of whether the lack of a superordinate authority means international law is not law.

> No matter how eloquently the existence of international law is proved, the fact of the absence of an organizational force, which could coerce a state with the same ease as a state coerces an individual person, remains a fact. The only real guarantee that the relationships between bourgeois states ... will remain on the basis of equivalent exchange, i.e. on a legal basis (on the basis of the mutual recognition of subjects), is the real balance of forces.[106]

Each time Pashukanis points out the contingency of organised external coercion to law, international law is exemplary.

> [M]odern international law recognises no coercion organised from without. Such non-guaranteed legal relations are unfortunately not known for their stability, but this is not yet grounds for denying their existence.[107]

---

[105] Pashukanis, in Beirne and Sharlet, *Pashukanis*, p. 108.
[106] E. Pashukanis, 'International Law', in Beirne and Sharlet, *Pashukanis*, p. 179.
[107] Pashukanis, *Law and Marxism*, p. 89, n. 9.

However, he goes further than this. For Pashukanis, law itself – in its earliest, embryonic form – is a product precisely of the *lack* of an overarching authority or particular state form, historically:

> The development of law as a system was evoked not by the requirements of the state, *but by the necessary conditions for commercial relations between those tribes which were not under a single sphere of authority*. ... Commercial relations with foreign tribes, with nomads, and plebeians [in Rome] ... ushered in the ius gentium, which was the prototype of the legal superstructure in its pure form. In contrast to the ius civile, with its undeviating and ponderous forms, the ius gentium discards all that is not connected with the goal – with the natural basis of the economic relation.[108]

For the international legal scholar, this is a stunning theoretical illumination. An interminable question for the discipline has been how, with the lack of a superordinate authority, international law can be law. Pashukanis has here, in passing, solved the most tenacious problem of the legality of a decentralised legal system. Pashukanis's claim that (proto-)international law historically predates domestic law has nothing to do with any putative ontological primacy of the international sphere: it is, rather, because law is thrown up by, and necessary to, a systematic commodity exchange relationship, and it was between organised but disparate groups without such overarching authorities rather than between individuals that such relationships sprang:

> As a separate force which set itself off from society, the state only finally emerged in the modern bourgeois capitalist period. But it by no means follows from this that the contemporary forms of international legal intercourse, and the individual institutions of international law, only arose in the most recent times. On the contrary, they trace their history to the most ancient periods of class and even pre-class society. To the extent that exchange was not initially made between individuals, but among tribes and communities, it may be affirmed that the institutions of international law are the most ancient of legal institutions in general.[109]

3.2.3. 'Club law is law': self-help as legal regulation

There is a conundrum for Pashukanis. On the one hand, he stresses the 'law-ness' of legal relationships without superordinate authorities. On the other, we have seen that at one point he alleges that coercion 'as the

---

[108] Pashukanis, in Beirne and Sharlet, *Pashukanis*, p. 69 (emphasis added).
[109] Pashukanis, 'International Law', p. 175.

imperative addressed by one person to another, and backed up by force' is inimical to commodity relations.[110] If law requires force, as it clearly does, and as Pashukanis makes clear that it does,[111] then where does the coercive violence in law without an abstract state come from?

I have argued that violence and coercion are immanent in the commodity relationship itself. Once this is accepted, the conundrum disappears as it is clear that self-help – the coercive violence of the legal subjects themselves – will regulate their legal relation. The importance of this solution to Pashukanis's paradox cannot be overstated. It is also abundantly clear that, notwithstanding his own occasional comments to the contrary, Pashukanis throughout his work – particularly when discussing international law – realised this. He cites 'inter-dependence' or 'reciprocity' 'under the conditions of the balance of power'[112] or 'the real balance of forces'[113] – a backdrop of force-mediated relations – as at the basis of international legal regulation.

Contradicting his own later assertion that coercion is antipathetic to the commodity relationship, Pashukanis claims that:

> [l]egal intercourse does not 'naturally' presuppose a state of peace just as trade does not . . . preclude armed robbery, but goes hand in hand with it. Law and self-help, those seemingly contradictory concepts are, in reality, extremely closely linked.[114]

To understand, as Pashukanis clearly does, that robbery (non-consensual possession of another's commodity) goes 'hand in hand' with trade (consensual exchange of commodities), is to understand that violence is implicit in the commodity – and therefore legal – form. If 'mine' implies force to keep it from becoming 'yours', then robbery is the failure of that force, and the success of someone else's. '[O]rder is actually a mere tendency and end result (by no means perfected at that), but never the point of departure and prerequisite of legal intercourse',[115] Pashukanis makes clear. Coercion is fundamental to his theory of the legal form.

---

[110] Pashukanis, *Law and Marxism*, p. 143.
[111] Pashukanis, in Beirne and Sharlet, *Pashukanis*, p. 108 and elsewhere. For example, stressing the distinction between legal and moral conduct, Pashukanis observes that legal conduct is such 'irrespective of the motives which produce it. Whether a debt is repaid because "in any event I will be forced to pay it", or because the debtor considers it his moral obligation to do so, makes no difference from the juridic perspective. It is obvious that the idea of external coercion . . . constitutes an essential aspect of the legal form' (p. 108).
[112] *Ibid.*, p. 108. [113] Pashukanis, 'International Law', p. 179.
[114] Pashukanis, *Law and Marxism*, p. 134. [115] *Ibid.*, p. 135.

Compared to this, the failure of mainstream international legal theory to make sense of sanctions and violence is marked. One senses a petulance at the very tenacity of this problem, and a concomitant evasion of analysis dressed up as a high-minded refusal to be bogged down in vulgar details. Akehurst claims that:

> [i]t is unsound to study any legal system in terms of sanctions. It is better to study law as a body of rules which are usually obeyed, not to concentrate exclusively on what happens when the rules are broken. *We must not confuse the pathology of law with law itself.*[116]

Here the abject failure of mainstream undialectical analysis is stark. The notion that breaches of law, disputes moderated by coercion, are pathological to law, rather than inextricable elements of the legal fabric, is remarkable. In contrast, as Pashukanis points out, 'deviation from a norm always constitutes their premise'.[117]

Pashukanis understands that law and violence are inextricably linked as regulators of sovereign claims. He can therefore square two seemingly opposed points of view in Marx. One is the stress on juridical equality and exchange of equivalents; the other is Marx's claim that '[e]ven club law is law'.[118] The solution is to be found in another remark of Marx's that spans those two conceptions: 'between equal rights, force decides.'

On the one hand, law is an abstract relationship between two equals; on the other, the naked imposition of power is claimed as a legal form. 'This is not a paradox', Pashukanis makes clear – against his own occasional oppositions between coercion and contract – because 'law, like exchange, is an expedient resorted to by isolated social elements in their intercourse with one another'[119] – as is violence. In the absence of an abstract 'third force', the only regulatory violence capable of upholding the legal form, and of fleshing it out with a particular content, is the violence of the participants. This is why '[l]aw and self-help . . . are, in reality, extremely closely linked',[120] and that is why, in the absence of a sovereign, '[m]odern international law includes a very considerable degree of self-help (retaliatory measures, reprisals, war and so on)'.[121]

---

[116] M. Akehurst, *A Modern Introduction to International Law* (London: Unwin Hyman, 1987), p. 7 (emphasis added).
[117] Pashukanis, in Beirne and Sharlet, *Pashukanis*, p. 110 (emphasis added).
[118] Marx, quoted in Pashukanis, *Law and Marxism*, p. 134. The original is in K. Marx, *Grundrisse* (New York: Vintage, 1973), p. 88. In this translation, it reads: '[t]he principle of might makes right . . . is also a legal relation'. I have chosen to quote the former, as it is a starker formulation.
[119] Pashukanis, *Law and Marxism*, p. 134.   [120] *Ibid.*, p. 134.   [121] *Ibid.*, p. 134.

Violence is intrinsic to law, but in the absence of a sovereign the violence retains its particularistic, rather than abstract impersonal (state) character:

> [T]he armed individual (or, more often, group of people, a family group, a clan, a tribe, capable of defending their conditions of existence in armed struggle), is the morphological precursor of the legal subject with his sphere of legal power extending around him. This close morphological link establishes a clear connection between the lawcourt and the duel, between the parties to a lawsuit and the combatants in an armed conflict. But as socially regulative forces become more powerful, so the subject loses material tangibility.[122]

Where there is no such 'socially regulative forces', however, that coercion remains embedded in the participants, and their sanctions such as self-help. Though it is shared at all levels of law, the morphological proximity of the legal subject and the armed unit is much closer and more clear in international law.

3.2.4. Putting the content in the legal form: power and its political economy

In his essay on international law, Pashukanis makes clear what the specific social content of particular international laws is:

> The historical examples adduced in any textbook of international law loudly proclaim that *modern international law is the legal form of the struggle of the capitalist states among themselves for domination over the rest of the world.*[123]

That struggle is the 'real historical content hidden behind' the legal form.[124]

Pashukanis never systematically theorises the interests being pursued by the capitalist states. However, on this topic he quotes Lenin's *Imperialism* approvingly[125] (although unaccountably ending his quote just before the nub of the matter):

> The epoch of modern capitalism shows us that certain relations are established between capitalist alliances, based on the economic division of the world; while parallel with this fact and in connection with it, certain relations are established between political alliances, between states, on the basis

---

[122] *Ibid.*, p. 118.   [123] Pashukanis, 'International Law', p. 169 (emphasis in original).
[124] *Ibid.*, p. 169. See also p. 172.   [125] *Ibid.*, pp. 169–70.

of the territorial division of the world, of the struggle for colonies, of the 'struggle for economic territory'.[126]

The struggle between capitalists is based on the economic division of the world, and that economic division will be brought about politically by the state, which relies in turn on the capitalist economic system. This is a preliminary theoretical justification for the intuition that the struggle between capitalist states is more than a struggle between states that happen to have capitalist internal economies. It is a struggle for resources for capital. That is what makes the state a capitalist state.

If we agree with Pashukanis, therefore, that the 'real historical content of international law' is an ongoing and remorseless struggle for control over the resources of capitalism, that will often as part of that capitalist ('economic') competitive process spill into 'political' violence:

> [E]ven those agreements between capitalist states which appear to be directed to the general interests are, in fact, for each of the participants a means for jealously protecting their particular interests, preventing the expansion of their rivals' influence, thwarting unilateral conquest, i.e. in another form continuing the same struggle which will exist for as long as capitalist competition exists.[127]

What has emerged is a fascinating circularity. Capitalism is based on commodity exchange and, contrary to appearances (and to some of Pashukanis's comments), such exchange contains violence immanently. However, the universalisation of such exchange has tended to lead to the abstraction of a 'third force' to stabilise the relations, and that force has been the state. Thus politics and economics have been separated under the generalised commodity exchange which reaches a zenith under capitalism. In the same moment, the flipside of that separation and the creation of a public political body was the investiture of that body – the state – as the subject of those legal relations which had long inhered between political entities, and which now became bourgeois international law. But that process itself necessitated the self-regulation of the legal relation internationally by its own subjects, which was a simultaneously 'political' and 'economic' function, and a manifestation of the collapse of the distinction between politics and economics inherent in the very dynamic which had separated them.

---

[126] V. I. Lenin, *Imperialism* (New York: International Publishers, 1939), p. 75.
[127] Pashukanis, 'International Law', p. 170.

We have identified the social relations – the competition between capitalist states – which make up the content of international law. We have also seen that 'might makes right', that the necessary coercive force will be held by the participants to the legal relations. And, of course, it will not be held equally:

> [B]ourgeois international law in principle recognizes that states have equal rights yet in reality they are unequal in their significance and their power. For instance, each state is formally free to select the means which it deems necessary to apply in the case of infringements of its right: 'however, when a major state lets it be known that it will meet injury with the threat of, or the direct use of force, a small state merely offers passive resistance or is compelled to concede.' These dubious benefits of formal equality are not enjoyed by those nations which have not developed capitalist civilization and which engage in international intercourse not as subjects, but as objects of the imperialist states' colonial policy.[128]

Although both parties are formally equal, they have unequal access to the means of coercion, and are not therefore equally able to determine either the policing or the content of the law. The policing of the form and therefore its interpretation – its investiture with particular content – is down to the subjects themselves. This is why a less powerful state either 'offers passive resistance or is compelled to concede'. And that is how the particular contents and norms that actualise the general content of social relations are invested into the legal form.

4. Imperialism and international law

4.1. 'Serving two masters': the imperialism of freedom

Imperialist actions are framed in juridical terms. And not just for propagandist reasons, but more fundamentally because the imperialism and the international law are part of the same system. Modern capitalism is an imperialist system, and a juridical one. International law's constituent forms are constituent forms of global capitalism, and therefore of imperialism.

Nevertheless, the mainstream view is still one that sees imperialism as incidental or opposed to the equal sovereign state form which underpins international law. Joseph Lockley, discussing the US policy of

---

[128] *Ibid.*, p. 178. The quote (emphasis mine) is from V. E. Grabar, *The Basis of Equality between States in Modern International Law* (1912).

'pan-Americanism', the crucial element of which was 'the independence and equality of the American nations',[129] expressed this starkly:

> The one [policy] is expressly intended to create and maintain a community of equal, cooperating nations; and the other is intended, presumably, to create and maintain an empire. The two policies, the two courses of action, lead in different directions. In which of these directions does the United States move? It cannot move in both at one and the same time. It cannot serve two masters.[130]

Of course, it had long been evident that there is in fact no contradiction between the spread of the sovereign state form and imperialism. States categorically can serve the two masters of pushing for regional or even world dominance and of supporting the independent sovereign state form on the basis of their own overwhelming power. The United States has for decades been uniquely placed to succeed in this strategy.

Internationally, there is no authority to act as final arbiter of competing claims, and no body with a monopoly of violence with which to enforce them, and the means of violence remains in the hands of the very parties disagreeing over the interpretation of law. 'There is here, therefore, an antinomy, of right against right, both equally bearing the seal of the law of exchange. Between equal rights, force decides.'[131] And, of course, that force, the capacity for coercive violence which has underpinned the legal relation, is not distributed equally.

This is why strong states are able to enforce their own interpretations of law. Intrinsically to the legal form, a contest of coercion occurs, or is implied, to back up the claim and counterclaim. And in the politically and militarily unequal modern world system, the distribution of power is such that the winner of that coercive contest is generally a foregone conclusion. The international legal form assumes juridical equality and unequal violence – the political violence of imperialism.

International disputes are part of the juridical system of sovereignty and are assiduously legally argued on both sides, by formally equal subjects – even when one side's interpretations represent an extremely minority position.[132] Their outcomes are expressed in legal terms and establish legal facts on the ground. And these outcomes are rarely in doubt, given

---

[129] J. Lockley, 'Pan-Americanism and Imperialism' (1938) 32 *American Journal of International Law* 233 at 234.

[130] *Ibid.*, 234. [131] Marx, *Capital*, vol. 1, p. 344.

[132] To take just one example, see the ingenious applications of international law by the US to justify 'Operation Just Cause', the invasion of Panama, at the end of 1989. Despite the bulk of international legal opinion being against them, the US legal case was carefully worked out, involving a descending claim about the necessity for humanitarian intervention; an

the unequal military coercion one side can use to enforce its legal interpretation. This, of course, is never more the case than when the United States is one of the parties to a dispute.

4.2. Post-imperial international law?

In the face of the opposition of the colonised, 'by the late 1950s it had become clear to the surviving old empires that formal colonialism had to be liquidated'.[133] 'After the cataclysm of World War II the nation-state tide reached full flood. By the mid-1970s even the Portuguese Empire had become a thing of the past.'[134] 'What began as a sort of Euro-American club [the UN General Assembly] ... has become a predominantly African and Asian organisation.'[135] As Benedict Anderson argues, '[t]he "last wave" of nationalisms, most of them in the colonial territories of Asia and Africa, was in its origins a response to the new-style global imperialism made possible by the achievements of industrial capitalism'.[136]

'The need of a constantly expanding market for its products chases the bourgeoisie over the whole face of the globe. It must nestle everywhere, settle everywhere, establish connections everywhere.'[137] So with the juridical relations that this market implies. For the establishment of independent territories in opposition to direct colonial rule, this must mean the establishment of sovereign states, the subjects and agents of international law.

International law has been profoundly changed by this historical shift, exemplified in the proclamations of the UN. 'Instead of a special colonial international law, there was now only a multitude of independent and formally equal member-States.'[138] Though the colonial powers – or,

---

ascending claim about sovereign rights of a state during war (based on Noriega's hyperbolic declaration that a war existed between the countries); a principle of 'intervention by invitation', claiming the sanction of Endara, the opposition candidate; and a claim of legitimate intervention as part of a campaign against drugs by the ingenious application of a 50-year-old Arbitration between the US and Canada designed to minimise cross-border air pollution.

[133] E. Hobsbawm, *Age of Extremes* (New York: Pantheon Books, 1994), p. 221.

[134] B. Anderson, *Imagined Communities* (London and New York: Verso, 1991), p. 113. For a comprehensive and chronological list of the expansion of the UN from 51 members in 1945 to 185 by 1997, see M. Marín-Bosch, *Votes in the UN General Assembly* (Leiden: Martinus Nijhoff, 1998), pp. 7–8.

[135] Marín-Bosch, *Votes in the UN*, p. 12.   [136] Anderson, *Imagined Communities*, p. 139.

[137] K. Marx and F. Engels, *The Communist Manifesto* (New York: Pathfinder Press, 1987), pp. 19–20.

[138] W. Grewe, *The Epochs of International Law* (Berlin and New York: Walter de Gruyter, 2000), p. 649.

more exactly, certain sections of the ruling class in each colonial power – resisted the changes,[139] 'the vast majority of UN members sought to set in motion an irreversible process of decolonization'.[140] The United Nations, the 'raison d'être' of which is '[t]he codification of International Law',[141] 'has . . . striven for universality'.[142]

It is not enough to claim that 'international law is now more open and cosmopolitan', or that it 'promoted the process of decolonization by formulating doctrines of self-determination where once it formulated doctrines of annexation and *terra nullius*':[143] this tends to imply that the emphasis is on the differences between pre- and post-war international law. The continuities are even more important, as they trace the dynamic of international legal development. Embedded even in colonialist international law doctrines was the germ-seed of self-determination and sovereignty.

This sense of a tendential logic is expressed in Jackson's observation that '[e]quality is infectious',[144] and Miller's claim that once sovereignty

---

[139] See the discussion of Portugal and France in Marín-Bosch, *Votes in the UN*, pp. 50–2.
[140] *Ibid.*, p. 52.   [141] *Ibid.*, p. 151.   [142] *Ibid.*, p. 9.
[143] A. Anghie, 'Finding the Peripheries: Sovereignty and Colonialism in Nineteenth-Century International Law' (1999) 40 *Harvard International Law Journal* 1 at 75. Though they are not his conclusions, it is interesting and somewhat surprising to see Anghie make such claims: it would be obnoxious not to point out, as an earlier draft of this article unfortunately failed to do, that arguments over these formulations notwithstanding, overall Anghie's work is indispensable precisely for its vivid stress on the embeddedness of colonialism in the fabric of international law.
[144] R. Jackson, 'Quasi-States, Dual Regimes, and Neoclassical Theory: International Jurisprudence and the Third World' (1987) 41 *International Organization* 519 at 538. Jackson distinguishes between juridical sovereignty and 'empirical statehood', and sees the modern international legal system of juridical equality as based on 'the contemporary moral-legal framework of the accommodative juridical regime' (at 536), in contrast to the 'traditional empirical foundation of the competitive states-system' of 'positive sovereignty: the national will and capacity to become and remain independent'. 'International law in this sphere', he claims, 'is an acknowledgement of real statehood that is a consequence of successful state-building' (at 536). He sees the focus on the 'juridical' rather than the 'real' aspects of sovereign statehood as underlying many of the problems of the third world – essentially, this is a problem of an 'accommodative' system. For a devastating critique of Jackson's liberal construction which completely writes out the complicity of the colonial powers in the very problems of underdevelopment that he terms 'quasi-statehood', see S. Grovogui, *Sovereigns, Quasi-Sovereigns and Africans* (Minneapolis, MN: University of Minnesota Press, 1996), pp. 182–4 and 202–3. While, of course, Jackson is right that the various states of the world have vastly different capabilities, it is not a pathology or mistake that has led them to be treated as juridically equal – such a coexistence of real inequality and juridical equality is precisely the condition of capitalist modernity that must be explained. He describes the situation as a 'new dualism' (Jackson, 'Quasi-States', p. 536) which it emphatically is not. To that extent, his putatively 'liberal' solutions, revolving around the move away from juridical equality towards 'a greater variety of international

is granted to some politically weak polities, 'the tendency is irresistible to qualify still other members of the society as well'.[145] With the theoretical tools developed throughout this thesis we can more exactly express this: the post-war drive to self-determination is thus not merely a change in the structure or content of international law, but the culmination of the universalising and abstracting tendencies in international – legal – capitalism.

Though for many years formal colonialism was expressed in international legal terms, and without for a moment downplaying the struggles of the colonised to achieve self-determined status, the recent conversion of international law to decolonisation also represents the self-actualisation of international law – the universalisation of the abstract juridical equality of its subjects. With the end of formal empire comes the apogee of the empire of sovereignty, and of international law.

With the universalisation of the legal form, modern international law is usually deemed antipathetic to imperialism:

> There is in existence today a peremptory norm of general international law, a rule, that is to say, of *jus cogens*, which provides for the right of self-determination and thus prohibits colonial domination.[146]

This position does not have to equate to a naïve belief that with the new international legal epoch, imperialism domination comes to an end. Umozurike, for example, warns of 'neo-colonialism', and is perfectly hard-headed about its coexistence with universal international law and self-determination.[147] However, he still sharply counterposes such 'neo-colonialism' from international law itself.

---

statuses including more intrusive forms of international trusteeship' (R. Jackson, *Quasi-States: Sovereignty, International Relations, and the Third World* (Cambridge: Cambridge University Press, 1991), p. 202 are profoundly conservative, and conservatively utopian, harking nostalgically back to the mandate era.

[145] L. Miller, *Global Order: Values and Power in International Relations* (Boulder, CO: Westview Press, 1985), p. 49.

[146] E. Udechuku, *Liberation of Dependent Peoples in International Law*, 2nd edn (London: African Publications Bureau, 1978), p. 15. For an almost identical formulation, see U. Umozurike, *International Law and Colonialism in Africa* (Enugu, Nigeria: Nwamife Publishers, 1979), p. 85: '[i]n present international law, colonialism is illegal for it runs against the *jus cogens* rules of self-determination and respect for fundamental human rights.'

[147] Umozurike, *International Law and Colonialism in Africa*, pp. 126–38. See also Chimni, *International Law and World Order*, p. 235: '[i]mperialism, it bears repeating, is just not another word for "colonialism" but refers to a particular stage in the global development of capitalism . . . For those who associate imperialism with colonialism, the former phenomenon was extinguished with decolonisation or continues only in so far as decolonisation is not complete. Such a view veils the fact that colonialism not only existed before what is termed "the monopoly stage of capitalism" but is survived today by neo-colonialism.'

International law, he says:

> must now provide the legal framework within which the New International Economic Order [of more equitable distribution] can be achieved. Though the main actions to redress neo-colonialism must be internal, international law is an additional medium.[148]

Here, 'neo-colonialism' – the continued existence of imperialism – is held to be a political phenomenon which can be remedied, in part, by recourse to international law, which by its nature is held to oppose imperialism. However, this construction is supported neither by the facts of post-war history, nor by the analysis of international law and the legal form.

This is not to say that the ending of the era of formal colonialism was not a historically progressive moment: as Koskenniemi puts it, '[f]ormal sovereignty is useful . . . as an absolute barrier by a weak community against a more powerful one'.[149] This is why, though '[s]overeignty is a dry, legal question for those nations who have acquired statehood . . . [it is] a passionate crusade for those who do not have it'.[150]

However, imperialism outlasts the transition to universalised juridical sovereignty, and not because postcolonial sovereignty is incomplete.[151] Such imperialism is not something international law can successfully oppose – it is embedded in the very structures of which international law is an expression and a moment.

The imperialism of international law, then, means more than just the global spread of an international legal order with capitalism – it means that the power dynamics of political imperialism are embedded within the very juridical equality of sovereignty. Formal equality is a powerful weapon in the hands of the state whose overwhelming coercive power will actualise content in the legal form. For the state that knows its interpretation will 'win', that it has the power to effect authoritative interpretation, the spread of juridical equality is not only no block to domination: it can be conducive of it.

This coexistence of formal freedom and imperialist subjugation has long been a fact of the international system, and where it has been invisible to many international lawyers, it has been obvious to the agents of imperialism themselves. In 1824, when the countries of Latin America

---

[148] Umozurike, *International Law and Colonialism in Africa*, p. 138. See also pp. 128–9.
[149] M. Koskenniemi, 'International Law and Imperialism', the Josephine Onoh Memorial Lecture 1999 (2000), p. 16.
[150] L. Farley, *Plebiscites and Sovereignty: The Crisis of Political Illegitimacy* (Boulder, CO: Westview Press, 1986), p. 9.
[151] Grovogui, *Sovereigns, Quasi-Sovereigns*, p. 196: 'The current postcolonial crises suggest that the results of the dominant African had significant political and theoretical implications.'

were winning independence from Spanish control, Britain was quick to recognise the new states (over which it had a great deal of economic control). The 'flexible' foreign secretary Canning[152] straddled the dialectic of formal freedom and factual control in the new imperialism admirably: 'Spanish America is free, and if we do not mismanage our affairs sadly she is *English*.'[153] Formal sovereign independence not only does not preclude domination but can be the very institution by which domination is exercised.

This is not about the ultimate triumph of some hypostatised 'power politics', a Morgenthau-ist claim that '[p]olitics is focal and law secondary'.[154] The point, rather, is that the 'power politics' of modernity are the power politics of a juridically constructed system. The most realist, cynical, power-maximising state in the modern world-system is a realist, cynical and power-maximising juridical form. The agents of what realists might fondly suppose is 'pure power' are, in fact, defined by the abstract, juridical structures of generalised commodity exchange. There is no separation of these juridical forms from 'pure politics' because there is no pure politics: there are instead the politics of juridical units.

5. From commodity form to class law

The violence in the legal form shows that the legal subjects must also be the agents of violence. However, at this level of abstraction, this is the violence of the market, of the commodity and of the legal form, but it is not class violence. The necessity of coercion inheres in the exchange of commodities, not on a particular mode of production and exploitation.

Here, the insights of Lenin – and Bukharin, on whose towering analysis Lenin based his own more pamphleteering account of the state-capital relation in capitalism[155] – on the structure of the imperialist state can inform Pashukanis's legal theory. In an epoch of mature capitalism, of the consolidation and monopolisation of capitals, the state cannot be understood as autonomous from those capitals. The penetration of capitalist concerns into the state remains vital to explain imperialism. As imperialist

---

[152] E. Hobsbawm, *The Age of Revolution* (Cambridge: Cambridge University Press, 1967), p. 131.
[153] Quoted in J. Rosenberg, *The Empire of Civil Society* (London: Verso, 1994), p. 170 (emphasis in original). Of course, British ambitions were dashed. 'In point of fact, the British did mismanage their affairs very sadly' (C. Hitchens, *Blood, Class and Nostalgia* (New York: Farrar, Straus & Giroux, 1990), p. 154).
[154] Koskenniemi, *From Apology to Utopia*, p. 168.
[155] N. Bukharin, *Imperialism and World Economy* (New York: International Publishers, 1987).

states, they are powered by capitalist economics, and operating according to capitalist concerns. The very imperialism of each state is a function of its capitalist nature. When it comes to international law, then, the point is that the more powerful state, with the coercive force to enforce its own interpretation of the legal rules, is a more powerful *capitalist* state. Its interpretations and its coercive efforts are deployed for capital, which is predicated on class exploitation.

This is emphatically not to say that the more powerful state in an international legal relation is taking the role of 'capitalist' and its opponent that of 'proletarian', nor that in any crudely instrumentalist way capitalist states only come to blows over narrowly economic issues. It is only to say that the strategic logic of capitalist states, including of course the powerful imperialist states, is ultimately derived from the exploitative logic of capitalism.

The international legal form assumes juridical equality and unequal violence. In the context of modern international capitalism, that unequal violence is imperialism itself. The necessity of this unequal violence derives precisely from the juridical equality of the sovereign states: one of the legal subjects will make law out of the legal relation by means of their coercive power – their imperialist domination.

In other words, specifically in its universalised form, predicated on juridical equality and self-determination, international law assumes imperialism. At the most abstract level, without violence there could be no legal form. In the concrete conjuncture of modern international capitalism, this means that without imperialism there could be no international law.

6. The rule of law

6.1. *The new cosmopolitan advocates*

Among the various criticisms levelled at Pashukanis, one is the accusation that his theory 'is ultimately a theory against law'.[156] It would be possible in defending Pashukanis to point out that he stressed that the legal form would continue to inhere in the USSR for some time after the revolution of 1917, that he did not advocate the active destruction of law, that his work as a jurist showed his commitment to the progressive application of law, and so on. All this is true, but it rather misses the point. Pashukanis was,

---

[156] Von Arx, 'An Examination', p. 8.

absolutely, hostile to law, inasmuch as he understood it to be a reflection of capitalist property relations, an integral part of a class society where the market had a commanding role, and he did not believe that it would last as communism flowered. To criticise Pashukanis for this view is to decide in advance that law is to be defended.

Given the widespread though mistaken belief that law is counterposed to power and war, the desire for a rule of law makes sense. The extension of the rule of law is held to be an emancipatory project, both internationally and domestically. The rule of law 'is necessary to achieve a well-ordered society in which the problems of knowledge, interest, and power are handled'.[157] According to one writer, in fact, it 'could ... make possible the birth of a new civilization of unparalleled brilliance and enlightenment'.[158]

Recently, calls for an international rule of law have been deployed by the critical modern liberal project known variously as 'cosmopolitan democracy',[159] 'global governance', 'democratic governance',[160] but that I follow Peter Gowan in terming 'liberal-cosmopolitanism'.[161] Humanitarian intervention is seen as having 'chipped away'[162] absolute sovereignty in the search for a just international law:[163] for the liberal-cosmopolitans the rule of law must 'involve a central concern with distributional questions and matters of social justice'.[164]

---

[157] R. Barnett, *The Structure of Liberty* (Oxford University Press, 1998), p. 325.
[158] G. Walker, *The Rule of Law* (Melbourne: Melbourne University Press, 1988), p. 406.
[159] D. Archibugi and D. Held, *Cosmopolitan Democracy* (Cambridge: Polity and Blackwell Publishers, 1995).
[160] See Global Governance Reform Project, *Reimagining the Future: Towards Democratic Governance* (Bundoora, Australia: La Trobe University, 2000).
[161] P. Gowan, L. Panitch and M. Shaw, 'The State, Globalisation and the New Imperialism: A Roundtable Discussion' (2001) 9 *Historical Materialism* 3 at 4. The choice of terminology is important. In Gowan's words: '[t]hese people are not talking about a global democratic state. They are not, therefore, talking about cosmopolitan democracy ... What they are talking about is global governance ... That's why I say that these people are cosmopolitan liberals, not actually democrats, even though they may well say that they are democrats, and no doubt they are good democrats when it comes to domestic activities' (at 5). Panitch points out that '[t]here are ... cosmopolitan liberals who are liberal democrats' (at 12), citing David Held, but this does not undermine Gowan's point, and neither does Shaw's attempt to distinguish himself from Held (at 21–2).
[162] K. Mills, *Human Rights in the Emerging Global Order: A New Sovereignty?* (London: MacMillan Press and New York: St Martin's Press, 1998), p. 41.
[163] This is clearly exemplified in the title of M. Glennon, 'The New Interventionism: The Search for a Just International Law' (1999) 78(3) *Foreign Affairs* 2.
[164] D. Held, *Democracy and the Global Order* (Cambridge: Polity, 1995), p. 248.

The notion that this represents a new era is predicated on the erroneous claim that the 'traditional' view of sovereignty was 'anti-interventionist'.[165] In fact, of course, sovereignty has always been overridden by intervention. 'Great Powers', Callinicos says, 'have always asserted a right of intervention in the affairs of small countries':[166] international law presumes the capacity for the organised violence of intervention, sovereignty assumes its own abnegation, and it is the Great Powers which are particularly able to effect that. And though the ideology of humanitarianism has recently been particularly stressed, it is in no way a new justification for intervention: '"Humanitarian intervention" played an increasingly important role in the numerous cases of intervention which occurred during the nineteenth century.'[167] The 'apology' of state sovereignty operates in a contradictory unity with the 'utopia', a normativity the power of which inheres in its constant penetration of sovereignty.

6.2. Against the rule of law

Whether envisaged by the liberal-cosmopolitans or more traditional writers, the rule of law is not a self-evident good. It is a concept that needs unpacking, and it has long had its critics.[168] Generally speaking, these criticisms revolve around the fact that the rule of law is an abstract, formal construction that is not only incapable of reflecting the complexities of reality, but actually serves to obscure them. '[T]he formal conception of the rule of law was always a mask for substantive inequalities in power.'[169] This criticism – that the rule of law is abstracting – is quite correct, if itself rather abstract. With the analysis that has been constructed here,

---

[165] Glennon, 'The New Internationalism', p. 2.
[166] A. Callinicos, *Against the Third Way* (Cambridge: Polity, 2001), p. 93.
[167] Grewe, *Epochs of International Law*, pp. 489–490.
[168] For an overview of the debates, see P. Craig, 'Formal and Substantive Conceptions of the Rule of Law: An Analytical Framework' (1997) *Public Law* 467. Perhaps most famous of the critics is Roberto Unger, in R. Unger, *Law in Modern Society* (New York: Free Press, 1977), pp. 176–81. See also the writers collected with A. Hutchinson and P. Monahan (eds.), *The Rule of Law: Idea or Ideology* (Toronto, Carswell, 1987), particularly the editors themselves. For a particularly splenetic attack on the Critical Legal Studies movements approach to the rule of law, see Walker, *The Rule of Law*, pp. 256–87. Walker produces very much more heat than light, but is interesting as an example of the defensive outrage with which mainstream jurisprudence is capable of reacting to attacks on the fetishised object of its attention. Some of Walker's claims – for example, that there is a 'CLS-clerisy monopoly of legal coverage in the mass media' (p. 378) – are nothing short of absurd.
[169] Craig, 'Formal and Substantive Conceptions', p. 474. See also A. Hutchinson and P. Monahan, 'Democracy and the Rule of Law', in Hutchinson and Monahan (eds.), *The Rule of Law*, p. 114.

that critique can be brought to bear on the desire for an international rule of law between states, and can also be concretised.

The question of legal nihilism, or the 'deniers', to use Lachs's phrase, has 'often confused the question of whether international law is "law" with the problem of the effectiveness and enforcement of international law'[170] (Lachs himself blurs that distinction).[171] Obviously, in focusing precisely on the specific 'law-ness' of the legal form, and in elaborating that the international state system is intrinsically constituted by the juridical forms that underpin international law, I do not see international law as a weak or non-existent force between states, and am a denier in neither of those senses. However, I am a 'denier' in an alternative sense – one also touched on by Lachs and others, but never with a sense of it specificity[172] – in that I see no prospect of any systematic progressive political project or emancipatory dynamic coming out of international law.

International law is made actual in the power-political wranglings of states, ultimately at the logic of capital, in the context of an imperialist system. In other words, the very social problems which liberal-cosmopolitan writers want to end are the result of the international system, which is the international legal system. The forms and relations of international law are the forms and relations of imperialism.

Attempts to reform law can only ever tinker with the surface level of institutions. It would, obviously, be fatuous to deny that law could ever be put to reformist use. Marx himself discusses the Factory Acts of the nineteenth century and certainly sees in them 'progress'. But the recourse

---

[170] Malanczuk, *Akehurst's Modern Introduction*, p. 5.
[171] He describes as deniers those for whom 'the prevailing lawlessness offered no evidence of any rule of law among nations' (M. Lachs, *The Teacher in International Law* (The Hague: Martinus Nijhoff, 1987), p. 10), but he lumps together Austin, who famously denied that international law was law 'properly so-called', asserting instead that it was only 'positive morality' (p. 15), and Morgenthau, who asserts that 'law will give way to politics' (H. Morgenthau, *In Defense of the National Interest* (New York: Knopf, 1981), p. 144).
[172] When Lachs says that 'at the opposite end of the spectrum' from the deniers are the Utopians (Lachs, *The Teacher*, p. 18), those utopians are writers who envisage 'an ideal State or world' (p. 19) brought about by that law. They are therefore, in fact, the 'opposite' neither of those who do not believe that international law is law, nor those who believe that international law has a negligible effect on states' actions, but of those who believe that international law can never systematically be used to improve the world. When Schachter considers 'the sceptics of international law' it is this third strand of denial that he focuses on: he is concerned with 'those who doubt . . . that international law can contribute significantly to international order' (O. Schachter, *International Law in Theory and Practice* (Leiden: Martinus Nijhoff, 1991), p. 5).

to law can only ever be of limited emancipatory value, and not just, as Marx argues, because such 'progress' is always hedged by 'retrogression'.[173]

One limiting factor is specific to international law. For Marx, the 'formulation, official recognition and proclamation by the state . . . [of the Factory Acts was] the result of a long class struggle'.[174] Very crudely, the contending classes fought quite directly to fill the legal form with specific content, and at particular points the working class triumphed. That the ruling class was often able to turn these triumphs to its own advantage does not mean the battles were not worth having, or that the successes were not manifest in 'progressive law'. However, at an international level, the class struggle over the legal form is far more mediated. States, not classes or other social forces are the fundamental contending agents of international law – though of course other agents are sometimes the subjects of such law – and while their claims and counterclaims are certainly informed by their own domestic class struggles, they do not 'represent' classes in any direct way – it is generally the opposing ruling classes of the different states which are clashing with the legal form. This is certainly not to foreclose any possibility of a 'progressive' international legal decision, but it is to argue that such moments will be more tenuous, unstable and unlikely than their domestic counterparts, because, exceptional circumstances aside, every international legal decision represents the triumph of (at least) one national ruling class – it is they, after all, who have had recourse to the legal form – rather than of any exploited classes or oppressed groups at all.

There is also a more fundamental sense in which radical change, or even the systematic amelioration of social and international problems, cannot come through law. As Pashukanis's form-analysis shows, the system which throws those problems up is the juridical system which underpins the law attempting to solve them. Law is a relation between subjects abstracted of social context, facing each other in a relationship predicated on private property, intrinsically dependent on coercion. Internationally, law's 'violence of abstraction' is the violence of war.

Fundamentally to change the dynamics of the system it would be necessary not to reform the institutions but to eradicate the forms of law – which would mean the fundamental reformulation of the political economic system of which they are expressions. The political project to achieve this is the best hope for global emancipation, and it would mean the end of law.

---

[173] Marx, *Capital*, vol. 1, p. 395.   [174] *Ibid.*, p. 395.

The commodity-form theory of international law is in its early stages, and might hopefully be built on with examinations of specific historical moments and fields within international law, as part of a wider research project. But of all the insights that this approach offers, none is more important than the unapologetic response offered to those who call for the rule of law. The attempt to replace war and inequality with law is not merely utopian – it is precisely self-defeating. A world structured around international law cannot but be one of imperialist violence.

The chaotic and bloody world around us *is the rule of law*.

4

Positivism versus self-determination: the contradictions of Soviet international law

BILL BOWRING

1. Introduction

The Soviet theory and practice of international law, if it is the subject of any consideration today at all, is usually dismissed as a purely historical example of an extreme species of positivism, and of no contemporary interest. Most often it is ignored. For example, in his essay 'What should international lawyers learn from Karl Marx?',[1] Martti Koskenniemi does not mention Soviet international law at all. Even an avowed Marxist scholar of international law does little more. In his essay, 'An outline of a Marxist course on public international law',[2] B. S. Chimni contrasts the definition of 'treaties' in what he terms 'Mainstream International Law Scholarship':

> with the definitions offered by the Soviet scholars Korovin and Pashukanis: 'Every international agreement is the *expression of an established social order, with a certain balance of collective interests*';[3] 'A treaty obligation is nothing other than *a special form of the concretization of economic and political relationships*'.[4] These definitions, through drawing in extra-textual reality, offer greater insight into the meaning of a treaty than the formal definition offered by MILS. They refer us to both the fact of an established (capitalist) social order and to its concretization as economic and political rules embodying a certain balance of collective (class) interests.[5]

---

[1] Chapter 1 in this volume. [2] Chapter 2 in this volume.
[3] E. Korovin, 'Soviet Treaties and International Law' (1928) 22 *American Journal of International Law* 753 at 763 (emphasis added).
[4] E. Pashukanis, *Pashukanis: Selected Writings on Marxism and Law*, p. Bierne and R. Sharlet (eds.) (London: Academic Press, 1980) p. 181 (emphasis added).
[5] B. Chimni, 'An outline of a Marxist course'.

However, these authors are not introduced save as 'Soviet scholars', no context at all is given, nor the fact that they were bitter enemies. Soviet international law, even in this Marxist account, barely exists; in the standard genre of the history of international law it is mentioned only to be dismissed.

I wish to take a very different position. I seek to argue in the following paragraphs that the contradictions of Soviet international law have generated some of the most important propositions and principles of contemporary international law, and are of continuing relevance.

This chapter starts with a typical description in the standard genre, by a distinguished contemporary international legal scholar. I then trace the development of Soviet international law through a double refraction: what it said about itself, in some bitterly fought theoretical struggles; and what was said about it by the attentive scholars of the United States. For this purpose I trace the trajectory of Yevgeny Pashukanis, the best-known Marxist theorist of law in the West, in part as refracted in the writings of US scholars of international law. I show that, despite following developments in Soviet international law with close interest, these observers entirely misunderstood what they sought to analyse. It should be said that the leading Soviet theorists did so too. This tradition of misunderstanding has continued until the present day. I contend that this is true also of the most sophisticated and committed of contemporary Marxist scholars of international law, China Miéville. I engage respectfully with his impressive work.

More importantly, however, there was on my contention a clear-cut contradiction between the positivism of the legal textbooks, and the actual practice of the Bolshevik and then Soviet doctrine of the 'Right of Peoples to Self-Determination'. Thus, the USSR gave enormous material and moral support to the National Liberation Movements, and led the successful drive to see the principle and then right to self-determination placed at the centre of public international law in the twentieth and twenty-first centuries.

2. 'Taking the dogma for a walk'

Western scholars are familiar with what is generally termed the 'Marxist-Leninist theory' in international law, and with its standard characterisation.[6] Ian Scobbie in a recent comparison of Soviet and 'New Haven' theories, refers to 'the Soviet theory of international law propounded by G. I. Tunkin'.[7] For Scobbie, Soviet theory amounted to a 'constitutive' (rather than a 'facilitative') theory.[8] It relied on 'the objective rules of societal development and the historical inevitability of socialism'.[9] That is, it was thoroughly mechanical in spirit and exposition.

There can be no surprise that Scobbie refers only to Tunkin. William Butler's translation of Tunkin's textbook made available to a Western audience the only substantial Soviet text in English on international law.[10] Tunkin, born in 1906 and died, aged 87, in 1993, while completing the last edition of his *Theory of International Law* and having just submitted an article – on customary international law – to the *European Journal of International Law*. Here he wrote of the attempt 'to create a new world order based on the rule of law'.[11]

Scobbie comments that Soviet theory was structurally highly traditional, and firmly rooted in Marxist-Leninist theory to the extent that 'at times it seems simply to amount to taking the dogma for a walk.'[12] This was certainly true of Tunkin's textbook. It was also very conservative, recognising only rules and state consent to rules: as Damrosch and Müllerson explained it, Soviet theory treated 'the existing corpus of international law as a system of sufficiently determinate principles and norms which all states are obliged to observe in their mutual relations.'[13] As a direct consequence, Soviet theory rejected 'the general principles of law recognised by the civilised nations'.[14]

The existence of two opposed social systems meant that the only norms of 'customary' or 'general' international law could be those which were neither socialist nor capitalist. Tunkin asserted that: 'only those

---

[6] I. Scobbie, 'Some Common Heresies about International Law: Sundry Theoretical Perspectives', in M. Evans (ed.), *International Law*, 2nd edn (Oxford: Oxford University Press, 2006), p. 83 at p. 84.
[7] *Ibid.*, p. 92. [8] *Ibid.* [9] *Ibid.*, p. 96.
[10] G. Tunkin, *Theory of International Law* (Cambridge MA: Harvard University Press, 1974).
[11] G. Tunkin, 'Is General International Law Customary Only?' (1993) 4 *European Journal of International Law* 534 at 534.
[12] Scobbie, 'Some Common Heresies', p. 97.
[13] L. Damrosch and R. Müllerson, 'The Role of International Law in the Contemporary World', in J. F. Damrosch, G. M. Danilenko and R. Müllerson (eds.), *Beyond Confrontation: International Law for the Post-Cold War Era* (Boulder, CO: Westview Press, 1995) p. 9.
[14] Article 38(1)(c) of the Statute of the International Court of Justice.

international legal norms which embrace the agreement of all states are norms of contemporary general international law.'[15] Thus, Soviet theory recognised only treaties and custom – narrowly defined as above – as sources of international law.

The US scholar Alwyn Freeman (1910–1983),[16] writing much earlier, also noted that Soviet international law embraced:

> [T]he most extreme form of positivism . . . The Soviet brand of positivism is much more restricted, much narrower, and is, in sum, a rejection of a great portion of international legal principles . . . Soviet positivism has been distinguished by the exclusion of customary practice as a source of international obligations. It views international law as embracing only those principles to which states have expressly consented through an international agreement or have otherwise manifested their acquiescence.[17]

Indeed, writing in 1948, at the time of his frenetic activity in the United Nations as leader of the Soviet delegation, the notorious Andrey Vyshinsky[18] wrote that:

> the Soviet theory of international law regards the treaty, resting on the principles of sovereign equality of peoples and the respect for mutual interests and rights as the basic source of international law. This secures for international law and its institutions full moral as well as juridical force since at their base will lie the obligations agreed to and voluntarily assumed by nations.[19]

---

[15] G. Tunkin, *Theory of International Law* (Cambridge, MA: Harvard University Press, 1974) pp. 250–1.

[16] Freeman was an editor of the *American Journal of International Law* from 1955 to 1972, worked on international claims cases while in the US State Department, and served in the Army Judge Advocate General's Office in World War II, on the staff of the Senate Committee on Foreign relations, and as an official of the IAEA.

[17] A. Freeman, 'Some Aspects of Soviet Influence on International Law' (1968) 62 *American Journal of International Law* 710 at 713.

[18] Andrey Vyshinsky was born in Odessa, Russia, on 28 November 1883. As a young man he joined the Social Democratic Party. In the 1903 split, he sided with the Mensheviks. Vyshinsky became a lawyer and after the October Revolution he joined the Bolsheviks. He taught law at Moscow State University until becoming a state prosecutor. Between 1934 and 1938 Vyshinsky was the leading prosecutor in the 'show trials' of Stalin's opponents. In 1940 he was given the responsibility of managing the (illegal) occupation of Latvia. He also helped establish communist rule in Romania before becoming Soviet foreign minister in March, 1949. He survived the purge that followed the death of Joseph Stalin in 1953 and continued as the Soviet representative in the United Nations. Vyshinsky died in New York on 22 November, 1954.

[19] A. Vyshinsky, 'Mezhdunarodnoye pravo i mezhdunarodnaya organisatsiya (International Law and International Organisation)' (1948) 1 *Sovetskoye gosudarstvo i pravo* (*Soviet State*

There is, however, a point at which this conservatism shows another, opposite side. Freeman did not fail to notice it in his discussion of sovereignty. He explained that the Soviets:

> retain the classical, strict conception of states alone as the subjects of international law, with a rigid insistence on sovereignty in its most extreme form, a form which must deny the paramount nature of international law over national law. They do, however, recognise an exception in favour of peoples fighting for 'national liberation.'[20]

It is very odd, however, that Freeman did not notice the basis for such a claim: the right of peoples to self-determination. This 'principle' had become a 'right' as the common first article of the two International Covenants of 1966 – the 'International Bill of Rights'.

Scobbie quite rightly notes the notorious so-called 'Brezhnev doctrine', that relations between socialist states are not based on 'peaceful co-existence', but on 'proletarian internationalism'. This hypocritical policy justified the invasions of Hungary in 1956, Czechoslovakia in 1968, and Afghanistan in 1980.[21] But, curiously, he says nothing about the application of the 'right of peoples to self-determination' to Soviet support for the national liberation struggles of three decades from World War II.

In the next section of this chapter, therefore, I analyse the origins of the Soviet doctrine of the right of nations to self-determination. It should be noted that in Russian, as in many other languages, 'nation' and 'people' are practically synonymous.

3. The Bolsheviks and international law

3.1. Bolshevism versus Austro-Marxism

The Bolshevik and then Soviet doctrine of the right of nations to self-determination had its origin in the uncompromising pre-World War I struggle between Lenin, Stalin and Trotsky (and orthodox Marxists with

---

and Law) 22, cited in J. Triska, 'Treaties and Other Sources of Order in International Relations: The Soviet View' (1958) 52 *American Journal of International Law* 699 at 713.

[20] Freeman, 'Some Aspects of Soviet Influence', 716.
[21] Scobbie, 'Some Common Heresies', 99.

Karl Kautsky at their head) on the one side, and the Austro-Marxist theorists such as Karl Renner and Otto Bauer on the other.[22]

Austro-Marxist ideas of non-territorial personal autonomy, developed as a possible antidote to the dissolution of the multi-national Austro-Hungarian Empire, found a ready audience among the Jews of the Russian Empire. The Jews had no 'historic' or 'consolidated' territory. The Jewish 'Bund' (*Algemeyner Yidisher Arbeter Bundin Lite, Poyln un Rusland*) was founded in Vilna (now Vilnius, capital of Lithuania) in 1897, as a Jewish political party espousing social democratic ideology as well as cultural Yiddishism and Jewish national autonomism.[23] The First Congress of the Russian Social Democratic Labour Party in 1898 decided that the Bund 'is affiliated to the Party as an autonomous organisation independent only in regard to questions specifically concerning the Jewish proletariat'.[24] It was from the start influenced by the ideas of Renner and Bauer, although Renner's model did not allow for diasporas or scattered minorities.[25] As Yves Plasseraud points out:

> The leaders of the Bund and the Jewish Socialist Workers Party therefore took on the task of adapting Renner's ideas to the situation of the Yiddish-speaking Jews of Central and Eastern Europe ... The Bundist leaders proposed that Russia, like the Austro-Hungarian Empire, should become a federation of autonomous peoples.[26]

Vladimir Ilich Ulyanov (Lenin), the leader of the Bolsheviks following the split in the RSDLP in 1903, was a bitter opponent of the Bund and of the Austro-Marxist prescription. In October 1903 he published an article entitled 'The Position of the Bund in the Party'.[27] He was especially critical of the Bund's idea of a Jewish nation. He argued that:

---

[22] B. Bowring, 'Burial and Resurrection: Karl Renner's controversial influence on the "National Question" in Russia', in E. Nimni (ed.), *National-Cultural Autonomy and its Contemporary Critics* (London: Routledge, 2005).

[23] In the Bund Archive at the Russian State Archive of Social and Political History (GRASPI), Moscow.

[24] *The CPSU in Resolutions and Decisions of Its Congresses, Conferences and Plenary Meetings of the Central Committee* (Moscow: Progress, 1954), Pt 1, p. 14.

[25] Y. Plasseraud, 'How to solve Cultural Identity Problems: Choose your own nation', *Le Monde Diplomatique*, May 2000, p. 4, available at www.globalpolicy.org/nations/citizen/region.htm.

[26] Plasseraud, 'How to Solve Cultural Identity Problems', p. 4.

[27] V. I. Lenin, *Complete Collected Works*, 2nd edn, (Moscow: Progress, 1968), vol. 7, p. 92, first published in *Iskra*, 22 October 1903, n. 51.

Unfortunately, however, this Zionist idea is absolutely false and essentially reactionary. 'The Jews have ceased to be a nation, for a nation without a territory is unthinkable', says one of the most prominent of Marxist theoreticians, Karl Kautsky.

Lenin was wholly in agreement with Kautsky on this point.

Lenin thus adopted Kautsky's orthodox 'scientific' definition of the concept 'nationality', with two principal criteria: language and territory.[28] Both Lenin and Kautsky were in favour of Jewish assimilation.

At the January 1912 Conference of the RSDLP(B), the Jewish Bund declared that it had been influenced by Austro-Marxist theories of personal or non-territorial national cultural autonomy. Consequently, at the August conference of the RSDLP(B), it adopted a resolution 'On National Cultural Autonomy', including it in the programme of the Bund.[29]

Lenin's reply was uncompromising. In 1913, in his 'Draft Platform of the 4th Congress of the Social Democrats of the Latvian Area', he denounced the 'bourgeois falsity' of the slogan of 'cultural national autonomy'. He asserted that in Russia only the Jewish Bund members – 'together with all the Jewish bourgeois parties' – had so far defended this concept.[30] Later that year, he devoted an article to 'Cultural-National Autonomy'.[31] He once more denounced this plan, as 'an impossibility':

> A clear grasp of the essence of the 'cultural-national autonomy' programme is sufficient to enable one to reply without hesitation – it is absolutely impermissible. As long as different nations live in a single state they are bound to one another by millions and thousands of millions of economic, legal and social bonds. How can education be extricated from these bonds? Can it be 'taken out of the jurisdiction of the state', to quote the Bund formula?

---

[28] K. Kautsky, (1903)2 *Neue Zeit*.
[29] V. Filippov. 'Natsionalno-Kulturnaya Avtonomiya: klassicheskaya kontseptsiya i yeyo sovremennaya interpretatsiya (National-Cultural Autonomy: the classical conception and its contemporary interpretation)', in Y. Filippova (ed.), *Natsionalno-Kulturnaya Avtonomiya: problemy i suzhdeniya (National-Cultural Autonomies: problems and evaluation)* (Moscow: Etnosfera, 1998), Materials from the Round Table organised by the 'Etnosfera' Centre, p. 66.
[30] V. I. Lenin *Complete Collected Works*, 2nd edn, (Moscow: Progress, 1968) vol. 19, p. 117, first published in *Za Pravda*, 28 November 1913, n. 46.
[31] *Ibid*, p. 503, n. 30.

Lenin particularly mocked the references to Austria:

> [W]hy should the most backward of the multinational countries be taken as the *model*? Why not take the most advanced? This is very much in the style of the bad Russian liberals, the Cadets, who for models of a constitution turn mainly to the backward countries such as Prussia and Austria, and not to advanced countries such like France, Switzerland and America!

3.2. Stalin's 'scientific' contribution

Also in early 1913, J. V. Stalin published, under Lenin's instruction, his one substantial work of theory, *Marxism and the National Question*.[32] This devoted a whole chapter to 'Cultural-National Autonomy', and was primarily designed as a reply to the Bund. Stalin attempted his own definition of a nation:

> A nation is a historically constituted, stable community of people, formed on the basis of a common language, territory, economic life and psychological make-up manifested in a common culture.

It is noteworthy that Stalin's definition of the nation is not so far from contemporary orthodoxy. Anthony D. Smith defines *ethnie* as:

> [A] named unit of population with common ancestry myths and shared historical memories, elements of shared culture, a link with a historic territory, and some measure of solidarity, at least among the elites.[33]

Note the importance of the link to territory. Again, he defines the modern nation, in ideal-typical terms, as 'a named human population sharing a historic territory, common myths and historical memories, a mass, public culture, a common economy and common rights and duties for all members'. John Hutchinson, too, contends that 'Nations are distinguished in addition by a commitment to citizenship rights, and the possession of a high literate culture, a consolidated territory and a unified economy'.

They are all agreed on the importance of territory.

Stalin's next move was a critique of Renner and Bauer, insisting on the importance of territory: 'Bauer's point of view, which identifies a nation

---

[32] J. Stalin, *Marxism and the National Question* (1913) 3–5 *Prosveshniye (Enlightenment)*, available at www.marxists.org/reference/archive/stalin/works/1913/03.htm.

[33] A. Smith, 'Nations and History', in M. Guibernau and J. Hutchinson (eds.), *Understanding Nationalism* (London: Polity, 2001), pp. 9–31 at p. 19. See also A. D. Smith, 'Dating the Nation', in D. Conversi (ed.), *Ethnonationalism in the Contemporary World: Walker Connor and the Study of Nationalism* (London: Routledge, 2002), pp. 53–71.

with its national character, divorces the nation from its soil, and converts it into an invisible, self-contained force.' Stalin's answer was as follows:

> there is no doubt a) that cultural-national autonomy presupposes the integrity of the multi-national state, whereas self-determination goes outside the framework of this integrity, and b) that self-determination endows a nation with complete rights, whereas national autonomy endows it only with cultural rights.

And he further warned that 'Springer's and Bauer's cultural-national autonomy is a subtle form of nationalism'.

3.3. The Bolshevik origins of the right to self-determination

Applying his definition and critique to the national question in Russia, Stalin started from the assertion that 'the *right of self-determination is an essential element* in the solution of the national question'. For 'crystallised units', such as Poland, Lithuania, the Ukraine, the Caucasus etc., he believed that *national* autonomy could not solve the problem, and the only correct solution was *regional* autonomy, for a definite population inhabiting a definite territory. The national minorities in each of these territories need not fear the result: 'Give the country complete democracy and all grounds for fear will vanish.' This would include equal rights of nations in all forms – liberty of conscience, liberty of movement, languages, schools, etc.

In December 1913 Lenin began himself to write on the question of the 'right of nations to self-determination'. In a short polemic[34] on the question of independence for Ukraine, he insisted on '*freedom* to secede, for the *right* to secede', while conceding that 'the *right* to self-determination is one thing, of course, and the *expediency* of self-determination, the secession of a given nation under given circumstances, is another'. Later in December 1913[35] he again declared that: 'A democrat could not remain a democrat (let alone a proletarian democrat) without systematically advocating, precisely among the Great-Russian masses and in the Russian language, the

---

[34] V. Lenin, 'The Cadets and "The Right of Nations to Self-Determination"', (1913) 4 *Proletarskaya Pravda*; Lenin *Collected Works*, vol. 19, pp. 525–527, available at www.marxists.org/archive/lenin/works/1913/dec/11.htm.

[35] V. Lenin, 'National-Liberalism and the Right of Nations to Self-Determination' (1913) 12 (20) *Proletarskaya Pravda*; *Collected Works*, vol. 20, pp. 56–58, available at www.marxists.org/archive/lenin/works/1913/dec/20.htm.

"self-determination" of nations in the political and not in the "cultural" sense.' The latter, he said, meant only freedom of languages.

In April–June 1914 Lenin published his own substantial work on the question, a polemic against Rosa Luxemburg, who opposed the break-up of the Tsarist Empire, 'The Right of Nations to Self-Determination'.[36] In the first chapter, he insisted that 'it would be wrong to interpret the right to self-determination as meaning anything but the right to existence as a separate state'.[37] Furthermore, 'the national state is the rule and the "norm" of capitalism: the multi-national state represents backwardness ... from the standpoint of national relations, the best conditions for the development of capitalism are undoubtedly provided by the national state'.[38]

His understanding of the historical significance of the demand is highly significant for this chapter:

> The epoch of bourgeois-democratic revolutions in Western, continental Europe embraces a fairly definite period, approximately between 1789 and 1871. This was precisely the period of national movements and the creation of national states. When this period drew to a close, Western Europe had been transformed into a settled system of bourgeois states, which, as a general rule, were nationally uniform states. Therefore, to seek the right to self-determination in the programmes of West-European socialists at this time of day is to betray one's ignorance of the ABC of Marxism.
>
> In Eastern Europe and Asia the period of bourgeois-democratic revolutions did not begin until 1905. The revolutions in Russia, Persia, Turkey and China, the Balkan wars – such is the chain of world events of *our* period in our 'Orient'. And only a blind man could fail to see in this chain of events the awakening of a *whole series* of bourgeois-democratic national movements which strive to create nationally independent and nationally uniform states. It is precisely and solely because Russia and the neighbouring countries are passing through this period that we must have a clause in our programme on the right of nations to self-determination.[39]

Thus, Lenin's conception of self-determination in 1914 was wholly and necessarily relevant, not only to the Tsarist Empire but also to the European colonial empires.

---

[36] Published in the journal *Prosveshcheniye* Nos. 4, 5 and 6; *Collected Works* (1972) vol. 20, pp. 393–454, available at www.marxists.org/archive/lenin/works/1914/self-det/index.htm.
[37] See www.marxists.org/archive/lenin/works/1914/self-det/ch01.htm, p. 2.
[38] See www.marxists.org/archive/lenin/works/1914/self-det/ch01.htm, p. 5.
[39] See www.marxists.org/archive/lenin/works/1914/self-det/ch03.htm.

He spelt this out further in 1915, in a polemic with his fellow revolutionary Karl Radek:

> We demand freedom of self-determination, i.e., independence, i.e., freedom of secession for the oppressed nations, not because we have dreamt of splitting up the country economically, or of the ideal of small states, but, on the contrary, because we want large states and the closer unity and even fusion of nations, only on a truly democratic, truly internationalist basis, which is inconceivable without the freedom to secede. Just as Marx, in 1869, demanded the separation of Ireland, not for a split between Ireland and Britain, but for a subsequent free union between them, not so as to secure 'justice for Ireland', but in the interests of the revolutionary struggle of the British proletariat, we in the same way consider the refusal of Russian socialists to demand freedom of self-determination for nations, in the sense we have indicated above, to be a direct betrayal of democracy, internationalism and socialism.[40]

Finally, in 1916, in a long article entitled 'The Discussion on Self-Determination Summed Up',[41] Lenin wrote, with regard to the colonies:

> Our theses say that the demand for the immediate liberation of the colonies is as 'impracticable' (that is, it cannot be effected without a number of revolutions and is not stable without socialism) under capitalism as the self-determination of nations, the election of civil servants by the people, the democratic republic, and so on—and, furthermore, that the demand for the liberation of the colonies is nothing more than 'the recognition of the right of nations to self-determination'.

It is, therefore, perfectly clear that Lenin's conception of self-determination had nothing in common with that propounded by US President Woodrow Wilson after World War I. It should be recalled that standard texts on international law usually refer only to Wilson as progenitor of the concept. For Wilson, self-determination applied – and applied only – to the former Ottoman, Austro-Hungarian and Russian empires. The British, Belgian, French, Dutch, Spanish and Portuguese Empires were in no way to be threatened. And American interests in Puerto Rico and the Philippines were also sacrosanct. Lenin's approach, on the other hand, was consistent, and revolutionary.

---

[40] V. Lenin, 'The Revolutionary Proletariat and the Right of Nations to Self-Determination', *Collected Works*, vol. 21, pp. 407–14, available at www.marxists.org/archive/lenin/works/1915/oct/16.htm.

[41] (1916) 1 *Sbornik Sotsial-Demokrata*; *Collected Works*, vol. 22, pp. 320–60, available at www.marxists.org/archive/lenin/works/1916/jul/x01.htm.

4. The Soviet practice of self-determination

I wish to maintain strongly that, for Lenin at least, self-determination was not a mere slogan, but a principle he put into practice with immediate effect within the former Russian Empire following the Bolshevik Revolution. According to Igor Blishchenko (1930–2000), one of the best Soviet scholars of international law,[42] in a text published, ironically, in 1968, the year that the USSR crushed the 'Czech Spring', Lenin's Decree on Peace of 26 October 1917, for the first time extended the principle of the right to self-determination to all peoples, thereby discarding the imperialist distinction between 'civilised' and 'uncivilised' nations.[43]

In fact, the Decree declared that:

> By annexation or seizure of foreign territory the government, in accordance with the legal concepts of democracy in general and of the working class in particular, understands any incorporation of a small and weak nationality by a large and powerful state without a clear, definite and voluntary expression of agreement and desire by the weak nationality, regardless of the time when such forcible incorporation took place, regardless also of how developed or how backward is the nation forcibly attached or forcibly detained within the frontiers of the [larger] state, and, finally, regardless of whether or not this large nation is located in Europe or in distant lands beyond the seas.
>
> If any nation whatsoever is detained by force within the boundaries of a certain state, and if [that nation], contrary to its expressed desire whether such desire is made manifest in the press, national assemblies, party relations, or in protests and uprisings against national oppression, is not given the right to determine the form of its state life by free voting and completely free from the presence of the troops of the annexing or stronger state and without the least desire, then the dominance of that nation by the stronger state is annexation, i.e., seizure by force and violence.[44]

In his article, Blishchenko moved next to answer a series of Western scholars who argued that the Decree was entirely hypocritical, first having no application to peoples within the USSR and, second, having been applied

---

[42] I worked with Blishchenko for a number of years, in particular on the draft of the Rome Statute of the International Criminal Court; for a touching obituary by the International Committee of the Red Cross: see www.icrc.org/Web/eng/siteeng0.nsf/html/57JREV.

[43] I. Blishchenko, *Antisovyetism i mezhdunarodnoye pravo* (*Antisovietism and International Law*) (Moscow: Izdatelstvo IMO, 1968), p. 69.

[44] See www.firstworldwar.com/source/decreeonpeace.htm.

only to Finland in the former Tsarist Empire. He pointed to the substantial autonomy, if short of secession, enjoyed by Union and Autonomous Republics in the USSR in accordance with Article 17 of its Constitution. More importantly, he underlined the extent to which the principle was indeed put into practice by Lenin in the early years of the USSR. What he failed to point out, not surprisingly in 1968, is the fact that one of Lenin's most bitter struggles with Stalin concerned independence for Georgia.[45]

In a much later text,[46] Blishchenko showed that the early Soviet government was entirely consistent in implementing self-determination. On 4 (17) December 1917 the Soviet government recognised the right to self-determination of Ukraine. In response to the request of the Finnish government, the Soviet of Peoples' Commissars on 18 (31) December 1917 resolved to go to the Central Executive Committee with a proposal to recognise Finland's independence. In fact, it was the Whites, seeking to restore the Empire, who opposed Finnish independence. By a Decree of 29 December 1917 (11 January 1918) the right of the people of 'Turkish Armenia' to self-determination was recognised. In answer to a request from the government of Soviet Estland, on 7 December 1918 Lenin signed a Decree on recognition of the independence of Estonia, Latvia and Lithuania.

On 5 February 1919 the Presidium of the All-Union Central Executive of Soviet Russia insisted, in a principled manner, that, in implementing the principle of self-determination, the issue was resolved by the self-determining nation itself, by the people itself. The dictatorship of the proletariat was not a condition for self-determination, which applied equally to bourgeois independence movements. Thus, the Soviet government recognised the republics of Bukhara and Khorezm, which were not socialist.

This was the profoundly significant historical context in which Yevgenii Pashukanis became the acknowledged theoretician and leader of a Marxist account of law and of international law.

[45] See M. Lewin, *Lenin's Last Struggle* (Ann Arbor, MI: University of Michigan Press, 2005).
[46] I. Blishchenko, 'Soderzhaniye prava narodov na samoopredeleniye' ('The content of the right of peoples to self-determination'), in A. Ossipov (ed.), *Pravo Narodov na Samoopredeleniye: Ideya i Voploshcheniye (Right of Peoples to Self-Determination: Idea and Realisation)* (Moscow: Zvenya 1998), p. 71; see also, on national liberation movements, D. I. Baratashvili, 'Natsionalno-osvoboditelnoye dvizheniye i razvitiye mezhdunarododnovo prava' ('The national liberation movement and the development of international law') (1967) 9 *Sovetskoye gosudarstvo i pravo (Soviet State and Law)* 69–75.

5. Soviet Legal Doctrine: Yevgeny Pashukanis

5.1. Pashukanis's history

Pashukanis was born in what is now Lithuania in 1891, and was liquidated in 1937, condemned as a member of a 'band of wreckers' and 'Trotsky-Bukharin fascist agents'.[47] He was a pupil of the Latvian-born legal theorist Piotr I. Stuchka, his senior by twenty-five years (Stuchka lived from 1865 to 1932, when, unusually for those times, he died of natural causes).[48] Chris Arthur has described Pashukanis's 'important contribution to the materialist critique of legal forms' as 'to this day the most significant Marxist work on the subject'.[49] I do not disagree. At the same time, I hope to demonstrate that the paradoxical effects of Soviet practice (as opposed to the positivist theory they propagated) played a key role in developing and putting in place one of the most important principles of international law, the right of peoples to self-determination.

Pashukanis was, from 1925 to 1936, the leading theorist of law in the USSR, recognised as such by none other than Stuchka himself, who wrote that the *General Theory of Law and Marxism* was 'to the highest degree a valuable contribution to our Marxist theoretical literature on law and directly supplements my work, which provides only an incomplete and greatly inadequate general doctrine of law'.[50] This was a period of 'passionate legal debate', well analysed by Michael Head.[51]

Pashukanis was the Director of the Institute of Law of the Soviet Academy of Sciences, and effectively the country's director of legal research and legal education. He made significant changes to legal education, including the virtual elimination of civil law subjects from the educational curriculum, and replacing them with an emphasis on economics and economic administration.[52] John Hazard (1909–1955),[53] who studied

---

[47] C. Arthur, 'Introduction', in Y. Pashukanis, *Law and Marxism: A General Theory. Towards a Critique of the Fundamental Concepts* (London: Pluto Press, 1983), p. 10.

[48] I. Stuchka, *Selected Writings on Soviet Law and Marxism* R. Sharlet, P. Maggs and P. Beirne (ed. and trans.) (Armonk: M. E. Sharpe, 1988), pp. x–xi.

[49] Arthur, 'Introduction', p. 9.

[50] Stuchka, *Selected Writings*, p. xvii.

[51] M. Head, 'The Passionate Legal Debates of the Early Years of the Russian Revolution' (2001) 14 *Canadian Journal of Law and Jurisprudence* 3. See also the extracts from Pashukanis and Stuchka in Z. Zile, *Ideas and Forces in Soviet Legal History: A Reader on the Soviet State and Law* (Oxford: Oxford University Press, 1992).

[52] E. Garlan, 'Soviet Legal Philosophy' (review of J. Hazard (intr.), *Soviet Legal Philosophy* (1951)) (1954) 51 (10) *Journal of Philosophy* 300 at 303.

[53] Hazard was a founder of the field of Soviet legal studies in America who taught at Columbia for forty-eight years. Upon his graduation from Harvard Law School, he was sent by the

under him, recalled another side of his character: in the Institute the situation where he 'projected a theory said to be infallible, and where those who strayed from Pashukanis's line were castigated like Korovin or denied faculty appointments, promotions and salary raises was novel to me'.[54] That is probably disingenuous of Hazard, a native of American academe; but seems to be accurate.

Edwin Garlan, writing in 1954 for an American audience during the Cold War, identified two conclusions reached by Pashukanis on the basis of his analysis of basic legal categories. First:

> Only bourgeois-capitalist society creates all the conditions essential to the attainment of complete definiteness by the juridic element in social relationships[55]

And, second:

> The dying out of the categories . . . of bourgeois law by no means signifies that they are replaced by new categories of proletarian law – precisely as the dying out of the category of value, capital, gain and so forth will not (with the transition to expanded socialism) mean that new proletarian categories of worth, capital rent and so forth appear. The dying out of the categories of bourgeois law will in these conditions signify the dying out of law in general: that is to say, the gradual disappearance of the juridic element in human relations.[56]

As Garlan notes, it follows from these propositions that the transition period of the dictatorship of the proletariat had to take the form of bourgeois law. Thus, the task of transition law was to eliminate itself, by way of a rapid movement to policy – technical – administration as opposed to civil and criminal law.[57]

> Institute of Current World Affairs as the first American to study Soviet law at the Moscow Juridical Institute. Only a handful of scholars were concerned with Russian diplomacy and business then, and scholarship on Russia was limited principally to historical studies. He approached the field of Soviet law as a pioneer and received the certificate of the Juridical Institute in 1937. He was the author of widely used textbooks and studies of Soviet law and public administration, and served the US government during World War II, helping to negotiate the Lend-Lease agreement with the Soviet Union.

[54] J. Hazard, 'Memories of Pashukanis', Foreword to *Evgeny Pashukanis, Selected Writings on Marxism and Law* (London: Academic Press, 1980), pp. 273–301, available at www.marxists.org/archive/pashukanis/biog/memoir.htmHazard.

[55] Y. Pashukanis, *The General Theory of Law and Marxism* (1924), republished in Pashukanis, *Selected Writings on Marxism and Law*, pp. 168–83, at p. 110.

[56] Pashukanis, *The General Theory of Law and Marxism* in *Selected Writings on Marxism and Law*, pp. 168–83, at pp. 184–5.

[57] Garlan, 'Soviet Legal Philosophy', p. 303.

5.2. Pashukanis revived: China Miéville

China Miéville, with his re-working of the 'commodity-form theory of international law',[58] has provided the most serious and sophisticated attempt in recent years at a Marxist account of international law.[59] The final sentence of his powerful book truly sums up his conclusion: 'The chaotic and bloody world around us *is the rule of law*'.[60] International law and human rights are at best distractions, on his account, and at worst potent weapons in the hands of the enemy. As he points out in his Introduction to *Between Equal Rights*, Miéville draws extensively from Pashukanis, who was one of the most serious Marxist legal theorists of the USSR or anywhere. Miéville traces and explains his arguments in Chapter 3 of this book, and seeks, through 'immanent reformulation', to answer some criticisms of Pashukanis.[61]

China Miéville identifies in Critical Legal Studies, and other so-called 'New Stream' theories of international law, an 'implicit theory of the social world, an idealist constructivism',[62] in which international law is sometimes depicted as a 'constraining myth' inherited from the past, or where structures of everyday life such as international law are deemed to be 'the accretion of ideas.' For Miéville, this privileges 'abstract concepts over the specific historic context in which certain ideas take hold, and how'.

Miéville upholds a resolutely 'classical' version of Marxism.[63] As it happens, I agree with this. However, as explained by Miéville, Pashukanis argues that *the logic of the commodity form is the logic of the legal form*. In commodity exchange, he continues:

> each commodity must be the private property of its owner, freely given in return for the other... Therefore, each agent in the exchange must be i) an owner of private property, and ii) formally equal to the other agent(s). Without these conditions, what occurred would not be commodity exchange. The legal from is the *necessary form* taken by the relation between these formally equal owners of exchange values.[64]

For Miéville, law is called forth as a 'specific form of social regulation... *That form is law*, which is characterised by its abstract quality, its being based on the equality of its subjects and its pervasive character in

---

[58] C. Miéville, 'The Commodity-Form Theory of International Law', Chapter 3 in this volume.
[59] C. Miéville, *Between Equal Rights: A Marxist Theory of International Law* (Leiden: Brill, 2005).
[60] *Ibid.*, p. 319. [61] *Ibid.*, pp. 6–7. [62] Chapter 3 in this volume.
[63] *Ibid.* [64] Miéville, *Between Equal Rights*, p. 78.

capitalism'.[65] Miéville refers with approval to Pashukanis's assertion that 'private law [rather than public law] is the "fundamental, primary level of law"'.[66] The rest of the legal superstructure can be seen as essentially derived from this.

In fact, Pashukanis's assertion goes rather further, and is as follows:

> Yet while civil law, which is concerned with the fundamental, primary level of law, makes use of the concept of subjective rights with complete assurance, application of this concept in public-law theory creates misunderstandings and contradictions at every step. For this reason, the system of civil law is distinguished by its simplicity, clarity and perfection, while theories of constitutional law teem with far-fetched constructs which are so one-sided as to become grotesque. The form of law with its aspect of subjective right is born in a society of isolated bearers of private egotistic interests...[67]

It is clear that Pashukanis knew Marx's *On the Jewish Question*,[68] and it must be said that the passage just cited is highly reminiscent of what Marx had to say about the 'rights of man':

> None of the so-called rights of man, therefore, go beyond egoistic man, beyond man as a member of civil society, that is, an individual withdrawn into himself, into the confines of his private interests and private caprice, and separated from the community.[69]

Later in the same passage, Marx expressed ironic puzzlement that in the French Declaration of 1789 'finally, it is not man as *citoyen*, but man as *bourgeois* who is considered to be the *essential* and *true* man'.

6. Pashukanis's limitations

I am also a great admirer of Pashukanis's early work. However, I doubt very much that his work on the commodity theory of law can really serve as the basis for a new theory of international law. Miéville himself at several points recognises Pashukanis's limitations and contradictions. Here are some important objections.

---

[65] *Ibid.*, p. 79.   [66] Miéville, Chapter 3 in this volume; and *Between Equal Rights*, p. 86.
[67] Y. Pashukanis, *Law and Marxism: A General Theory. Towards a Critique of the Fundamental Concepts*, C. Arthur (ed.) (London: Pluto Press, 1983), p. 103.
[68] *Ibid.*, p. 132, n. 43.
[69] K. Marx 'On the Jewish Question', in K. Marx and F. Engels, *Collected Works* (New York: International Publishers, 1975), vol. 3, pp. 146–74 at p. 164.

First, Pashukanis's theory strongly suggests that there was no law as he defines it before the development of the commodity form, which only appeared with the development of capitalism. That must be either wrong or circular, a definition that depends upon itself. Miéville does not neglect this problem, and effectively criticises Pashukanis for 'eliding' the distinction between the *logical* movement from simple to capitalist commodity exchange, and the *historical* movement from exchange of commodities under pre-capitalist societies to that in capitalism itself.[70] Miéville is forced to assert that: 'A history of the development of the legal form *can* be developed using Pashukanis's theory'.[71] Chris Arthur notes this problem from a different point of view in his *Introduction*:

> A difficulty that arises from a Marxist point of view is that the bourgeois regime is one of *generalised* commodity production; that is, it treats labour-power as a commodity and pumps out surplus labour from the wage-workers. Yet Pashukanis makes reference to commodity exchange without taking account of the various forms of production that might involve production for a market...[72]

In other words, Pashukanis has failed to take into account the whole of human pre-capitalist history.

Second, Miéville, it seems to me, takes insufficient notice of Bob Fine's critical remarks, which go to the heart of this particular re-appropriation of Pashukanis. First, as Fine points out: 'Whereas Marx derived law from relations of commodity production, Pashukanis derived it from commodity exchange'.[73] This, according to Fine, leads Pashukanis to a conclusion that was plainly wrong:

> Instead of seeing both the content and the forms of law as determined by and changing with the development of productive relations, Pashukanis isolated law from its content and reduced quite different forms of law, expressing qualitatively different social relations, to a single, static and illusory 'legal form'.[74]

And any 'legal form' must be bourgeois. As Fine explains, this led Pashukanis in 1924 to argue that the Soviet Union of the New Economic Policy (NEP) was not yet ready for the abolition of law, and that, since law is in any event bourgeois, there can be no such thing as proletarian law. More

---

[70] Miéville *Between Equal Rights*, pp. 96–7.   [71] *Ibid.*, p. 97.
[72] Arthur, 'Introduction', at p. 29.
[73] B. Fine, *Democracy and the Rule of Law. Marx's Critique of the Legal Form* (Caldwell, NJ: Blackburn Press, 2002), p. 157.
[74] *Ibid.*, p. 159.

to the point, Pashukanis was obliged by the logic of his own position to see the transition from capitalism to socialism simply as the replacement of commodity exchange by planned production, that is, the replacement of bourgeois (legal) forms by socialist (technical forms).[75] Thus, as Fine points out, in 1929 he accepted Stalin's view that communism was being achieved through the first Five-Year Plan.[76] Miéville has read Fine;[77] but seems entirely to have missed the point of his criticism.

Third, Miéville's reprinting and discussion of Pashukanis's short essay on international law[78] from 1925, fails to take account not only of the fact of Pashukanis's intellectual trajectory until his death at the hands of Stalin in 1937, but, more importantly, the way in which that trajectory was already determined by Pashukanis' early accommodation to Soviet technicism. Indeed, the essay formed part of the three-volume *Encyclopaedia of State and Law*, which was launched and edited by Stuchka. Pashukanis's contribution was entirely consistent with Stuchka's overall line and policy. But the reasons for this went deeper than a mere desire for conformity, which in any event was not in Pashukanis's character. As Fine explains:

> Not only did Pashukanis invert the relationship between law and bureaucracy envisaged by Marx, he lost all sight of the democratic nature of Marx's critique of the state, according to which its withering away was to be the result of its ever more radical democratisation.[79]

7. Pashukanis's official trajectory

Pashukanis was a staunch loyalist in relation to the regime – by conviction rather than any sort of pressure. Thus, by 1932, Pashukanis, by then editor in chief of the official law journal *Soviet State*, was able to write a 'hallelujah' in response to Stalin's letter, 'Some questions on the history of Bolshevism'.[80] Pashukanis's major work on international law, *Essays*

---

[75] *Ibid.*, p. 167.   [76] *Ibid.*, p. 168.
[77] See Miéville, *Between Equal Rights*, p. 101, n. 122, n. 123.
[78] *Ibid.*, pp. 321–35; Y. Pashukanis, *Mezhdunarodnoye pravo, Entsiklopediya gosudarstva i prava* (*International Law, Encylopedia of state and law*) (Moscow: Izd. Kommunisticheskoi akademii, 1925), vol. 2, pp. 858–74. From Pashukanis, *Selected Writings on Marxism and Law*, available at www.marxists.org/archive/pashukanis/1925/xx/intlaw.htm, pp 184–5.
[79] Fine, *Democracy and the Rule of Law*, p. 169.
[80] Y. Pashukanis, *Pismo tov. Stalina i zadachi teoreticheskovo fronta gosudarstvo i pravo* ('The letter of comrade Stalin and the tasks of the theoretical front of state and law') (1932) 1 *Sovetskoye gosudarstvo* (*Soviet State*) 4–48, cited in E. A. Skripilev, '*Nashemy zhurnalu – 70 let*' ('Our journal is 70 years old') (1997) 2 (17) *Sovetskoye Gosudarstvo i Pravo* (*Soviet State and Law*) 17.

in International Law, appeared in 1935.[81] Within two years he was dead, following *Pravda*'s announcement on 20 January 1937 that he had been found to be an enemy of the people – just two months after he had been named by the regime to supervise the revision of the whole system of Soviet codes of law. Michael Head's analysis leads to a critical assessment of Pashukanis's legacy:

> He offered profound insights into the economic roots of the legal form, even if displaying several basic confusions in Marxist economics. However, he was weaker on the ideological and repressive role of law and the state apparatus. And key aspects of his theory served the interests of the emerging Stalinist bureaucracy, with whom he aligned himself against the Left Opposition.[82]

Indeed, scholars such as Christine Sypnowich, who presents Pashukanis as an orthodox Marxist, coupling 'Marx and Pashukanis',[83] and Ronnie Warrington,[84] for whom, following the US scholar Robert Sharlet, Pashukanis was an orthodox 'Old Bolshevik',[85] miss the extent to which Pashukanis's theories led him inexorably to support for Stalin's policies.

As I show below, Pashukanis also entirely missed the revolutionary context for his analysis of international law. Moreover, his denunciation in 1937 and, posthumously, for the remainder of the Stalin period, was based on the assertion that he failed to point out that 'international law must be defined as class law in terms so simple and expressive that no one could possibly be deceived'.[86] According to the US scholar Hazard, the Soviet reader was supposed by Soviet orthodoxy to be able to find 'simple proof of the theoretician's argument that foreign policy is shaped to fit the demands of the struggle between the classes, and that international law as the tool of that policy is no more than a reflection of class conflicts calling for some attempts at solution'.[87]

---

[81] Y. Pashukanis, *Ocherki po Mezhdunarodnomu Pravu (Essays in International Law)* (Moscow: lzd. Kommunisticheskoi akademii, 1935).
[82] M. Head, 'The Rise and Fall of a Soviet Jurist: Evgeny Pashukanis and Stalinism' (2004) 17 *Canadian Journal of Law and Jurisprudence* 269 at 272.
[83] C. Sypnowich, *The Concept of Socialist Law* (Oxford: Clarendon Press, 1990), p. 8.
[84] R. Warrington, 'Pashukanis and the Commodity Form Theory' (1981) 9 *International Journal of the Sociology of Law* 1 at 3, reprinted in C. Varga (ed.), *Marxian Legal Theory, International Library of Essays in Law and Legal Theory* (New York: New York University Press, 1993), p. 181.
[85] This, as Michael Head shows, is quite wrong – Pashukanis, like Vyshinsky, was a Menshevik and only joined the Bolsheviks in 1918: see Head, 'The Rise and Fall of a Soviet Jurist', 274.
[86] J. Hazard, 'Cleansing Soviet International Law of Anti-Marxist Theories' (1938) 32 *American Journal of International Law* 244 at 246.
[87] Ibid.

As against Korovin, for whom a change of form must follow a change of substance, so that the Soviet Union had brought with it a new form of international law, the 'international law of the transition period', Pashukanis had argued for a continuation of old forms, including diplomatic immunity, the exchange of representatives, and the customary law of treaties, not least since these gave the Soviet Union considerable protection.

Pashukanis roundly condemned Korovin's doctrine:

> [S]cholars such as Korovin who argued that the Soviet Government should recognise only treaties [as a source of] international law and should reject custom are absolutely wrong. An attempt to impose upon the Soviet Government a doctrine it has nowhere expressed is dictated by the patent desire to deprive the Soviet Government of those rights which require no treaty formulation and derive from the fact that normal diplomatic relations exist.[88]

Pashukanis also came in for particular criticism because he called the principle *rebus sic stantibus* 'healthy'.[89]

Most copies of the *Essays* were destroyed after he was denounced in 1937, but in this culminating work he declared that any attempt to define the 'nature of international law' was scholastic.[90] In his view, such attempts were the result of the continuing influence of bourgeois legal methodology, which, he said, rested on the association of law with substance developing in accordance with its own internal principles. For him, in 1935, international law was a means of formulating and strengthening in custom and treaties various political and economic relationships between states, and that the USSR could use international law to further Soviet interests in the struggle with capitalist states. He saw no reason to believe that, in using these principles of international law for its own purposes, the USSR was compromising its principles, in a world in which most states were capitalist. For Pashukanis there was no point in seeking to determine whether international law was 'bourgeois' or 'socialist'; such a discussion would be 'scholastic'.[91]

This approach to international law is as far as it could be from a 'commodity-form' theory. It is utterly positivist in its approach, in precisely the manner described by the 'standard genre' to which I referred

---

[88] Pashukanis, *Essays in International Law*, ch. 2, cited in J. Triska, 'Treaties and Other Sources of Order in International Relations: The Soviet View' (1958) 52 *American Journal of International Law* 699 at 704–5.
[89] Hazard, 'Cleansing Soviet International Law', 250.
[90] Pashukanis, *Essays in International Law*, p. 16, cited in J. Hazard, 'Pashukanis is No Traitor' (1957) 51 *American Journal of International Law* 385 at 387.
[91] See Hazard, 'Pashukanis is No Traitor', at 387.

above. For Pashukanis, international law is composed simply of the treaties concluded by states, and such customary law as every state could agree on.

It should be no surprise that Pashukanis's apparent theoretical stance changed as it did between 1925 and 1935. The context had completely changed. In his 1925 essay, Pashukanis was writing when the world appeared to be divided into two camps – capitalism and workers' power – and when much of the planet was subject to colonialism. He wrote, quite correctly:

> The historical examples adduced in any textbook of international law loudly proclaim that *modern international law is the legal form of the struggle of the capitalist states among themselves for domination over the rest of the world.*[92]

In the 1935 textbook, he said that international law as practised between capitalist states was one of the forms with the aid of which imperialist states carry on the struggle between themselves for territory and super-profits.[93] He also declared that the earliest international law appeared with the earliest class society; that is, with the development of the slave holding state which grew out of the tribal civilisation of primitive man as division of labour and acceptance of the concept of private property stratified society into classes.[94]

Vyshinsky, Pashukanis's nemesis – and Stuchka's theoretical successor – was diametrically opposed to this:

> Only one who is consciously falsifying history and reality can perceive in capitalist society the supreme and culminating point of legal development . . . Only in socialist society does law acquire a firm ground for its development. . . . As regards the scientific working out of any specific problems, the basic and decisive thought must be the aspiration to guarantee the development and strengthening of soviet law to the highest degree.[95]

Indeed, Pashukanis's 1935 textbook is absolutely standard in the ordering and style of its presentation. The exception is Chapter III, '*Istoricheskii ocherk mezhdunarodnoi politiki i mezhdunarodnovo prava* (Historical

---

[92] Y. Pashukanis, *Mezhdunarodnoye pravo, Entsiklopediya gosudarstva i prava (International Law, Encyclopedia of state and law)* (*Izd. Kommunisticheskoi akademii*, 1925–1926) Moscow, vol. 2, 858–74; from Pashukanis, *Selected Writings on Marxism and Law*, 184–5.
[93] Summarised in Hazard, 'Cleansing Soviet International Law', 245–6.
[94] Pashukanis, *Essays in International Law*, p. 20, cited in Hazard, 'Cleansing Soviet International Law', p. 251.
[95] Cited in E. Garlan 'Soviet Legal Philosophy' (review of J. Hazard (intr.), *Soviet Legal Philosophy* (1951)) (1954) 51 (10) *Journal of Philosophy* 300 at 304.

sketch of international policy and international law)',[96] which presents, with some references to Comrade Stalin, and 'the thesis of the victory of socialism in a single country', a strictly factual account of the history of international law and policy from ancient times to 'International relations in the period of the breakdown of capitalist stabilisation and the struggle of the USSR for peace', with the most attention given to the October Revolution of 1917 and the post-World War period.

Pashukanis's 1925–27 conception that '[t]he real historical content of international law, therefore, is the struggle between capitalist states'[97] rapidly gave way to 'socialism in one country' and 'peaceful co-existence'. As Hazard pointed out in 1938: 'throughout the whole of any future discussion, the (Soviet) writer must re-emphasise the struggle for peace which is being waged by the USSR, and show how this struggle rests upon the sanctity of treaties and the observance of international obligations'.[98] The political context for this new orientation was the fact that the USSR was admitted to membership of the League of Nations on 18 September 1934, and, until its aggression against Finland in December 1939, it was the leading protagonist of the League and of 'collective security'.[99]

Within a year, the Molotov-Ribbentrop pact and Hitler's attack on the Soviet Union would bring an end to such political and scholarly imperatives.

In the circumstances, Pashukanis could not possibly have predicted the thoroughly contradictory developments which followed World War II, in particular the creation and transformation of the United Nations, the development of the great multilateral – in some cases universal – international treaties, and the consolidation of political principles such as self-determination into fundamental principles – legal rights – of international law. Indeed, it was his own theoretical position which prevented him from doing so. His great protagonist E. A. Korovin, writing as early as 1923, placed particular emphasis on '[s]overeignty as national self-determination', '[t]he legal form of self-determination', '[b]ourgeois self-determination and the method of "Balkanisation"'.[100] Korovin was much more a Bolshevik – a Leninist – than Pashukanis ever was.

---

[96] Pashukanis, *Essays in International Law*, pp. 24–64.
[97] Miéville, *Between Equal Rights*, p. 325.
[98] Hazard 'Cleansing Soviet International Law', 252.
[99] C. Prince, 'The USSR and International Organisations' (1942) 36 *American Journal of International Law* 425 at 429.
[100] E. Korovin, *Mezhdunarodnoye pravo perekhodnovo vremeni (International law of the Transitional Period)* (Moscow: lzd. Kommunisticheskoi akademii, 1923), Ch. IV, Pt 2, 26–35.

8. Why did Pashukanis miss self-determination?

At this point there is an absence in Pashukanis's work which is key to the argument of this chapter. He made only one reference to the 'right of nations to self-determination', despite the fact that this was the centre of Lenin's approach to international policy in the immediate post-1917 period. A factual account of 'imperialist usurpation' is analysed only in relation to Lenin's work on 'imperialism as the highest stage of capitalism'. On Pashukanis's 1935 account, the 'basic fact of world history' after the October Revolution is the 'struggle of two systems': capitalism, and socialism as constructed in the USSR. The most important feature of the 'Decree on Peace' of 8 November 1917 is the rejection of secret treaties. At this point, Pashukanis introduced the following: 'The declaration of the rights of the peoples of Russia proclaimed the right of each people to self-determination right up to secession and forming an independent state'.[101] Pashukanis said nothing about any significance this might have for the imperialist and colonial systems.

Pashukanis noted the creation of several new states on the ruins of the Austro-Hungarian and Ottoman Empires, and the existence in most of them of significant national minorities – but he did not breathe a word on self-determination. The same is true of his account of the recognition by the USSR and conclusion of treaties with Estonia (2 February 1920), Lithuania (12 July 1920), Latvia (11 August 1920) and Finland (14 October 1920).[102] The whole analysis is centred on the USSR and its interests. Thus, Pashukanis related that 'the sympathy of the oppressed peoples of the colonies for the Soviet Union aroused the anger of the imperialists'.[103] The Soviet Union, on the other hand, was 'guided by support for the workers within the countries and in the whole world'.[104]

Pashukanis was quite clear that the many bilateral treaties concluded by the USSR from 1932, when Hitler came to power, onwards, were not directed against any third state, but were based on the policy of supporting peaceful relations with all states 'and guaranteeing our socialist construction against the threats of intervention'.[105] Thus, the culmination of Soviet diplomatic efforts by 1935 was the invitation by thirty-four states on 15 September 1934 for the USSR to join the League of Nations, and its accession on 18 September 1934, with only three states voting against and seven abstentions.[106] According to Pashukanis, the 'brilliant success' of Soviet foreign policy was based on the internal policy of strengthening

---

[101] Pashukanis, *Essays in International Law*, p. 38.   [102] *Ibid.*, p. 44.   [103] *Ibid.*, p. 49.
[104] *Ibid.*, p. 50.   [105] *Ibid.*, p. 55.   [106] *Ibid.*, p. 62.

the dictatorship of the proletariat and construction of a classless socialist society. The 'thesis of the possibility of the victory of socialism in one country' had determinate significance for resolving the problems of foreign policy. A list of principles contains, after breaking with the policy of the Tsarist and Provisional Governments, exit from the wars, proposing peace to all warring countries, publishing and denouncing all secret treaties, cancelling debts:

> winning the trust and sympathy of the proletariat and oppressed peoples of the whole world, the proclamation of the principle of self-determination of nations and brotherly solidarity of the proletariat and the colonial peoples of the whole world ...[107]

Pashukanis was incapable of recognising the significance of self-determination for international law. In my view, this was not simply the result of the limitations imposed by the period in which he was living, or the necessity to adapt to Stalin's ideology, but was the direct consequence of his own theoretical position, worked out in the early 1920s.

Miéville does, of course, notice these developments, in particular the fact that the UN Charter proclaimed the 'equal rights and self-determination of peoples'.[108] However, although he acknowledges that the struggles for de-colonisation after World War II represented a radical change in international law in relation to colonisation, he argues that it its *content* it is a mere continuation of the universalising trend in the *form*. By this he means that the logic of international law is and was 'universalising', or, in other words, imperialist. Following Eric Hobsbawm's *Age of Extremes*,[109] Miéville notes the fact that waves of decolonisation struggles broke out first in Asia, then North Africa and the Middle East, then Sub-Saharan Africa. This was the point at which the United Nations General Assembly, twice the size that it was at the foundation of the UN, adopted the watershed *Declaration on the Granting of Independence to Colonial Countries and Peoples*.[110]

Miéville fails to note the following salient points. First, as I have already outlined, 'self-determination of nations' was the principled position thoroughly worked out by V. I. Lenin before World War I, and put into practice by him in the context of the former Russian empire after that war. Second, the principle was anathema to the Western imperialist powers, which were

---

[107] *Ibid.*, p. 63.   [108] Miéville, *Between Equal Rights*, p. 264.
[109] E. Hobsbawm, *Age of Extremes: The Short Twentieth Century* (London: Abacus, 1995).
[110] UN GA Resolution 1514 (XV) 947th plenary meeting, 14 December 1960; text at www.gibnet.com/texts/un1514.htm (last accessed 19 March 2006).

content for the former Russian, Austro-Hungarian and Ottoman Empires to break up into new nations. Self-determination limited to these cases was quite acceptable to the major imperialist powers. Third, the UN Charter contains a statement of principles including self-determination, but does not proclaim a right. This was a victory of the Western allies over the USSR and its partners. Fourth, it is significant that only in the context of victories of the national liberation movements did the principle of self-determination become a right in international law.

In fact, both Pashukanis and Miéville seem to overlook the significance of the principle, then right, to self-determination. Pashukanis's emphasis on the commodity form, and insistence that law only comes into its own in the context of capitalism, blinded him to the importance for international law of the political events in the midst of which he lived and worked. This may well have been a consequence of the perspective given to him by his own time and place. But it was much more the inevitable consequence of his own theoretical position.

9. The USSR and self-determination after World War II

9.1. De-colonisation

Blishchenko, writing in 1968, celebrated the break-up of the colonial system of imperialism, and the broad national liberation movements in Asia, Africa and Latin America after World War II, which had posited the right of peoples to self-determination with new force. He asserted, with reason, that the USSR had done everything to ensure that the right became one of the fundamental principles of contemporary international law. This was due in part the work of the Soviet Delegation at the San Francisco Conference[111] which drafted the Charter of the UN, as a result of which Article 2(1) of the Charter refers to 'respect for the principle of equal rights and self-determination of peoples . . .'.[112]

As Morsink points out,[113] in 1914 Lenin calculated that more than one half of the world's population lived in colonies, which covered

---

[111] United Nations Conference on International Organisation, 1945, v. III, 622; and see G. I. Tunkin, *Leninskiye printsipi ravnopraviya i samoopredeleniya narodov i sovremennoye mezhdunarodoye pravo* ('Lenin's principles of equal rights and the self-determination of peoples in contemporary international law') (1970) 2 *Vestnik Moskovskovo Universiteta* (*Bulletin of Moscow University*) 62 at 67.

[112] Blishchenko, *Antisovietism and International Law*, p. 75.

[113] J. Morsink, *The Universal Declaration of Human Rights. Origins, Drafting and Intent* (Philadelphia: University of Pennsylvania Press, 1999), p. 96.

three-quarters of the world's territory, a calculation that was still roughly correct at the end of the 1940s. The UN's Universal Declaration on Human Rights was drafted just as the European empires began to break up. Two leading participants, Malik from Lebanon and Romulo from the Philippines, were from countries which became independent in 1946, together with Syria. India, Burma and Pakistan gained their independence in 1947, and Ceylon in 1948. India and Pakistan were both active players in the drafting process.

Andrei Zhdanov, Stalin's favourite, delivered the key speech at the founding meeting of the Cominform (Communist Information Bureau), and announced that the world was divided into two camps, 'the imperialist and anti-democratic camp' led by the United States, and the 'democratic and anti-imperialist camp' led by the USSR. He asserted that there was a 'crisis of the colonial system' and that 'the peoples of the colonies no longer wish to live in the old way. The ruling classes of the metropolitan countries can no longer govern the colonies on the old lines.'[114] Cassese relates that the Dumbarton Oaks Proposals, the basis for the UN Charter, did not contain any reference to self-determination, but this was reconsidered at the end of April 1945, at the UN Conference on International Organization in San Francisco – at the insistence of the USSR.[115] Thus, a draft was presented referring to 'respect for the principle of equal rights and self-determination of peoples'.

As Tunkin noted in 1970, at the Second Session of the UN General Assembly the Soviet delegation proposed an article for the Universal Declaration on Human Rights as follows:

> Each people and each nation has the right to national self-determination. A state which has responsibility for the administration of self-determining territories, including colonies, must ensure the realisation of that right, guided by the principles and goals of the United Nations in relation to the peoples of such territories.

However, under pressure from the colonial powers this proposal was rejected, with the result that the principle of self-determination does not appear in the UDHR.[116]

---

[114] Cited in Morsink, *Universal Declaration*, p. 97.
[115] A. Cassese, *Self-Determination of Peoples: A Legal Reappraisal* (Cambridge: Cambridge University Press, 1995), p. 38.
[116] Tunkin, 'Lenin's Principles of Equal Rights', p. 69.

Dmitrii Grushkin notes[117] that one key factor at the end of World War II was the strengthened role of the USSR and the appearance of a whole bloc of states oriented towards it. Further, a bi-polar system took shape in international relations in which the contradictory interests of the two sides could be clearly traced. Third, the role of the mass character of politics significantly grew during World War II: 110 million people from seventy-two states took part. It was a war of peoples, not of governments. Fourth, in place of the League of Nations, a global international organisation appeared with real resources and much more effective instruments. The UN sought to create on the basis of new principles (human rights, self-determination, sovereign equality of states) a powerful and effective international legal system. In the documents adopted by the UN, the idea of self-determination received new support, but also aroused bitter disputes. However, the USSR, with the support of the socialist countries and the newly independent states of Asia, campaigned for the establishment of practically unlimited right to self-determination of colonial and dependant countries and peoples.

At the Tenth Session of the UNGA in 1955, the opponents of including the right to self-determination into the Covenants argued that the UN Charter refers only to a 'principle' and not a 'right' of peoples to self-determination, and that in various instruments the principle is interpreted in different ways. To the extent that the right to self-determination is a collective right, then it was inconsistent to include it in a document setting out the rights of individuals. Supporters, however, responded that despite the fact that the right to self-determination is collective, it affects each person, and that to remove it would be the precondition for limiting human rights. Furthermore, a state accepting the UN Charter and recognising it, must respect the 'principle of self-determination' and the 'right' flowing from it. The latter point of view triumphed, and the new 'right' found its way into the common Article 1 of the International Covenants on Civil and Political Rights, and Social, Economic and Cultural Rights, respectively.[118]

---

[117] D. Grushkin, *Pravo Narodov na Samoopredeleniye: Istoriya Razvitiya i Voploshcheniye Ideyi* ('Right of Peoples to Self-Determination: History of the Development and Realisation of the Idea'), in A. Ossipov (ed.), *Pravo Narodov na Samoopredeleniye: Ideya i Voploshcheniye (Right of Peoples to Self-Determination: Idea and Realisation)* (Moscow: Zvenya, 1997), p. 10.

[118] Grushkin, 'Right of Peoples to Self-Determination', p. 12.

9.2. The right to self-determination in international law

Heather Wilson reminds us[119] that the admission of seventeen newly independent states at the opening of the Fifteenth Session of the General Assembly had a decisive effect on the UN. On 23 September 1960, the Soviet Union, grasping the opportunity presented by this dramatic development, requested the addition of a 'declaration on the granting of independence to colonial peoples and countries and peoples' to the agenda.[120] This is a truly climactic moment in the development of contemporary international law.

It was the USSR which submitted to the Fifteenth Session of the UN General Assembly the draft of the historic Resolution 1514 (XV) of 14 December 1960, the 'Declaration on the granting of independence to colonial countries and peoples'. This historic resolution aroused a whole wave of reactions and protests, but was, nonetheless, adopted. This document noted the connection between the right of peoples to self-determination and individual freedoms. Following on the heels of Resolution 1514 (XV) came a whole series of documents of a similar type: Resolution 1803 (XVII) of 14 December 1962 on 'Inalienable sovereignty in relation to natural resources'; Resolution 2105 (XX) of 20 December 1965 'On the realisation of the Declaration on the granting of independence to colonial countries and peoples' – the General Assembly recognised the legitimacy of the struggle of colonial peoples against colonial domination in the exercise of their right to self determination and independence, and it invited all states to provide material and moral support to national liberation movements in colonial territories.

In the 1966 Covenants on human rights, which to begin with were developed as a single document, it was decided that the provision on self-determination be included on the basis that:

(a) it 'is the source or essential foundation for other human rights, since there cannot be authentic realisation of individual rights without realisation of the right to self-determination';
(b) in drafting the Covenants the realisation and protection of the principles and goals of the UN Charter must be taken into account, including the principles of equal rights and self-determination of peoples;

---

[119] H. Wilson, *International Law and the Use of Force by National Liberation Movements* (Oxford: Clarendon Press, 1988) pp. 67–8.
[120] UN Doc A/4501, 23 September 1960.

(c) a series of provisions of the Universal Declaration of Human Rights are directly connected to the right to self-determination;
(d) if the right was not included in the Covenants, they would be incomplete and ineffective.[121]

Writing in 1970, Tunkin also pointed out that if in 1919 as many as 64 per cent of the population of the planet lived in colonies and semi-colonies, then at the start of 1969 only 1 per cent of humanity remained in colonies. It was on this basis that both the International Covenants have a common Article 1, on the right in international law of peoples to self-determination. This was a remarkable achievement by the USSR and its allies in the de-colonised world.[122]

9.3. The national liberation movements

The success of the USSR and its allies in the 1960s had momentous consequences for the legal and political process of decolonisation. Later resolutions of the UNGA ensured that the so-called 'national liberation movements'[123] were recognised as the 'sole legitimate representatives' of the relevant peoples. In other words, ex-territorial social and political organisations were in fact made equal to sovereign subjects of international law. Examples were the Palestine Liberation Organisation (PLO), the South West African Peoples Organisation (SWAPO), the African National Congress (ANC) and the Pan African Congress (PAC). In 1973 the UN declared that it recognised SWAPO as the 'sole authentic representative of the people of Namibia'. And in 1974 the PLO was recognised by the majority of member states of the UN as the lawful representative of the Palestinians, with corresponding status at the UN.

There are writers such as Christopher Quaye, who ignore the Soviet role in promoting the legal right to self-determination or supporting the national liberation movements.[124] However, Galia Golan, although seemingly unaware of the international law dimension, wrote in the context of

---

[121] Grushkin, 'Right of Peoples to Self-Determination', p. 12, citing A. Kristesky, *Pravo narodov na samoopredeleniye: istoricheskoye i sovremennoye razvitiye* (*Right of peoples to self-determination: historical and contemporary development*) (New York: UN ECOSOC, 1981).

[122] Tunkin, 'Lenin's Principles of Equal Rights', p. 70.

[123] See G. Golan, *The Soviet Union and National Liberation Movements in the Third World* (Boston: Unwin Hyman, 1988).

[124] C. Quaye, *Liberation Struggles in International Law* (Philadelphia: Temple University Press, 1991).

national liberation movements that: 'The term preferred by the Soviets [to "independence"] as an overall, all-inclusive type of objective was self-determination'.[125] Her book demonstrates the huge resources devoted by the USSR to support of all kinds for a very wide range of national liberation movements in the Third World. Tables she prepared list forty-three movements in twenty-six countries, with thirteen instruments of 'Soviet behaviour'.[126] Roger Kanet noted that 'Soviet trade with the developing nations increased more than eleven times from 1955 to 1970'. In 1970 it increased an additional 15.7 per cent.[127] Furthermore, Bhabani Sen Gupta pointed out that:

> in cultivating friendly, viable forces, the Soviet union has persistently tried to satisfy some of the *felt* needs of the power elites of Third World societies. In South Asia, they have come forward to provide aid for industrialisation programs in India, for which the Indians could not secure resources either domestically of from Western nations.[128]

I would contend, contrary to these authors, that it was not as a result of Soviet propaganda, but through the logic of the new international law, developed through the efforts of the USSR and its allies, that a people with the right to self-determination faced with aggressive attempts to deny that right enjoyed the right of self-defence under Article 51 of the Charter, and was in all respects considered a subject of international law. Thus, Portugal was at that time waging war against the peoples of Angola and Mozambique; those peoples were therefore victims of aggression and enjoyed the right of self-defence, and third party states had the right and duty to come to their assistance.[129] G. I. Tunkin, a year earlier, in a more formal article, defending the dubious concept of 'proletarian internationalism', also linked the 'struggle for international peace and security' with the 'struggle for the freedom and independence of peoples', with reference especially to Resolution 1514 (XV).[130]

---

[125] *Ibid.*, p. 136.   [126] *Ibid.*, pp. 262–7.
[127] R. Kanet, 'The Soviet Union and the Colonial Question 1917–1953', in R. Kanet (ed.), *The Soviet Union and the Developing Nations* (Baltimore: Johns Hopkins University Press, 1974), pp. 1–26 at p. 1.
[128] B. Gupta, 'The Soviet Union in South Asia', in R. Kanet (ed.), *The Soviet Union*, p. 123.
[129] Blishchenko, *Antisovietism and International Law*, pp. 76–7.
[130] G. Tunkin, *Borba dvukh kontseptsii v mezhdunarodnom prave* ('The Struggle of Two Conceptions in International Law') (1967) 11 *Sovetskoye Gosudarstvo i Pravo (Soviet State and Law)* 140 at 144–6.

10. Vietnam and the Czech Spring: further contradictions in self-determination

1968 was not only the year of the Soviet invasion of Czechoslovakia, but also a crucial moment in the US war in Vietnam. The invasion of Czechoslavkia took place against the background of the emergence of a new 'socialist international law', with a new approach to traditional concepts of sovereignty. G. I. Tunkin published a revised second edition of his textbook on international law.[131] According to him, it appeared to commentators in the United States that the new Soviet position could be dated back to Pashukanis's conclusion in the 1920s that the Soviet Union could and did utilise generally accepted norms of domestic and international law both in the administration of the state affairs and in conducting relations with foreign states. Through this practice, it gave the bourgeois norms a new socialist content.[132]

Dealing with the Czechoslovak events, Tunkin argued that these were a logical extension of the concept already well developed and applied in Hungary in 1956. This was the legal prevention of inroads by capitalist influences into a socialist state.[133] The international law framework is provided through an analysis of the concept of sovereignty. Tunkin noted that both general and socialist international law respected the concept of 'sovereignty', but concluded that respect is not the same thing in the two systems.[134] Socialist states would continue to insist on respect for the principle as developed in general international law when speaking of the relationships between themselves and capitalist states so as to prevent capitalist states from intervening in the internal affairs of Socialist states, but the concept of sovereignty had evolved within the conceptual framework of 'proletarian internationalism' as regards the mutual relationships of socialist states. His translator, William Butler, commented:

> The Soviet invasion of Czechoslovakia plainly was a difficult moment for his approach to international law, and his treatment of a 'socialist international law' impressed, rightly or wrongly, as something less than enthusiastic'.[135]

---

[131] Tunkin, *Theory of International Law*.
[132] J. Hazard, 'Renewed Emphasis Upon a Socialist International Law' (1971) 65 *American Journal of International Law* 142 at 143.
[133] Tunkin, *Theory of International Law*, p. 493, cited in Hazard, 'Renewed Emphasis', 145.
[134] Tunkin, *Theory of International Law*, p. 495.
[135] W. Butler, 'The Learned Writings of Professor G I Tunkin' (2002) 4 *Journal of the History of International Law* 394 at 394.

Tunkin's arguments should be contrasted with what, in the same year, the US scholar Alwyn Freeman was able to write:

> In the years following World War II increasing interest has been evidenced in the extent to which Soviet theory and practice may have influenced the development of the law of nations. This is to be expected in view of the prominence and power which the USSR has come to enjoy in the world community.[136]

Freeman denounced what he saw as a 'political dogma dressed in treacherous legal trappings', namely the official Soviet doctrine of 'peaceful coexistence'. He referred, as do so many American scholars of the period, as well as President Kennedy in his post-inauguration speeches, to an alleged address by Khrushchev to a Soviet Communist Party audience on 6 January 1961.[137] In one account:

> Soviet Premier Nikita Khrushchev delivered a speech behind closed doors in which he asserted that 'a mighty upsurge of anti-imperialist, national-liberation revolutions' was sweeping through the 'third world'. He went on to say that 'Communists fully and unreservedly support such just wars ... of national liberation'.[138]

The impact of Khrushchev's words was felt in the US itself and in its subsequent policy:

> The speech, published in the Soviet press just two days before the newly elected President John F. Kennedy took his oath of office, had a profound effect on the new administration which regarded it as a portent of wars to come. Kennedy and his advisers concluded that the Cold War was entering a new phase which would take place in the 'third world,' and would be characterized by guerrilla wars. Accordingly, they sought to improve the nation's ability to conduct counter insurgency warfare by dramatically expanding the Army's Special Forces or, 'green berets'. Before Kennedy's assassination in Dallas in 1963, he had dispatched over 16,000 of them to South Viet Nam in order to engage in just such a conflict. The war for the 'third world', and a new phase of the Cold War had gotten under way in earnest.[139]

---

[136] A. Freeman, 'Some Aspects of Soviet Influence on International Law' (1968) 62 *American Journal of International Law* 710 at 711.

[137] Quoted in the American Bar Association *Peaceful Coexistence: A Communist Blueprint for Victory* (Chicago, 1964), p. 14.

[138] See http://hnn.us/roundup/comments/19470.html.

[139] R. Speed, 'Review of Christopher Andrew and Vasili Mitrokhin', *The World Was Going Our Way: The KGB and the Battle for the Third World* (New York: Basic Books, 2005), posted

This address may well be apocryphal; it has proved impossible for me to track down a definite reference. But there is every reason to believe that its effect was as described.

It had its effect on the scholars too. For Freeman, while accommodations of mutually acceptable principles were possible in 1968, no progress in international law was possible until 'the Soviet Union is prepared to abjure its messianic and compulsive espousal of the doctrine of world revolution'.[140] Freeman was, of course, writing at the height of the Vietnam War: he expresses outrage that the public opinion barrage orchestrated by the USSR 'actually inhibited the United States from using tear gas where such use was in the interest of humane treatment of the civilian population'.[141]

The leading Soviet scholars were, in the end, obliged to abandon both positivism and the revolutionary content of self-determination. Writing in 1991, just before the dissolution of the USSR, and using the new language of 'perestroika', 'common human values' and 'common European home', Blishchenko also argued for:

> re-thinking the periodisation of the contemporary history of international law, and for reading its formation not in the October Revolution of 1917 but the French bourgeois revolution, for the first time promoting such generally recognised norms and principles of international law as the right of peoples to self-determination.[142]

However, the principle, then right, of self-determination played in my view a much more significant role, both in its practical effects in the international order, and as the 'obscene other' of Soviet positivism in international law.

This paradoxical, dialectical aspect of Soviet international law is entirely missed by Miéville. In this, it has to be said, he takes his place in a well-established tradition of the critique of 'socialist law'. It seems to me that a radical re-working of Pashukanis' contribution is required in order to account satisfactorily with the role of law in a world in which capitalism has – as it must, and as Marx predicted – spread to every corner. Turbulence has grown proportionately with interdependence. The Iraq adventure is

---

on Saturday, 17 December 2005 at George Mason University, History News Network: http://hnn.us/roundup/comments/19470.html.

[140] Freeman, 'Some Aspects of Soviet Influence', 722.   [141] *Ibid.*, p. 720.

[142] I. Blishchenko, '*Nekotoriye problemy sovetskoi nauki mezhdunarodonovo prava*' ('Some problems of the Soviet science of international law') (1991) 3 *Sovetskoye gosudarstvo i pravo* (Soviet State and Law) 134 at 135–6.

a compelling example not of the omnipotence of US power, but of its radical limitations, and the indomitable human spirit.

What Miéville quite rightly draws from Pashukanis is what he terms 'materialism', that is, the crucial importance of economic and political investigation and analysis for analysing developments in law, without forgetting law's real existence and relative autonomy as a constant but endlessly metamorphosing aspect of human existence – like religion, with which, as a human construct, it has so much in common.

The right of peoples to self-determination in international law achieved the status of a right in the context of de-colonisation and – thoroughly paradoxical and hypocritical – Soviet support both for the principle and for national liberation movements. It was law, indeed a pillar of the international rule of law.

11. Conclusion – another account

At this point I would like to propose an alternative reading to China Miéville's relentlessly pessimistic account of the post-World War II movements for de-colonisation, and 'peoples' rights', especially the right to self-determination and the right to development – the 'New International Economic Order' which he mentions in passing.

Here a thoroughly dialectical case can be made. There is no question that the movements for colonial freedom and de-colonisation were, as shown above, bitterly opposed by all the imperialist powers. In each case – France in Vietnam and Algeria, Britain in Kenya and Malaysia, the United States, to this day, in Puerto Rico, Portugal in Mozambique and Angola, the South African and Israeli experiences – the response of imperialism was ferocious and bloody. It is not enough to note that some of these became petty imperialisms in their own right, or in many ways simply served the interests of the former colonial power.

For me, it is vitally important to note that the demand for self-determination became a vitally important part of the external legitimation and ideological self-empowerment of these movements. In a paradoxical – and dialectical – fashion, the USSR, despite the profound deracination of its approach to international law, as exemplified by Vyshinsky[143] and Tunkin,[144] found itself obliged to give very considerable material support

---

[143] A. Vyshinsky, *The Law of the Soviet State*, H. W. Baab (trans.) (Westport, CT: Greenwood Press, 1979).
[144] Tunkin, *Theory of International Law*.

to self-determination struggles, despite the fact that this was not only materially costly but often contrary to its own geo-political self-interest. I mean dialectical in the following way: the content of the proposed norm often came into sharp conflict with its juridical form, and in the process the content was imbued with a new significance, in due course transforming the form as well.

In every case the process was not ideal – it was not the work of professors – but thoroughly material. This is what Patricia Williams in *The Alchemy of Race and Class* refers to as the subversion and appropriation of bourgeois legal norms – a process of alchemy.[145] Thus, the United Nations itself was transformed, not in effectiveness or ultimate independence, but in the unique possibility it gives for the less powerful states – and international civil society – to gather and speak.

[145] P. Williams, *The Alchemy of Race and Rights* (Cambridge, MA: Harvard University Press, 1991).

5

Marxism and international law: perspectives for the American (twenty-first) century?

ANTHONY CARTY

1. Introduction

Rumours of the death of socialism have been accompanied, oddly enough, by rumours of the disappearance of the United States. Post-structuralists tell us that we are all victims now but that, somehow, the multitude will arise against 'the powers'. Power enslaves us all in its impersonality, but resistance is everywhere. A primary focus of this study is Michael Hardt and Antonio Negri's *Empire*, a post-structuralist and, at the same time, post-Marxist critique of globalisation.[1] This paper will argue, against the book, that an updated theory of capitalist imperialism convincingly captures the contemporary international scene. The brutal power of the United States is everywhere. It is infinitely destructive of international law. Postmodernism is the exhausted moral spirit of the old Europeans, and the ghosts of Marxist interpretations of imperialism offer us the most convincing explanations as to why the violence of the United States increases by the year.

In this view, Marxism does not offer a theory of international law as such, but merely a contemporary, up-to-date explanation as to why it is being systematically, or structurally, violated. Marxism is presented as a vision, an analysis of a condition, essentially pessimistic in its tracing of an increasing intensification of exploitation on a global scale, violently promoted and protected by the United States and its allies, the so-called 'coalition'. So the contradictions of capitalism are reflected in the contradictions of international law.

However, *law as such* is not merely an ideological legitimisation of capitalism. It is also a positivist identification or equation of the idea of law with that of the state, in particular the United States. Law, as an instrument

[1] M. Hardt and A. Negri, *Empire* (Cambridge, MA: Harvard University Press, 2000).

of coercion by the state, as a concentration of capitalist power, facilitates the fragmentation and oppression of the world community. However, *international law as such*, in the Western tradition going back at least to Westphalia, is definitely not an ideological instrument in this programme. Its flagrant violation points the way back to an ordered humanity based on principles of the equality of states, and economic and social justice, reached through negotiation and dialogue, but having to rest on an equilibrium of force.

2. Post-structuralism and the end of Marxism

The greatest strength of post-structuralism is essentially emotional, atmospheric. It reflects the collapse of the revolutionary spirit of May 1968 in France, and the decay of Keynesian social democracy and of 'real existing socialism' in the former Soviet bloc. The onward march of monetarism and neoliberal economics makes it appear that every micro-decision is a profit-and-loss accounting exercise, whether in the running of a hospital, a university, a company or a nation-state. The latter is supposedly powerless to regulate a molecular capital monetary flow that appears to permeate every nook and cranny of social being.[2] Economic nationalism and social democracy all have to give way to the inexorable drive of market opportunity. The rhetoric is that the market-state provides the open forum for opportunity, in contrast to the nation-state that attempted to impose legal regulations on behalf of particular moral commitments.[3] The reality appears to be that the relentless drive of the all-consuming market sweeps away all social democratic attempts to direct investment or stem speculative currency transactions that play havoc with democratic controls of the economy. These arguments have to maintain that capital has no significant territorial location and no particular social concentration. Yet in *Empire* they become an irrational cult of pessimism and even nihilism in the face of the impossibility of social change for which the *call of the multitude* to arise is a hopeless remedy.

From within the international law confraternity perhaps the strongest and most authoritative recent espousal of these views comes from Martti Koskenniemi.[4] In rather a forceful tone, Koskenniemi announces:

[2] The term 'molecular' is taken from D. Harvey, *The New Imperialism* (Oxford: Oxford University Press, 2003), pp. 29–32.
[3] P. Bobbitt, *The Shield of Achilles. War and Peace and the Course of History* (New York: Anchor, 2002), p. xxxii.
[4] In his contribution to M. Byers and G. Nolte (eds.), *United States Hegemony and the Foundations of International Law* (Cambridge: Cambridge University Press, 2003), p. 98.

> The time of conspiracy theories is over. There is neither an overall 'plan' nor overarching wisdom located in the United States, or elsewhere . . . But instead of making room for only a few non-governmental decision-makers I am tempted by the larger vision of Hardt and Negri that the world is in transit towards what they, borrowing from Michel Foucault, call a biopolitical Empire, an Empire that has no capital, that is ruled from no one spot but that is equally binding on Washington and Karachi, and all of us. In this image there are no interests that arise from states – only interest positions that are dictated by an impersonal, globally effective economic and cultural logic. This is a structural Empire which is no less powerful as a result of not being ruled by formal decision-making from anywhere.

It is quite possible that international lawyers should simply absorb what I have already called the atmosphere of post-structuralist gloom. In *Cultural Pessimism, Narratives of Decline in the Post-modern World*, Oliver Bennett places economic developments since the early 1970s in a wider context of Western cultural decay.[5] He traces the immediate cause of contemporary economic anomie to the break from fixed to floating currency exchanges in 1973. This marked the end of the balance between organised labour, large corporate capital, and the nation-state.[6] The post-1973 shift to speculative financial markets ($1.5 trillion in 1997) means that these speculative markets amount to more than fifty times the level of daily world trade. The role of futures and derivatives – a global bond market of $200 billion a day compared with a $25 billion trade in equities – marks the independent force of global finance with its own laws. The same measureless expansion in the role of the trade of multinational enterprises (MNEs) comes to $16.3 trillion a year by 1998, growing at 8 per cent, with intra-MNE trade at about 50 per cent of all international trade. Transport costs are negligible in comparison to savings in raw materials and labour costs, brought about by mobility.[7]

What is crucial is the socio-political impact of these developments. The commitments of shareholders to companies can be cut by a telephone call, leading to slash-and-burn restructuring strategies. Factor-price equalisation means that workers' salaries can be kept at a lowest global common denominator, and for 70 per cent of US employees salaries are stagnant or declining. It is impossible to tax corporate profits that can so easily move to cheaper locations. As a percentage of US revenue they are down from 39 per cent in 1939 to 12 per cent in the 1990s, meaning huge public borrowing commitments and budget deficits. The greater inequality of the

---

[5] O. Bennett, *Cultural Pessimism, Narratives of Decline in the Post-Modern World* (New York: Columbia University Press, 2001).
[6] *Ibid.*, p. 146.   [7] *Ibid.*, pp. 153–4.

new capitalism means a propensity to uncontrollable structural change, merging, downsizing, with a consequent breakdown of all connective ties of family, friendships, and communities. This is the economic background to crime, divorce, and other social breakdown – an untrammelled individualism in transactional societies – where long-term co-operative relationships are replaced by short-term market transactions governed by expediency and self-interest. These market values spread into medicine, education, and so on, and signify the end of common interest.[8] Some predict an imminent disintegration of the global capitalist system, with a new capitalism locked into a negative dialectic with tribalist identity politics, where a mounting scarcity of resources and conflicts of interests are matched by a decreasing capability for co-operation.[9]

Bennett places these economic developments alongside developments in politics, sciences and the arts, pointing to a general culture indicating marks of clinical depression. Global capitalism leads individuals into feeling trapped, with no control over their lives. Rampant individualism is accentuated by maladaptive social comparisons, pressurising with overwhelming idealised standards, in an environment of unprecedented levels of competitive assessment in education and employment – a modern plague of the law of self-esteem. This is all within a framework of consumerism focused on increased personal insufficiency – which operates with an increased differentiation of products whose built-in deterioration engenders perpetual dissatisfaction in the consumer.[10]

A political development to parallel the economic ones described above has been the nuclear stand-off of the Cold War. The threat of nuclear extinction has caused a moral sickness or nausea, necessitating a dissociation from feeling in order to be able to live in a society threatened by annihilation. The widespread numbing of a moral sense encourages a Dionysian immersion in sensation, leading to ever-increasing levels of schizophrenia and anomie. Chaos paradigms of world society multiply, as there is breakdown of the governing authority of states, and a transfer of power to sectarian groupings, criminal organisations, and private security agencies. The most obvious source of immediate political danger comes from the growing sectors of Third-World societies dropping out of the world economy, providing a source of increasing resentment which leads easily to terrorism, given the access to arms, explosives, and other means of aggression.[11]

---

[8] *Ibid.*, pp. 160–1.   [9] *Ibid.*, pp. 170–2.   [10] *Ibid.*, pp. 162, 190.   [11] *Ibid.*, pp. 61–5.

The prevalence of terrorism, for Bennett, is best understood in the wider climate of total political disintegration, marked by epidemics of torture, genocide and politicide (government-sponsored murder), which McBride, speaking for Amnesty International in the 1960s, described as marking a massive breakdown of public morality and of civilization itself.By the 1980s, over a third of the world's governments used torture, and Amnesty was able to note that public campaigning made no difference. There was no public outrage. The figures for genocides and politicides range to 9 million and 20 million respectively. The crucial dimension is 'comparison fatigue' and the failure of any 'political' process of response.[12]

The criticism that Marxists make of post-structuralist elaborations of this picture is the depoliticising impact they provide. They offer an alternative ideology that does lead to the multiple resistances of which Koskenniemi speaks, but they add significantly to the realistic, empirical picture that Bennett has presented. Foucault's anti-Marxist, decentralised contestation of power resists what it sees as any attempt to replace one set of social relations with another – which would only be a new apparatus of power-knowledge. Rather than being unitary, power is a multiplicity of relations infiltrating the whole of the social body, with no causal priority to the economic. This process does not simply repress and circumscribe people, but constitutes them. Power evokes resistance, albeit as fragmentary and decentralised as the power relations it contests.[13]

The constitutive character of knowledge has been identified as a key epistemological foundation of cultural pessimism. Bennett points to the argument that knowledge as a way of life is impossible – either we are on the outside – in which case its essence eludes us – or we are on the inside and too close.[14] For Foucault also, power is always already there – one is never outside or on the margins. Resistance is possible, but it is nothing more than the oppositional other of the prevailing apparatus of power – knowledge, minor, local knowledges in opposition to the scientific hierarchisation of knowledges. This can appear as a theoretical foundation for pluralism – opposition to a so-called will to totalise that is a refusal to accept the possibility of difference and discontinuity. Instead, it should be recognised that there are irreducibly different perspectives, each in its way critical of existing social reality. This approach reflects the rise of a medley

---

[12] *Ibid.*, pp. 65–75.
[13] A. Callinicos, *Against Postmodernism* (Cambridge: Polity Press, 1989), p. 82.
[14] Bennett, *Cultural Pessimism*, p. 16.

of social movements – feminists, ecologists, black nationalists, and so on. They all insist on change without a totality, piecemeal. Yet the Foucault perspective, in a Marxist view, is itself a total vision that evacuates any political content from the concept of resistance, objecting to any political action except waging war on the totality.[15]

These ideas are reproduced in Empire, and the argument here will be that the ideas do not, in spite of the metaphysical halo of postmodernism, become good political–economic theory or empirical analysis. The rhetorical, virtually magical style of this work makes it difficult to engage with its arguments. Its mystical adulation of speculative currency flows and MNEs is irrepressible. For instance, the following is typical of the authors' style: '[t]he huge transnational corporations construct the fundamental connective fabric of the biopolitical world in certain important respects', and so on. Now they (the MNEs, not the authors!) 'directly structure and articulate territories and populations', and so on.[16] In the same nonsensical style they pronounce that the supposedly complex apparatus that selects investments and directs financial and monetary manoeuvres determines 'the new biopolitical structuring of the world'. They tell us that '[t]here is nothing, no "naked life", no external standpoint, that can be posed outside this field permeated by money; nothing escapes money'. The authors stand in hopeless awe of what they call the great industrial and financial powers which produce not just commodities, but subjectivities, that is – wait for it – 'agentic subjectivities within the biopolitical context: they produce needs, social relations, bodies, and minds – which is to say, they produce producers'.[17] In metaphysical terms what Hardt and Negri are doing is simply to deny any dialectic between structure and agency. Structure is everything. This makes it metaphysically impossible for them to conceive of anyone or any particular grouping having actions ascribed to them. So they tell us that '[t]he machine is self-validating, autopoetic – that is systemic. It constructs social fabrics that evacuate or render ineffective any contradiction; it creates situations which, before coercively neutralizing difference, seem to absorb it in an insignificant play of self-generating and self-regulating equilibria',[18] and so on.

There are 400 pages of this convoluted rhetoric. In the space of a chapter it is proposed to highlight the flourishes with which the authors dispose of the nation-state as a possible form of political defence of social democracy, and then to consider the economic power of the United States, the crisis

---

[15] Callinicos, *Against Postmodernism*, pp. 84–6.   [16] Hardt and Negri, *Empire*, p. 31.
[17] *Ibid.*, p. 32.   [18] *Ibid.*, p. 34.

of 1973, financial deregulation, and the relation of the United States to the MNEs.

Hardt and Negri object that the concepts of nation and national state faithfully reproduce the patrimonial state's totalising identity of both the territory and the population. Relying on sovereignty in the most rigid way, nation and national state make the relation of sovereignty into a thing, often by naturalising it, 'and thus weed out every residue of social antagonism. The nation is a kind of ideological shortcut that attempts to free the concepts of sovereignty and modernity from the antagonism and crisis which define them',[19] and so on. Apparently, Hardt and Negri know that Luxemburg's most powerful argument was 'that nation means dictatorship and is thus profoundly incompatible with any attempt at democratic organization'.[20]

The nation or the people it produces is contrasted with the multitude. The former is something that is one, having a will, and to whom one action may be attributed; it commands. While the multitude is:

> a multiplicity, a plane of singularities, an open set of relations, which is not homogeneous or identical with itself and bears an indistinct, inclusive relation to those outside of it . . . The construction of an absolute racial difference is the essential ground for the conception of a homogeneous national identity.[21]

Even the nation as the dominated power will, in turn, play an inverse role in relation to the interior they protect and suppress internal differences, and so on.[22]

In contrast, the United States has a constitution that favours the productive synergies of the multitude rather than trying to regulate them from above. This encourages the expansiveness of capitalism, which, supposedly, does not know an outside and an inside (i.e. it is all-absorbing). The US Constitution provides the opportunity for the decentred expansion of capital.[23] This apparently makes the United States especially suited as an instrument of the global events since the early 1970s. Hardt and Negri's account is rather neutral: 'Little by little, after the Vietnam War the new world market was organized: a world market that destroyed the fixed boundaries and hierarchical procedures of European imperialisms.' After American power had destroyed European colonialisms, 'the army of command wielded its power less through military hardware anymore

---

[19] Ibid., p. 95. [20] Ibid., p. 97. [21] Ibid., p. 103. [22] Ibid., p. 106.
[23] Ibid., pp. 161–7.

through the dollar ... an enormous step forward towards the construction of Empire'.[24]

The second mechanism for its construction was a process of decentring the sites and the flows of production. The transnationals transferred the technology necessary for constructing the new productive axis of the subordinate countries and mobilised the labour force and local productive capacities in these countries. Rather strangely, the authors conclude this part of their argument as follows:

> These multiple flows began to converge essentially towards the United States, which guaranteed and co-ordinated, when it did not directly command, the movement and operations of the transnationals. This was a decisive phase of Empire. Through the activities of the transnational corporations, the mediation and equalization of the rates of profit were unhinged from the power of the dominant nation-states'.[25]

So one might ask why Nixon had the wit to decouple the dollar from the gold standard and put a surcharge of 10 per cent on all imports from Europe to the United States, a transfer of the entire American debt to Europe? It 'thus reminded the Europeans of the initial terms of the agreement, of its [US] hegemony as the highest point of exploitation and capitalist command'.[26]

Yet nation-state resistance must always be rejected as an option, being a metaphysical impossibility. If it is argued that, through the imposition of imperialist domination, the underdevelopment of subordinated economies was created and then sustained by their continued integration into dominant capitalist economies, it is still an invalid conclusion that disarticulated developing economies should aim for relative isolation in order to achieve their own full articulation. Instead, the tendential realisation of the world market should destroy any notion that today a country or region could isolate itself or delink itself from the global networks of power. The interactions of the world market have resulted in a generalised disarticulation of all economies.[27]

The fetishisation of the US economic policy decisions of the 1970s follows. In italics the authors announce that the state has been defeated and the corporations rule the earth. Politics have disappeared and consensus is determined by economic factors such as the equilibria of trade balances and speculation on the value of currencies. The mechanisms of political

[24] *Ibid.*, p. 246.   [25] *Ibid.*, p. 247.   [26] *Ibid.*, p. 266.   [27] *Ibid.*, pp. 283–4.

mediation function through the categories of bureaucratic mediation and managerial sociology. This means that single government has been disarticulated and invested in a series of separate bodies, banks, international organisms of planning, and so on.[28] Notwithstanding these categorical statements, the authors still insist that at the top of the pyramid of world power are the United States and a group of nation-states which:

> control the primary global monetary instruments and thus have the ability to regulate international exchanges. Only the United States itself has the global use of force. On a second tier, under this umbrella come the transnationals that organize what the authors call the networks, already many times described.[29]

Never tired of contradicting themselves, the authors go on to tell us once again that it is foolish to harbour nostalgia for the nation-state, as either a cultural or an economic–juridical structure. Its decline can be traced through the evolution of a whole series of bodies, such as the General Agreement on Tariffs and Trade (GATT), its successor the World Trade Organization (WTO), the World Bank, and the International Monetary Fund (IMF). Even if the nation were to try to resist, it could only make things worse, since 'the nation carries with it a whole series of repressive structures and ideologies'.[30]

The resistance to a dichotomised focus on Third-World nation-state and imperialism is in favour of the postcolonial hero 'who continually transgresses territorial and racial boundaries, who destroys particularisms . . . liberation means the destruction of boundaries and patterns of forced migrations'. For the most wretched of the earth, 'its new nomad singularity is the most creative force . . . The power to circulate is a primary determination of the virtuality of the multitude, and circulating is the first ethical act of a counter-imperial ontology'.[31] So the authors are not denying the focused power of the United States and its imperial allies. Rather, they claim that this power is irrelevant to the future liberation of their post-modern hero. The means to get beyond the crisis of empire 'is the ontological displacement of the subject'.[32] They offer a kind of millennial spirituality. Calling on Saint Francis of Assisi, they say that, once again, we find ourselves in Francis's situation, 'posing against the misery of power the joy of being . . . biopower, communism, co-operation and

---

[28] *Ibid.*, p. 308.   [29] *Ibid.*, pp. 309–10.   [30] *Ibid.*, p. 336.   [31] *Ibid.*, p. 363.
[32] *Ibid.*, p. 384.

revolution remain together, in love, simplicity and also innocence... This is the irrepressible lightness and joy of being communist.'[33]

3. National sovereignty and economic reform

Poststructuralist pessimism poses the danger of political resignation and passivity, or simply total moral and intellectual confusion. What if it were the case that responses to imperialism, or what might condescendingly be described as the conspiracy of imperialism, were possible? Maybe there are perfectly obvious and feasible responses to the ills of the global economy that states cannot implement because these responses are resisted by other, more powerful states whose own interests argue against them. First, one needs simply to set out what reforms are required and then explain how they are being blocked. Then, hopefully, the mist of *Empire* will pass away.

Joseph Stiglitz, a former chief economist to the World Bank, and a chief economic adviser to US President Bill Clinton, considers that it is possible to adopt a non-mystical approach to international monetary problems, particularly as they affect developing countries.[34] He sets out two starting principles for his argument in favour of government intervention in the market. It should happen where there is imperfect information and where social cohesion is threatened. In this event, an economy will not function rationally. Starting from these principles, Stiglitz, argues quite simply that no case has been made for capital market liberalization.

In summary, for Stiglitz, monopoly concentration of capital in the interests of a small number of creditor states, particularly the United States, operating through a secretive, undemocratic IMF, serves acutely dysfunctionally the interests of most developing – that is, poor – countries. The creditor states resist change simply because it is in their financial interest to do so. Immediate prospects for the necessary political reform at the global level are not good.[35] The IMF rhetoric that liberalisation would enhance world economic stability by diversifying sources of funding is nonsense. Banks prefer to lend to those who do not need money. The limited competition in financial markets means that lower interest rates do not follow. The so-called freedom of capital flow is very bad for developing countries, because there is no control of the flow of hot money in and out of countries – short-term loans and contracts that are usually only bets

---

[33] *Ibid.*, p. 413.
[34] J. Stiglitz, *Globalization and its Discontents* (London: Allen Lane, 2002).
[35] *Ibid.*, pp. 223–8.

on exchange rate movements. It consists of money that cannot be used to build factories, for example, because companies do not make long-term investments with it. Such a financial climate can only destabilise long-term investments. There are bound to be adverse effects on growth in this environment, because countries have to set aside in their reserves amounts equal to their short-term foreign-denominated loans. Thus if country A borrows $100 million at 18 per cent, it should deposit the same in US Treasury bills at 4 per cent – losing 14 per cent.[36]

Where benefits are not paid for, or compensated, global collective action is necessary – that is, externalities to achieve global economic stability. The mindset of the IMF is that it will vote to suit creditors, and weighted voting cannot be changed with the United States using its effective veto. Yet contributions are actually coming from the developing countries, since the IMF is always repaid. Stiglitz is not sanguine that the necessary reforms to this institution will come. If there were to be open debate in the IMF, perhaps the interests of workers and small businesses would fare better against those of creditors. As things are, secrecy always allows special interests full sway and engenders suspicion.[37]

The institutional solutions are clear. Banking and tax restrictions must be imposed to ensure effective restrictions on short-term capital flows. There is needed a bankruptcy provision that expedites restructuring and gives greater presumption in favour of a continuation of existing management – thereby inducing more diligence in creditors. The IMF role in debt restructuring is fundamentally wrong. The IMF is a major creditor, representing major creditors, and a bankruptcy system can never allow creditors to make bankruptcy judgments.[38]

The rest of the institutional changes necessary are perfectly clear. They have nothing to do with bureaucracy and efficiency and everything to do with the equity which political choice must realise. The risk-based capital adequacy standards imposed on developing-country banks are inappropriate. The IMF must be required to expand substantially its Special Drawing Rights to finance global public goods to sustain the world economy. The risks of currency fluctuation must be absorbed by the creditors, and the concerns of workers and small businesses have to be balanced against those of creditors. There must be global taxation to finance development. It is quite simply because alternative policies affect different groups differently that it is the role of the political process – not international bureaucrats – to sort out the choices.[39]

[36] *Ibid.*, pp. 65–7. [37] *Ibid.*, pp. 223–8. [38] *Ibid.*, p. 237. [39] *Ibid.*, pp. 238–48.

So why has Stiglitz cause not to be sanguine about these obvious reforms to the world financial system?

4. Characteristics of late capitalism and the structure of international relations

There are several apparent contradictions in capitalism. Industrial or productive capitalism tends to become, gradually, financial capitalism. That is, such productive capitalism accumulates greater and greater profit, which it then has increasing difficulty in placing, since it is not necessary, or perhaps even possible, to reinvest the capital in productive processes to serve an ever-shrinking market. This is because of the exploitative conditions inherent in the ownership of the means of production under capitalism. Profit comes from the transfer of the surplus value of labour, necessitating a reduction in the scope and extent of consumer demand.[40] It then drifts into increasingly scarce – because demanded – assets, such as derivatives and property, which acquire speculative values.

The surplus capital is exported into production abroad that then becomes significantly competitive with the home producers, while still competing for the same limited consumer markets. In their classical study *Chaos and Governance in the Modern World System*, Arrighi and Silver set out the historical framework of modern capitalism in its development from industrial to finance capitalism.[41] Just as the hegemony of the Dutch Republic, and after it, the British Empire, exported capital to finance their eventual rivals, so also did the United States from 1945 until the 1970s. The crisis of US hegemony was marked with the abandonment of the dollar–gold standard and the floating of currencies in the early 1970s. Just as with the former hegemonies, the United States had built effective rivals out of western Europe, Japan, and, increasingly, the Pacific Rim. Because of the capitalism-induced concentration of markets, almost the only effective outlet for the increased productive capacity of these rivals is the United States itself. Equally, the consumer boom in the West, and particularly the

---

[40] E. Todd, *Weltmacht USA. Ein Nachruf* (München: Piper, 2003), p. 95, referring to the taboo nature of discussion of shrinking demand among economists considering globalisation. The only exception he can find is C. Johnson, *Ein Imperium verfällt Wann endet das Amerikanische Jahrhundert?* (München: Karl Blessing Verlag, 2000), p. 252.

[41] G. Arrighi and B. J. Silver (eds.), *Chaos and Governance in the Modern World System* (St. Paul, MN: University of Minnesota Press, 1999), generally, and esp. ch. 1, 'Geopolitics and High Finance', pp. 37–96.

United States, is credit-led, marked by the capacity of oligarchies of the United States and its 'coalition' to corner surplus liquidity.[42]

So international economic relations are increasingly marked by a dependency of the greatest consumer of world manufactures and natural resources, the United States, on the producers, Western Europe, Japan and the Pacific Rim, through the medium of increasing United States debt. An advantage that the United States has had from the period following 1945, when it dominated world production and trade, is the dollar. By fixing the value of its own currency as the world currency, it can pay its debts by printing money.[43] This is where the Stiglitz critique can become focused. The absence of world monetary reform has nothing to do with the 'money, money everywhere' rhetoric of Hardt and Negri. It has everything to do with the usefulness of the fiscal and monetary control of one world currency by a single power.

However, the full context of the usefulness of this power can only be understood if another aspect of the concentration of wealth and avoidance of income redistribution is stressed. The way out of surplus production for the United States, since the 1930s, has been the war economy, military production financed by the state, first through domestic income but eventually through the control of world liquidity.[44] That is, the United States found its way out of the Great Depression by adopting the 'warfare–welfare' economy of armaments, which, after the defeat of Germany and Japan, retained its impetus through the Czech crisis (the Prague communist coup of February–March 1948) and the Korean War.

Since then, the United States has remained primarily a war economy, driven by the need to confront external danger at a global level. This feeds effectively on the paranoid style that is fundamental to US foreign policy. David Harvey explains that the internal configurations of power that were able to resist Roosevelt's modest attempts through the New Deal to rescue the economy from its contradictions through redistribution of wealth, meant instead the paranoid style of politics. The difficulty of achieving internal cohesion in an ethnically mixed society characterised by intense individualism and class division made for the construction of

---

[42] Todd, *Weltmacht USA*, pp. 32–6, identifies this feature of advanced capitalism as affecting equally all the so-called Western democracies, and France and Britain, in particular, are governed by remote oligarchies that preside over increasingly polarised societies.

[43] The least disputable aspect of this argument: see Arrighi and Silver (eds.), *Chaos and Governance*, p. 284; Harvey, *The New Imperialism*, pp. 128–9; Todd, *Weltmacht USA*, pp. 117–19.

[44] Arrighi and Silver (eds.), *Chaos and Governance*, pp. 137, 147.

American politics around the fear of some 'other' (such as Bolshevism, socialism, anarchism).[45] This aggressive policy extends to an unequal military alliance system which ensures transfers of profit back to the United States through compulsory purchases of US armaments, an effective export of the 'warfare–welfare' economy.[46]

It is widely recognised that these economic contradictions accentuate further political contradictions. First, there is the changing character of US military dominance at the global level. This dates from 1945 and the US reconstruction of Germany and Japan as semi-sovereign states, as protectorates. Under a US military umbrella, they were free to redevelop their own industrial potential. By the time of the Korean War, the United States had ringed the Soviets and Chinese with an unprecedented number of military bases, which meant that not merely were there only two superpowers, there were, in fact, in the classical (Westphalia) international law sense of the term, only two (maybe three) sovereign states in the world, i.e. states with the power to declare and wage war. Turkey, Israel, Japan, Germany, the United Kingdom, Italy and many other states were no longer autonomous, even legally.

The major distinction of the argument of Arrighi and Silver is to place in historical context the limitations of the Westphalia system of international law, based on the sovereign equality of states. This was reflected in the original Dutch system of hegemony which prevailed from 1648 until the Napoleonic Wars. When British hegemony replaced the Dutch in the nineteenth century, other states enjoyed only a nominal independence at a time when British industrial and naval supremacy guaranteed a global Pax Britannica. Britain called into independence the Latin American states, but they remained under British economic tutelage until 1914. With the coming of US hegemony after 1945, even the semblance or fiction of the Westphalia system disappeared. However, since the 1970s there has been a radical bifurcation of military and financial global power. This was most remarkable in the 1980s, when the Reagan military build-up was financed through manipulation of interest rates for the dollar to suck world liquidity into the United States.[47]

The difficulty with overwhelming US global military dominance at present rests in the transformation of its capital base. As long as military production was financed from within the United States, the latter saw no security threat to itself. Now that the finance to support these

---

[45] Harvey, *The New Imperialism*, pp. 48–9.   [46] Todd, *Weltmacht USA*, pp. 115–16.
[47] Arrighi and Silver (eds.), *Chaos and Governance*, pp. 88–96, 284.

military structures has started to come from outside, the picture becomes more uncertain. US military power is accompanied by increased indebtedness of the American state to foreign capital seeking profit within the United States, either on the stock exchange or in government securities. This began in the 1970s, but it became acute in the course of the 1990s. These concrete developments are central to the whole 'global financial expansion that in the 1980s and 1990s reflated the power of the US state and capital and correspondingly deflated the power of the movements that had precipitated the crisis of US hegemony'.[48] The United States has become financially dependent on its industrial protectorates, Germany and Japan, as well as on Arab oil states and Chinese diaspora interests (Singapore, Hong Kong and Taiwan). These entities may not be hostile to the United States, but they are not necessarily committed to US political–military policies. At the same time, they do have the economic power to limit US action, even if self-destructively. Besides, even now, the United States does not have the military and political resources to constrain positively the direction of these states and city-states. This creates uncertainty in the United States about how to behave towards its erstwhile protectorate-allies.[49] Todd sees here a fundamental weakness in the global order. The United States lays sole claim to military dominance at a global level, but it is, in fact, neither financially nor militarily capable of ensuring the monopoly of the use of force which has to be, since Max Weber, the characteristic of legality in modernity.[50]

Another political contradiction of late capitalism concerns the relations between the United States, its 'coalition' and the so-called developing world. Again, Arrighi and Silver have challenging insights into a true history of international law. These are completed by Harvey, with his theory of accumulation through dispossession. Capitalism has always been global, and has always involved a huge transfer of value from the developing to the developed world. Dutch wealth was based on the plunder of Spanish Indies' gold and silver bullion. The exploitation from the eighteenth century of the Empire in India was utterly crucial to Britain's world hegemony. British power was further enhanced through the humiliation of China in the nineteenth-century Opium Wars that allowed the full realisation of India's potential.[51]

---

[48] *Ibid.*, p. 284.
[49] An identical argument by Todd, *Weltmacht USA*, pp. 110–11, who points to the particular role of Germany and Japan as subordinate powers, suffering huge military bases which they finance indirectly.
[50] *Ibid.*, p. 119.   [51] Arrighi and Silver (eds.), *Chaos and Governance*, pp. 219–46.

The central thesis has to be that the so-called global order has always been and never ceased to be based on plunder. As Harvey puts it, the market-state will never produce a harmonious state in which everyone is better off. It will produce ever greater levels of social inequality. He argues that Marxism must not:

> regulate accumulation based upon predation, fraud and violence to an 'original stage' that is no longer considered relevant... A general re-evaluation of the continuous role and persistence of the predatory practices of 'primitive' or 'original' accumulation within the long historical geography of capital accumulation is, therefore, very much in order.[52]

There is no longer even the pretence of a global project to integrate the formerly colonial world into a common world order. In the 1950s to 1970s there had been a project of development, Truman's 'Fair Deal', although there was no real transfer of resources to the developing countries. It appeared as if there were a US and even a European postcolonial alternative to the subordinated and openly exploitative treatment of the non-Western world during the previous four centuries. Agriculture should have been the basis of the transfer of resources to a growing industrial base within developing countries, encouraging the strengthening of nation-state based economies. This process was to be supported by foreign investment and soft development finance, through the World Bank and the IMF, which allowed a place for monetary policy to reduce unemployment and inflationary pressure. Nonetheless, there was no Western acceptance of cross-society political alliances within developing countries. These were seen as 'extremist' and destabilising in the context of the Cold War. They could only survive with Soviet support. They were caught up in the ideological conflict of the Cold War and subjected to periodic Western military interventions, such as in Guatemala, the Dominican Republic, Chile, Vietnam, Angola and many other instances. Consequently, there were the severest international political constraints standing in the way of assuring the widening of the purchasing power and consumer demand of non-Western societies.[53] Even the neo-Keynesian development project was abandoned in the 1980s and replaced by a once again openly predatory transfer of capital resources from the developing countries to the West. This has covered suppression of natural resource prices, protection and subsidisation of the exports of Western agriculture, and simply

---

[52] Harvey, *The New Imperialism*, p. 144.
[53] Arrighi and Silver (eds.), *Chaos and Governance*, pp. 205–11.

the buying up and destruction of local industrial capacity, in the context of devaluation of assets and debt rescheduling. Market and opportunity mean simply removing any redistributive element from politics. Such redistributive politics are branded as 'extremist' or 'illusory'.

The crucial weapon or instrument in the implementation of these policies has been the United States' control of the world currency, the dollar. Once again, it is a direct link between the political impossibility of monetary reform and the continued pillage of the third world – vindicating Stiglitz's sceptical prognosis. As Will Hutton graphically explains, it was raw power that enabled the United States to insist on the dollar as the international unit of account in 1944.[54] However, at the time government policy was still Keynesian, with the aim of achieving income equality, employment and economic stability. There was to be no devaluation of the dollar against gold, with full convertibility. Yet, in the early 1970s, the United States imposed a world financial system in which the dollar would be the number one currency against which the others would float, but it accepted no obligations in managing its own currency. While the dollar fell, it had no rival currency and so the United States was able to appropriate 80 per cent of the industrialised West's current surplus for its own strategic and military purposes. Without interest rate ceilings or reserve requirements, US banks lending out of London could come to dominate global banking.

The creation of a new world currency, managed by a world central bank – a currency that Stiglitz suggested might be made out of expanded Special Drawing Rights managed by an IMF whose voting system was reformed – was out of the question for simple reasons of national interest. US President Reagan abandoned tax on dividends paid to foreign holders of US financial assets. By the end of the 1980s, most countries had been forced to remove outward capital controls, and by 1999 virtually 80 per cent of the world's current-account surplus had been won for the United States. The structures for US deficit financing of its consumer boom and armaments programme were in place. These developments 'have been the results of a series of consistent policy choices over thirty years reflecting essential US reflex dispositions towards unilateralism'.[55]

Such a stranglehold on credit has offered huge possibilities of enrichment. The increase in interest rates for the dollar in the 1980s not only

---

[54] W. Hutton, *The World We Are In* (London: Little, Brown, 2001), pp. 234–9.
[55] Ibid., pp. 240–2, esp. p. 242. Also Harvey, *The New Imperialism*, pp. 127–32, 'The Powers of Mediating Institutions'.

ensured the inflow of capital to finance the arms race, it forced most Latin American economies, with huge dollar debts, into recession, into devaluation of their currencies and into debt–equity swaps that facilitated a general US buy-up of productive assets.[56] The same pattern was repeated with the Asian financial crisis of 1997, when the United States picked up large sectors of South Korean industry at knock-down prices, so that US dollar loans could be repaid. The dollar is used for 77 per cent of international loans and 83 per cent of foreign exchange transactions – as much as in 1945. Hutton warns that this has not been irrational economic dogma: 'It was the dogma of the expanding superstate. The international financial system has been shaped to extend US financial and political power, not to promote the world public good.'[57] Hutton succinctly describes the global political deficit of the international financial system in social democratic terms. There is no equality of opportunity, nor an equitable sharing of risk. Nor is there a social contract for the redistribution of income, the investment in social, physical, and human capital.[58]

Harvey resorts to more familiar Marxist language. He insists that the fundamental drive to accumulation by dispossession is as old as capitalist imperialism itself. The crisis could not be happening 'if there had not emerged chronic problems of over-accumulation of capital through expanded reproduction coupled with a political refusal to attempt any solution to these problems by internal reform'.[59] He describes the opportunities open to those who can manipulate a monopoly of credit mechanisms in traditional Marxist terms. Monopoly control of credit systems allows unlimited possibilities for operating a credit squeeze, forcing a drying-up of liquidity and forcing enterprises into bankruptcy.[60] Accumulation by dispossession allows the release of a set of assets (including labour power) at very low (and in some instances zero) cost. Over-accumulated capital can seize hold of such assets and immediately turn them to profitable use.[61] These 'money, money, everywhere' activities are as old as the hills:

> Some of the mechanisms of primitive accumulation that Marx emphasized have been fine-tuned to play an even stronger role now than in the past. The credit system and finance capital became, as Lenin, Hilferding, and Luxemburg all remarked at the beginning of the twentieth century, major levers of predation, fraud, and thievery. The strong wave of financialization

[56] Hutton, *The World We Are In*, pp. 243–5.
[57] *Ibid.*, pp. 247–51, esp. p. 251. Also Harvey, *The New Imperialism*, pp. 137–82, 'Accumulation by Dispossession'.
[58] Hutton, *The World We Are In*, p. 247.   [59] Harvey, *The New Imperialism*, p. 181.
[60] *Ibid.*, p. 155.   [61] *Ibid.*, p. 149.

that set in after 1973 has been every bit as spectacular for its speculative and predatory style. Stock promotions, ponzi schemes, structured asset destruction through inflation, asset-stripping, through mergers and acquisitions, and the promotion of levels of debt incumbency that reduce whole populations, even in the advanced capitalist countries, to debt peonage, to say nothing of corporate fraud and dispossession of assets (the raiding of pension funds and their decimation by stock and corporate collapses) by credit and stock manipulations – all of these are central features of what contemporary capitalism is about. The collapse of Enron dispossessed many of their livelihoods and their pension rights. But above all we have to look at the speculative raiding carried out by hedge funds and other major institutions of finance capital as the cutting edge of accumulation by dispossession in recent times.[62]

5. The shaping of international law agendas

Law may refer to the command enforced by a sovereign state, the positivist's equation of law with the state. The word 'law' in 'international law' may refer more generally to the legal relations among equal and independent states according to the Westphalia system, in existence since 1648. Marxism can easily identify the first sense of 'law' as an instrument of 'the capitalists' who control the state. This is a very useful shorthand for the assumption of a rule-of-thumb political sociology that a state bureaucratic apparatus is effectively controlled by a clique or oligarchy in its own interests. The difficulty is how to understand the relations between a dominant capitalist state and a whole range of other states in the international system. Concretely, this means asking how the United States relates to the other major Western powers, including Japan and, then, to what are loosely called the developing, or simply significantly poorer countries, including China, India, Brazil and innumerable other smaller countries. This chapter has relied on an updated classical Marxist analysis of contemporary capitalist imperialism that insists there is nothing new in the name of the so-called 'new imperialism'. Now it will be asked whether international law can offer any autonomous prescriptions in response by delving also among the first Marxist theories of imperialism and the nation,[63] while considering specifically the quality and possibilities of US relations with other powers.

---

[62] *Ibid.*, p. 147.
[63] V. Kubalkova and A. Cruickshank, *Marxism and International Relations* (Oxford: Oxford University Press, 1989). One could give weight to Soviet or Chinese doctrines of

Arrighi and Silver consider most exhaustively the historical dimension of a series of capitalist hegemonies and identify the original structure of international law as attributable to the character of Dutch hegemony:

> When it was first established under Dutch hegemony, national sovereignty rested on a mutual recognition by European states of each other's juridical autonomy and territorial integrity (*legal* sovereignty), and on a balance of power among states that guaranteed their *factual* sovereignty against the attempts of any state to become so powerful as to dominate all the others.[64]

After 1945, the British fiction of a balance of power that could still assure a *factual* sovereign equality of states was discarded even as a fiction: 'As Anthony Giddens has pointed out, US influence on shaping the new global order both under Wilson and under Roosevelt "represented an attempted incorporation of US constitutional prescriptions globally rather than a continuation of the balance of power doctrine".'[65] In other words, while the symptoms of the present crisis in international law are clear to all, the nature of recent developments in US international law policy is seriously misunderstood. It is not now that the Westphalia model of international law is being challenged. This was buried, at the latest, with the onset of World War II, perhaps even with the Treaty of Versailles. The United States never in the twentieth century accepted that the constitution of a state was an internal matter. The export of its own constitutional model was the object of two world wars. The semi-sovereign German and Japanese protectorates were its models for the organisation of world society. There was no dissent about this from the West.

It is a mistake to claim that it is now, for instance, that the UN Charter is being ignored or the equality of states is being denied. There is not a present and unprecedented US overthrow of international norms. The US project of international society, at least since 1945 (and in terms of its war aims), was always quite different from classical international law. It was the export of its constitutional model of market democracy against the totalitarian socialism of the Soviet Union and China. By the early 1950s, it had locked the whole planet into a coalition to this end. The difference now is that the changing underlying economic structures of international

---

international law, or also the whole range of other post-1945 Marxist theories of international relations, but the turn of the millennium, remarkably, allows focus on issues in a manner similar to the immediate pre-1914 period, that is, when there is a crisis of hegemony, this time of the United States, while earlier of Britain.

[64] Arrighi and Silver (eds.), *Chaos and Governance*, p. 92 (emphasis in original).
[65] *Ibid.*, p. 93. See again, most extensively, Bobbitt, *The Shield of Achilles*.

society mean that the United States does not have the material resources to be assured of its ability to enforce its project against possible new foes, nor can it any longer rely on its economically resurgent erstwhile allies. This leads it to change from acting as a hegemonic power which continues to enjoy international legitimacy, to becoming a power which, clearly since its invasion of Iraq in spring 2003, tries to rely exclusively on its own political and military strength to force through its will.

The main preoccupation of the international law agenda of the United States, here acting alone except for UK support, has been to develop doctrines of pre-emptive attack, armed intervention, and the spreading of military bases, through agreement with host states and the global strengthening of military policing against terrorism. This agenda now dominates the international scene. There are US military protectorates in Afghanistan and Iraq. Others may be in the offing for North Korea, Iran and Syria. While there is less enthusiasm for intervention in Africa and Latin America, further protectorates, or very large measures of military assistance and cooperation are in place, or are likely at least, in Sierra Leone, Colombia, the Democratic Republic of the Congo and Liberia. The underlying principle of both US and UK policy is that such states are not sovereign and equal members of international society. Hence the United States undertakes international military actions, first, without troubling to find the consent of the UN and, second, without even looking to have the support of NATO. In the Federal Republic of Yugoslavia, Afghanistan and Iraq, the United States has waged wars which are all in contravention of the basic international law norms of the sovereign equality of states and of the elementary need for community authority to legitimate the exercise of force against individual members of the society of states.

The question is how this can be explained, and also whether any constructive response is possible. Writing in 1999, Arrighi and Silver do not consider that serious conflict between the United States, its erstwhile Western allies and the significant Pacific Rim states is inevitable, despite the bifurcation of military and financial global power, provided that there is not 'US resistance to the loss of power, and prestige (though not necessarily of wealth and welfare) that the recentering of the global economy on East Asia entails'.[66] Capitalism is a global phenomenon. Even China has long embarked on a process of primitive accumulation, which Harvey characterises as an internally imposed accumulation by

---

[66] Arrighi and Silver (eds.), *Chaos and Governance*, p. 270. They see a balance of power in East Asia as possible.

dispossession, comparable to the Tudor enclosures.[67] Todd also acknowledges that advanced capitalism affects social structures, democracy and the rule of law in all major Western societies, including France.[68] Probably, insofar as Hardt and Negri's work draws, eclectically of course, on Marxism, it also clearly fits into this picture.

An early Marxist theory of 'ultra-imperialism' at the beginning of the twentieth century proposed that a peaceful adjustment of the relations of production (including international relations) to the worldwide forces of production was possible. Karl Kautsky thought that this adjustment could be brought about by capitalism itself. Capitalism would go through an additional state, which would see an aggrandisement of the policy of cartels into a foreign policy:

> This phase of ultra- or super-imperialism involving the union of imperialists across the globe would bring to an end their struggles with one another. The notion, in other words, of a co-operative effort in the Grotian tradition enabling a joint exploitation of the world by internationally merged finance capital.[69]

However, writing at the end of 2002 and in late spring 2003, respectively, Todd and Harvey consider that present US foreign and, consequently, international law policy do indicate a very firm intention to resist any loss of power and prestige. The United States is evidently fully willing to accept open conflict with other powers. For both authors, the US actions are necessitated by the internal contradictions of its political–military and economic–social relations, above all, with its allies. Political relations with its allies have broken down because this is the wish of the United States. Political and military will have to be asserted to compensate for economic and social weakness within the United States. Economic structures shape the agenda of contemporary international law in the following respects. Most importantly, the United States realises that its economic pre-eminence in the global system is very seriously threatened in the medium term. Its economic dependence on its Western allies, particularly Japan and the European Union, means that it feels compelled to choose issues on which to exercise its political power in a primarily

---

[67] Harvey, *The New Imperialism*, pp. 153–4.
[68] Todd, *Weltmacht USA*, pp. 32–6.
[69] Kubalkova and Cruickshank, *Marxism and International Relations*, p. 52. This assumption underlies my own contribution to A. Qureshi (ed.), *Perspectives in International Economic Law* (The Hague: Kluwer Law International, 2002), 'The National as a Meta-Concept of International Economic Law', pp. 65–79.

coercive military dimension, in order to force an acknowledgement of its supremacy.[70]

This is where the exact nature of the evidence Todd and Harvey adduce to arraign the United States is interesting. Presumably, the post-structuralist view of the global penetration of 'capital discourse' means that it is impossible to speak of independent agency in international relations. In this sense, the United States does not exist as an entity, and, *ipso facto*, it can hardly have a plan of world domination. The United States is deconstructed as having no essence prior to international society. Intentionality is a mere effect of discourse and not a cause in its own right. Following Saussure's linguistic structuralism meaning stems from relations of difference between words rather than reference to the world, in this case the consciousness of individuals.[71] Todd's French discourse of critique of the United States is, perhaps, embedded in the French hostility to the United States which may be traceable back to Roosevelt's treatment of de Gaulle in North Africa in the winter of 1942–3. That opposition itself may be followed back into the mists of time. Wittgenstein has called 'mentalism' the belief that subjective mental states cause actions. Instead, we merely ascribe motives in terms of public criteria which make behaviour intelligible. Therefore, it is better for social scientists to eschew intentions as causes of actions and focus on the structures of shared knowledge which give them content.[72] This would place Todd firmly within a huge literary industry of French anti-Americanism.

Capitalism is a discourse that produces resistances, because it has to strive to both absorb and exclude its 'other', whatever is not capitalist. Harvey has no difficulty with using post-modern political theory to describe the workings of capitalism.[73] Capitalism can be said necessarily to create its own 'other'. It can make use of some non-capitalist formation or it can actively manufacture its 'other'. There is an organic relation between expanded reproduction and the often violent processes of dispossession that have shaped the historical geography of capitalism. This forms the heart of his central argument about accumulation by

---

[70] This is the clear overall argument of both their books.
[71] A. Wendt, *Social Theory of International Politics* (Cambridge: Cambridge University Press,1999), p. 178.
[72] *Ibid.*, p. 179.
[73] See, for instance, D. Harvey, *The Condition of Postmodernity* (Oxford: Blackwell, 1989), which explains the break from fixed to floating currencies as marking the end of the balance between organised labour, large corporate capital, and the nation-state, and which Bennett highlights as a watershed in the spread of modern cultural pessimism: *Cultural Pessimism*, p. 146.

dispossession.[74] However, Harvey objects to placing all struggles against dispossession 'under some homogenising banner like that of Hardt and Negri's "multitude" that will magically rise up to inherit the earth'.[75] Wendt makes a similar objection to post-structuralism or what he calls 'wholism' in social theory. He argues that no matter how much the meaning of an individual's thought is socially constituted, all that matters for explaining his behaviour is how matters seem *to him*. In any case, what is the mechanism by which culture moves a person's body, if not through the mind or the Self: 'A purely constitutive analysis of intentionality is inherently static, giving us no sense of how agents and structures interact through time.'[76] Individuals have minds by virtue of independent brains and exist partially by virtue of their own thoughts. These give the Self an 'auto-genetic' quality, and are the basis for what Mead calls the 'I', an agent's sense of itself as a distinct locus of thought, choice, and activity: 'Without this self-constituting substrate, culture would have no raw material to exert its constitutive effects upon, nor could agents resist those effects.'[77]

So the vital distinction that the historian has to struggle to make is between the following two styles of argument. Wittgensteinians say that, in the proverbial hypothetical court case, the jury can only judge the guilt of the defendant – having no direct access to his mind – by means of social rules of thumb to infer his motives from the situation (a history of conflict with the victim, something linking him to the crime scene, etc.). They go further and argue that the defendant's motives cannot be known apart from these rules of thumb and so there is no reason to treat the former as springs of action in the first place.[78] At the same time, many now distinguish between two kinds of mental content. 'Narrow' content refers to the meanings of actions in a person's head which motivate his actions, while 'broad' content refers to the shared meanings which make the actions intelligible to others.[79] While Wendt draws these distinctions from the philosophy of agency and structure, they are always perfectly familiar to historians. The difficulties of contemporary history are what face the polemics of Todd and Harvey. They have relatively little access to the primary archives, whether official or private, that would satisfy the most rigorous historian, but the value of knowledge is also relative to the circumstances in which it is constructed, whether individually or socially.

---

[74] Harvey, *The New Imperialism*, pp. 141–2.   [75] *Ibid.*, p. 169.
[76] Wendt, *Social Theory of International Politics*, pp. 180–1.   [77] *Ibid.*, pp. 181–2.
[78] *Ibid.*, p. 179.   [79] *Ibid.*, p. 181.

Todd's argument is, very much like Wittgensteinian public criteria, based on an analysis of the material situation of the United States and the material consequences of its actions. The United States is no longer necessary for the maintenance of 'freedom', democracy and the rule of law in the world, given the disappearance of the 'socialist world'. The country has, since the 1970s and especially since 1995–2000, seen its economic situation radically altered to its disadvantage – the world's largest debtor, and significantly less productive than its main trade rivals. The same United States embarks upon apparently ludicrous military adventures against extremely weak third-world countries and penetrates into the Central Asian landmass, under the pretext of pursuing a terrorism that it equates with the Arab–Muslim region, despite the limited pull of militant Islam outside Pakistan and Saudi Arabia. It acquires bases in several former Soviet Central Asian republics, Afghanistan and, eventually, Iraq (Todd is writing in December 2002), all through unilateral action, without consulting either NATO or the United Nations. A centrepiece of this policy is to block any settlement of the Palestinian–Israeli conflict and to keep the European Union marginal to a mediation of the conflict.

Europe, Japan, China and Russia have no immediate interest in quarrelling with one another and especially no economic interest in confronting the Arab and Muslim world. They have every assurance that energy will be supplied because the Arabs and Iran need to do so for their own development. At the same time, Israel's quarrel with the Palestinians is a serious source of conflict of interest for all of the United States' traditional allies. It could weaken or complicate their relations with the source of an essential energy supply. So the assertion of unqualified US solidarity with Israel fits together with a plan to maintain literally physical control of the oil resources of the Middle East. It enables the United States to view with equanimity the possible destabilisation of the source of its allies' oil supplies through a generalised Arab–Muslim hostility towards 'the West'.[80]

The kernel of Todd's structural argument is that the United States is behaving irrationally because both its internal and international situation have become unstable. It is fixated on the unilateral use of force to ensure control of territory and oil in the Middle East and Central Asia as a way of maintaining dominance over its erstwhile allies. In this context, the Westphalian and UN Charter rules of international law do not apply to the United States' relations with the Middle East and Central Asia.

[80] Todd, *Weltmacht USA*, pp. 36–8, 56–8, 146–54, 164–82.

Doctrines of pre-emptive strike against terrorist states, or humanitarian intervention against brutal dictatorships can be variously used, and are being used, to underpin a volatile Western–Middle East relationship. The balancing of Israeli and Palestinian rights to self-determination is not important compared to keeping the European Union marginal to the political relations of the Middle East.

Writing in spring 2003, Harvey is in possession of the fact that the war with Iraq is in full swing. He agrees with Todd that the starting point of US action is its increasingly serious economic weakness. His argument has a classical Marxist framework, considering the options between a Kautsky-style 'ultra-imperialism' of the Western powers and Lenin's scenario of a violent competition among the imperialist powers – meaning, effectively, all powers, including China.[81] He is also influenced by the tradition of geo-politics of the 1900s of Halford Mackinder that treats control of the Eurasian landmass as central to world domination. However, beyond that, Harvey relies primarily on an 'intentionalist' explanation of US policy. He refers to planning documents of US leaders, which are openly available, and also to the writings of influential opinion leaders within the United States. These are not the equivalent of open access to the minutes of meetings of key decision-makers, but they suppose that access to US elite intentions is possible. At the same time, these elites are, for the moment, able to direct the course of US power.[82]

Harvey considers that both intentions and actions, for example the defence strategy documents of 1991–2 and the language justifying the invasion of Iraq, show a clear opinion in favour of a military solution to the weakness of the United States. Alliances and traditional international law are to be discarded in favour of unilateral, also military, action in US interests. These actions are to demonstrate its absolute military and political global supremacy. Territorial and physical control of Middle East oil is sufficient for the United States to maintain its dominance for the near future.[83] As Harvey puts it:

> if it [the United States] can move on (as seems possible) from Iraq to Iran and consolidate its position in Turkey and Uzbekistan as a strategic presence in relation to Caspian basin oil reserves (which the Chinese are desperately trying to butt into), then the US, through firm control of the global oil

---

[81] Harvey, *The New Imperialism*, pp. 75, 209, and see also, more generally, Kubalkova and Cruickshank, *Marxism and International Relations*, pp. 52–3, that the development of capitalism is so uneven that conflict is inevitable.
[82] Harvey, *The New Imperialism*, pp. 18–25, 74–86, 183–212.   [83] *Ibid.*, p. 19.

spigot, might hope to keep effective control over the global economy and secure its own dominance for the next fifty years.[84]

All this dramatic confrontational strategy is understandable, given the immense danger that the present international economic situation poses for the United States. The constructive alternative would be for the United States to turn away from imperialism and engage in both a massive redistribution of wealth within its borders and a redistribution of capital flows into the production and renewal of physical and social infrastructures. This would mean an internal reorganisation of class power relations and transformation of social relations that the United States has refused to consider since the Civil War. More deficit financing, much higher taxation and strong state direction are what dominant class forces within the United States will not even consider.[85] At the same time the economic, particularly financial, threat from East Asia is huge. Arrighi and Silver think that the immediate major task for the United States is to accommodate itself to this constructively. Harvey thinks that, on balance, the United States is unlikely to take this course. The ferocity of the primitive capital accumulation that is taking place in China may well spark in China a rate of economic growth capable of absorbing much of the world's capital surplus. There may be revolution and political breakdown in China caused by the stress of present social change. However, if there is not:

> the drawing off of surplus capital into China will be calamitous for the US economy, which feeds off capital inflows to support its own unproductive consumption, both in the military and in the private sector . . . In such a situation, the US would be sorely tempted to use its power over oil to hold back China, sparking a geopolitical conflict at the very minimum in central Asia and perhaps spreading into a more global conflict.[86]

The Leninist scenario of violent competition among capitalist blocs is most likely. The more explicit the US project becomes the more it will almost certainly force an alliance between France, Germany, Russia and China, which more reflective US figures, such as Henry Kissinger, believe will not necessarily lose in a struggle with the United States.[87] Arguing from within social democratic parameters, Hutton and Todd hope that the European Union can balance the economic power of the United States more peacefully. The key instrument is the aggressive use of the euro as a political weapon, to enforce European social policies both within the

---

[84] Ibid., p. 78. [85] Ibid., pp. 75–6. [86] Ibid., pp. 208–9. [87] Ibid., p. 200.

European economic area and in international development aid policy.[88] However, Harvey insists that such a project cannot hope to be realistic unless it involves an explicit rejection of neo-liberal economic policy—which indeed both Todd and Hutton would also advocate. There must be a strong revival of sustained accumulation through expanded reproduction (read: curbing the speculative powers of finance capital, decentralising and controlling monopolies, and significantly redistributing wealth). Otherwise, this Kautsky-style benevolent 'New Deal' imperialism can only move deeper into the quagmire of a politics of accumulation by dispossession throughout the world in order to keep the motor of accumulation from stalling.[89]

Contemporary US policy, that for the moment enjoys UK support, appears nihilistic in relation to the existing Westphalian international legal order, making it a pure fiction. It appears at the same time, consciously but completely unrealistically, to be a project to restore the political control of large parts of the non-Western world that was temporarily relinquished in the 1950s and the 1960s. There is much argument that the granting of independence was premature and that it has to be undone because there are simply no adequate political institutions, namely state structures, in large parts of the globe.[90] Again, as with the present US treatment of its erstwhile allies, this apparently radical suspension of traditional Westphalian and UN Charter law in relation to large parts of the South has to be seen in its longer historical context. It is, in terms of timescale, merely a phase in the development of international law since the sixteenth century. Arrighi and Silver have most brilliantly captured this phase as one of a crisis of US capitalist hegemony. They give full place to changing developments in the history of international law since Dutch hegemony ushered in the Westphalia system. The League of Nations and the United Nations mark the transition from British to US hegemony. The latter's hegemony is now fundamentally in question. The US attempt to reverse the course of history, to reintroduce colonial-type international protectorates, is another aspect of the nihilism that will simply not face the responsibilities of global management in terms of necessary economic and social change.

---

[88] Todd, *Weltmacht USA*, pp. 211–38; Hutton, *The World We Are In*, pp. 400–11.
[89] Harvey, *The New Imperialism*, pp. 211–12.
[90] This is argued most forcefully by such British figures as R. Cooper ('The New Imperialism', *Observer*, 7 April 2002), an adviser to Tony Blair, and Niall Ferguson, a historian of the British empire and international economic and financial history.

Optimistic European voices argue that a reassertion of an economic balance of power between Europe, Russia, Japan, China and others (possibly eventually India and Brazil) and the United States make inevitable a return to the dialectics of dialogue in the resolution of international conflict. This supposes that the Americans adjust to a reduced but still significant role in the international economy. In relation to the South, this optimistic Europeanism argues that European, Japanese, and Chinese capitalism are more socially oriented than the predatory Anglo-American neo-liberal market economy states. Unlike the United States and the United Kingdom, they can negotiate compromise relations with different cultures, premised on a slow process of gradualist reform and on integration. Concretely, this means Europe absorbing Russia and the Middle East into its economic–social zone, in which a post-modern, agnostic absence of the military dimension to politics will prevail. Arguably, Japan and China can take the same lead in East Asia. In this picture, the United States goes off altogether into the wilderness from which it emerged at the beginning of the twentieth century. It is left with the North American Free Trade Agreement (NAFTA). Todd and Hutton, from England and France, place plenty of hope in developments in such directions. They can point to the failure of neo-liberalism to make a decisive breakthrough in France and Germany, not to mention reversals of economic strategy in Putin's Russia and, finally, the great enigma of China.

None of this optimism can be grounded in the rather more Leninist imperialist scenario outlined by Harvey. The concrete flaw in European optimism is that the United States is aware of its strategic precariousness and has already moved to anticipate it. It enjoys a political military precedence, if not dominance, which can impede any alternative global project. Japanese, other East Asian and European capital is locked into the radically skewed US capital market as part of capital's natural search for maximum profit. European and East Asian industrial production is equally locked in the embrace of this US market. The latter is not only skewed but also twisted, since an integral part of the consuming power of this market is the surplus capital of the exporters to the United States.

On the outside stands the economically marginal, disenfranchised world proletariat, threatening, or being seen to threaten, illegal immigration, international crime (especially people- and drug-trafficking), and, of course, terrorism. Marxism would surely require that this proletariat must become more radical as it becomes more economically marginal. The latter must happen because of the continuing transfer of capital resources from the South to the North, an uninterrupted process since the sixteenth century. The will and the means do not really exist in the West (Europe and Japan will not go along with the United States) to restore political control over the South. So the disorder it represents will gradually engulf the West. That is, unless a social democratic alternative – whether or not dubbed Kautsky-style 'ultraimperialism' – can support a true development of the same social democratic model, a substantive economic self-determination of peoples in the developing world.[91] However, Marxist analyses of the impact of the international political economy on the general structure of international law remain the most convincing for the present.

[91] As the author has already suggested, particularly in 'The National as a Meta-Concept of International Economic Law', and also in A. Carty, 'Liberal Rhetoric and the Democratization of the World Economy' (1988) 98 *Ethics* 742.

6

Toward a radical political economy critique of transnational economic law

A. CLAIRE CUTLER

[T]he tradition of all the dead generations weighs like a nightmare on the brain of the living. And just when they seem engaged in revolutionising themselves and things, in creating something that has never yet existed, precisely in such epochs of revolutionary crisis they anxiously conjure up the spirits of the past to their service and borrow from them names, battle-cries, and costumes in order to present the new scene of world history in this time-honoured disguise and this borrowed language.

Karl Marx[1]

[H]istory is an immanent necessity which finds its justification in the culture, the economic forms, and the ways of living of human society as determined by past developments.

Antonio Gramsci[2]

1. Introduction

This chapter argues that the contemplation of international law on the left in the context of international trade law necessarily implies engaging in a radical political economy critique of transnational economic law in the form of historical materialist analysis. There are two parts to this claim. The first part is that international trade law is best regarded as a form of transnational and not international economic law. The remit of the law of international trade is expanding to include economic relations that touch upon most every dimension of existence and which defy classification as domestic or international, private or public, and local or global. The

---

[1] *The Eighteenth Brumaire* of *Louis Bonaparte* (London: Lawrence and Wishart, 1984 [1869]), p. 10.
[2] P. Cavalcanti and P. Piccone (eds.), *History, Philosophy and Culture in the Young Gramsci* (St Louis: Telos Press, 1975), p. 56.

contemporary trade regime institutionalised in the World Trade Organization (WTO) governs matters that extend well beyond border controls to reach deeply inside the domestic jurisdiction of states. But the WTO is itself just one dimension of a broader transnational economic order that encompasses global and regional trade, investment, financial and monetary relations, as well as multiple systems of dispute resolution. Indeed, international trade law takes on a distinctive form and content under more general conditions of late capitalism and postmodernity. Late capitalism in law is reflected in the increasing recourse to law to facilitate the displacement of welfare states by competition states through liberalisation, deregulation and privatisation, in the intensification and expansion of legal disciplines facilitating transnational capital accumulation, and in the related tendency to flexible accumulation and the 'soft' re-regulation of labour relations, consumer protection, environmental practices and corporate ethics.[3] Late capitalism, in turn, gives rise to a specifically postmodern form of law.[4] Postmodernity in law reflects the global expansion and deepening of the logic of the market at the level of culture, collapsing distinctions between economy and culture and giving rise to legal pluralism and interlegality, as multiple legal orders cross-sect and overlap, simultaneously occupying the same space as they erase territorial borders by linking local and global political economies and societies in complex ways.[5]

---

[3] D. Harvey, *The Condition of Postmodernity: An Enquiry into the Origins of Cultural Change* (Cambridge, MA: Blackwell, 1990) and *The New Imperialism* (Oxford and New York: Oxford University Press, 2003). F. Jameson in *Postmodernism or the Cultural Logic of Late Capitalism* (Durham: Duke University Press, 1991), pp. xviii-xix notes that the term 'late capitalism' was originally used by the Frankfurt School to capture Foucault-like bureaucratic and administrative control and the interpenetration of government and big business. Today, it has taken on a specific content in the context of the emergence of transnational corporations: 'the new international division of labour, a vertiginous new dynamic in international banking and the stock exchanges (including the enormous Second and Third world debt), new forms of media interrelationship (very much including transportation systems such as containerisation), computers and automation, the flight of production to advanced Third World areas, along with all the more familiar social consequences, including the crisis of traditional labour, the emergence of yuppies and gentrification on a now-global scale.' This marks a 'vision of a world capitalist system fundamentally distinct from the older imperialism, which was little more than a rivalry between various colonial powers'.

[4] Jameson, *Postmodernism*, p. xxii notes that while the term 'postmodern' is 'not merely contested, it is also internally conflicted and contradictory', we 'cannot *not* use it' but must do so aware of these internal contradictions. 'The concept, if there is one, has to come at the end, and not at the beginning, of our discussions of it.'

[5] *Ibid.* And see B. de Sousa Santos, 'Law: A Map of Misreading. Toward a postmodern conception of law' (1987) 14 *Journal of Law and Society* 297.

Late capitalist and postmodern trade law today takes the form of a transnational regulatory order that is hegemonic in facilitating the transnational expansion of capitalism and privatised regimes of accumulation, which secure the interests of an increasingly transnational capitalist class.[6] Transnational law, as conceived by the classic definition of Philip Jessup, includes 'all law which regulates actions or events that transcend national frontiers. Both public and private international law are included, as are other rules which do not wholly fit into such standard categories.'[7]

Transnational economic law and the theories underpinning it are co-extensive with late capitalism. The law and capitalism are co-extensive in that postmodern subjectivity in international law, premised as it is on the deterritorialising tendencies of delocalised transactions and dispute settlement procedures, along with global networks of transnationally organised law firms, enables an expansion and deepening of the logic of capitalism, empowering a transnational elite, whilst simultaneously disabling and disempowering certain peoples and groups who depend upon their particularly situated places and spaces to resist.[8]

The second part of the claim is that historical materialism is the best method for analysing transnational economic law. Transnational economic law links local and global political economies and societies through increasingly dense and complex networks of overlapping and crosssecting global, regional and national regimes regulating, trade, investment, finance, dispute resolution and related social relations. The transnational economic order constitutionalises neoliberal economic discipline, fetishistic understandings and practices of law and private, exclusionary

---

[6] See A. C. Cutler, *Private Power and Global Authority: Transnational Merchant Law in the Global Political Economy* (Cambridge: Cambridge University Press, 2003); W. Robinson, *A Theory of Global Capitalism: Production, Class, and State in a Transnational World* (Baltimore, MD: Johns Hopkins University Press, 2004); K. van der Pijl, *Transnational Classes and International Relations* (London: Routledge, 1998); L. Sklair, *The Transnational Capitalist Class* (Oxford; Blackwell, 2001).

[7] P. C. Jessup, *Transnational Law* (New Haven: Yale University Press, 1956), p. 2. While this discussion adopts Jessup's expansive definition of transnational law, it does not embrace the faith that Judge Jessup held in liberal internationalism. See A. C. Cutler, 'Locating the "Transnational:" Boaventura de Sousa Santos and the New Legal Common Sense', presented at the University of Glasgow Faculty of Law Workshop on 'Law, Politics, and Power in the Global Age: The legal and social theory of Boaventura de Sousa Santos' (2006).

[8] A. C. Cutler, 'Transnational Law and Privatized Governance', in W. Coleman and L. Pauly (eds.), *Institutions, Governance, and Global Ordering* (Vancouver: University of British Columbia Press, forthcoming) and 'Critical Reflections on Westphalian Conceptions of International Law and Organization: A Crisis of Legitimacy', (2001) 27 *Review of International Studies* 133. And see S. Gill, *Power and Resistance in the New World Order* (Houndsmill: Palgrave Macmillan, 2003).

institutions that marginalise and alienate large populations of the world. It gives rise to a dialectic of affirmation and negation that works to legitimate the de facto legal subjectivity of some non-state entities, such as transnational corporations and powerful private business associations, whilst simultaneously marginalising whole populations and peoples, by denying international legal personality to other non-state entities, such as individuals and indigenous peoples. The transnational economic order is thus ripe for the development of a radical political economy critique in the nature of historical materialist analysis.

Historical materialism is here conceived of as a philosophy of praxis and as a method of critical analysis. Historical materialism conceptualises world order as an historical bloc comprised of material, ideological and institutional forces that embody both the traces of the past and seeds of the future.[9] As a form of critical theory, historical materialism is inherently and unavoidably transformative:

> [e]ntailing practices of critical scholarship, the traditions of historical materialism share a set of family resemblances: they aim at de-reifying the apparently natural, universal, and politically neutral appearances of capitalist social reality, explicitly to re-situate those abstract appearances in relation to the processes and social power relations implicated in their production, and thereby to enable their transformation by the human social agents whose socially productive activity constitutes their conditions of existence.[10]

As a form of immanent critique, the philosophy of praxis directs attention to identifying and transforming the social forces that give rise to laws that create and sustain a world characterised by increasing inequalities.[11] It involves unmasking formalistic analyses of international trade law which posit law to function neutrally in the 'efficient' management of the world economy. Rather, international trade law is analysed and theorised as an historically effective social force with both oppressive and emancipatory potential.

---

[9] See R. Cox with T. Sinclair, *Approaches to World Order* (Cambridge: Cambridge University Press, 1996) for the adaptation of Antonio Gramsci's conceptions of historical bloc and hegemony to the analysis of the conditions of world (dis)order. And see Cutler, *Private Power*.

[10] M. Rupert and H. Smith (eds.), 'Editors' Introduction', *Historical Materialism and Globalization* (London and New York: Routledge, 2002), p. 1.

[11] For an excellent elaboration of the philosophy of praxis as a form of immanent critique, see A. D. Morton, 'A Double Reading of Gramsci: Beyond the Logic of Contingency', in A. Bieler and A. D. Morton (eds.), *Images of Gramsci: Connections and Contentions in Political Theory and International Relations* (London and New York: Routledge, 2006), pp. 45–59.

However, there is scant evidence of such critique or analysis in international law books. Classic texts on international trade law tend to take as given the presumed benefits flowing from transnational economic law.[12] They accept liberal theories of political economy and liberal institutionalist analysis that posit enhanced global wealth through the realisation of mutual gains from liberalised trade and the efficiencies flowing from locking these gains in through hard legal regulation.[13] These theories rely upon the liberal economic doctrine of comparative advantage, rational choice theories and game theoretic models to explicate the benefits of an expansionary geographic and substantive trade regime as self-evident truths.[14] They provide no sense of the significance that transnational regulation plays in the promotion of a one-dimensional market civilisation and the fetishism of commodified legal forms and institutions that work profound asymmetries in power, wealth and influence. There is little recognition that transnational legality operates on one side of what Boaventura de Sousa Santos insightfully describes as 'the great abyssal line' between knowledge and law on one side and on the other side, 'no knowledge', 'incomprehensible beliefs, opinions, intuitive or subjective understandings', the 'a-legal, the lawless, the non-legal and even the legal according to non-officially recognized law'.[15] Santos argues that modern thinking is, quintessentially, an 'abyssal thinking':

> Western modern thinking is an abyssal thinking. It consists of a system of visible and invisible distinctions, the invisible ones being the foundation for the visible ones. The invisible distinctions are established through radical lines that divide social reality into two realms, the realm of 'this side of the line' and the realm of 'the other side of the line'. The division is such that 'the other side of the line' vanishes as reality, becomes non-existent,

---

[12] See R. R. Hudec, *Enforcing International Trade Law: The Evolution of the Modern GATT Legal System* (Salem, NH: Butterworth Legal Publishers, 1993); Jon R. Johnson, *International Trade Law* (Concord, Ont: Irwin Law, 1998); R. K. Paterson, M. Band, J. Finlayson and J. Thomas, *International Trade and Investment Law in Canada* 2nd edn (Scarborough, Ont: Carswell, 1994).

[13] See R. Posner, *Economic Analysis of Law* (Toronto: Little Brown, 1986) and D. C. North, *Institutions, Institutional Change and Economic Performance* (Cambridge: Cambridge University Press, 1990).

[14] For the theoretical foundations of liberal international political economy and related accounts of law, see R. Keohane, *After Hegemony* (Princeton: Princeton University Press, 1984); K. Abbot, R. Keohane, A. Moravcsik, A. Slaughter and D. Snidal, 'The Concept of Legalization', (2000) 54 (3) *International Organization* 401.

[15] 'Beyond Abyssal Thinking: From Global Lines to Ecologies of Knowledges', presented at the University of Glasgow Faculty of Law Workshop on 'Law, Politics, and Power in the Global Age: The Legal and Social Theory of Boaventura de Sousa Santos' (2006).

and is indeed produced as non-existent. Non-existent means not existing in any relevant or comprehensible way of being. Whatever is produced as non-existent is radically excluded because it lies beyond the realm of what the accepted conception of inclusion considers to be the other. What most fundamentally characterizes abyssal thinking is thus the impossibility of the co-presence of the two sides of the line. To the extent that it prevails, this side of the line only prevails by exhausting the field of relevant reality. Beyond it, there is only non-existence, invisibility, non-dialectical absence.

Significantly, international law lies on the side of Western modernity, where civil society and forces of regulation and emancipation vie for supremacy. But this contestation is rooted in a deeper conflict on the other, the colonial side, between forces of appropriation and violence. However, the universalist pretensions of Western modernity render the colonial side invisible and non-existent as pre-scientific, non-rational and anarchic, in the sense of a pre-contractual state of nature and thus an unknowable terrain that is inappropriate for rational, regulatory and emancipatory politics. However, this asymmetry is obscured because 'the hegemonic eye, located in civil society, ceases to see and indeed declares as non-existent the state of nature', thus leaving the claim of Western modernity to universality uncompromised.

For Santos, post-abyssal thinking in law[16] involves an 'unthinking' of modern law, legal reasoning, categories and disciplines. This chapter seeks to contribute to the conceptualisation of international law on the left by unthinking international trade law. It identifies the contours of a radical political economy critique that exposes the internal contradictions in capital's law, the law of transnational economic relations, and explores the emancipatory potential of this law. The next section reviews the history and nature of international law and situates international trade law as an imperial regime with global pretensions. This regime operated historically as a mechanism of exclusion that contributed to the construction of and today maintains the great abyssal divide. The following section then develops a radical critique of the General Agreement on Trade in Services (GATS) negotiated during the Uruguay Round of multilateral trade negotiations. It articulates the commodity form theory of law as a first step towards establishing a radical political economy critique of transnational economic law. The concluding section then proposes the praxis conception of transnational economic law as a promising means for

---

[16] This Santos calls counter-hegemonic and subaltern cosmopolitanism. See *Toward a New Legal Common Sense* 2nd edn (London: Butterworths, 2002), ch. 9.

exploring the sites and openings for emancipatory politico-legal strategies that contest an increasingly one-dimensional neoliberal market civilization.

2. International trade law and the empire of capital

International law has always been about conquest, imperialism and empire.[17] As China Miéville observes, international law:

> is a *world-historic* result of the early colonial experience of transatlantic and eastern trade ... it is the dialectical result of the very process of conflictual, expanding inter-polity interaction in an age of early state forms and mercantile colonialism.... international law *is* colonialism.[18]

Thus it is that Santos muses that the first modern abyssal line was probably drawn by the Tordesillas Treaty of 1494 between Portugal and Spain, which divided the world between them, but was unmistakable in the amity lines of the sixteenth century.[19] The amity lines clearly differentiated between the European 'sphere of peace and the law of nations from an overseas sphere in which there was neither peace not law'.[20] These articulations of global divisions between Europeans and non-Europeans also marked the beginnings of modernist legal conceptions of international legal personality or subjectivity, generating debate, for example, over the legal rights and status of indigenous peoples and the beginnings of their characterisation as objects in the periphery of international society.[21] Special legal doctrines were also developed to facilitate the commercial activities of the great trading companies who were granted trading monopolies and

---

[17] Thus it is challenging to consider how and why it is that as M. Koskenniemi, *The Gentle Civilizer of Nations: The Rise and Fall of International Law 1870–1960* (Cambridge: Cambridge University Press, 2001), p. 99, n. 6 observes that: '[v]ery little has been written on imperialism and international law. Not only does there seem to exist no full-length study of the matter, there is almost complete silence on it. . . . . . "Imperialism" always appears as a political, economic, military, social or cultural "fact," a series of incidents or relationships instead of a normative category . . .'

[18] *Between Equal Rights: A Marxist Theory of International Law* (Leiden and Boston: Brill, 2005), pp. 168–9 (original emphasis).

[19] B. de Souza Santos, 'Beyond Abyssal Thinking'. And see Miéville, *Between Equal Rights*, p. 171.

[20] Grewe, quoted in Miéville, *Between Equal Rights*, p. 180.

[21] See A. Anghie, 'Finding the Peripheries: Sovereignty and colonialism in nineteenth century international law' (1999) 40 *Harvard International Law Journal* 1; A. C. Cutler, 'The Globalization of International Law, Indigenous Identity and the "New Imperialism"', in W. Coleman and J. C. Weaver (eds.), *Property Rights: Struggles over Autonomy in a Global Age* (Vancouver: University of British Columbia Press, forthcoming).

state-like powers as they engaged in colonial expansion.[22] Prior to the establishment of the European states system at a time when the public/private distinction had not yet crystallised, these trading companies were created by royal charters and later by letters patent and regarded as royal patrimony, exercising powers of imperium, antecedent to the concept of sovereignty.[23]

The drawing of abyssal lines also foreshadowed the development of the standard of 'civilisation' established by Western, Christian nations as a criterion of inclusion and exclusion and the foundation for differential treatment under international law. Initially framed as *jus gentium*, or the principles of law common to all peoples, international law was gradually circumscribed by methodological and ontological doctrines that reflected the growing significance of state sovereignty. Legal positivism was the analytical method used to facilitate the imposition of European international law upon peoples encountered in the Americas, in the annexation of Australia, the conquest of large parts of Asia and the partitioning of Africa.[24] The result was the articulation of a racialised order wherein international legal subjectivity was associated with the cultural characteristics 'essential to the membership of the family of nations' and emanating from European international society.[25] Legal doctrines of dispossession, such as the Roman doctrine of *terra nullius*, were developed in international law to appropriate indigenous lands, while different standards of civilisation gave rise to distinctions between sovereign and 'not-full sovereign', states resulting in different legal rights and entitlements. Asian states, for example, were regarded as having the necessary legal capacity to enter into treaty relations, thus requiring special treaties of capitulation. In contrast, African tribes were regarded as incapable of entering into treaty relations and so occupation was sufficient to establish title to land.

The great trading companies were complicit in these arrangements and benefited greatly by the growing statist focus of international law. They too could not figure as international law's 'subjects', but were analogous

---

[22] These included the rights to trade, wage war, make peace, impose customs duties, and to create money.

[23] J. McLean, 'The Transnational Corporation in History: Lessons for Today?' (2004) 7 *Indiana Law Journal* 363.

[24] J. Anaya, *Indigenous Peoples in International Law*, 2nd edn (Oxford: Oxford University Press 2004).

[25] T. Lawrence, *The Principles of International Law* (London: Macmillan, 1895), p. 58.

to individuals and peoples as 'objects' of international law.[26] The growing statist orientation of the analytical foundations of international law thus appeared to level the colonial playing field by creating an appearance of juridical equality and equalising the relationships amongst non-state entities, such as indigenous peoples and business corporations. 'The legal framework tended to portray the colonial encounter as a clash between individuals', because the trading companies could operate legally as private persons, acquiring and disposing of lands and so forth.[27] This obscured the fact that, rather than being configured in the periphery of law and empire, the great trading corporations were the main engines of colonial dispossession.

By the nineteenth century, during the second wave of colonial expansion, trading corporations were regarded as creatures of national corporate law, but of ambiguous status, described as they were by John Westlake as 'mediate sovereigns'.[28] McLean notes that:

> [t]heir ambiguous status served the interests of the chartering state well and had the effect of portraying the colonial encounter as an encounter between 'equals.' Trade was a pure and liberal endeavour abroad without necessarily engaging the European powers in hostilities at home. A separate and flexible law of nations developed: not a universal law of nations, but a separate French, English, or German colonial law. This prevented transfer to the colonial sphere of the European concept[s] of the nation state, sovereignty, and territorial borders. The concept of natural frontiers, which was central to the European concept of statehood, would not apply in the colonies.[29]

Indeed, as McLean concludes, the 'history of colonial expansion is capable of being viewed as a history of the corporate form'.[30] One might add that this history is intimately connected to the specificity of the relation between imperial expansion and the legal forms that capitalism took.[31] As Ellen Meiksins Wood notes, imperialism had for a long time hinged not upon 'the appropriation of territory, settlement or resource extraction,

---

[26] See R. Higgins, 'Conceptual Thinking About the Individual in International Law', in R. Falk, F. Kratochvil and S. Mendolvitz (eds.), *International Law: A Contemporary Perspective* (Boulder, CO: Westview Press, 1985), p. 476 for what continues to be an insightful discussion of the distinction between subjects and objects under international law.
[27] McLean, 'The Transnational Corporation', 371.   [28] Quoted in *ibid.*, 370.
[29] *Ibid.*, 371.   [30] *Ibid.*, 363.
[31] See A. C. Cutler, 'Historical materialism, globalization, and law: competing conceptions of property,' in Rupert and Smith, *Historical Materialism*, pp. 230–256 for analysis of the significance of different conceptions of property to the capitalist mode of production. And see C. Miéville, 'The Commodity-Form Theory of International Law', Chapter 3 in this volume.

but dominance in international trade'.[32] The Arab, Muslim, Venetian and Dutch empires were fuelled by commercial supremacy, which was in turn facilitated by international law. For example, Hugo Grotius contributed greatly to Dutch commercial dominance in the seventeenth century by articulating the principle of freedom of the high seas, thus challenging the Portuguese maritime trade monopoly. But it is England that Wood credits with the creation of the first 'form of imperialism driven by the logic of capitalism'.[33] She traces this to a 'new logic of capitalist appropriation' generated by developments in the political economy of agriculture and in the creation of new property rights, which were then transferred to imperial expansion.

> This, then, was the logic of agrarian capitalism, which was gradually enveloping the English countryside; and with it came new principles of imperial expansion. The history of early agrarian capitalism – the process of domestic 'colonization', the removal of land from the 'waste', its 'improvement', enclosure and new conceptions of property rights – was reproduced in the theory and practice of empire.

Indeed, empire was conceived through property in the development of the Lockean theory of private property that permitted the colonial appropriation of unused and unimproved lands without the consent of the inhabitants.[34] The rationale was that, because such lands were not used for profit or production, they gave rise to no improvement or exchange value and, hence, to no real property. In Polanyian terms, only upon commodification and entry into the market system did land become appropriable as private property and subject to claims of private right.[35] Moreover, such improvement was regarded as inherently linked to the 'civilising' move of the colonial encounter. Wood emphasises the crucial role played by Locke's labour theory of value and the specificity that changing understandings of private property had on the imperial project by facilitating imperial

---

[32] E. M. Wood, *Empire of Capital* (London: Verso, 2003), p. 45.   [33] *Ibid.*, p. 73.
[34] Wood traces this to Thomas More's belief that colonisers could rightfully seize colonial lands and displace the inhabitants if the latter were unwilling to develop and improve the lands. 'But if the natives refuse to conform themselves to their laws, they drive them out of those bounds which they mark for themselves, and use force if they resist. For they account in a very just cause of war, for a nation to hinder others from possessing a part of the soil of which they make no use, but which is suffered to lie idle and uncultivated; since every man has by the law of nature a right to such a waste portion of the earth as is necessary for his subsistence, Thomas More, *Utopia*, quoted in Wood, p. 75.
[35] K. Polanyi, *The Great Transformation: the political and economic origins of our time* (Boston, MA: Beacon Press, 1944).

expansion through dispossession.[36] This transformed imperialism from a coercive, military relationship to a:

> directly economic relationship, even if that relationship required brute force to implant and sustain it. That kind of relationship could be justified not by the right to rule, nor even simply the right to appropriate, but by the right, indeed the obligation, to produce exchange-value.[37]

The insight that market ideology, which in its 'strongest and most comprehensive metaphysical version' 'associates the market with human nature',[38] identifies possibly the single most important historical and analytical link between the classical imperialism of the past and the 'new imperialism' of the present.[39] While variations on these ideas are evident in the works of the great international lawyers, such as Grotius and Vattel, and other thinkers who contributed to the development of modern international law,[40] and it is commonplace to regard international law as a fundamentally liberal project,[41] the linkage between empire and the natural obligation/right to produce exchange-value takes us to the heart of the intersection of international trade law and empire. Today it forms the foundation for law's co-extensity with capitalism. Today, imperial expansion through international trade takes on the character of natural law principles and inherent rights to market access. Indeed, these principles are constitutionalised in trade disciplines that extend well beyond trade relations and reach deep inside states to govern matters once regarded as the proper subjects of domestic public policy and national social regulation.

---

[36] Wood, *Empire of Capital*, pp. 99–100: 'Early modern England, no less than other commercial powers, engaged in the same international rivalries; and, needless to say, the expansion of the British empire would continue to require massive military force and a particularly powerful navy. But there was already something new in both the theory and practice of empire, and we find its best early expression in Locke. Here, we see the beginnings of a conception of empire rooted in capitalist principles, in pursuit of profit derived not simply from exchange but from the creation of value in competitive production. This is a conception of empire that is not simply about establishing imperial rule or even commercial supremacy but about extending the logic and the imperatives of the domestic economy and drawing others into its orbit. Although capitalist imperialism would never dispense with more traditional means of justifying imperial expansion, it had now added wholly new weapons to the ideological arsenal, just as it had pioneered new social property relations, which had their effects both in the domestic economy and in the strategies of imperial expansion.'
[37] *Ibid.*, p. 99 (emphasis added). [38] Jameson, *Postmodernism*, p. 267.
[39] See Harvey, *The New Imperialism*.
[40] See Wood, *Empire of Capital*, ch. 5 for a discussion of Grotius and Vattel.
[41] See M. Koskenniemi, *From Apology to Utopia: The Structure of International Legal Argument* (Cambridge: Cambridge University Press, 2005).

However, Wood notes the analytical difficulty of capturing or isolating the role of the forces that sustain 'the system of economic compulsion, the system of property (and propertylessness) and the operation of markets'.[42] This problem is even more acute today in analysing the 'new imperialism', where physical occupation through military force and the forfeiture of wealth, which were once fairly transparent processes, have been replaced by a complex architecture of local and global economic disciplines that knit the word together into asymmetrical relations of power and influence and new legal forms and patterns of dispossession. The specific role that the international trade law plays in securing the stability and expansion of this architecture may be seen most vividly in the regime evolving to regulate international trade in services. This regime is advancing a highly privatised order with new mechanisms of dispossession and exclusion and may be fruitfully approached through the commodity form theory of transnational economic law, to which attention now turns.

3. GATS and the commodity form theory of transnational economic law

The significance of new forms of property to the development and expansion of capitalism underlies the relationship between law and capitalism and is probably analysed most incisively by Karl Marx.[43] Marx suggested, and others have further developed, the notion that law takes on a distinctive form under capitalism that reflects and, indeed, is homologous with the 'commodity form'.[44] He noted that commodities have a 'use-value', which differs from commodity to commodity in that it embodies a particular amount of human labour. Commodities also have an 'exchange-value', which emerges upon the entry of a commodity into the market and which equalises differences in value among commodities by translating their value into monetary terms. The exchange-value thus obscures the human labour that went into the creation of the product, working a process of commodification that masks the link between the product

---

[42] *Empire of Capital*, p. 4.
[43] *Capital: A Critique of Political Economy* vol. 1, B. Fowkes, trans (London: Penguin, 1976), ch. 1. For a fuller discussion of a the commodity form theory of law, see A. C. Cutler, 'Gramsci, Law, and the Culture of Global Capitalism', in Bieler and Morton, *Images of Gramsci*, p. 133.
[44] *Ibid.*, p. 138. See I. Balbus, 'Commodity Form and Legal Form: An Essay on the "Relative Autonomy" of the Law' (1977) 11 *Law and Society* 571. See also E. Pashukanis, *Law and Marxism: A General Theory* (London: Pluto Press, 1978) and Miéville, Chapter 3 in this volume.

and its human creator and alienates the labourer from the fruits of her labour. This process of commodification abstracts form from content and transforms quality into quantity, and, by separating the commodity from its creator, infuses the product, now a commodity, with the appearance of independence from its producer and with a life of its own. This process of commodification Marx identified as the fetishism of commodities, to which he attributed the 'metaphysical subtleties', 'mystery' and 'enigmatic character' of commodities under capitalism.[45]

Unfortunately, Marx did not have a great deal to say about the role that law plays in the fetishism of commodities under capitalism. However, others have developed the analysis, theorising that law takes on a specific form under capitalism that both mirrors the commodity form and works a co-extensive or parallel fetishism of the legal form.[46] Just as the commodity form creates the appearance that all products are equal, the legal form creates an appearance of equality between individuals as legal subjects. The presumption of juridical equality thus undergirds capitalist market relations, equalising sellers and consumers of goods or suppliers and purchasers of services. This masks and conceals class and social inequalities that inhere in capitalist production. Moreover, legal regulation empties economic relations of politics and contestation by configuring the laws governing property and contract as part of the domain of civil society, economic markets, and free and equal exchange between juridical equals. The legal structure thus neutralises and depoliticises the fetishism of commodities and produces a fetishism of law by presenting the communal legal protection of private property rights and entitlements as natural incidents of the capitalist production and exchange.

Law in the commodity form thus conceals the asymmetries in power and influence and the political economy of capitalist economic relations, presenting as rational and equitable relations that are inherently oppressive and unequal. As Balbus notes, the legal form in creating illusory forms of equality and in precluding genuine equality, is a specifically 'bourgeois' form.[47]

The commodity form of law forms the template for late capitalist and postmodern legal regulation. It establishes market ideology as the *grundnorm* for global economic regulation by opening up ever greater and novel vistas for liberalisation, flexible accumulation and appropriation. While this is evident in a number of areas of transnational economic law, it

---

[45] Marx, *Capital*, vol. 1, pp. 163–4.   [46] See the references, above notes at 43 and 44.
[47] 'Commodity Form and Legal Form', p. 580.

is probably most visible in the emerging regime governing international trade in services.[48] The General Agreement on Trade in Services (GATS) forms part of the larger international trade regime and was negotiated within the World Trade Organization (WTO) Uruguay Round of multilateral trade negotiations. The GATS marked a profound and fundamental transformation in the way in which cross-border telecommunications, finance, transportation, management, consulting, accounting, legal and other services relating to sports, schools, universities, research establishments, hospitals, electricity, libraries and so on are conceptualised and regulated. Traditionally regarded as matters of domestic public policy and national legal regulation, the GATS privatises these services, transforming them into commodities to be regulated in the same delocalised manner as trade in goods is regulated under the WTO/GATT (General Agreement on Tariffs and Trade) regime. In privatising service provision, the GATS advances a particular understanding of development and poverty that critics argue 'disregards the social context of provision, the lived experiences of the poor and dismisses and/or reinforces the way in which deprivations are constituted'.[49]

While the GATS was resisted by many states, and particularly less developed states in the past, the 'shift to trade discourse was a revolution in social ontology: it redefined how governments thought about the nature of services, their movement across borders, their roles in society, and the objectives and principles according to which they should be governed'.[50] This revolution was driven initially by powerful transnational corporations seeking to expand their market opportunities in the services sectors and to lock governments in to hard legal disciplines that limit their abilities to regulate foreign service providers. Unable to secure constitutionalised protections for foreign direct investment under the failed Organization of Economic Cooperation and Development (OECD) initiative on the

---

[48] It is also evident in the developing intellectual property regime, which is globalising a commodified conception of indigenous identity, but this is beyond the scope of this chapter. See Cutler, 'Globalization of International Law'.

[49] R. Higgott and H. Weber, 'GATS in Context: Development. An evolving *lex mercatoria* and the Doha Agenda' (2005) 12(3) *Review of International Political Economy* 435 at 442, the authors note that the provision of health care, education and publicly provided sanitary care were once regarded as matters of 'public' policy; but under the GATS are redefined as commercial services. For a critical analysis of the commodification of nature and the environment under the GATS, see M. Weber, 'The "nature" of environmental services: GATS, the environment and the struggle over the global institutionalization of private law' (2005) 12(3) *Review of International Political Economy* 456.

[50] W. J. Drake and K. Nicolaïdis, 'Ideas, Interests, and Institutionalization: "trade in services" and the Uruguay Round', (1992) 46 *International Organization* 37 at 38.

Multilateral Agreement on Investment (MAI), corporate interests turned their attention to developing a new strategy that would flatten out distinctions between trade in goods and the provision of services by characterising the latter as an analogous matter of trade regulation. The extension to services provision of GATT-like disciplines imported into the regulation of services related liberal political economy assumptions and normative presumptions that liberalised, deregulated and privatised 'free' trade is the best, most efficient and desirable standard against which policies should be measured. Thus it is that GATT-like disciplines and technical language operationalising the commitments to progressive liberalisation and non-discrimination are adopted to govern the policies of states concerning services regulation concerning four modes of delivery (cross-border supply, consumption abroad, establishing a commercial presence, and temporary presence of services personnel). The latter two modes clearly relate to the services 'supplier'. Mode 3 limits the host state's abilities to regulate foreign direct investment (FDI) in services sectors, while mode 4 has implications for national immigration laws. However, as Jane Kelsey notes, the characterisation of services provision as trade in services is an 'artificial construct' that implies the equivalence of trade in goods and trade in services, thus obscuring a recognition of the distinctive nature of service provision as rooted in everyday life and personal relationships that extend 'into families, communities and societies' and 'serve purposes that are intrinsically social, as well as environmental, cultural and economic'.[51] The societal dimension of service provision is lost as service provision enters the marketplace as any other commodity. Possibly most important though, is the concealing move of law, for through the equalisation of many diverse services under the language of trade regulation, market ideology trumps any potentially competing non-market value and obscures the underlying asymmetry in power relations embodied in the modes. For example, Kelsey observes that most Northern states want mode 3 commitments to benefit their transnational corporations, but want to limit the influx of foreign workers under mode 4. In contrast, many Southern states, while dependant on FDI, are reluctant to bind themselves under mode 3 commitments, but want access for their workers under mode 4. However, the negotiations 'do not take place on a level playing field. Pressures on Southern countries seem much more likely to be effective than their corresponding demands that richer

---

[51] J. Kelsey, 'Legal Fetishism and the Contradictions of the GATS' (2003) 1(3) *Globalisation, Societies and Education* 267.

countries liberalise even temporary unskilled immigration'.[52] Moreover, the GATS advances marketised and commodified conceptions of poverty and development that empty these conceptions of meaning.[53] In Polanyian terms, the commodification of service provision disembeds this activity from social regulation and control with the burden of adjustment falling most heavily on those with the weakest bargaining power.[54] The authority of the GATT/WTO regime lends legitimacy to the marketisation of service provision and provides a language, a culture and a set of legal concepts that fetishise the legal form of service provision: 'the juristic form is, in consequence, made everything and the economic content nothing.'[55]

Under the GATS, the commodity form of law operates to fetishise services:

> services have become fetishised, a process that distorts reality by assimilating many diverse features of social life within a unified ideological category. Diverse dimensions are reduced to the simple form of the production and sale of commodities, where everything only exists to be bought and sold.[56]

The GATS legitimises the fragmentation of trade in services into separate modes of delivery, taking services discourse into 'a technical realm that is stripped of any social or political dimension' or 'other ways of perceiving them that might raise more objections'.[57] Moreover, the service provider is described as the 'supplier,' a 'neutral and disembodied term' that disguises the overwhelming dominance of major transnational enterprises in these activities.[58] The GATS thus facilitates the transnational expansion of capital by opening services markets to foreign competition and setting limits to domestic regulation.

While initiated by transnational corporate interests, this movement was later joined by international agencies and key governments, such as the United States, and ultimately even the less developed countries supported the transformation in regulation. Drake and Nicolaïdes characterise this movement as an 'epistemic community' comprised by those with direct

---

[52] Ibid., 273. She notes the controversy over the implications of mode 3 on services ranging from retail, to railway, education and water and also identifies asymmetrical impacts of modes 1 (cross-border supply) and 2 (consumption abroad). Modes 1 and 2 'disguise further controversies, such as the provision of tele-medicine and internet education, and medical tourism for purposes of cosmetic surgery or unconventional treatment in foreign clinics'.
[53] See Higgott and Weber, 'GATS in Context'.   [54] Polanyi, *The Great Transformation*.
[55] Kelsey, 'Legal Fetishism', 269 quoting Engels (1958), p. 397.   [56] Ibid., p. 276.
[57] Ibid., p. 272.   [58] Ibid.

interests in liberalising services (governments, international agencies and private firms) and others who articulated the ideological framework for adopting a market-oriented regulation to services provision (academics, lawyers, industry specialists and journalists).[59] Together, they worked to create the ideological climate for the commodification of services, presenting their position as '"scientifically objective" and susceptible to truth tests' and creating the appearance of benefiting 'the international community as a whole'.[60] This is, indeed, how the fetishism of law in the commodity form operates, as the concluding section will explore.

4. Beyond the abyssal divide: the praxis conception of law

Unthinking the GATS involves conceptualising transnational economic law as an historically effective social force. It involves unmasking the political economy and power relations underlying the GATS by revealing how the agreement fetishises services provision. This is a potentially daunting task in the light of Marx's observation that 'the tradition of all dead generations weighs like a nightmare on the brain of the living'. Indeed, conceptualising the GATS as an historically effective social force involves challenging traditions that resist conceptualising legal forms as active social forces. Both legal positivism and political realism, the dominant traditions in international law and in international relations, raise obstacles that bear in one way or another on the problem of 'locating' law in the ensemble of social forces at work in the world. For scholars of international relations, the tendency to regard international law unhistorically and as an epiphenomenal dimension of the superstructure, overlying a power/interest-based order, precludes its conceptualisation as a determinative influence in world affairs.[61] For scholars of international law, the drawing of sharp distinctions between international politics and international law and between international economics and international law, coupled with a tendency to legal formalism, work against understanding law as a foundational and constitutive element of a global order with roots in distinctive historical blocs. Because neither discipline adequately

---

[59] Ibid., p. 39.   [60] Ibid.
[61] Interestingly, distinctions between the base and superstructure of the capitalist state have also worked against the conceptualisation of law as an historical force for Marxist scholars, as well. These analytical and theoretical obstacles to conceptualising law as an historically effective social force are addressed at length in Cutler, *Private Power and Global Authority* and in 'Critical historical materialism and international law: Imagining international law as praxis', in S. Hobden and J. Hobson (eds.), *Historical Sociology of International Relations* (Cambridge: Cambridge University Press, 2002), p. 181.

locates the law so as to capture its significance in the constitution of global inequalities and asymmetrical power relations, neither is able to envision law as a potentially emancipatory force.

The praxis conception of law, as developed in a fragmentary way by Gramsci, conceives of law, dialectically, as an effective historical force that gives rise to potentially oppressive and emancipatory social forces. The praxis conception is rooted in an understanding of historical materialism as a philosophy of praxis. In keeping with Marx's critique of political economy 'that set out to overcome the essential separation of philosophy, economics, and politics',[62] the philosophy of praxis postulates the immanent unity of material and ideational conditions in an historical process of becoming. Gramsci conceptualised the law as operating dialectically, both coercively, as the arm of the state, and consensually, within civil society, 'turning necessity and coercion into "freedom"'.[63] Gramsci's understanding of law is thus intimately related to his understanding of hegemony.[64] For Gramsci, hegemony is the process by which the ruling class establishes the material, ideological and institutional conditions to establish control. Significantly, this is not achieved through force alone, but through ideologically capturing popular support and conditioning it as the articulation of the public interest or common sense.[65] In this, the role of 'organic intellectual' is crucial in manufacturing consent and in 'creating a social conformism which is useful to the ruling group's line of development'.[66] By this process, 'the Law is the repressive and negative aspect of the entire positive, civilising activity undertaken by the State', but it also 'renders the ruling group "homogeneous" and legitimate'.[67] The law's role in creating coercive and consensual social relations is described as the 'double face of the law', which forms a dialectic specific to the bourgeois conception of law.[68] This conception Gramsci regarded as an 'ethical conception', whereby the 'bourgeois class poses itself as an organism in continuous movement, capable of absorbing the entire civil

---

[62] Morton, 'A Double Reading of Gramsci', p. 54.
[63] A. Gramsci, *Selections From the Prison notebooks of Antonio Gramsci*, Q. Hoare and G. N. Smith (ed. and trans.) (London: Lawrence and Wishart, 1971), p. 242.
[64] It is important to note that Gramsci did not develop a detailed account of the role of law in creating hegemony, but provides a suggestive line of analysis. See Cutler, *Private Power and Global Authority* for elaboration.
[65] C. Mouffe, 'Hegemony and Ideology in Gramsci', in C. Mouffe (ed.), *Gramsci and Marxist Theory* (London: Routledge and Kegan Paul, 1979), p. 168.
[66] Gramsci, *Selections from the Prison Notebooks*, p. 247. [67] *Ibid.*, pp. 247, 195.
[68] M. Cain, 'Gramsci, the State and the Place of Law', in D. Sugarman (ed.), *Legality, Ideology and the State* (London: Academic Press, 1983), p. 95.

society, assimilating it to its own cultural and economic level'.[69] Law thus becomes an effective social force when it cements society and economy together and binds subordinate groups to the will of the ruling group. The praxis conception of law articulates the dialectical nature of law's coercive and consensual faces as it operates in practice and in lived experience; a conception 'freed from every residue of transcendentalism and from every absolute'.[70]

Gramsci theorised that the role of the organic intellectual is central to the absorption and assimilation of subordinate groups. The organic intellectual functions to provide 'homogeneity and an awareness of its [the social groups] own function not only in the economic but also in the social and political fields'.[71] He noted that these 'deputies' create the conditions necessary to advance the interests of their specific group as those of the common interest: '[t]he capitalist entrepreneur creates alongside himself the industrial technician, the specialist in political economy, the organizers of new culture, of a new legal system...' Significantly, organic intellectuals:

> do not simply produce ideas, but they concretise and articulate strategies in complex and contradictory ways ... It is the task of the organic intellectuals to organise the social forces they stem from and to develop a 'hegemonic project', which is able to transcend the particular economic-corporate interests of their social group by binding and cohering diverse aspirations, interests and identities into an historical bloc.[72]

In the context of the GATS, a fundamental transformation in the conceptualisation of services was required in order to legitimate their commodification. This was achieved by lawyers, government officials, corporate actors and journalists who, as part of an epistemic community, functioned as the organic intellectuals. They assisted in creating the ideological climate that legitimated treating services in the same conceptual and legal terms as tradable commodities. Indeed, through their work, the commodification of public services has become the standard against which the common interest and common sense are measured. Significantly, as Kelsey underlines, the generally accepted concept of trade under the GATT regime 'gave the artificial construct of "trade in services" some intrinsic legitimacy'. It was achieved by 'this fluid group as an "epistemic community" of like-minded technocrats driven by rationality ... They

[69] *Selections from the Prison Notebooks*, p. 260. [70] *Ibid.*, p. 246. [71] *Ibid.*, note at p. 5.
[72] A. Bieler, 'Class Struggle over the EU Model of Capitalism: Neo-Gramscian Perspectives and the Analysis of European Integration', in Bieler and Morton (eds.), *Images of Gramsci*, p. 124.

were the organic intellectuals of capital constructing a new hegemony.'[73] Indeed, the commodification of services was achieved through fetishised legal forms that worked to naturalise, rationalise and universalise capitalist social relations and market ideology.[74]

In this, the convergence of beliefs amongst powerful corporations and business interests, governments, journalists and academic groups from developed states and even developing states, who initially opposed the agreement, was crucial in achieving agreement that treating trade in services just like trade in goods was the commonsensical thing to do and would serve the world well as part of the neoliberal project of global restructuring.[75] While it appears to be accepted that powerful corporate interests drove the reconceptualisation of public services as tradable commodities, what is not at all clear is the political economy of the distributional outcomes: the 'who gets what' under the ontological shift. Echoing the crucial insight of critical theory that all theories serve purposes,[76] it is necessary to understand those purposes served by the GATS. This involves examining the social impact and distributional consequences of the GATS and determining whether developing states continue to reap disproportionately fewer benefits from the GATS regime as they do from the more general WTO/GATT regime.[77] It also requires debunking the myths of progress that inhere in liberal internationalist understandings of international law and recognising the history of international law as an exclusionary imperial project.

Conceiving transnational economic law as praxis directs attention to the dialectical nature of the law and suggests that law is a 'constitutive component of the social totality', whose dialectical operation gives rise to potentially emancipatory and liberating practices.[78] Here, the exercise

---

[73] Kelsey, 'Legal Fetishism', p. 270.
[74] See D. Litowitz, 'Gramsci, Hegemony, and the Law' (2000) 2 *Brigham Young University Law Review* 515; D. Kennedy, 'Antonio Gramsci and the Legal System' (1982) 6(1) *American Legal Studies Forum* 32.
[75] Drake and Nicolaïdis, 'Ideas, Interests, and Institutionalization', p. 40 observe that the 'very act of defining services transactions as "trade" established normative presumptions that "free" trade was the yardstick for good policy against which regulations, redefined as non-tariff barriers (NTBs), should be measured and justified only exceptionally'. Initially Anglo-American in composition, the group of organic intellectuals came to embrace a more European approach to managed liberalism as the negotiations over services proceeded, which in the end even developing states accepted.
[76] Cox, *Approaches to World Order*.
[77] See A. Narlikar, *The World Trade Organization: A Very Short Introduction* (Oxford: Oxford University Press, 2005).
[78] K. Klare', 'Law-Making as Praxis' (1979) 40 *Telos* 128.

of human agency to challenge the hegemony of market ideology and the fetishism of services under the GATS is a first step in unthinking abyssal law. In this journey, historical materialism provides both theoretical and practical inspiration. The commodity form theory of transnational economic law assists in understanding and explaining the co-extensity of the law and capitalism. But it also reveals potential openings and sites for contesting neoliberal economic and social restructuring. The praxis conception of law reveals the dialectical nature of law and its practical potential for working emancipatory purposes. The first obstacle to overcome is understanding the detailed operations of the fetishised commodity form of law. A more challenging obstacle is to translate that recognition into practical resistance to law, through law. However, following Herbert Marcuse, 'to engage in praxis is not to tread on alien ground, external to the theory [of historical materialism]', for the theory 'itself is already a practical one; praxis does not only come at the end, but is already present in the beginning of the theory'.[79] A praxis conception of transnational economic law directs attention to the human dimension of law-making and the realisation that just as people make laws, so too can they modify or change them.

---

[79] 'Foundations of Historical Materialism,' in H. Marcuse, *Studies in Critical Philosophy* J. De Bres (trans.) (London: New Left Books, 1972), p. 5.

7

Marxian insights for the human rights project

BRAD R. ROTH

Across the globe for well over a century, the ideas of Karl Marx held a special fascination for movements seeking to transform economic, political and social conditions in favour of the 'have-nots'. That this fascination endured a spectacular array of disappointments, defeats and disasters – ranging from the failure of Marxian predictions about the historical trajectory of capitalism to the massive commission of ignominious crimes in the name of Marxism – merely testifies to the power of those ideas to capture and hold the imagination of those who have yearned to transform the conditions of the disempowered and the deprived.

By now, however, the continued relevance of the Marxian inspiration stands in serious question. Experiments in socialist revolution are widely discredited. Insofar as there remains a global activist project to secure the conditions of a dignified human existence for all, the initiative seems to lie with the human rights movement – quintessentially a liberal design, and one historically in tension with Marxism.

Can Marxian political thought make a positive contribution to the contemporary project of international human rights advocacy? Marxism is ordinarily understood to assert the 'ideological' (and thus obfuscatory) character of rights claims and the impossibility of a justice that transcends class interests. The characteristic Marxian 'debunking' of rights, justice, and the rule of law is thus thought not only to preclude a rights-oriented critique of capitalism but, far worse, to disparage any rights-oriented constraint on the pursuit of the imperative social transformation, thereby lending itself to apologism for abusive practices of regimes cloaked in revolutionary garb. Furthermore, it is argued, even if Marx's work can be successfully disassociated from the dictatorial practices perpetrated in its name, a rehabilitation of Marx's ideas would be of purely academic significance, as Marx's normative ideas are too thin to have application: their specific prescriptions are relevant only to a materially-conditioned historical moment (the ultimate crisis of capitalist production) that is not, and will never be, upon us,[1] and the underlying vision of genuinely self-directed human activity (for which end-stage communist society is anticipated to furnish the material basis), however congenial, adds nothing useful to the conception of human flourishing expounded in the main current of contemporary liberal thought.

A retrieval of Marxian thought from the dustbin of activist history – and a retrieval of the human rights project from the conservatising grip of conventional doctrine – call for a response to this conventional wisdom. Marxian approaches to the instrumentalities of revolutionary rule entail no general rejection of human rights-oriented constraint, procedural or substantive, on the exercise of power in the name of the revolution. Moreover, a Marxian orientation contributes to the human rights project normative insights not supplied by, and in some respects at odds with, the main current of contemporary liberalism. It counters complacency about *status-quo*-oriented conceptions of the rule of law, rights, and democracy, and inspires an affirmative vision of the human potentialities that a well-ordered society must nurture.

Marxism retains its relevance in the current period, not as a comprehensive replacement for liberal human rights theories, but as a source of critique that challenges those theories on the basis of the very values of human freedom and dignity that they espouse, and as a source of alternative gauges of whether particular policies advance those values. A human-rights-friendly reading of Marx is thus both available and edifying.[2]

---

[1] See G. A. Cohen, *If You're an Egalitarian, How Come You're So Rich?* (Cambridge, MA: Harvard University Press, 2000).

[2] To be sure, Marx's work cannot be reconciled with a 'natural rights' approach that attributes to rights a metaphysical existence that transcends human institutions, nor can Marx be interpreted to embrace the view that 'moral rights' are a distinctively useful construct in reasoning about political morality. The same can be said, however, about any number of thinkers, including John Stuart Mill, whose contributions to the human rights project are beyond cavil. Human rights advocates are united by the belief that certain legal norms pertaining to basic conditions of human flourishing ought, on the basis of moral considerations, to be promulgated and implemented globally; they are not united by any one particular elaboration – be it theological, deontological, utilitarian, or perfectionist – of those moral considerations. The question at hand is whether Marxian thought can furnish intellectual resources for the political struggle to establish legal norms conducive to human flourishing, not whether Marx qualifies as a 'rights theorist'.

1. Marxism's compatibility with the rule of law

Any effort to reconcile Marxian thought with the human rights project must confront the familiar claim that Marxism, in proposing the establishment of a 'dictatorship of the proletariat', intends a regime, purportedly transitional but of indefinite duration, that is inimical to the rule of law, and thus to all institutionalisation of human rights. That claim finds highly sophisticated expression in the work of Martin Krygier.

Krygier argues that the absence of the rule of law under the Eastern and Central European regimes can be traced in significant part to Marx's analysis of the liberal state and civil society.[3] He contends that Marx's tendency to view law's role as subordinate to social forces and as a mask for ruling class interests systematically engenders a disrespect for legality:

> Many of Marx's comments on law seek to *unmask* it and its pretensions. As a limit to the power of the powerful it is either illusory and systematically partial – for law is involved in class exploitation and repression – or useful to ruling classes as an ideological emollient and mask for their real social power, a power which, however well disguised, is fundamental – at least, Engels came to add after Marx's death, 'ultimately', 'in the last analysis'. It was necessary, not that law fulfill any mythical essence, . . . but that it disappear along with the state, and with the civil society which supported them and which they supported.
>
> . . . That [law] might . . . be *liberating* was only conceded by Marx in comparison with the feudal past or with worse versions of the capitalist present, certainly not in comparison with the socialist and communist future. So to ask Marxist revolutionaries to make space for restraint by the rule of law would be to voice a quaint liberal demand for which they were not *theoretically* – let alone temperamentally – programmed.[4]

This is not an idiosyncratic charge. According to Lenin, after all, '[t]he revolutionary dictatorship of the proletariat is rule won and maintained by the use of violence by the proletariat against the bourgeoisie, rule that is unrestricted by any law'.[5] In the Leninist interpretation of Marx, to

---

[3] M. Krygier, 'Marxism and the Rule of Law: Reflections After the Collapse of Communism' (1990) 15 *Law and Social Inquiry* 633.

[4] *Ibid.*, 651 (footnotes omitted).

[5] V. I. Lenin, 'The Proletarian Revolution and the Renegade Kautsky' [1918], in R. C. Tucker (ed.), *The Lenin Anthology* (New York: W. W. Norton & Co., 1975), p. 461 at p. 466. The need for this polemic against the then leading theoretician of European Marxism itself demonstrates the controversial nature of Lenin's interpretation. At any rate, Lenin acknowledged that 'dictatorship does not necessarily mean the abolition of democracy for the class that exercises the dictatorship over other classes'. *Ibid.*, p. 465. His answer to

exalt any of the attributes of 'bourgeois democracy' in abstraction from that system's class content was at once to mistake form for substance and to shield a class enemy bent on subverting the real democratic triumph of proletarian power. As Krygier observes, this interpretation is not confined to Communist apologetics; the supposed Marxian hostility to legal restraint appears to find confirmation, for example, in the charges of apostasy that some Marxist-oriented Western scholars levelled at E. P. Thompson after the latter notoriously characterised the rule of law as an 'unqualified human good'.[6]

Marx never had occasion to deal directly with the question of the rule of law in the transitional society that follows the overthrow of capitalism and precedes the end stage of communism. Throughout his career, from *On the Jewish Question* (1843)[7] to *Critique of the Gotha Program* (1875)[8] and beyond, he criticised the bourgeois-revolutionary achievements of 'political emancipation' and equal rights as embodying an incomplete – and therefore, in a sense, false – freedom. These statements have frequently served as the bases for extrapolations rationalising despotic concentrations of power in the name of socialist revolution.

But such extrapolations are remarkably 'undialectical'. The relentless theme of Marx's critique of liberal accomplishments is that these fail to overcome the underlying conditions that at once necessitate them and

---

Kautsky emphasised both the workers' democratic participation in the soviets (councils) and their concrete realisation of freedoms that had in the past been nominally guaranteed to all, but effectively enjoyed only by the bourgeoisie. Thus, the new Soviet state was 'a million times more democratic than the most democratic bourgeois republic.' *Ibid.*, pp. 470–1.

[6] Compare E. P. Thompson, *Whigs and Hunters* (New York: Pantheon, 1975), pp. 258–69; with M. J. Horwitz, 'The Rule of Law: An Unqualified Human Good?' (1977) 86 *Yale Law Journal* 561, 566; A. Merritt, 'The Nature of Law: A Criticism of E. P. Thompson's "Whigs and Hunters,"' (1980) 7 *British Journal of Law and Society* 194. Horwitz's response to Thompson is a classic:

> [The rule of law] undoubtedly restrains power, but it also prevents power's benevolent exercise. It creates formal equality – a not inconsiderable virtue – but it promotes substantive inequality by creating a consciousness that radically separates law from politics, means from ends, processes from outcomes. By promoting procedural justice it enables the shrewd, the calculating, and the wealthy to manipulate its forms to their own advantage. And it ratifies and legitimates an adversarial, competitive, and atomistic conception of human relations.

Horwitz, 'The Rule of Law', 566.

[7] K. Marx, 'On the Jewish Question', in R. C. Tucker (ed.), *The Marx-Engels Reader* (New York: W. W. Norton & Co, 2nd edn, 1978) [hereafter *MER*], p. 26.

[8] K. Marx, 'Critique of the Gotha Program', *MER*, p. 525.

render largely illusory their benefits for the subordinate class. For Marx, the promise of these accomplishments can be genuinely realised only when the fundamental oppositions to which they respond are fully overcome. The evidence is very thin for the proposition that Marx intended – or would even have found tolerable – the abolition of legal constraints on the exercise of political power in advance of the eradication of the conditions that occasion the existence of political power itself.

In *On the Jewish Question*, Marx analysed liberal rights as reflected in prominent documents from the American and French revolutions. Marx criticised the liberal conception of liberty as follows:

> Liberty is . . . the right to do everything which does not harm others. The limits within which each individual can act are determined by law, just as a boundary between two fields is marked by a stake. It is a question of the liberty of man regarded as an isolated monad, withdrawn into himself. . . . [L]iberty as a right of man is not founded upon relations between man and man, but rather upon the separation of man from man. It is the right of the *circumscribed* individual, withdrawn into himself.[9]

The practical application of this asocial liberty, Marx maintained, reduces to the right to private property, which consists in 'the right to enjoy one's fortune and to dispose of it as one will, without regard for other men and independently of society. It is the right of self-interest.'[10]

For Marx, this impoverished conception of liberty reflected the essential contradictions of bourgeois political life. The French Declaration of the Rights of Man and of the Citizen drew the distinction between 'man', a member of civil society,[11] on the one hand, and citizen, a member of the political community, on the other. Marx discerned in this distinction a thorough subordination of the political community to civil society, to the arena of private interest and egoism. 'The end of every political

---

[9] *Ibid.*, p. 42.   [10] *Ibid.*
[11] The term 'civil society' is a source of great confusion. Marx, following Hegel, used that term to demarcate a realm of social life within which individuals pursue their private interests, as distinct from 'political community' (for Hegel, 'the state'), a realm in which they pursue a common good. (This is an oversimplification, but a useful one.) Since the 1980s, however, the term has come to denote, especially in regard to Eastern Europe, a realm of civic association developing independently of the tentacles of the totalitarian state. These two uses of 'civil society' have overlapping elements, and it is frequently (but quite wrongly) imagined that Marx championed the crushing of civil society, in both senses, by the all-powerful socialist state. Thus arises Krygier's assertion that Marx was hostile 'not to particular aspects of civil society, but to civil society tout court', that he 'hated and considered rightly doomed what the whole of eastern Europe is now wondering how to build or rebuild'. M. Krygier, 'Marxism, Communism, and Narcissism' (1990) 15 *Law and Social Inquiry* 707 at 717. This assertion is, to put it mildly, highly misleading.

association', stated the Declaration, 'is the preservation of the natural and imprescriptible rights of man'. All of the 'rights of man', Marx observed, concerned the 'individual separated from the community, withdrawn into himself, wholly preoccupied with his private interest and acting in accordance with his private caprice'.[12] Such a vision of political association assumes that '[t]he only bond between men is natural necessity, need and private interest, the preservation of their property and their egoistic persons'.[13]

Liberal institutions establish a political community that exists only as means of preserving the prerogatives of egoism, so that 'species-life itself – society – appears as a system which is external to the individual and as a limitation of his original independence'. Man there functions as a species-being only in an 'allegorical' sense, in the abstract role of citizen that is subordinated to his concrete role as a self-seeking individual. Accordingly:

> we observe that the political liberators [liberals] reduce citizenship, the *political community*, to a mere *means* for preserving these so-called rights of man, and consequently, that the citizen is declared to be the servant of egoistic 'man,' that the sphere in which man functions as a species-being is degraded to a level below the sphere where he functions as a partial being, and finally that it is man as a bourgeois and not man as a citizen who is considered the *true* and *authentic* man.[14]

Genuine human emancipation, to the contrary, requires a supersession of this opposition, so that 'the real, individual man has absorbed into himself the abstract citizen', and the 'individual man, in his everyday life, in his work, and in his relationships ... has become a *species-being*'.[15] The achievement of genuine human freedom for Marx depends on 'the return of man himself as a social, i.e., really human, being, a complete and conscious return which assimilates all wealth of previous development'. This entails nothing less than 'the *genuine* resolution of the conflict between man and nature and between man and man'.[16]

In Marx's conception, rights, like the state itself, ultimately disappear as a result of elaborate historical processes, not simple acts of will. Indeed, as he noted in *Critique of the Gotha Program*, even bourgeois economic

---

[12] MER, p. 43.   [13] Ibid.   [14] Ibid.
[15] Ibid., p. 46. The point was not to disparage 'political emancipation', but to expose its limitations: '*Political* emancipation certainly represents a great progress. It is not, indeed, the final form of human emancipation, but it is the final form of human emancipation *within* the framework of the prevailing social order. It goes without saying that we are speaking here of real, practical emancipation.' *Ibid.*, p. 35.
[16] K. Marx, 'Economic and Philosophic Manuscripts of 1844,' MER, p. 66 at p. 84.

rights, such as the right to payment according to one's work, remain and cannot be transcended until the development of productive forces and 'the all-round development of the individual' make possible the fulfillment of the formula, 'from each according to his ability, to each according to his needs'.[17] There is thus no reason to assume that civil and political rights (corresponding to the historical circumstances of socialist revolution) can be transcended before all opposing interests, and thus all need for coercion (and, therefore, for the state itself, as history has known it), are themselves transcended.[18]

More concretely, for Marx, unlike for many of his self-appointed continuators, working class power was not an abstraction. The 'dictatorship of the proletariat' entailed the actual control by ordinary people of government operations on a day-to-day basis. Indeed, such control, as Marx described in his account of (*cum* projection upon) the 1871 Paris Commune,[19] was not to be limited to the workers, but extended to the peasantry as well, notwithstanding the latter's distinct set of interests:

> The rural communes of every district were to administer their common affairs by an assembly of delegates in the central town, and these district assemblies were again to send deputies to the National Delegation in Paris, each delegate to be at any time revocable and bound by the *mandat impératif* (formal instructions) of his constituents. ... While the merely repressive organs of the old governmental power were to be amputated, its legitimate functions were to be wrested from an authority usurping pre-eminence over society itself, and restored to the responsible agents of society. Instead of deciding once in three or six years which member of the ruling class was to misrepresent the people in Parliament, universal suffrage was to ... [permit the people] if they for once make a mistake, to redress it promptly.[20]

---

[17] Marx, 'Critique of the Gotha Program', p. 525 at p. 531.

[18] Engels characterised the transitional state as 'at best an evil inherited by the proletariat' whose 'worst sides' are to be 'lopped off' but that will persist in some form 'until such time as a generation reared in new, free social conditions is able to throw the entire lumber of the state on the scrap heap'. Engels, 'Introduction to "The Civil War in France"', *MER*, p. 629.

[19] As Shlomo Avineri points out, 'despite its superficial appearance as a narrative of the Commune's achievements', *The Civil War in France* was more an account of what Marx took to be its potential achievements. S. Avineri, *The Social and Political Thought of Karl Marx* (New York: Cambridge University Press, 1968), p. 241. Marx did not (Engels' subsequent exuberance notwithstanding) regard the uprising as the true dawn of socialist revolution (the term 'Commune' it should be noted, referred not to communism but to the historical name of the Paris municipal government), but he did seize the opportunity to project the initial direction of such a revolution. See *ibid.*, pp. 198–201, 239–49.

[20] Marx, *The Civil War in France*, *MER*, p. 618 at p. 633.

'The Commune', Marx believed, 'would have delivered the peasant of the blood tax – would have given him a cheap government – transformed his present blood-suckers, the notary, advocate, executor, and other judicial vampires, into salaried communal agents, elected by, and responsible to, himself.'[21] To himself *literally*, it may be added, not merely 'objectively,' as in subsequent Communist distortions of the concept of representation.

True accountability of the revolutionary state apparatus to the working class requires that citizens be protected against that apparatus. Engels's 1891 Introduction to Marx's account of the Paris Commune contains a derisive description of a vanguardist faction among the Communards, the Blanquists:

> Brought up in the school of conspiracy, and held together by the strict discipline which went with it, they started out from the viewpoint that a relatively small number of resolute, well-organised men would be able, at a given favourable moment, not only to seize the helm of state, but also by a display of great, ruthless energy, to maintain power until they succeeded in sweeping the mass of the people into the revolution and ranging them round the small band of leaders. This involved, above all, the strictest, dictatorial centralization of all power in the hands of the new revolutionary government.[22]

Engels therefore warned that the working class must 'safeguard itself against its own deputies and officials, by declaring them all, without exception, subject to recall at any moment'.[23]

It follows that, notwithstanding their bourgeois origins, political rights retain their relevance, at least in some form, well beyond the overthrow of the bourgeoisie. And indeed, one finds nowhere in Marx's critique of the French Declaration of the Rights of Man and Citizen any attack on the rights of citizens, which included the right to 'speak, write and publish freely' (Art. XI) and the 'right to determine the necessity of the public contribution, either in person or by their representatives, to consent freely thereto, to watch over its use, and to determine the amount, base, collection and duration thereof' (Art. XIV).[24] To the contrary, just a year before writing *On the Jewish Question*, Marx condemned Prussian censorship

---

[21] *Ibid.*, p. 637.   [22] Engels, 'Introduction to *The Civil War in France*', pp. 626–27.
[23] *Ibid.*, p. 627.
[24] Marx pointed out that under the French constitution, freedom of the press is denied 'when it endangers public liberty'. This, for Marx, is another example of how liberalism subordinates the rights of the citizen to the imperative of preserving 'the rights of man', i.e., order in 'civil society', by which Marx meant the realm of competitive self-seeking: 'On the Jewish Question', p. 44.

in terms that extended, beyond the immediate context, to the period of French Revolutionary rule for which he had the most sympathy:

> The writer is exposed to the most dreadful terrorism, the jurisdiction of suspicion. Tendencious [sic] laws, laws that do not supply objective laws, are laws of terrorism, as they were thought out by the necessity of the state under Robespierre and by the corruption of the state under the Roman emperors. Laws that take as their criteria not action as such, but the state of mind of the actor, are nothing else than the positive sanction of lawlessness.[25]

Rosa Luxemburg's criticisms of the early course of the Bolshevik revolution thus appear as fully authentic emanations from what little of the Marxian canon pertains to an anti-capitalist dictatorship established by a revolutionary clique claiming to represent the objective interests (and the latent will) of the proletariat. She proclaimed:

> Freedom only for supporters of the government, only for the members of one party – however numerous they may be – is no freedom at all. Freedom is always and exclusively for the one who thinks differently. Not because of any fanatical concept of 'justice' but because all that is instructive, wholesome and purifying in political freedom depends on this essential characteristic, and its effectiveness vanishes when 'freedom' becomes a special privilege.[26]

While she did not shrink from harsh measures to extirpate the old regime, Luxemburg objected to the exclusion of any substantial part of the populace, proletarian or not, from political participation. She called for 'unrestricted freedom of press and assembly', and faulted Lenin's failure to allow for 'the most unlimited, the broadest democracy and public opinion'.[27] She recognised that, in the absence of pluralism, popular participation is necessarily reduced to the role of rubber-stamping the leadership's decisions:

> Without general elections, without unrestricted freedom of press and assembly, without a free struggle of opinion, life dies out in every public institution, becomes a mere semblance of life, in which only the bureaucracy remains as the active element . . . [What remains is] not the dictatorship of the proletariat . . . but only the dictatorship of a handful of politicians, that is[,] a dictatorship in the bourgeois sense. . .[28]

---

[25] Marx, 'Notes about the New Prussian Censorship Regulations' [1842], quoted in Avineri, *The Social and Political Thought of Karl Marx*, p. 188; cf. Montesquieu, *The Spirit of the Laws* [1748], A. Cohler, B. Miller and H. Stone (eds.) (New York: Cambridge University Press, 1989), p. 198 (bk. XII, ch. 12) (vagueness of speech crimes destructive of liberty).
[26] R. Luxemburg, 'The Russian Revolution', in *'The Russian Revolution' and 'Leninism or Marxism?'* (Ann Arbor, MI: University of Michigan Press, 1970), p. 69.
[27] Ibid., p. 71.   [28] Ibid., pp. 71–2.

Even Leon Trotsky, a central target of Luxemburg's criticisms, belatedly came to embrace Luxemburg's as the genuine Marxist view (without, however, conceding that he and Lenin had been any more dictatorial than had been required by the dire exigencies of the years immediately following 1917). In 1936, the exiled Trotsky denied (albeit now rather conveniently) that the abolition of conflicting classes had removed any need for competing parties. To the Stalinist argument that 'the question where to go – whether back to capitalism or forward to socialism – is no longer subject to discussion', Trotsky answered that the 'choice of road is no less important than the choice of the goal', and that the Soviet working class could 'furnish adequate nourishing soil for several parties'. Quoting Victor Serge, he asked: 'What remains of the October Revolution . . . if every worker who permits himself to make a demand, or express a critical judgment, is subject to imprisonment?'[29]

And yet, whatever arguments for democratic accountability might be authentically derived from Marxian texts, Krygier is correct that, historically speaking, Marxism has furnished few resources to the struggle against the usurpations and brutalities of vanguardist dictatorships that ruled in its name.[30] This deficit is familiarly, and not altogether incorrectly, attributed to the Marxian fixation on economic divisions and dynamics as the factors ultimately driving political events. The danger that an autonomous political force might wrest control of both the state and the economy for its own ends simply did not occupy Marx's attention – even though, as Michael Harrington has pointed out, Marx had recognised explicitly that under pre-capitalist conditions (e.g., 'Asian despotism'), it is political power that determines the mode of economic life.[31]

---

[29] L. Trotsky, *The Revolution Betrayed* (New York: Pathfinder Press, 1972), pp. 268–70.

[30] Krygier's critique has both the strength and the weakness that it focuses on the 'Marxism' that has had a distinctive historical impact in its own name, at the expense of other variants, such as those that blended with liberalism to produce mainstream continental European social democracy. That focus leads him to count Lenin, Trotsky, and even Stalin as authentic continuators of Marxism, largely on the ground that they and their supporters sincerely believed them to be so. M. Krygier, 'Marxism, Communism, and Narcissism,' (1990) 15 *Law and Social Inquiry* 707 at 708 (his response to critics of the article cited above). Reading Marx through this lens, however, tends to overdetermine Krygier's conclusions, since communist interpretations of Marx were fashioned to reflect their authors' policy objectives, and thus could scarcely be expected to emphasise any politically inconvenient aspects of the underlying theory.

[31] M. Harrington, *The Twilight of Capitalism* (New York: Simon & Shuster, 1976), pp. 84–7. As Harrington notes, Stalin suppressed discussion of Marx's work in this area, precisely because it might have provided the basis for an indictment of Stalinist practice. *Ibid.*, p. 87.

Ironically, Marxism's relative inattention to the danger of vanguardist usurpation can be attributed, not to Marx's lack of familiarity with would-be vanguardist usurpers, but to the contempt for them that his familiarity bred. Marx was, indeed, intensely occupied with neo-Jacobin and Blanquist efforts to remake societies by force of political will. His 'scientific' approach to social transformation led him to view these efforts as doomed to futility.[32] His concern for their consequences was that they would lead the proletariat to premature uprisings, resulting in catastrophic defeats (and thus, setbacks for the revolutionary timetable). The suggestion that they would cause catastrophe through success did not quite arise.

Even Engels's berating commentary on the Commune's would-be usurpers, cited above, neglected to be alarmist; his faith in an historical *telos* caused him to regard dictatorial conspiracies more as irrelevant than as dangerous. Indeed, for Engels, the experience of the Commune demonstrated Blanquism to be as superfluous, in the presence of material conditions for a genuine revolutionary development, as it had been futile, in the absence of such conditions. According to Engels, the 'irony of history willed' that the Blanquists in Paris did just the opposite of what their doctrine prescribed: in power, their dictatorial stance gave way to a call for a free federation of Communes, and to the filling of all posts by universal suffrage with right of recall.[33] Engels's point was that the Commune, though led by non-Marxists with dubious theoretical credentials, inexorably found its way, driven by the forces of history, to the very democratic dictatorship of the proletariat prescribed by Marx. The problem solves itself.

A further difficulty is the vagueness of the primary literature's references to 'dictatorship of the proletariat'. Dictatorship classically denoted a constitutional republic's delegation, for a limited period, of all powers needed to address an emergency;[34] it thus involves, as Lenin suggested, 'rule that is unrestricted by any laws'. Even Lenin limited this characterisation to the relationship between proletarian political power and recalcitrant elements of the bourgeoisie. The dictatorship is to be exercised by

---

[32] See Avineri, *Social and Political Thought*, pp. 187–8 ('Marx explains the reign of terror as derived from the Jacobin attempt to realise a political order still lacking its socio-economic preconditions . . . Recourse to terror is, according to Marx, an ultimate proof that the aims the revolution wishes to achieve cannot be achieved at present').
[33] Engels, 'Introduction' to *The Civil War in France*, MER, pp. 626–28.
[34] See N. Machiavelli, *The Discourses* [1521] (New York: Penguin Books, 1970), p. 195 (bk. I, disc. 34); C. Schmitt, *Political Theology* [1922] (Cambridge, MA.: MIT Press, 1985), pp. 5–10; G. Schwab, *The Challenge of the Exception*, 2nd edn (New York: Greenwood Press, 1989), pp. 30–7.

the proletariat as a whole, for the sole purpose of assimilating elements of other classes to the universal class. This animating purpose implies that one's political role, rather than one's class origin, governs one's relationship to the dictatorship. As noted above, non-hostile elements from other classes, such as the peasantry, are participants in, not objects of, the dictatorship; in principle, this is true even of members of the bourgeoisie, as soon as they renounce their class identity. The implication is that the relationship of rulers to ruled, initially presented as a matter of class, is transformed into a matter of 'objective' role in a teleological process.

That implication arguably entails, however, that where members of the working class are deemed to be 'objectively' aligned with the bourgeois enemy – where they lack the consciousness that transforms the 'class in itself' into a 'class for itself' – they may properly be objects of, rather than participants in, the exercise of dictatorial authority.[35] Even worse, the 'proletariat' may be covertly transmogrified into a wholly non-empirical construct, constituted not by real workers but by an 'objectively correct' set of normative commitments.[36] Historically, this is the sleight-of-hand that often turned Marxism, ironically, into a rationalisation for the very Blanquist-style despotism that Marx and Engels expressly scorned.

Marx and Engels never engaged in this manoeuver, and there is little reason to believe that they would have approved of it, even if they unwittingly laid the groundwork for it. Their failure to grapple effectively with the dangers of a mis- or mal-directed revolutionary mobilisation

[35] It thus became possible for Trotsky to assert in 1921: 'the dictatorship does not base itself at every given moment on the formal principle of a workers' democracy, although the workers' democracy is, of course, the only method by which the masses can be drawn more and more into the political life.' The Party, he concluded, had the right 'to assert its dictatorship even if that dictatorship temporarily clashed with the passing moods of workers' democracy.' R. Miliband, *Marxism and Politics* (New York: Oxford University Press, 1977), p. 143, citing I. Deutscher, *The Prophet Armed* (London: Oxford University Press, 1954), p. 509. Even Lenin's foremost rival among Russian Marxist theoreticians, Georgy Plekhanov, affirmed that: 'The success of the revolution is the highest law. And if, for the sake of that success, it would be necessary temporarily to limit the application of one or another democratic principle, it would be a crime to shrink from such a restriction.' *Minutes of the Second Congress of the Russian Social Democratic Labor Party* (Moscow, 1957), p. 182, quoted in R. A. Medvedev, *The October Revolution*, George Sanders (trans.) (New York: Columbia University Press, 1979), p. 113.

[36] One is reminded of Bertold Brecht's poem facetiously suggesting, amid the 1953 East German uprising, that since 'the people had forfeited the confidence of the government', the solution was for the latter to 'dissolve the people and elect another' Brecht, 'The Solution', available at: www.revolutionarydemocracy.org/rdv4n2/brecht.htm.

legitimately counts against them in any historical assessment, but in no way does it make them accomplices of the dictators and thugs who subsequently invoked them. On the contrary, the work of Marx and Engels furnishes enduring intellectual resources to the project of actualising the conditions of a dignified human existence.

2. Marx as distinctive contributor to the human rights project

If Marxian thought is acquitted of the charge of espousing normative principles incompatible with the human rights project, its affirmative contribution remains to be explored. Contemporary liberal theory has moved well beyond the 'possessive individualism'[37] that provided such an easy target for Marx's critique in *On the Jewish Question*. Its egalitarian variants (developed most prominently by John Rawls and Ronald Dworkin, but also importantly by Martha Nussbaum, Will Kymlicka, Jeremy Waldron and many others)[38] have demonstrated the liberatory potential of liberal premises for a wide range of disempowered and deprived constituencies. Conversely, Marx, in fixating on the class dimension, provides little guide to the social dynamics that produce systematic subordination and exclusion on bases such as race, ethnicity, gender, sexual orientation and disability. Moreover, Marx's normative project presupposes not only exogenous developments (an ultimate crisis of capitalism that unifies the interests of the have-nots) that have failed to unfold, but also the establishment of material conditions (abundance superseding all conflict among genuine human needs) that appear beyond the realm of possibility. Why, then, do human rights advocates need Marx?

There is no reason to doubt that, a century and a quarter after Marx's death, there is much in the corpus of Marx's work that needs to be jettisoned, and that developments within the liberal tradition have generated substantial insights that a strictly Marxian framework does not supply or even accommodate. It would be misguided to assert a new 'Marxism' as a comprehensive replacement for 'bourgeois' approaches to political morality.

---

[37] See C. B. Macpherson, *The Political Theory of Possessive Individualism: Hobbes to Locke* (Oxford: Oxford University Press, 1962).

[38] Representative works include: J. Rawls, *A Theory of Justice*; R. Dworkin, *Sovereign Virtue: The Theory and Practice of Equality* (Cambridge, MA: Harvard University Press, 2000); M. C. Nussbaum, *Women and Human Development: The Capabilities Approach* (New York: Cambridge University Press, 2000); W. Kymlicka, *Liberalism, Community, and Culture* (New York: Oxford University Press, 1989); J. Waldron, *Liberal Rights* (New York: Cambridge University Press, 1993).

The discussion below nonetheless suggests two respects in which the Marxian inspiration continues to pose a worthy challenge to the main current of contemporary liberal approaches to human rights. The first concerns the implications of class divisions for the supposed universality of liberal rights. The second concerns liberalism's resistance to institutionalising a privileged conception of human flourishing.

2.1. Form and substance: beyond legality, rights and democracy 'without adjectives'

According to conventional wisdom, the Eastern European experience has refuted the assertion, associated with Marxism, of a 'socialist legality', 'socialist rights', and a 'socialist democracy' that rival the 'bourgeois' variants. The rule of law, individual rights and democracy, properly so called, are said to exist, where at all, only 'without adjectives'.[39] This conventional wisdom reflects the altogether worthy rejection of an ends-oriented conception of legality, rights and democracy that, in establishing the ruling clique as the authoritative interpreter of their defining ends, denuded these concepts of all practical content.

Nonetheless, the conventional wisdom's espousal of legality, rights and democracy 'without adjectives' throws out the baby of Marxian insight with the bathwater of Communist practice. Underlying this espousal is the claim that each of these concepts has an objective institutional content that stands above the ends that competing normative tendencies might seek to accomplish through it. The clash of normative visions, it follows, properly occurs in an arena bounded by the 'basic structure' of a liberal society, a structure constituted by principles of legality, rights and democracy that are neutral, internally coherent, and mutually reinforcing.

The Marxian contribution is to suggest that this neutrality and harmony of fundamental political values cannot be realised so long as a society's class antagonisms have not been transcended. Whereas liberalism's project is to devise a formula that renders the exercise of power rationally justifiable from the standpoint of every individual (*qua* distinct bearer of interests and values) subject to it, Marxism denies that such a formula is possible in a class-divided society.

The Marxian insight goes beyond the familiar observation that the differently situated realise differential benefits from liberal institutions. Liberals have long conceded that, in the words of Isaiah Berlin:

---

[39] See Krygier, 'Marxism and the Rule of Law', 639.

to offer political rights, or safeguards against intervention by the state, to men who are half-naked, illiterate, underfed, and diseased is to mock their condition; they need medical help or education before they can understand, or make use of, an increase in their freedom.[40]

Social-democratic liberals (often inspired by Marxian observations or under pressure from Marxist movements) have long advocated egalitarian socioeconomic reform to realise for all sectors of society the animating purpose of liberal norms: the furtherance of the individual's capacity for genuinely self-directed activity.

The difference is that, whereas social-democratic liberals regard this struggle as the development of the liberal project to completion, Marxists see this struggle as laying bare contradictory interests and values of a class-divided society that are reflected as contradictions within the concepts at the core of the liberal mission. Thus, whereas a liberal can expect social change to be accomplished without doing any violence to legality, rights and democracy as defined by prevailing conceptions – and would evaluate a revolutionary regime's human rights performance on its continuing to uphold those conceptions – a Marxist anticipates that a crisis of the old order will force a choice between, as it were, 'their democracy and ours'.[41]

Legality, rights and democracy all trade on promises that, in a class-divided society, they must necessarily betray. In a capitalist society, they will all naturally operate to reaffirm and reinforce the prevailing dynamics of economy and society, thus giving rise to a contradiction between the values they trade on and the effective conditions that the prevailing economic and social dynamics inflict on the subordinated classes. The class struggle will thus be played out as contestation over the essential meanings of these concepts.

2.1.1. Legality

The rule of law is illustrative. The concept is animated by a concern for predictability and accountability in the exercise of power, as these are necessary (though not sufficient) conditions for liberty and democracy, respectively. Absent the secure knowledge that within fixed confines, however narrow, the individual can act on her own free will without fear of reprisal, the individual has no possibility of pursuing her own life plan; she

---

[40] I. Berlin, 'Two Concepts of Liberty' [1958], in *Four Essays on Liberty* (New York: Oxford University Press, 1969), p. 118 at p. 124.

[41] The reference is to Trotsky's (highly inadequate) essay, 'Their Morals and Ours,' in L. Trotsky, J. Dewey and G. Novak, *Their Morals and Ours: Marxist vs. Liberal Views on Morality* (New York: Pathfinder Press, 1973), p. 13.

can protect herself (if at all) only by currying favor with those exercising power, and must forsake any agenda that might interfere with that imperative. Absent mechanisms effectively holding the exercise of governmental functions to fixed standards, the polity, however broadly and deeply participatory its processes, has no capacity to see to it that its decisions are faithfully executed.

These universal truths recommend a fundamental maxim of minimally tolerable governance: 'No power shall be exercised, but according to law.' Despite the manifest ambiguities of 'according to' (a spectrum of constraint on discretion leading all the way from 'as authorised by' to 'as dictated by') and 'law' (an ideal of fixity realised in actual statutes to widely varying extents), the maxim's defining purposes of predictability and accountability ensure at least a minimum of 'bite.'[42] Accordingly, the Marxian historian E. P. Thompson, in a work that otherwise elaborately illustrated the 'shams and inequities' that lay 'concealed beneath' legal forms in early-modern England, affirmed that 'the rule of law itself, the imposing of effective inhibitions upon power and the defence of the citizen from power's all-intrusive claims', is 'an unqualified human good'.[43]

Yet, in a class-divided society, the promises of legal protection from arbitrary imposition and of legal implementation of collective empowerment go largely unrealised. The rule of law, as conventionally conceived, ignores precisely those unpredictable and unaccountable exercises of power that most fully condition social life for those lacking command over resources: exercises of 'private' power. In a capitalist economy, decisions on matters of great human consequence (working conditions, firings, plant relocations, evictions, and so on) are decentralised. These decisions are typically attributed to 'the free market', a term that suggests a natural, non-political ordering process that operates independently of human will. Thus, standards appropriate to the exercise of public power

---

[42] One of the greatest exponents of the rule of law, Lon Fuller, attributed to law an 'internal morality' entailing a set of formal qualities (i.e., that enactments be general, public, non-retroactive, clear, not in contradiction of one another, susceptible of compliance, stable, and enforced according to their terms) that are supposed to be 'neutral toward substantive aims'. L. L. Fuller, *The Morality of Law*, revd edn (New Haven: Yale University Press, 1969), pp. 46–91, 153. Fuller recognised, however, that these qualities are realised in practice only to a greater or lesser extent, and that the internal morality is a matter of overall fulfillment of essential purposes ascribable to law. '[T]here would', for example, 'be a certain occult unpersuasiveness in any assertion that retroactivity violates the very nature of law itself.' L. L. Fuller, 'Positivism and Fidelity to Law: A Reply to Professor Hart' (1958) 71 *Harvard Law Review* 630 at 650.

[43] Thompson, *Whigs and Hunters*, p. 266.

are made to appear inapplicable. Nonetheless, actual private decisions over the conditions of others' lives are often highly discretionary (sometimes even whimsical), and these decisions, far from being genuinely outside the state realm, are governmentally recognised, facilitated and enforced. Moreover, the notion of 'the free market' (which in its best usage presupposes conditions such as free and equal access to market information, low barriers to market entry, and an inability of enterprises to 'externalise' their costs) tends to be invoked irrespective of concentrations of market power within the private sector, and even of direct and indirect governmental subsidies in aid of those concentrations.[44]

Thus, the substantive values at the core of the rule of law – protection from arbitrary deprivation of conditions essential to one's life plans, and the capacity to bring the decisions that affect one's life under some measure of collective control – are values systematically under-realised for the subordinate class in a capitalist society. Since this situation can be remedied only by the progressive imposition of popular will on the defining activities of the capitalist class, thereby largely reversing the roles, the result is in some measure a zero-sum game. It is no accident that pro-capitalist ideology often invokes rule-of-law considerations, not implausibly, precisely to block the extension of legal guarantees and popular control to the operation of private enterprise.[45] Consequently, one's class perspective may reasonably determine whether one deems a given measure to further or to erode the rule of law.

The point comes into starker relief in the 'public' realm when class and ideological conflict strain constitutional arrangements to the breaking point. Given the inherent woolliness of the demand that governmental power be exercised only 'according to law', the stakes of a situation tend to determine how much discretionary power is thought to be compatible with the rule of law. Crises typically occasion an increase in discretionary

---

[44] Marx, whose study of capitalism included a discourse on 'commodity fetishism', *Capital*, vol. 1, in *MER*, pp. 319–29 (the 'ultimate money-form of the world of commodities ... conceals, instead of disclosing, the social character of private labour, and the social relations between the individual producers'), would surely be amused by today's tendency to fetishise market relations. The free-market rhetoric goes beyond likening market forces to forces of 'nature' in the physical sense, since science and technology operate to free human beings from natural limitations (such as the inability to fly); instead, the 'nature' metaphor seems to be a teleological one, an appeal to a morally ordered universe analogous to the appeal that underlies the claim that homosexuality is 'unnatural'.

[45] Illustrative is F. A. Hayek, *The Constitution of Liberty* (London: Routledge & Kegan Paul, 1960), pp. 148–61. On the other hand, the same concerns about impositions of will can be adapted to justify casting redistribution of essential resources to the poor as a matter of unconditional right. See C. Reich, 'The New Property' (1964) 73 *Yale Law Journal* 733.

authority, whether through the adoption of broad legislative authorisations or through the invocation of emergency powers. The authorisation of such measures is typically justified on the ground that 'the Constitution is not a suicide pact', in terms that lay bare the substantive values that the constitutional structure supposedly exists to defend.[46] What is then exposed is that the constitutional propriety of such exercises of power turns principally on 'to whom' the Constitution ultimately belongs. As Carl Schmitt noted:

> Public order and security manifest themselves very differently in reality, depending on whether a militaristic bureaucracy, a self-governing body controlled by the spirit of commercialism, or a radical party organization decides when there is order and security and when it is threatened or disturbed.[47]

The Marxian insight is that the contradictions of a class-divided society are manifested as inherent tensions and indeterminacies within core liberal values. Extremists have appropriated this insight for the crude claim that the rule of law in bourgeois society is nothing more than a sham, and the still cruder claim that the problem to which the concept responds is overcome once the reins of power are seized by a revolutionary party representing the objective interests of the subordinated class. Neither of these claims follow from the Marxian premise. Not only did Marx acknowledge the legal forms of the bourgeois revolution to represent a genuine (if incomplete) emancipation, but he acknowledged these forms as genuine (if incomplete) responses to the social reality of domination and compulsion, to be overcome only when societal development transcends the oppositions that underlie all subjection of one human being to the will of others. A capitalist-oriented rule of law must, in the first instance, be supplanted by a socialist-oriented rule of law, itself animated by the imperatives of predictability and accountability in the exercise of power, in ways that maximise their relevance to the real lives of the broadest sectors of society.

Still, to speak of a rule of law 'without adjectives' is to neglect the essential partisanship with which any conception of the rule of law must,

---

[46] Compare G. H. Fox and G. Nolte, 'Intolerant Democracies' (1995) 35 *Harvard International Law Journal* 1 with M. Koskenniemi, B. R. Roth, G. H. Fox and G. Nolte, 'Responses' (1996) 36 *Harvard International Law Journal* 37 (debating the democratic merit of repressive measures against anti-democratic parties), reprinted as adapted in G. H. Fox and B. R. Roth (eds.), *Democratic Governance and International Law* (New York: Cambridge University Press, 2000), pp. 389–448.

[47] Schmitt, *Political Theology*, pp. 9–10.

consciously or unconsciously, be suffused. Such neglect lays the groundwork for a 'neutral' human rights scrutiny that will be systematically skewed against movements for radical social change operating outside the bounds of 'lawful' authority, and against revolutionary regimes seeking to restructure economic and social institutions over the entrenched opposition of privileged sectors. An approach informed by the Marxian insight will not rationalise whatever thuggery announces revolutionary pretensions, but at the same time will not misidentify as mere thuggery revolutionary activity that seeks to revise the terms of class relations.

2.1.2. Rights

The same analysis applies, *mutatis mutandis*, to the substance of rights. Traditional negative rights, such as those at the core of the International Covenant on Civil and Political Rights, have differential worth to those occupying privileged and subordinate positions, respectively, within economic and social institutions. Social-democratic liberals appreciate the truth underlying Anatole France's tart observation that: '[t]he law in its majesty draws no distinction, but forbids rich and poor alike from begging in the streets or sleeping in public parks.'[48] What is less widely appreciated is that the right to free expression protects soap-box ranters and media moguls alike in their efforts to affect social consciousness, whether to problematise or to normalise the subordination and exclusion of the disempowered.

Much of the freedom that negative rights protect amounts to a freedom to exercise power: at best, power over the conditions of one's own life and a proportionate share of power in collective processes of decision-making over the shared conditions of social life; at worst, a disproportionate share of power over the conditions of others' lives. Indeed, where this disproportionate power is exercised directly, as in the exclusion of racial minorities from privately owned public accommodations, liberals have come to acknowledge it and to advocate restrictions on it in the name of liberal freedom.

The economic and social power of a dominant class typically manifests itself less directly, but no less weightily. As Lukes has pointed out in his classic work on the 'three dimensions' of power, elites frequently possess the capacity, not merely to win such political conflicts as arise, nor merely even to frame the issues that arise, but further to dissuade

---

[48] H. Zinn, 'The Conspiracy of Law', in R. P. Wolff (ed.), *The Rule of Law* (New York: Simon & Shuster, 1971), p. 15 at p. 32.

the underprivileged from understanding their life difficulties as bases for political demands.[49] In particular, society's dominant forces act – in a mostly spontaneous but nonetheless structured fashion – to maintain and deepen a consumer-oriented culture, thereby impeding both the recognition of class interests and the development of habits of collective action. Cultural hegemony operates to sustain domination behind the mask of a formal regime of freedom and equality.

More concretely, rights can function as shields behind which privileged elites, when confronted by governments bent on economic and social reform or transformation, can act to mobilise resistance and to generate economic chaos. As illustrated in the history of populist and socialist governments in the Western Hemisphere (e.g., Guatemala in the early 1950s, Chile in the early 1970s, Jamaica in the late 1970s, Nicaragua in the 1980s, and Venezuela today), the struggle to implement structural change in stratified societies can culminate in political crises that raise serious questions about whether protection of the destabilising oppositional activities of entrenched elites serves or disserves the liberatory goals of the human rights movement.

This Marxian line of critique suffers from a bad reputation, owing to the crudity and one-sidedness of many of its former applications. Part of the problem is fairly attributed to errors within Marx's own thinking. Marx wrongly anticipated, on the one hand, a progressive unification of both the economic interests and the political consciousness of those diverse sectors lacking command over the major means of production, and, on the other hand, a progressive sharpening of capitalism's economic contradictions that would impel the unified have-nots to a root-and-branch rejection of the status quo. These predictions gave rise to an oversimplified understanding of the political aspects of economic conflict. In reality, different sectors of the have-nots are differently situated; the political task is not merely to reveal the inherent harmony of their economic needs, but affirmatively to develop a programme that reconciles them. Class interests are not so much 'objective' as subject to conflicting reasonable interpretations. The political choice is at all times not between intolerable economic conditions and a great leap into the dark, but between better and worse projected outcomes, which in turn can be gauged only according to competing normative understandings of what mixes and distributions of improvements and detriments count as just and beneficial.

An oversimplified understanding of what is at stake in political conflict has frequently led self-styled continuators of the Marxian tradition

---

[49] S. Lukes, *Power: A Radical View* (London: Macmillan Press Ltd., 1974), p. 24.

to a number of poorly reasoned conclusions about rights. These have ranged across a spectrum of embarrassments, from a simplistic inversion of the typical liberal-democratic prioritisation of civil and political over economic and social rights, to the notion that socialist civil and political rights properly exist 'in order to strengthen and develop the socialist system' and therefore are exercisable only 'in accordance with the aims of building communism', as these aims are authoritatively interpreted by the revolutionary leadership.[50] As noted above, whereas Luxemburg's interpretation of Marx properly understood socialism as the set of policies that the working people themselves choose – by collective decisions derived from the autonomous participation of each, in a process open to the expression of the widest range of disagreement – the Communists came remarkably close to defining the working people, the bearers of 'socialist rights', as the supporters of objectively progressive policies. By this logic, the rights of individuals are reducible to the right to play out a scripted role in a revealed historical drama. The incompatibility of any such notion with the human rights project is self-evident.

Notwithstanding these catastrophic mistakes of supposed Marxists, the essential Marxian insight remains unrefuted. Socioeconomic stratification, in rendering rights-bearers differently situated to a radical extent, renders the universal application of traditional liberal rights not only insufficient for the realisation of universal liberal values, but also, at least potentially in some circumstances, a detriment to efforts to effectuate that realisation for subordinated classes. The overcoming of class divisions is a necessary (whether or not sufficient) condition for dissolving the clashes within the liberal scheme of values, which otherwise need to be addressed case-by-case in a non-dogmatic effort to further the overall conditions of a dignified human existence.

2.1.3. Democracy

The shortcomings of 'democracy without adjectives' are still easier to demonstrate. Empirically oriented political scientists conventionally identify democracy with a set of institutional requisites: fair electoral processes, freedom to organise competing parties, an uncensored press, and so on.[51] This institutional definition is designed to abstract from

---

[50] The quoted words are from Articles 50 and 51 of the 1977 Soviet Constitution.
[51] The requisites typically cited track Robert Dahl's seven criteria of 'polyarchy' – essentially, constitutional rule based on fair elections, combined with freedom of expression and of association. See R. A. Dahl, *Democracy and Its Critics* (New Haven: Yale University Press, 1989), p. 233.

potentially contentious questions about the institutions' relationship to a presumed source of political authority (e.g., 'popular will') or to the ends with which democracy might be associated (e.g., equality of power over the conditions of social life).[52]

This same non-teleological approach to defining the phenomenon has recently been adapted to the normative claim for a right to democracy.[53] But whereas it is at least coherent (whether or not persuasive) to speak of fulfilment of other rights as representing an imperative independent of the purposes for which an individual right-bearer might choose to exercise it, the same cannot be said for a right to democracy. No-one values democracy for the sheer joy of going into a voting booth every few years to choose among different slates of candidates. (Even civic republicans, who regard the activity of political participation as end in itself, have in mind a much different conception of what that activity encompasses.) A right to democracy can be rooted only in the value of a democratic social reality that institutions are calculated to bring about, and so cannot ultimately be defined in abstraction from its animating purposes.[54]

---

[52] The contemporary comparative politics literature justifies rejecting teleological definitions of democracy on the ground that these render democratic performance inherently unmeasurable by social science techniques. This justification is understood by social scientists to entail lightening the term's normative baggage – that is, of identifying democracy as, at most, one of many political virtues. See S. Huntington, *The Third Wave: Democratization in the Late Twentieth Century* (Norman, OK: University of Oklahoma Press, 1991), pp. 5–13. Advocates of a human right to 'democratic governance' have nonetheless imported, rather dubiously, this simplification from the empirical into the normative realm.

[53] See T. M. Franck, 'The Emerging Right to Democratic Governance', (1992) 86 *American Journal of International Law* 46; G. H. Fox, 'The Right to Political Participation in International Law' (1992) 17 *Yale Journal of International Law* 539. For an overview of the issues raised by the claim, see G. H. Fox and B. R. Roth, 'Democracy and International Law' (2001) 27 *Review of International Studies* 327. For critical accounts of the 'democratic entitlement' claim, see B. R. Roth, *Governmental Illegitimacy in International Law* (New York: Oxford University Press, 1999); S. Marks, *The Riddle of All Constitutions* (Oxford: Oxford University Press, 2000). For a sampling of competing evaluations, see G. H. Fox and B. R. Roth (eds.), *Democratic Governance and International Law* (New York: Cambridge University Press, 2000).

[54] See B. R. Roth, 'Evaluating Democratic Progress: A Normative Theoretical Perspective' (1995) 9 *Ethics and International Affairs* 55, reprinted in Fox and Roth (eds.), *Democratic Governance*, p. 493; B. R. Roth, 'Democratic Intolerance: Observations on Fox and Nolte' (1996) 37 *Harvard International Law Journal* 235, reprinted in Fox and Roth (eds.), Democratic Governance, p. 441. For a remarkably ends-oriented account of liberal democracy, disparaging the conventional emphasis on electoral participation, see R. A. Dworkin, 'The Moral Reading and the Majoritarian Premise', in H. Hongju Koh and R. C. Slye (eds.), *Deliberative Democracy and Human Rights* (New Haven, Yale University Press, 1999), p. 81.

Competing normative theories, however, assign democracy differing, and often conflicting, animating purposes. The prevailing view, which the anti-Rousseauian Benjamin Constant articulated with great clarity almost two centuries ago, is that democracy aims to effectuate individual freedom, no longer in the sense of equal and direct participation in the decisions of a social whole ('the liberty of the ancients'), but in the sense of making society safe for the pursuit of diverse private interests ('the liberty of the moderns').[55]

In the long term, the Marxian hope is to overcome this dichotomy through a thoroughgoing transformation of economic relations. The liberty of the ancients, which Rousseau hoped could still be realised in the modern world, envisages a 'general will', arising from participatory processes, that holistically reconciles the freedom of each with the freedom of all. Rousseau understood that any such vision presupposes the overcoming of power disparities among classes, so that no citizen is 'wealthy enough to buy another, and none poor enough to be forced to sell himself'.[56] His intensive conception of 'generality' required that citizens be so similarly situated that the benefits and burdens of public acts would fall equally across the citizenry, leading each to identify his own interests with the interests of the whole.[57] In such circumstances, participation in common projects and enjoyment of public goods were expected to furnish a greater part of individual happiness, leaving less need to seek fulfilment through the furtherance of private interests.[58]

---

[55] B. Constant, 'The Liberty of the Ancients Compared with That of the Moderns', in *Benjamin Constant: Political Writings*, Biancamaria Fontana (trans.) (Cambridge: Cambridge University Press, 1988), pp. 307–28.

[56] J.-J. Rousseau, 'The Social Contract,' in *Rousseau, The Social Contract and Discourses*, G. D. H. Cole (trans.) (Toronto: J. M. Dent & Sons Ltd., 1973), bk. II, ch. 11, p. 163 at p. 204.

[57] In Rousseau's conception: 'every *authentic* act of the general will binds or favors all citizens equally; so that the Sovereign recognises only the body of the nation, and draws no distinctions between those of whom it is made up. . . . The Sovereign never has a right to lay more charges on one subject than on another, because, in that case, the question becomes particular, and ceases to be within its competency.' Rousseau, 'The Social Contract', bk. II, ch. 4, p. 163 at p. 188 (emphasis added). Since 'all continually will the happiness of each one', and every citizen considers 'each' to mean himself, every citizen will vote for the good of the whole in consideration of his own good. *Ibid.*, bk. II, ch. 4, pp. 186–7.

[58] *Ibid.*, bk. III, ch. 15, p. 240. The functioning of the general will does not require, however, that individuals no longer differ in their interests and values. 'If there were no different interests, the common interest would be barely felt, as it would encounter no obstacle; all would go on of its own accord, and politics would cease to be an art.' *Ibid.*, bk. I, ch. 9, p. 185, n. 1. Rousseau and Marx are harmonised by Will Kymlicka's astute observation that Marx's vision of end-stage communism entails the overcoming only of class antagonisms,

But, as Marx recognised, past efforts to reconcile 'citizen' (participant in political community) with 'man' (pursuer of private interests) had either lacked the economic requisites for the identification of the freedom of one with the freedom of all (thereby reducing to 'utopianism') or had been predicated on the assignment of productive labour to a large class of non-citizens (e.g., slavery in the ancient world). With the transcendence of scarcity, of the capitalistic division of labour, and therefore of external control over the individual's productive powers, Marx envisaged finally transforming a circumstance in which 'species-life itself – society – appears as a system which is external to the individual and as a limitation of his original independence' into one in which 'the real, individual man has absorbed into himself the abstract citizen' and the 'individual man, in his everyday life, in his work, and in his relationships . . . has become a *species-being*'.[59] Lucio Colletti summarises the point, if perhaps exaggeratedly, in his assertion that 'revolutionary "political" theory, as it has developed since Rousseau, is already foreshadowed and contained in The Social Contract', and that Marx and Lenin have added nothing, 'except for the analysis . . . of the "economic bases" for the withering away of the state'.[60]

Marx's immediate relevance, however, is to the shorter term, where the prevailing concern must remain a genuine extension of 'the freedom of the moderns' to the subordinated class. The Marxian observation here is that those sectors of society having real weight in political decision-making tend to win the conditions of freedom relevant to those sectors. The primary condition of freedom for those with command over resources is the protection of the individual from state encroachment, whereas the primary condition of freedom for the have-nots is an end to economic deprivation and insecurity and to social disempowerment and exclusion.

Although the right to democracy trades heavily on the ideal of political equality, what passes for democracy in the prevalent discourse is an institutional structure that both reflects and works to stabilise power disparities in the 'private' realm. While attention is focused on each citizen's free exercise of a single vote, 'insiders' determine the composition of

---

not of conflicting individual goals and projects. Kymlicka, *Liberalism, Community, and Culture*, pp. 118–19. Notwithstanding Marx's reservation of the word 'political' for modes of governance that entail class domination, it appears that end-stage communism's residual coordination authority was intended to embody a realisation of the Rousseauian scheme.

[59] Marx, 'On the Jewish Question', *MER*, pp. 43, 46.

[60] L. Colletti, *From Rousseau to Lenin: Studies in Ideology and Society*, J. Merrington and J. White (trans.) (London: NLB, 1972), p. 185.

candidate slates, candidates are beholden to campaign contributors, mass media outlets frame the political issues, and large commercial interests have macroeconomic leverage over local elected officials.[61]

The more rigid the social stratification and the more widespread the economic deprivation, the more frequently has formal political equality has been perceived to mock the moral authority associated with the word 'democracy'. Especially in underdeveloped countries, where these conditions are endemic, liberal-democratic procedures typically do little to enhance the power of the poor majority to influence the social decisions that affect their lives. The capacity to select periodically from among pre-packaged candidates of elite-controlled parties scarcely implies the rudiments of accountability, let alone genuine popular empowerment. Popular prerogative to reject one given set of administrators of the social order in favour of another, while not a trivial development, is very far from the power to make government responsive to popular initiatives, input or needs. Where opposition groups operate without resources in a context of widespread illiteracy, economic dependence and entrenched habits of deference to traditional authority, meager are the prospects for making real the promises associated with the democratic label.

A Marxian approach would posit as the essence of democracy the effective equality of power in social decision-making. An appropriate measure of democracy, then, is the extent to which the interests and views of the bottom half of the socioeconomic ladder have commensurate weight in political decision-making – a consideration notably absent in the literature on the right to democracy. On this view, fidelity to familiar electoral procedures should be subject to the overarching purpose of substantive social empowerment of the resource-deprived.

Accordingly, militant opposition to fairly elected governments, including tactics exceeding the bounds of legality, cannot be sweepingly dismissed as inimical to genuine democracy. Moreover, one cannot rule out, *a priori*, that authoritarian and coercive practices calculated to break the

---

[61] Susan Marks exposes the prevailing vision of democratisation as both shallow and narrow: shallow in that it identifies the democratic norm with a 'low-intensity democracy' that emphasises electoral competition among elites at the expense of mass participation and empowerment; narrow in that it aims at democracy within the boundaries of each state – 'pan-national democracy' – without concern for democratic control of those realms of decision-making that are increasingly transnational. See Marks, *The Riddle of All Constitutions*, pp. 50–100. In her view, assertions of an international democratic norm give an imprimatur to procedural reforms that are intended less as an opening to the thoroughgoing transformation of decision-making processes that govern economic and social life than as a strategy for deflecting pressures for such transformation.

effective hold of socioeconomic elites may, under certain conditions, be a more democratic alternative to 'free and fair elections' that, for structural reasons, systematically ratify the *status quo*.

This is not to say that *a posteriori* examination will frequently vindicate such measures, the historical consequences of which have tended to be setbacks to popular empowerment. It is also not to deny that liberal-democratic procedural mechanisms can constitute a real achievement that creates crucial space for agitation in favour of subordinated sectors of society – an achievement that Marx himself indisputably valued.

A Marxian orientation does, however, anticipate that in class-divided societies, internal tensions and contradictions will inevitably mark the application of the concepts of legality, rights and democracy, in striking contrast to the more conventional image of a seamless web of mutually reinforcing values. This insight qualifies as a substantial contribution to the intellectual infrastructure of the human rights project.

2.2. Socialist ends: beyond the right-good distinction

The second Marxian contribution to normative human rights theory is to call into question the 'neutralist' ethos predominant in contemporary liberal thought. Marx attributed to human beings an innate potential for creative self-expression that achieves realisation only in unalienated social labour. To achieve genuine human emancipation, the oppressed class must take collective action to forge new economic and social arrangements that will not only marshal economic resources to meet needs on an equal basis, but also will transform work into the vehicle for the fulfilment of creative powers. That process is envisaged progressively to overcome the egoistic opposition of individuals one to another, thereby bringing about 'the complete return of man to himself as a *social* (i.e., human) being'.[62] The project of social transformation presupposes a 'truly human' way of life to be pursued collectively (albeit one that exalts individual self-direction within the designated parameters), in contrast to a debased one under capitalism pursued by individuals in isolation.

Conversely, deontological liberalism rejects all political manifestations of 'perfectionism' – efforts to further, through compulsory collective decisions, a determinate conception of the good life – insisting instead on an equality of human beings *qua* individual end-choosers. Thus, Martha Nussbaum characteristically seeks to limit the political project to the

---

[62] Marx, 'Economic and Philosophic Manuscripts', *MER*, p. 84 (emphasis in original).

furtherance of 'central human capabilities', as opposed to the furtherance of any particular model of 'human functioning'. While acknowledging that Aristotle and Marx, her sources of inspiration, can be invoked for both projects, she asserts that 'there is a big difference between pushing people into functioning in ways you consider valuable and leaving the choice up to them'.[63]

If, however, 'capabilities' and 'functioning' are interdependent, the deontological wall of separation between 'the right' (moral judgments about fairness to human subjects) and 'the good' (moral judgments about the proper objects of human striving) cannot be sustained. Putting aside the debater's point that the distinction itself may be nothing more than a sleight-of-hand – proper functioning may effectively be the ultimate test of the true realisation of capabilities – interdependence is established if proper functioning is indispensable to the social conditions needed for capabilities to be developed. In refusing to take compulsory collective decisions that presuppose and reinforce the common pursuit of a new way of functioning, a society governed by neutralist liberalism may systematically neglect to produce the public goods (both tangible and intangible) that form the structural basis for development of new capabilities. If that proves to be the case, it would follow that deontological liberalism serves, in the guise of neutrality on the proper mode of 'human functioning', effectively to reaffirm and to reinforce an existing way of life that actually stunts the development of certain 'central human capabilities'.

The issue is not limited to abstractions or to projected policies for a remote future society, but rather pertains to concrete, present-day social-democratic practice. The neutralist approach, although favouring redistribution to reduce inequality among individual end-choosers, embraces markets as non-coercive instruments of co-ordination, not solely for the sake of efficiency, but for sake of neutrally empowering individual choice. In contrast, a social democratic perfectionism may pursue not merely a Rawlsian distributive justice (allowing only such inequalities as improve the conditions of the worst off),[64] but also societal goals derived from a peculiarly socialistic conception of the good life: e.g., relative equality *per se* (even where greater inequalities might increase somewhat the incomes of the poor); an ethos of frugality; broad and deep popular participation in collective projects; workers' control over the workplace environment;

---

[63] M. C. Nussbaum, *Women and Human Development: The Capabilities Approach* (New York: Cambridge University Press, 2000), p. 101.

[64] For an elaboration of the 'difference principle' as the basis for distributive justice, see Rawls, *A Theory of Justice*, pp. 75–83.

security against risks to basic material needs; and stability of the economic bases of local communities. Absent a collective decision, market-based aggregations of individual choices would tend, for structural reasons, to drive out these socialistic goals in favour of more individualistic ends. The collective non-decision, while purportedly neutral, would facilitate some modes of human 'functioning' while undermining others.

Genuine freedom, Marx insisted:

> can only consist in socialized man, the associated producers, rationally regulating their interchange with Nature, bringing it under their common control, instead of being ruled by it as by the blind forces of Nature; and achieving this with the least expenditure of energy and under conditions most favorable to, and worthy of, their human nature.[65]

According to Marx's early work on alienation, man is distinguished from lower animals in that he 'makes his life-activity itself the object of his will and of his consciousness'.[66] 'Activity and consumption, both in their content and in their *mode of existence*, are *social*; *social* activity and *social* consumption.'[67] Thus, even:

> when I am active *scientifically*, etc. – when I am engaged in activity which I can seldom perform in direct community with others – then I am *social*, because I am active as a *man*. Not only is the material of my activity given to me as a social product (as is even the language in which the thinker is active): my *own* existence *is* social activity, and therefore that which I make of myself, I make of myself for society and with the consciousness of myself as a social being.[68]

Social production, so understood, is humanity's life activity, the expression of human creativity and the prime need of a genuinely human existence; only through an organisation of productive activity that estranges man from his essential nature does he come to regard productive activity only as a means of life.

Marx observed that under the capitalist mode of production, which 'throws back some of the workers into a barbarous type of labor and turns the others into machines', man:

> in his work . . . does not affirm himself but denies himself, does not feel content but unhappy, does not develop freely his mental and physical energy but mortifies his body and ruins his mind . . . As a result, therefore, man

---

[65] Marx, *Capital*, vol. III, *MER*, p. 441.
[66] Marx, 'Economic and Philosophic Manuscripts of 1844', *MER*, p. 66 at p. 76.
[67] *Ibid.*, p. 85 (emphasis in original).   [68] *Ibid.*, p. 86 (emphasis in original).

(the worker) no longer feels himself to be freely active in any but his animal functions – eating, drinking and procreating, or at most in his dwelling and in dressing-up, etc.; and in his human functions he no longer feels himself to be anything but an animal. What is animal becomes human and what is human becomes animal.[69]

As a result, the individual's need to express himself through co-operative and socially useful productive activity is lost from consciousness, replaced by egoistic needs of the individual as consumer that capitalist processes systematically multiply to further the accumulation of capital:

> [E]very person speculates upon creating a *new* need in another, so as to drive him to a fresh sacrifice, to place him in a new dependence and to seduce him into a new mode of *gratification* and therefore economic ruin. Each tries to establish over the other an *alien* power, so as thereby to find the satisfaction of his own selfish need.[70]

Under capitalism, the supremacy of egoistic (pseudo-)needs assures that human beings are pitted against one another. Every man comes 'to see in other men, not the realization, but rather the *limitation* of his own liberty'.[71]

But under socialism, this ceases to be so: 'we shall have an association, in which the free development of each is the condition for the free development of all.'[72] The fulfilment of necessity, says Volume III of *Capital*, permits 'that development of human energy which is an end in itself, the true realm of freedom', the 'basic prerequisite' of which is 'the shortening of the working day'.[73] According to Volume IV (a work otherwise known as *Theories of Surplus Value*):

> [F]ree time, disposable time, is wealth itself, partly for the enjoyment of the project, partly for the free activity which – unlike labor – is not dominated by the pressure of an extraneous purpose which must be fulfilled, and the fulfillment of which is [instead] regarded as a natural necessity or a social duty, according to one's inclinations.[74]

---

[69] *Ibid.*, p. 74.   [70] *Ibid.*, p. 93 (emphasis in original).
[71] Marx, 'On the Jewish Question', *MER*, p. 26 at p. 42 (emphasis in original).
[72] Marx and Engels, 'The Manifesto of the Communist Party' [1848], *MER*, p. 469 at p. 491.
[73] *MER*, p. 441.
[74] Marx, *Theories of Surplus Value*, iii (Moscow: Foreign Languages Publishing House, 1962), p. 257, quoted in S. Lukes, *Moral Conflict and Politics* (Oxford: Oxford University Press, 1991), p. 207.

It follows that the shortening of the working day has an objective priority over the pursuit of superfluous – that is to say, low-pleasure-oriented and status-oriented – consumption, a pursuit that enlarges the realm of necessity and thereby increases the subjection of human labour to an alien power. A socialist society will, in bringing economic forces under rational control, have a collective interest in suppressing rampant consumerism and competitive quests for 'positional' goods.[75] Establishing the conditions of genuine human freedom requires establishing conditions conducive to the development of a consciousness of human beings' true nature and true needs – in other words, collective decisions presupposing a perfectionist commitment to a particular conception of the proper objects of human striving.

The dominant strain of contemporary social-democratic liberalism holds compulsory collective decisions to be admissible in aid of the production of 'neutral' public goods that furnish appropriate conditions for individual choice, but are inadmissible where they presuppose a controversial conception of the good.[76] Conversely, a social democratic perfectionism, though not seeking directly to impose one ideal way of life, is partisan among visions of the good life, and it attempts actively to effectuate the social requisites to lives it recognises as good.

These requisites are achievable only through a distinctively collective, rather than individual, mode of rationality. Without the assurance that their sacrifices lock others into a scheme of co-operation, individuals have no incentive to forgo an individual benefit for the sake of contribution to a public good. The logic of market rationality leads to the pursuit only of those goods that can be secured by one's own independent activity. Where all decisions that reflect a distinctive conception of the good life are left to individual choices, co-ordinated by market mechanisms, the

---

[75] The significance of a 'positional' good lies in the social status one gains by possessing it while others do not, or, more importantly, in the social status or access one loses by not possessing it while others do. A typical characteristic of positional goods is that most people would be better off if all entered into a binding agreement not to pursue them. See R. H. Frank, *Choosing the Right Pond: Human Behavior and the Quest for Status* (New York: Oxford University Press, 1985).

[76] Elizabeth Anderson asserts that: 'the capabilities citizens need to function as equals in civil society count as neutral goods for purposes of justice not because everyone finds these capabilities equally valuable, but because reasonable people can recognise that these form a legitimate basis for making moral claims on one another.' E. S. Anderson, 'What is the Point of Equality?' (1999) *Ethics* 109, 287, 330. Note, however, that this statement assumes it to be possible to make a 'neutral' assessment of 'what capabilities citizens need to function as equals in civil society'.

public goods conducive to co-operative development are systematically neglected.

To abjure 'non-neutral' collective decisions is thus to impose by default a determinate collective view of what individuals ought to be free to do. Teleology, turned away at the front door, comes in through the back. And the *telos* is an atomistic one, not by design, but by default.

The essential Marxian insight, then, is that liberalism's pretensions to neutrality, even in the highly nuanced form expounded by egalitarian liberals, mask its deep structural affinity for prevailing patterns of human functioning that reflect and reinforce existing hierarchies. This insight is applicable to the struggles to overcome social dynamics that produce systematic subordination and exclusion on bases other than those on which Marx focused, such as race, ethnicity, gender, sexual orientation and disability.[77]

Still more broadly, a Marxian sensibility is on guard against flawed arguments from neutrality that liberals typically invoke against tyrannical perfectionisms. Instead of unpersuasively dismissing conservatives' identification of meaningful freedom with embeddedness in a supportive social environment, sustained by a shared commitment to certain of what Wilmoore Kendall termed 'public truths' (i.e., 'standards upon whose validity a society is entitled to insist'),[78] human rights advocates will do better to take issue with the conservatives' 'public truths' on their merits. The Marxian inspiration contributes to a competing affirmative vision, thus providing a further resource to the human rights project.

3. Conclusion

Marxism retains its relevance in the current period, not as a comprehensive replacement for liberal human rights theories, but as a source of critique that challenges those theories on the basis of the very values of human freedom and dignity that they espouse. It thus helps to furnish alternative gauges of whether particular policies advance those values.

The theme of the Marxian critique is that, in a class-divided society, liberal institutions not only systematically fail to realise for all sectors the values on which they trade, but also tend, by virtue of their formal

---

[77] For my effort to apply a parallel analysis to the liberation of women, see B. R. Roth, 'The CEDAW as a Collective Approach to Women's Rights' (2002) 24 *Michigan Journal of International Law* 187.

[78] W. Kendall, 'The "Open Society" and Its Fallacies' (1960) 54 *American Political Science Review*, 972 at 974.

neutrality, to reaffirm and reinforce the structural dynamics of economy and society that maintain the disempowerment of subordinated sectors. Liberal theory normalises the indignities associated with the operation and maintenance of the prevailing order, while identifying as exceptional the harsh responses occasioned by that very order's contradictions. The contradictory interests and values of a class-divided society are thus reflected as contradictions within the core of the liberal mission. Whereas liberalism purports to represent a set of harmonious and mutually reinforcing values, a Marxian analysis reveals internal tensions that cannot be overcome until class antagonisms are themselves transcended. The class struggle is thus played out as contestation over the essential meanings of the normative concepts to which liberalism appeals.

Viewed in this light, the human rights movement's conventional rhetoric often appears as question-begging, and its prescriptions as one-sided and lacking in nuance. At the same time, a Marxian approach recommends no sweeping rejection of liberal values and practices, and in the greatest number of real-world instances reaffirms the liberal human rights mission, albeit on a somewhat different rationale. Marx further provides inspiration to an affirmative project of social democratic perfectionism, a political morality that extends beyond the limits of a 'neutral' distributive justice to demand the establishment, through collective decision, of economic and social conditions conducive to 'genuinely human' modes of functioning.

The twentieth century saw the refutation of a series of political experiments that invoked a Marxian aim of egalitarian social transformation. Nonetheless, the refutation of these experiments – all of which occurred in circumstances that Marx never foresaw and resorted to devices that Marx never recommended – does not invalidate the insights that prompted so many to embrace these experiments, often allowing their hopes to get the better of their reason. While no one should romanticise or seek to revisit these experiments, neither should one consign to the dustbin the ideas that inspired generations of activists to take up the cause of fundamental social change. Marxian thought remains a valuable source of insight for those pursuing the venerable aim of securing the conditions of a dignified human existence for all.

8

Marxian embraces (and de-couplings) in Upendra Baxi's human rights scholarship: a case study

OBIORA CHINEDU OKAFOR

1. Introduction

For a remarkably long period of time, the world over, Marxist ideas 'held a special fascination for movements seeking to transform economic, political, and social conditions in favour of the "have-nots"'.[1] But the not-too-distant fall of what was widely regarded as 'actually existing socialism' has led all too many commentators to declare (with varying degrees of thoughtfulness or the lack thereof) that the Marxian thought that seemed to inspire and animate that system had 'thus been rendered nugatory'.[2] Yet, there is increasing recognition among an epistemic community of those knowledgeable in the intricacies of Marxian and other socio-political thought that these sorts of announcements of the complete and total negation of the broadly Marxian theory of social, political and economic life are far too non-nuanced and totalising as to be accurate. Some, like Brad Roth and Martti Koskenniemi, have even gone as far as arguing (in separate papers) that Marx can even be retrieved to further the ends of either the human rights movement or of international law more generally.[3]

It is in this broad tradition of critical reflection on the continued (however limited) influence of Marxian thought on social scientific and international legal scholarship that this chapter is conceived. More particularly, the chapter is concerned with an understanding of the extent to which Marxian thought (understood more broadly than narrowly) has left its mark on the work of Upendra Baxi (emeritus professor of

---

[1] B. R. Roth, 'Marxian insights for the human rights project', Chapter 7 in this volume.
[2] See J. Muravchik, 'Marxism' (2002) 133 *Foreign Policy* 36 at 37.
[3] See Roth, 'Marxian insights'; and M. Koskenniemi, 'What should international lawyers learn from Karl Marx?', Chapter 1 in this volume.

law in development at the University of Warwick; former vice-chancellor of the University of Delhi; former president of the Indian law institute; one of the most accomplished scholars of our time; and certainly one of the most well-known and celebrated first generation critical Third World international law scholars).[4] Primarily for reasons of space limitations, this project will be undertaken and accomplished by focusing on Baxi's leading book-length contribution to the understanding of (international) human rights theory: the second edition of *The Future of Human Rights*.[5]

To be clear, the task at hand is not so much to discover if Baxi is a Marxist, as much as it is to map and reflect on the impact that his long and fruitful study of Marxian thought[6] has, or has not, had on his critical Third World approaches to international law (TWAIL) human rights scholarship.[7] In any case, for two major reasons, a focus on whether or not Baxi is a Marxist will not be as worthwhile as the latter strategy. First of all, Marxists do not always accept everything that Marx said or did as correct.[8] As such, by what functional measure of adherence are we to definitely identify a scholar as Marxist, especially when, like Baxi, that scholar's approach tends to be eclectic? Secondly, it may be somewhat problematic to describe Baxi, in monolithic fashion, as a Marxist if his even deeper TWAIL commitments are adequately factored into the equation.[9] On the whole then, the strategy

---

[4] The reference to Baxi as a Third World scholar is not intended to in any way limit the global impact of his remarkable career, but to underlie his own chosen position to write primarily from a Third World perspective. More will be said on this point in section 3. By *Third World* is meant the group of states and peoples who 'self-identify' as such. They are not a monolith, but a 'chorus of voices'. Save for the preceding explanation, I will bracket the long-standing debate over the existence and nature of this category, and refer the reader to my views on it in O. C. Okafor, 'Newness, Imperialism and International Legal Reform in our time: A TWAIL, Perspective' (2005) 43 *Osgoode Hall Law Journal* 171 at 174–6. For a fuller development of the 'chorus' metaphor used above, see also K. Mickelson, 'Rhetoric and Rage: Third World Voices in International Legal Discourse' (1998) 16 *Wisconsin International Law Journal* 353, at 360.

[5] See U. Baxi, *The Future of Human Rights*, 2nd edn (Oxford: Oxford University Press, 2006).

[6] Baxi's depth of appreciation of the tenets of classic and evolving Marxian thought is evidenced in part by his book-length commentary on Marxism: see U. Baxi, *Marx, Law and Justice* (Mumbai: NM Tripathi & Co.,1993).

[7] For more on this movement, see Mickelson, 'Rhetoric and Rage'; J. Gathii, 'Alternative and Critical: The Contribution of Research and Scholarship on Developing Countries to International Legal Theory' (2000) 41 *Harvard International Law Journal* 263; M. Mutua, 'What is TWAIL?' (2000) 94 *American Society of International Law Proceedings* 31; and Okafor, 'Newness, Imperialism and International Legal Reform' 174–80.

[8] See F. Tarrit, 'A Brief History, Scope, and Peculiarities of "Analytical Marxism"' (2006) 38 *Review of Radical Political Economy* 595 at 598–9.

[9] Baxi's deep commitment to a TWAILian approach will be examined in section 3.

adopted here, of mapping and assessing the impact of Marxian ideas on his scholarship (howsoever that body of writing is named) seems to be the more sensible one.

The hypothesis that is developed in the rest of the chapter is that while Marxism (broadly construed) is one of the two *disciplined approaches* to the understanding of human suffering that Baxi has drawn on the most in the course of producing a uniquely Baxian approach to human rights scholarship, his relationship with Marxian thought is far from linear or simplistic. Instead, that relationship is complicated and sophisticated. Needless to say, the other disciplined approach that has animated and influenced Baxi's human rights praxis the most is TWAIL. Baxi's broad emphasis and focus on the exploitation of the 'subaltern classes'[10] by formations of global capital has, alongside his deep and abiding TWAILian sensitivities to human suffering (especially but not exclusively) in the Third World, has provided him with the main intellectual building blocks and repertoires with which he has problematised, critiqued and built upon human rights law's often difficult relationships with the suffering of the subaltern classes. However, it should be noted at this juncture, that the focus of this chapter on the influence of Marxian insights on Baxi's human rights scholarship will not allow the full development, beyond the brief analysis in section 3, of the TWAIL character of his work.

In order systematically to develop this argument, the chapter has been organised into nine segments, this introduction included. Sections 2 and 3 are preliminary but necessary in nature. They set the stage for a fuller appreciation of the nature and extent of Marxian influence on Baxi's human rights scholarship. Without situating those Marxian influences in the context provided by these sections of the chapter, a nuanced and accurate assessment of their overall impact will be virtually impossible. In section 2, Baxi's abiding commitment to (a reformed version) of the human rights ethos will be examined. The aim of this enquiry is to seek to understand him – despite his critical posture in the area – as a practising, if highly advanced, scholar of that sub-discipline of international legal scholarship. In section 3, Baxi's impressive TWAIL credentials are established. As obvious as his qualifications are in the present respect, relatively short shrift is made of this task. It is therefore enough to make the extant point by examining some instances of his utilisation of many

---

[10] Like B. S. Chimni, Baxi uses this term as a historical category to include a whole range of people who inhabit a sharply subordinate socio-economic and political position. See B. S. Chimni, 'An outline of a Marxist course on public international law', Chapter 2 in this volume.

TWAIL tools in the book under study. It is in the next five sections that the extent to which Baxi's TWAIL human rights work has been impacted by Marxian ideas is considered. In section 4, Baxi's focus on and attention to a range of subaltern 'voices of suffering',[11] is examined for its Marxian credentials, or lack thereof. Section 5 deals with the extent to which Baxi's work in the book under study adheres to the Marxian theory of historical materialism. In section 6, Baxi's thesis on the emergence of a trade-related market-friendly human rights (TREMF) paradigm is examined for possible Marxian influences. Section 7 considers whether Baxi's approach to human rights movements and NGOs embraces any Marxian insights. Section 8 focuses on some of Baxi's de-couplings from Marxian thought in order to understand more fully the ways in which his relationship to this 'school of thought' may be complicated. Section 9 concludes the chapter.

2. Baxi the (international) human rights scholar

Given that Baxi is a critical human rights scholar who writes largely from a subaltern third world perspective, it may be tempting to view him from purely this oppositional perspective. Yet such a view would be a limited one, producing a distorted picture of Baxi's overall relationship to the human rights project. It is therefore important to examine, even if necessarily in brief, the evidence that completes the picture of Baxi's stance toward the human rights project.

One way in which to fully understand the depth of Baxi's commitment to human rights praxis is to contrast him with certain other critical scholars whose departures from mainstream and/or uncritical international (human rights) law scholarship is far more radical. One such scholar is China Miéville. Pointing to one instance of Miéville's very radical departure from the dominant international (human rights) law scholarship will suffice to make the rather uncontroversial point that is sought to be made here. To paraphrase and apply Miéville's thoughts, in his view, the rule of international law is *impossible* in the form envisaged in liberal (human rights) thought and even in the writings of many left-wing critics of liberalism, and the attempt to replace war and inequality with law is not merely utopian but is precisely *self-defeating*.[12] Miéville's view represents a

---

[11] See generally U. Baxi, 'Voices of Suffering, Fragmented Universality and the Future of Human Rights' in B. H. Weston and Stephen P. Marks (eds.), *The Future of International Human Rights* (New York: Transnational Publishers. Inc., 1999), p. 101.

[12] See C. Miéville, 'The commodity-form theory of international law', Chapter 3 in this volume.

segment of the critics of historically problematic attempts to bring equality and justice to the international plane. This point is so obvious as not to require more justification here.

Yet, as radical as Baxi's own work is, and as deeply sympathetic as he is to the complaints about the inequalities and problems within the human rights project itself,[13] in the end, like many scholars of his ilk,[14] Baxi does not subscribe to the kind of extremely radical point of view which asserts, in near-absolute terms, the virtual impossibility of international justice. Clear evidence for this proposition can be found in the following passage, in which Baxi begins by acknowledging and criticising the historical tendency to put human rights discourses to abusive use (especially against third world peoples), but ends up expressing a limited faith in the *possibility* (not inevitability) of human rights serving fruitfully the ends of justice:

> [T]he languages, logics, and paralogics of human rights also stand marshalled to authorise practices of mass cruelty on a global scale, whether in bourgeois, socialist, 'post-cold war' (post-liberal) and postmodern forms ... Even so, human rights languages, howsoever effete, remain perhaps all that we have to interrogate the barbarism of power.[15]

In another telling and compelling passage, Baxi tells and endorses the positive side of the story of many human rights movements. According to him:

> Through myriad struggles and movements throughout the world 'human rights has become an arena of transformative political practice that disorients, destabilises, and, at times, even helps destroy deeply unjust concentrations of political, social, economic, and technological power.[16]

Clearly, Baxi's stance is not one of radical de-coupling from the possibility of rights-inspired, or even rights-generated, international justice. From the above passages it is clear that, as critical as he is, he manages to retain a solid (though not blind) commitment to the human rights project. As he has himself written, he has devoted his whole life to 'the struggle for the implementation of "human rights".[17] Drawing from and paraphrasing Craven *et al.*, Baxi's concern then can be put in the following way: how

---

[13] See Baxi, *Future*, p. 11 (where he acknowledges that human rights can shelter a diverse range of politics, some good and some bad).
[14] For instance, Chimni, who has urged left internationalists to position themselves between those who assert the near complete objectivity of international law and those who assert its radical indeterminacy. See B. S. Chimni, 'An outline of a Marxist course'.
[15] See Baxi, *Future*, p. 4.   [16] *Ibid.*, p. 19 (emphasis added).   [17] *Ibid.*, p. 5.

can one seize the human rights ground without simultaneously being imprisoned by it?[18]

3. Baxi the TWAIL scholar

In order to establish that Baxi's human rights work is TWAILian, it is important first to outline in brief what is meant when a piece of scholarship is characterised as such. And the answer to this question depends almost entirely on what TWAIL as an approach to international law stands for. TWAIL is an umbrella signifier for a broad range of scholars who participate in what Makau Mutua has described as a dialectic of opposition to the generally unequal, unfair and unjust character of an international legal regime that all too often (but not always) helps subject the Third World to domination, subordination and serious disadvantage.[19] The key marker of TWAILness is a '*shared ethical commitment* to the intellectual and practical struggle to expose, reform, or even retrench those features of the international legal system that help create or maintain the generally unequal, unfair, or unjust global order' and to do so by centring and taking much more seriously than has hitherto been the case, the shared experiences, struggles, resistance and/or voices of suffering of subaltern third world peoples – including those of their experiences that are related to colonisation, decolonisation, and contemporary forms of empire.[20] This in turn entails a deep commitment to taking world history (as opposed to merely Western history) seriously; taking the equality of Third World peoples far more seriously than has hitherto been the case; being sceptical of unjustified universality claims since such claims tend to elide or mask an underlying politics of domination; and writing the resistance of third world peoples (and not necessarily states) into international law.[21]

The TWAILian character of Baxi's International (human rights) law work (as reflected by the book under study) will now be considered; albeit in a necessarily brief fashion. The first major indication of the TWAIL character of the Baxian human rights approach is its deep commitment to centring of the colonisation of the Third World in his analysis, and writing the associated experiences of Third World peoples into the human rights story. His work is replete with examples of this scholarly

---

[18] See M. Craven, *et al.*, '"We are Teachers of International Law"' (2004) 17 *Leiden Journal of International Law* 363 at 366.
[19] See Mutua, 'What is TWAIL?', 31.
[20] See Okafor, 'Newness, Imperialism and, International Legal Reform', 176–177.
[21] *Ibid.*, 177–80.

sensibility and method, but a few examples will suffice to illustrate the point. In the opening three pages of the book under study, Baxi speaks of – among other things – the importance of factoring in 'the extraordinary histories of the centuries-long political terrorism involved in the colonization of the non-European peoples'.[22] Elsewhere, he reminds us to retain this focus on (de)colonisation when mapping the transformation from what he refers to as the 'modern' human rights paradigm to its (more emancipatory) 'contemporary' successor. To Baxi, this last story even 'remains inconceivable outside movements for decolonization and self-determination'.[23] Furthermore, he points to the fact that what he refers to as the modern human rights paradigm justified the racist colonial recognition of 'the collective right of European nations to "own" other peoples, their territories, wealth, and resources' as a key reason for the poverty of that paradigm.[24] It is in this same vein that he strongly criticises those who have authored the dominant stories of human rights movements and NGOs for their inattentiveness to third world decolonisation and self-determination struggles.[25] Similar attentiveness to the imperative of writing the shared experiences of colonisation of third world peoples into human rights praxis characterises many other parts of Baxi's work in the book under study.[26] Importantly, there is little – if any – difference between these views, and those held by most of those whom Baxi has himself identified as TWAIL scholars.

As importantly, Baxi's commitment to factoring in the Third World's shared experience of colonial subjugation into the production of human rights knowledge(s) allows him to offer some insights into the workings of contemporary forms of empire. It also allows him to illuminate the effects that these 'new empires' have had on subaltern Third World peoples. Baxi's words are so important in this respect as to justify their extensive reproduction here. According to him:

> Most activist communities in the global South regard the role of the [principal] human messenger[s] . . . [the agents of some Western states, the IMF, and the World Bank] as obnoxious . . . The predatory power of the message commences its long career with the notion that subordinated/colonised peoples lack qualities that make them recognizably human. The peculiar notion of the White Man's Burden aimed at transforming 'savages' into recognizable human beings who then may be considered eligible and worthy recipients for the 'gift' of human rights.[27]

---

[22] Baxi, *Future*, p. 3.   [23] *Ibid.*, p. 19.   [24] *Ibid.*, pp. 44–5.   [25] *Ibid.*, pp. 71–2.
[26] For example, see *ibid.*, pp. 51, 30, 37 and 205.   [27] *Ibid.*, p. 34.

Part of the sense of this passage is that, even in the formally 'decolonised' world in which we now live, the colonialist praxis of tutelage, domination and exploitation continue to operate to the detriment of all too many Third World peoples in 'myriad and at times equally violent forms'.[28] The substantive inequalities of the global norm-negotiation processes, amidst a veneer of formal equality, and the not too subtle sense among many a powerful Western country's agents that international human rights surveillance is really meant to police almost exclusively a Third World that too many of them view and construct as 'benighted', are cited by Baxi as among the manifestations of this more contemporary forms of colonial praxis.[29] Another example of this kind of 'actually existing colonialism' that Baxi offers, is more epistemic. He is seriously dissatisfied with the strand of Western human rights thought that asserts the historical impossibility of indigenous Third World philosophies and cosmologies of human rights. He critiques adherents of this thesis as fostering 'Eurocentric' thought that 'smacks of overt racism'.[30] He also points out that such an approach 'disables any intercultural, multicivilizational discourse on the genealogy of human rights' and makes it far easier for some in 'the imperial "West" to impart (by a mix of persuasive and coercive means) to the "Rest" the gift of human rights'.[31] Virtually all TWAIL scholars would endorse the sense and sensibilities expressed by Baxi in the present connection.

If Baxi's TWAIL credentials still remain in doubt to the sceptical reader, his scholarly manoeuvre in writing Third World resistance (enacted in the form of the praxis of the G-77 and the non-aligned movement) into the story of the constitution of the post-Universal Declaration of Human Rights era of the struggle for human dignity is eminently TWAILian.[32] So is his reading of the renewal of international law that occurred as a result of such resistance as 'south-based'.[33] Indeed, this is the same kind of work that has been done by Balakrishnan Rajagopal in his germinal TWAIL work on the inscription of Third World resistance onto international legal texts and discourses.[34]

And although Baxi himself sometimes speaks of TWAIL in a way that suggests that that this appellation includes only third generation TWAIL scholars (such as Antony Anghie, James Gathii, Vasuki Nesiah and Balakrishnan Rajagopal) and thus excludes first generation TWAIL scholars

---

[28] *Ibid.*, p. 35.   [29] *Ibid.*, pp. 98 and 104.   [30] *Ibid.*, p. 39.   [31] *Ibid.*
[32] *Ibid.*, p. 237.   [33] *Ibid.*
[34] See B. Rajagopal, *International Law from Below* (Cambridge: Cambridge University Press, 2003).

(like himself, Christopher Weeramantry, Keba M'Baye, R.P. Anand and Mohammed Bedjaoui),[35] his work has been included in at least two collections of recent TWAIL writing and, as has been shown here, is *functionally* TWAILian in approach.[36] For the sake of clarity, an otherwise obvious point requires reiteration here. Although many first and second generation TWAIL scholars do not use the acronym *TWAIL*, most of them still describe or conceive of their work as lying within the broad 'third world approaches to international law' framework. All in all therefore, it is clearly justified to view Baxi's human rights work as located within the TWAIL tradition and framework.

Having completed in the last two sections the necessary, but preliminary, exercise of locating Baxi's work in the human rights and TWAIL traditions, it remains to consider at some length the relationship of his scholarship to Marxian thought. This task will be tackled in the next five sections of this chapter.

4. Baxi's 'new proletariat'

One important overarching theme in *The Future of Human Rights* is the extraordinary depth of Baxi's attentiveness to, focus on, and concern for the subaltern classes, howsoever conceived and named. He begins the book by vowing to articulate 'a distinctive subaltern perspective on human [rights] futures'.[37] Instructively, for Baxi, our naming of any human rights praxis as either 'good' or 'bad' must be firmly grounded in our knowledge of the ways in which the relevant groups of dispossessed and subaltern classes would view that praxis.[38]

The striking thing from the perspective of fathoming the impact, if any, that Marxian ideas have had on Baxi's human rights work is that Baxi's category of subalterns extends well beyond the classic Marxian category: the *working classes* or the *proletariat*. As even the most cursory reader of Marx's work knows, Marx's main concern was to advance the status of the working classes (or to teach us how history could be made to achieve that end). *Class* as a category and the conflict between the proletariat (the working classes) and the bourgeoisie (the capital-controlling classes)

---

[35] See Baxi, *Future*, pp. 48, 38ff.
[36] See A. Anghie, *et al.* (eds.), *The Third World and International Order: Law, Politics and Globalization* (The Hague: Martinus Nijhoff, 2003); and O. C. Okafor (ed.), 'Third World Approaches to International Law after 9/11' (2005) 43 *Osgoode Hall Journal of International Law* (special Issue) 1–222.
[37] See Baxi, *Future*, p. xxii.   [38] *Ibid.*, p. 10.

has always been central to Marxist theory.[39] More importantly for our purposes, class seems to have crowded out other kinds of subalterns from the classic Marxian imagination. To quote Roth: 'in fixating on the class dimension, [Marx] provides little guidance to the social dynamics that produce systematic subordination and exclusion on bases such as race, ethnicity, gender, sexual orientation, and disability.'[40]

Like many contemporary left-wing scholars,[41] Baxi avoids this serious limitation in classic Marxian thought by training his analytical lens on, and utilising, a broader and more inclusive set of subaltern classes. Without abandoning the proletariat as important members of this expanded category,[42] Baxi constructs a subaltern class that includes the stateless, the refugee, the massively impoverished, indigenous peoples and people living with disabilities.[43] This umbrella class also accommodates the illiterate, the have-nots, the tormented and those who suffer from a lack of the basic necessities of life.[44] Further, this class is flexible enough to give succour to culturally oppressed women, untouchables (e.g. the Indian *dalits*), trafficked females and child soldiers.[45] However, in describing what he includes and excludes within his expanded category of 'subaltern classes', Baxi takes pains, in all cases, to exclude 'those who suffer but only from a surfeit of pleasure'[46] and those who, not being part of the 'wretched of the earth', are a 'privileged miniscule of [elite] humanity'.[47]

It is therefore those who fall within these subaltern classes that – in my view – constitute Baxi's *new proletariat*. The members of this category are better seen as a new proletariat because Baxi seems metaphorically and conceptually to place them in a position that is similar (though not confined) to that occupied by the proletariat in classic Marxist thought. They do a similar 'job' for Baxi's human rights theory as the proletariat did for Marx's theory. In any case, given the expectation in classic Marxian thought that the proletariat will through revolution abolish the bourgeois classes, becoming the only remaining category, and thus creating a classless society, it is not altogether far fetched to imagine an expanded proletarian class that includes much more than the classic working classes. The narrow point that is being made here is that since the category of the proletariat

---

[39] See Miéville, 'The commodity-form theory'.
[40] See Roth, 'Marxian insights'.
[41] See B. S. Chimni, who defined his 'subaltern classes' to include 'all oppressed and marginal groups in society' where significant oppression and marginalisation is a function of historical context. See Chimni, 'An outline of a Marxist course'.
[42] See Baxi, *Future*, p. 2. [43] *Ibid.*, p. 2. [44] *Ibid.*, p. 23. [45] *Ibid.*, p. 29.
[46] *Ibid.*, p. 23. [47] *Ibid.*, p. 6.

is in the Marxian view even capable of expansion at all (albeit in a future communist time), notwithstanding that he expands that class in a different way, Baxi is on firm Marxian ground in seeking at all to author such an expansion. After all, Marx himself expected the proletarian class to absorb eventually all these other non-dominant classes. More promisingly, has not Ernst Fischer shown that Marx was not entirely inattentive to the existence of other non-bourgeois and subaltern classes and that, in reality, Marx did *subsume their history or at least their interests* within the struggles of the working classes, whose historical position was seen by Marx as likely to push them toward waging the anticipated socialist revolution?[48] However, it must be noted that Baxi's expanded class, his *new proletariat*, is not conceived in the Marxian sense of being the end product of the march of history, but as a 'here and now' umbrella of those who struggle to ameliorate their states of suffering, dispossession or abuse. Nevertheless, the utility of the Marxian proletarian metaphor is not thus negated. In any case, it is obvious that Baxi is not at all inattentive to the working classes themselves. Whole swathes of the book under study do examine the struggle of the proletariat against bourgeois capitalism and how that helped to write the human rights story.[49] The point here is that, even while expanding its limits, Baxi has evidently retained the classic Marxian focus on the proletariat. Given the, at least partial, sourcing from Marxian thought of his 'new proletariat' umbrella class – one of the key factors in his human rights analysis – is not his debt to Marxism evident? Put differently, is not his utilisation and improvement upon Marxian-style attentiveness to, focus on, and deep concern for the exploitation and domination of the working classes enriched by its Marxian sensibilities?

5. Is Baxi a historical materialist?

There is little, if any, doubt that classical Marxism is above all a rigorously materialist theory,[50] but in order to answer with any degree of accuracy the question raised by the above heading, the nature of the concept of historical materialism must first be explicated, however briefly. According to Marx, history is conditioned at each stage of its development by the way in which the relations of production are organised, or, to put it differently,

---

[48] See E. Fischer, *How to Read Karl Marx* (New York: Monthly Review Press, 1996), p. 74.
[49] For example, see *ibid.*, pp. 234–75.
[50] See Miéville, 'The commodity-form theory'.

the way in which the division of labour and class relations have evolved.[51] I thus agree with Fischer that:

> The essential thing about the philosophy of history developed by Marx is that *it always proceeds from social reality*, not from abstract categories: from the 'simple material production of life' not from intellectual constructs: from practice, not from a set of self-generating, self-developing, self-resolved ideas.[52]

Indeed, Marx departed from previous materialist doctrine on the basis that they 'overlooked practice as a world changing activity'.[53]

The question asked by the heading of this section is, of course, conditioned and limited by the nature of the enquiry in this chapter. The chapter is, of course, not concerned as much with providing a comprehensive analysis of the influence of Marxian thought on the enormous entirety of Baxi's contribution to international law. What the chapter is concerned to achieve is to shed some light on the impact of Marxian ideas and methods on his work in *The Future of Human Rights*. As such, the real question here is the extent to which Baxi's work in the aforementioned book reveals an adherence to the historical materialist methodology that characterises much Marxian thought.

Baxi's slightly complicated relation to, and sophisticated understanding of, the Marxian historical materialism thesis is illustrated by many a statement in the book under study. However, two passages stand out in this respect. First, Baxi's deployment of a form of historical materialism in developing his critique of the *excessive* focus in some (human rights) theories on discourse is self-evident when he declares that:

> [D]iscourse theorists often maintain that discursive practice constitutes social reality; there are no violators, violated, and violations outside discourse. But it ignores or obscures non-discursive or material practices of power and resistance. This talk *disembodies human suffering here-and-now*, for future ameliorative/redemptive purposes, whose status (at least from the standpoint of those that suffer) is *very obscure, indeed to a point of cruelty of theory*. The non-discursive order of reality, the materiality of human violation is just as important, if not more so, from the standpoint of the violated.[54]

Second, Baxi's measured reliance on and slight scepticism of aspects of Marxian historical materialism is illustrated by the following passage from

---

[51] See Fischer, *How to Read Karl Marx*, p. 89. [52] *Ibid.*, p. 98.
[53] *Ibid.*, p. 99.   [54] See Baxi, *Future*, pp. 23–4.

The Future of Human Rights in which he seeks to understand how we may narrate stories about globalisation as the march of global capitalism.[55] In his words:

> Would it mark a triumph of hope over experience to regard, in autopoetic theory terms, varieties of global capitalism as '*self-dissipating structures*'? What historic influences may we draw when we acknowledge fully, with and since Karl Marx, the global social fact that these forms remain wholly crisis-ridden? Are we to narrate the new social movements... or an impressive array of anti-globalization protests as *ineluctable* manifestations of the crises of late capitalism?[56]

Here Baxi stands with more contemporary Marxian theory in his justified scepticism of the historical 'ineluctability' of the collapse of capitalism, or even of that economic system's descent into seriously damaging crisis. But, as the same passage shows, this does not then mean that Baxi rejects the historical materialist thesis. What is more, he has written the historical materialist thesis into other aspects of the book under study.[57]

In any case, when the passages reproduced above are read closely and in conjunction with the analysis, in sections 4 and 6, of Baxi's focus on how human rights has, in different historical epochs (the modern, the contemporary, and the emergent) related to the concrete material conditions in which the working classes and other members of his new proletariat have lived, then Baxi's position as a modified historical materialist, whose work draws from, but is not determined by, that methodological and analytical perspective, becomes even clearer. And if any doubt still remains in this connection, did Baxi not explicitly argue in the book under study that 'while human rights practices are relatively autonomous, they also remain situated within the *structure of production*'?[58] Did Baxi not also suggest – following Wendy Brown – that some human rights languages may in fact mask '*material conditions* of unemancipated inegalitarian civil society?'[59]

6. Marxian currents in the Baxian TREMF thesis

As Robert Wolff has noted, 'the heart and soul of Marx's lifework was a massive critical analysis of the political economy of bourgeois capitalism'[60] and the 'pivotal concept of Marx's critique of capitalism' is

---

[55] *Ibid.*, p. 243. [56] *Ibid.* (emphasis added). [57] *Ibid.*, pp. xxiii, xxiv, 60 and 62.
[58] *Ibid.*, p. 60 (emphasis added). [59] *Ibid.*, p. 62 (emphasis added).
[60] See R. Wolff, *Understanding Marx: A Reconstruction and Critique of Capital* (Princeton, NJ: Princeton University Press, 1984), p. 3.

'exploitation'.[61] In a similar vein, Nicola Taylor and Ricardo Bellifiore suggest that 'the main aim of Marx's Das Kapital ... is to understand the conditions that make possible the existence and growth of capital on the basis of the exploitation of labour'.[62] Putting this reading of Marx in a more contemporary light, Brad Roth notes that the Marxian insight on the achievement of a truly democratic society is that the main condition for the subaltern classes, that is the have-nots, to be free is an end to economic deprivation and insecurity and to their social disempowerment and exclusion.[63] This contrasts with the primary condition for those who command the means of production to be free, which is their protection from state encroachment.[64] Each of the scholars referenced above will also be comfortable with the relatively uncontroversial notion that Marxism is also concerned to further our understanding of the processes of (global) capitalist expansion, especially when it functions to exploit workers and the other subaltern classes.

A consideration of the Marxian influence on Baxi's TREMF thesis may suggest a number of intimately related questions: Is the heart and soul of this Baxian thesis in any sense a massive critical analysis of the political economy of (global) bourgeois human rights praxis? Is the pivotal concept of Baxi's critique of (global) capitalism *exploitation*? Is his contribution in his TREMF thesis best understood as a critical demonstration of the ways in which the political economy logics of various forms of bourgeois capitalism inflects, shapes, constrains and limits the dominant contemporary human rights praxis? Is part of Baxi's aim in developing his TREMF thesis to understand the ways in which this emergent human rights paradigm renovates and re-furnishes the tool houses, kits and repertoires of various formations of global capital, and thus augments the exploitative capacities of these agents and structures, much to the detriment of the subaltern classes? In all these cases, does his approach to the questions asked draw further from Marxian ideas, idioms, insights and sensibilities? That is, are his ethical commitments Marx-like in being firmly located on the side of the working and other subaltern classes – the *new proletariat*? This last question is important, for merely examining the ways in which the emergent human rights paradigm supports the growth and flourishing of formations of global capital at the expense of workers and the other

---

[61] *Ibid.*, p. 103.
[62] See N. Taylor and R. Bellofiore, 'Marx's Capital I, the Constitution of Capital: General Introduction', in N. Taylor and R. Bellifiore (eds.), *The Constitution of Capital* (Basingstoke: Palgrave Macmillan, 2004), p. 1.
[63] See Roth, 'Marxian insights'.   [64] *Ibid.*

subaltern classes is *insufficient* on its own to justify affixing the Marxian label on a scholar's work. After all, that scholar may well attack that objective from some other autonomous perspective. No answers to these questions may be found without an analytical turn to a consideration of Baxi's writing on this subject.

In *The Future of Human Rights*, Baxi developed a germinal thesis on the steady supplanting in our time of the human rights paradigm that is grounded in logic of the Universal Declaration of Human Rights (UDH) by what he referred to as an emergent trade-related market-friendly human rights (TREMF) paradigm. As this TREMF thesis is one of his most important contributions to human rights theory, it will be outlined in some limited detail before a fruitful analysis of the Marxian influence on its character is conducted.

Baxi's overarching TREMF thesis is that:

> The paradigm of the Universal Declaration of Human Rights is being steadily, but surely, *supplanted* by that of trade-related, market-friendly human rights ... under the auspices of globalization. This new paradigm seeks to demote, even reverse, the notion that universal human rights are designed for the attainment of dignity and well-being of human beings and for enhancing the security and well being of socially, economically and civilisationally vulnerable peoples and communities.[65]

In the course of fleshing out his thought-provoking TREMF thesis, Baxi developed a number of distinguishable but intimately related sub-claims. Only some of these sub-claims concern us here. The first such sub-claim is that the emergent TREMF paradigm (unlike the UDH paradigm) insists on promoting and protecting the collective *human* rights of various formations of global capital mostly at the direct expense of human beings and communities.[66] The distinctive quality here is Baxi's notion of the assignment of *human* (as opposed to ordinary legal) rights to various formations of global capital in order to augment the status of these formations of capital at the expense of the subaltern classes. To Baxi, the UDH paradigm differs from the TREMF paradigm in this way because, although the UDH did make provision for a right to property that can be read to benefit any person (including presumably corporations and business associations), in the end the notion of property in the UDH is itself left substantially unsettled.[67] On the other hand, the TREMF paradigm

---

[65] See Baxi, *Future*, p. 235.
[66] *Ibid*. Baxi uses a pluralist notion of global capitalist actors because he argues that 'global capital is itself faction-ridden (as Marx sought to educate us all)'. See *ibid.*, p. 247
[67] *Ibid.*, p. 253.

makes the protection of the property interests of various formations of global capital central to its conception of the global social order. What is more, none of the two legally binding human rights covenants (the international covenant on civil and political rights and its sister covenant on economic, social and cultural rights), which – alongside the UDH – constitute the so-called international bill of rights, make provision for property rights.[68] Thus, to Baxi, 'to say that the [TREMF paradigm] ... is just an unfoldment of the potential of [the] UDHR is plainly incorrect'.[69]

The second sub-claim is that, much more than in the past, the progressive state – or at least the progressive 'Third World' state – is now conceived as one that is a good host state to global capital; as one that protects global capital (and its profits) against political instability and market failure, usually at a significant cost to the most vulnerable among its own citizens; and as one that is in reality more accountable to the IMF and the World Bank than to its own citizens; especially the most impoverished and vulnerable sections of that citizenry. According to this TREMF mindset, progressive states are those states that are much more soft than hard toward global capital.[70]

The third Baxian sub-claim is that the new global order also requires the instrumental reproduction of a core of internal hardness within these same generally soft states. Thus, to paraphrase Baxi, a progressive state is also conceived under the TREMF paradigm as a state that is market efficient in suppressing and de-legitimating the human rights-based practices of resistance of its own citizens and that is also capable of unleashing (and, when necessary, does in fact unleash) a reign of terror on some of its citizens, especially those of them that actively oppose its excessive softness toward global capital.

The fourth such sub-claim is that, unlike the UDH paradigm, the TREMF paradigm denies a significant redistributive role to the state.[71] In fleshing out this fourth sub-claim, Baxi argues that the UDH paradigm which 'assigned human rights responsibilities to states ... to construct, progressively and within the community of states, a just social order, national and global, that will at least meet the basic needs of human beings', is being pushed aside to a worrisome extent by a TREMF paradigm that, in contrast, 'denies any significant redistributive role to the state; calls upon the state [and world order] to free as many spaces [and economic resources] for capital as possible, initially by pursuing the three-Ds of

[68] Ibid., p. 254.   [69] Ibid.   [70] Ibid., pp. 248–52.   [71] Ibid., pp. 248–9.

contemporary globalization: *deregulation, denationalization,* and *disinvestment*.[72]

The point of this section is not to analyse these sub-claims for their accuracy and validity. Rather, it is to tease out the extent to which – on the whole – the TREMF thesis, which these sub-thesis together constitute, bears the imprimatur of Marxian thought. Do warm 'human life-giving' Marxian currents flow into and circulate within the even more germinal waters of Baxi's TREMF thesis?

First of all, it is crystal clear from even a cursory reading of *The Future of Human Rights* that the heart and soul of the Baxian perspective on the TREMF paradigm is a critique of what he sees as the increasingly anti-subaltern political economy logic of contemporary (global) bourgeois human rights praxis – a very Marx-like thing to do! It is also as clear that the pivotal concept of Baxi's critique of (global) capitalism's framing and constraining of human rights futures is what he sees as the TREMF-legitimised *exploitation* of the subaltern classes by various formations of global capital. Here again, Baxi's approach is, at the very least, very Marx-like. In developing his TREMF thesis, he focuses on the strengthening of the status of global capital in our time;[73] critiques the ongoing attempts to present to us 'a world without alternatives to global capitalism and associated transformations in state sovereignty;'[74] argues against the prevailing concrete reality regarding assumed state boundaries that are, in fact, borderless for Unocal, Monsanto and other such massive transnational corporations while remaining 'cruelly bordered for the violated victims subject to the practices of cruelty';[75] decries the fact that human genetic material can now be 'commodified' and exploited by corporations (via the instrumentality of electronic or genetic databases);[76] and demonstrates that the inability effectively to end toxic waste dumping in the Third World is, in part, due to the TREMF-style turn to frameworks of rights promotion and protection that are 'by and large, congenial to transnational capital'. To Baxi, this last situation is so because the TREMF-constitutive frameworks (such as the so-called 'Global Compact') mandate uneven partnerships between global capital (on the one hand) and subalterns (on the other hand); including far too many Third World states and peoples.[77]

Further evidence of the circulation of Marxian currents within the stream of Baxi's TREMF thesis may be deciphered from the very content

[72] Ibid., p. 248.   [73] Ibid., p. 249.   [74] Ibid., p. 239.   [75] Ibid., p. 247.
[76] Ibid., p. xxiii.   [77] Ibid., pp. 250–1.

of his enunciation of this thesis. It is quite clear that what bothers Baxi *the most* about the emergent TREMF paradigm and each of the characteristics of that paradigm that are identified by his four sub-claims, is its promotion of the interests of global capital while fostering in tow the augmentation of significant socio-economic and political inequality both within and among states, nations and peoples. This concern to articulate as exploitative the relationship between global capital and the (new) proletariat is definitely Marx-like. The attribution and conferment of collective human rights to various formations of global capital that Baxi identifies, and the increasing TREMF-style promotion and protection of such rights, would not worry Baxi as much if these did not work to exploit, degrade and/or violate the subaltern classes. The TREMF-style characterisation of the good (Third World) states as one that is 'more soft than hard' toward the various formations of global capital would also not agitate the Baxian intellect as much were it not for these same reasons. The TREMF-ish framing of the ideal (Third World) state as one that is 'more hard than soft' toward its own subaltern peoples would again not be as problematic were it not for the exploitative and violative relations that it augments. And, lastly, the fact that the TREMF paradigm increasingly works to 'legitimise' the denial of any significant redistributive role to the state and serves the interests of those who call upon the (Third World) state to pursue the three-Ds of contemporary globalisation – *deregulation, denationalisation* and *disinvestment* – would not furrow Baxi's brows as much were it not for the negative effects of these policy stances on the welfare of the subaltern classes. One of Baxi's achievements in developing and expounding his TREMF thesis was therefore that he has systematically shown us some of the ways in which this emergent human rights paradigm renovates and re-furnishes the normative tool houses and intellectual repertoires of the various formations of global capital, and thus functions to augment the exploitative capacities of these agents and structures, much to the detriment of the subaltern classes. Needless to say, this is also a most Marx-like thing to do. His other contribution in this respect was that he has critically demonstrated the ways in which the political economy logics of various forms of bourgeois global capitalism inflects, shapes, constrains and limits the dominant contemporary human rights praxis, at the cost of the effective protection of the dignity of the less privileged and the dispossessed. Once again, the Marxian influence is reasonably palpable here.

Putting the question of the influence of Marxian thought on his TWAIL human rights scholarship beyond all reasonable doubt, Baxi himself has described the intellectual activities he undertook in the course of developing his TREMF thesis as an attempt at the 'understanding and demystification of the complexity of global capitalism' and as a 'Marx-like labour'.[78] In any case, firmly located as they are on the side of the working and other subaltern classes, Baxi's ethical commitments are definitely Marx-like. This much is evident when he argues that:

> The emergent [TREMF] paradigm insists upon the promotion and the protection of the collective human rights of global capital, in ways which 'justify' corporate well-being and dignity even when it entails continuing gross and flagrant violations of human rights of actually existing human beings and communities.[79]

The book under study is replete with similar examples.

While in certain respects, Baxi's TREMF thesis diverges from, and improves upon, traditional Marxism, the focus of the chapter and space limitations do not allow their full development here. Suffice it to point out that a Baxi scholar may argue – with some validity – that while classic Marxism tends to envisage the virtually relentless march of capitalism from one lower stage to a higher one, toward greater socialism, and leading to the triumph of communism, the TREMF thesis actually demonstrates the hardening and strengthening of global capitalism in our time without necessarily envisaging light at the end of the tunnel, in terms of the enthronement of global socialism, what more communism. Although one could counter, in the traditional Marxian dialectical way, that the TREMF paradigm presents a new *synthesis* that will become a *thesis* of its own that will beget an *anti-thesis*, there seems to be much validity to the opposing view.

7. Marxian embraces in the Baxian approach to human rights movements and NGOs

The broadly Marxian perspective on social struggle is deeply connected to Marx's philosophy of history/knowledge. Thus, for one, Joan Rytina and Charles Loomis are correct that 'Marx held that thought and action cannot be separated because the purpose of knowing is to act, and one can know the truth only by observing action'.[80] As such, as Ernst Fischer has noted, although Marx occasionally overemphasised the 'natural laws' of history,

---

[78] Ibid., p. 18.   [79] Ibid., p. 234.
[80] See J. H. Rytina and C. P. Loomis, 'Marxist Dialectic and Pragmatism: Power as Knowledge' (1970) 35 *American Sociological Review* 308 at 309–10.

he never overlooked the fact that it is men [and women] themselves who make their history.[81] In his *The Holy Family*, Marx famously declared that:

> History does nothing . . . it 'wages no battles.' It is man [and woman], real living man [and woman], that does all that, that possesses and fights; history is not a person apart, using man [or woman] as a means for its own particular aims; history is nothing but the activity of man [and woman] pursuing his [or her] aims.[82]

Thus, to Marxists, practice (when intimately linked in a non-linear way with thought and reflection) is 'the world changing activity'.[83]

Therefore, the masses are (or ought to be) seen as a source of ideas about our social world, as well as the main agents of their own emancipation. Celebrated (albeit modified) Marxists like Rosa Luxemburg and Antonio Gramsci recognised and held dear this basic tenet of the Marxian view of social struggle and societal progress. As Mark Neufeld has shown, a point of commonality between Rosa Luxemburg's work and the Gramscian framework is the stress upon the masses as active agents of history; what has been described as writing history from the bottom up.[84] In this world view, the future is seen as made via *self-conscious mass struggle* and not as a result of the inexorable tendencies working themselves out behind the backs of social agents. The stress in classical Marxist theory on the idea-generating, even norm-bearing, role of the masses has, more recently, been emphasised by Ronaldo Munck.[85]

Thus, whatever Marxists think about human rights movements and NGOs (and they do not always agree on this point), for most of them, the basic overarching test for the 'ideal' human rights movement or NGO, the virtuoso, is: how well and fully does the given movement or NGO engage in and perform 'self-conscious mass struggle?' How well and fully does it give expression to the voices and interests of the subaltern and the dispossessed classes (that is, the masses)? Indeed, as Winberg Chai has noted, 'becoming divorced from the masses' has historically been one of the most damning charges that could be made against a Marxist or

---

[81] See Fischer, *How to Read Karl Marx*, p. 94.
[82] See K. Marx, *The Holy Family* (Moscow: Foreign Languages Publishing House, 1956), p. 52.
[83] See Fischer, *How to Read Karl Marx*, p. 99.
[84] See M. Neufeld, 'Democratic Socialism in a Global(-zing) Context: Toward a Collective Research Programme', TIPEC Working Paper 02/4, available at www.trentu.ca/org/tipec/2neufeld4.pdf (last visited 9 February 2007), p. 9.
[85] See R. Munck, 'Farewell to Socialism? A Comment on Recent Debates' (1990) 17 *Latin American Perspectives* 113 at 116.

socialist.[86] Thus, an elitist human rights movement or NGO would not pass the Marxian test for the ideal NGO. As such, in the Marxian view, this kind of NGO would require much re-orientation if it is to optimise its emancipatory potential. It remains to tease out the extent to which this basic Marxian test of NGO effectiveness and legitimacy, and other Marxian ideas and sensibilities, have helped shape Baxi's approach to human rights movements and NGOs.

Though not in any sense exclusive of other influences, the influence of Marxian thought on Baxi's view of human rights movements and NGOs is relatively deep. Several distinct but interrelated points at which he embraces a broad spectrum of both classic and later-day Marxian ideas of social struggle can be isolated. First, in the Baxian approach, even the very history of human rights movements and NGOs cannot be properly and accurately told without including and centering the history of working class movements which 'signify the proto-history of all contemporary human rights movements'.[87] To Baxi, this proto-history has much to teach us about contemporary human rights movements and NGOs because:

> [T]he histories of working class struggles narrate the transformative labour of practices that, as it were, confront the miniscule [that is the dominant classes] with the prowess of the multitude [the subaltern classes]. In contrast, much of human rights production [today] remains the work of human rights elites and entrepreneurs.[88]

This is so clearly a Marx-like thing to do that it requires no further analysis to suggest that it is one indicator of the influence that Marxian thought has had on Baxi's perspective on human rights movements and NGOs.

A second clear indicator of the Baxian embrace of Marxian ideas is suggested by his repeated and characteristic valorisation of the *people's* (as opposed to the *elite's*) human rights or human dignity struggles – what he refers to as the 'massification' of struggle – as tending to be far more legitimate than alternative modes, since these people's struggles tend to be much more rooted in the direct experience of pain and suffering.[89] This much is evident from the following passage, which is so revealing as to deserve reproduction *in extenso*:

---

[86] See W. Chai, 'The Ideological Paradigm Shifts in China's World Views: From Marxism-Leninism-Maoism to the Pragmatic-Multilateralism of the Deng-Jiang-Hu Era' (2003) 30 *Asian Affairs: An American Review* 163 at 165–7.
[87] See Baxi, *Future*, pp. 69–70.   [88] *Ibid.*   [89] *Ibid.*, pp. 5 and 26.

> [T]he perplexities here arise in deciphering the upward and downward linkages between mass movements for transformation and their representation by an incredible variety of non-governmental organizations (NGOs) in close interaction with national, regional, and international power formations. The NGOs, who so pre-eminently lead these movements, vary in their levels of 'massification.' This variation also marks the richness or poverty, as the case may be, in terms of their potential to articulate the voices of the violated and authenticating their visions of a just world. As such, they do not yet, fortunately, exhaust the emancipatory potential.[90]

Thus, like most Marxists would, Baxi applies the 'massification' or 'self-conscious mass struggle' test as a way of assessing the extent to which human rights movements and NGOs approach their ideal type. The more a human rights movement or NGO is 'massified,' the more it approaches the ideal type or virtuoso.

Third, even the nature of the Baxian notions of 'activism' and 'human rights realism' tell an important part of the story of Baxi's embrace in the present respect of some Marxian ideas. He constructs his preferred concept of human rights activism by fusing elements of the Marxian notion of 'struggle' with aspects of the notion of 'resistance' (which he sees as more ideology-imbued).[91] His modified concept of human rights realism is also firmly grounded in Marxian thought. Baxi begins his brief development of this concept by endorsing the classic Marxian view that 'human rights are created by people's praxis of resistance and struggle', and ends by offering examples that bear out its validity.[92]

Fourth, Baxi utilises Marxian thought in order to add much punch to his argument that to become far more successful, human rights movements and NGOs ought to form more meaningful partnerships with other progressive social forces. He suggests that it would be 'an egregious error to narrow the domain of human rights activism to specifically human rights NGOs' and notes that 'Karl Marx's *Kapital*' which describes:

> [in] great and grave detail how partnership with progressive – or at least, broadly human rights-inclined policy and political actors and the learned professions emerged to give birth to, and further progressively encode, the Magna Carta of worker's rights through the regulation of hours of work, as well as the progressive outlawry of carceral exploitation,

already makes 'this question entirely superficial'.[93]

---

[90] Ibid., p. 20.　[91] Ibid., p. 66.　[92] Ibid., pp. 94–5.　[93] Ibid., p. 64.

Fifth, Baxi's critical (though deeply committed) relationship to human rights movements and NGOs (broadly construed) has, in a nuanced and complicated way, also been affected significantly (though not exclusively) by the Marxian legacy. In the first place, he is attentive to the tendency within classical Marxism to be sceptical, or at least critical, of the potential of human rights movements and NGOs to emancipate the subaltern classes.[94] In his words:

> Marxian discourse resist[s] description of human rights movements as emancipatory movements... Although human rights emerge as the plentiful 'necessities of class struggle,' the very notion of human rights was regarded, in the final analysis, as the marker of a 'radically deficient' social order.[95]

He goes further to deploy Marxian insight in illustrating one of the contradictions that are too often generated when human rights movements seek to pursue emancipatory projects by seeking to disempower the state vis-à-vis the individual, while at the same time needing to re-empower it in contexts of ameliorating systemic patterns of domination and suffering, with the result that the desired real life emancipation is too often not achieved. According to Baxi, 'the subjects of human rights movements (as Marx showed in relation to the histories of the working classes) break away from the "iron cage" only to be further bound "in silken strings"'.[96]

Yet this last argument only reflects one (partial) dimension of Baxi's relationship to the Marxian critique of human rights movements and NGOs. While Baxi's thesis on human rights movements and NGOs draws quite significantly from Marxian ideas related to the necessity for human rights praxis to be grounded in mass social struggle, it diverges from classic Marxian thought (or at least some versions of it) in at least one notable way. It does not share as deep a scepticism as do these versions of Marxism regarding the potential of such movements and NGOs to bring about meaningful social change via their utilisation of the human

---

[94] See Roth, 'Marxian insights' (showing that Marxism seeks to demonstrate the ideological and obfuscatory character of human rights claims). See also Koskenniemi, 'What should international lawyers learn' (Marx would have had none of the tendency in some of the literature to uncritically endorse the informal social power of groups like human rights movements and NGOs, etc.).
[95] *Future*, p. 205.
[96] *Ibid.*, p. 204. (A Foucauldian influence on Baxi's work, however slight, is also palpable here.)

rights language. That Baxi is not himself entirely wedded to the (more absolutist versions of) the Marxian scepticism of human rights movements and NGOs is illustrated by his view of these movements as relatively autonomous of both 'bourgeois human rights formations' and 'the revolutionary socialism of Marxian imagination'.[97]

On the whole, his complicated view of the nature, operations, and emancipatory potential of human rights movements and NGOs is represented by his conclusion that these categories can shelter a diverse range of politics, ranging from those who practice a politics of domination to those who practice a politics of insurrection.[98] This view is itself also a reflection of the equally complicated relationship of the Baxian approach to human rights movements and NGOs to those strands of Marxian thought that have tended to be far more cynical of the potential of these movements and NGOs.

8. Some Baxian de-couplings from Marxian praxis

In the spirit of the last two paragraphs, which suggest that Baxi is far from a Marxian ideologue and that *The Future of Human Rights* is not an echo chamber or repeater station for Marxian thought, it remains to point out or consider more fully, the ways in which Baxi de-couples his human rights theory from certain versions and forms of Marxian praxis.

The first major way in which he does so is in his limited adoption of the Marxian historical materialism theory. As Baxi's complicated relationship to historical materialism has already been discussed at some length in section 5 above, suffice it to reiterate here that Baxi stands shoulder to shoulder with most of the more contemporary self-described Marxian theorists in his justified scepticism of the historical 'ineluctability' of the collapse of capitalism, or even of that economic system's much hoped for descent into seriously damaging crisis. Like the better versions of Marxian thought, he rather suggests that well-constituted and 'conscienticised' mass struggle can, under certain conditions, improve the lives of the subaltern classes. This is not, of course, as much a complete departure from Marxian thought as it is a de-coupling from certain versions of Marxism.

The second de-coupling from versions of Marxian thought that is evident in *The Future of Human Rights* is Baxi's escape from the treacherous waters of working class reductionism. As has already been seen, it is

[97] *Ibid.*, p. xxiii. [98] *Ibid.*, p. 11.

not, of course, a controversial point that 'class' as a category and 'class struggle' have always been key to Marxist thought.[99] The fact that much Marxist thought was historically fixated on the working classes is also so well established that its demonstration need not detain us here. Suffice it to note that although Marx himself did not entirely ignore the other classes, in the end, he focused his energies on the working class as the only class that raised the prospect of socialist revolution against the dominant classes.[100] As we have seen already, Baxi is more in tune with more contemporary Marx-influenced scholars such as the accomplished TWAILer, B. S. Chimni, in adopting a more expanded notion of class that admits and takes much more seriously the victims of other primarily non-economic forms of domination and exploitation.[101] It is in this sense that Baxi's approach to class is de-coupled from some versions of Marxism.

Third, as Branwen Jones has noted, while Marx never set out a fully developed theory of colonialism, scholars have been divided as to whether he himself (as opposed to the Marxists that followed him), held a favourable view of colonialism as a progressive force in the third world.[102] Despite the lack of clarity on this crucial point, some, like Sarah Bracking and Graham Harrison, have suggested that Marx held a strongly negative view of the European colonisation of most of the Third World.[103] They argue that Marx accused 'bourgeois civilisation' of going 'naked' in its 'barbarism' in Europe's then (Third World) 'colonies'.[104] Fortunately, a significant portion of post-Marx Marxist thought (as, for example, the work of Lenin) more clearly and fully rejects the colonial exploitation of the Third World.[105] The point here though is that, as was made clear in section 3, being the TWAILer that he is, Baxi would strongly reject any version of Marxian theory which tends to favour colonialism or which does not clearly reject that system.

Fourth, as a committed, if still critical, human rights theorist and activist, Baxi clearly de-couples his approach and theses from the more troubling aspects of the praxis of Soviet-style 'actually existing socialism'.

---

[99] See Mieville, 'The commodity-form theory'; and Wolff, *Understanding Marx*, p. 5.
[100] See Fischer, *How to Read Karl Marx*, p. 74.
[101] See Chimni, 'An outline of a Marxist course'.
[102] See B. G. Jones, 'The Civilised Horrors of Over-work: Marxism, Imperialism and Development' (2003) 95 *Review of African Political Economy* 33 at 35.
[103] See S. Bracking and G. Harrison, 'Africa, Imperialism and New Forms of Accumulation' (2003) 95 *Review of African Political Economy* 5 at 5.
[104] *Ibid.*
[105] See esp. V. I. Lenin, *Imperialism: the Highest Stage of Capitalism* (New York: International Publishers, 1933), pp. 80–116.

Baxi is, of course, not unique in adopting this 'anti-gulag' posture. Since the fall of the Berlin wall, have not so many fled from the troubled position of affording intellectual support to the Soviet attempt to practice with much brutality a (perverse) form of socialism? The first indication of this Baxian stance in the book under study is his lament, early on in the development of the book, that 'Marxian imagination... legitimised many a *gulag*'.[106] Later on in the book, he decries what he sees as the excesses of the kind of 'socialist human rights evangelism' that was theorised and practiced by those who built the 'actually existing socialism' of our era. In his view:

> Socialist human rights evangelism [just like the bourgeois human rights project] conceived all human beings exploited by bourgeois capitalism as insufficiently human, inviting pursuits of a worldwide revolutionary project of violent overthrow of global capitalism and the transformation of the insufficient bourgeois human into a global socialist comrade-citizen. This coequally violent project in critically discrediting the notion of the White Man's Burden also reconstituted it.[107]

Lastly, if classic Marxist thought has, as some have charged,[108] been *fundamentally* hostile to rule of law talk, Baxi is – to the same extent – clearly not in favour of classic Marxism. As much of this chapter shows, Baxi is quite sceptical of the lofty promises of the rule of law without succumbing to the kind of legal nihilism that characterises some criticisms of the possibility of the rule of law. Baxi recognises the serious contingency and limits of the promise that law can restrain the barbarisms of certain praxis of power, and sees 'the rule of (international) human rights law' as capable – under certain conditions – of limiting (not ending) the dispossession and abuse of the subaltern classes by some among the more dominant. Although Baxi would likely not subscribe to the notion that the rule of law is likely to ever become unnecessary, his view on this issue seems closer to Brad Roth's interpretation of Marx's work. To Roth, Marx's approach to the rule of law is far from nihilist, in that although Marx envisages the disappearance of law after the end of capitalism and with the anticipated triumph of communism, he nevertheless insisted that law and rights will remain necessary for governing society in the transitional period before the ideal communist state is achieved.[109] Thus, if E. P. Thompson famously described the rule of law as 'an unqualified human good', Baxi may go only as far as describing it as a *contingent* and

---

[106] See Baxi, *Future*, p. xxiii. [107] *Ibid.*, p. 35.
[108] See Roth, 'Marxian insights'. [109] *Ibid.*

much limited human good. Yet Baxi's view on this matter – that is on the possibility of a rule of an (international) human rights law that serves to a significant extent the interests of the subaltern classes – is closer to Thompson's than to that of far-too-many traditional Marxists. In this way is Baxi's theory of human rights de-coupled, at least in large measure, from certain versions of Marxism.

The discussion in this section serves to highlight the complicated and sophisticated relationship of Baxi's TWAIL human rights scholarship to Marxian thought. It clearly shows that, while his work has been influenced by Marxian thought, the latter body of ideas has not imprisoned it. However, part of that discussion (especially the portion on his difference with certain brands of Marxism on the question of colonialism) also suggests that Baxi's 'TWAIL sensibilities' were definitely at play in the construction of his relatively 'unique' theory on the future of human rights. These are some of the main points that will be highlighted in the concluding section of this chapter.

9. Conclusions

A keen student of Marx has recently declared that:

> [I]f Marxian thought is to have twenty-first century relevance in the political and juridical realms, it will almost certainly not be in the form of a comprehensive set of analytical and normative principles, but as a continued source of insight and inspiration within more eclectic theoretical systems.[110]

As has been made clear in the previous sections, the analysis of the impact of Marxist thought on Baxi's TWAIL human rights scholarship that has been conducted in this chapter, primarily via a close examination of such influences in his *The Future of Human Rights*, yielded results that are broadly consistent with this claim. Baxi's TWAIL human rights scholarship is definitely 'more eclectic'. To name just a fraction of the whole, it draws from intellectual resources as diverse as the critical theory of the Frankfurt school and the political philosophy of Mahatma Ghandi.[111] And Marxism has definitely provided many of the insights and inspirations that allowed his unique approach to form.

---

[110] *Ibid.* [111] See Baxi, *Future*, pp. 223 and 205, respectively.

Thus, *The Future of Human Rights* is no mere echo-chamber for Marxian views. The relationship of Baxian human rights praxis to Marxism is as complicated as it is sophisticated. Baxi does not simplistically worship at the feet of some Marxian oracle. He does not turn to Marxian thought in a deterministic way to find answers to the questions that animate his work. Instead, his long study of, and reflection on, Marxist thought did ease open one important valve (among many) within the heart of his TWAIL human rights scholarship, and this has allowed a strong Marxian current to flow into, and mix within, the already well-watered arteries of his thoughts – helping to give them form, force and, above all, meaning. This is amply reflected in the ways in which Marxian thought has played important roles in the development of Baxi's human rights praxis by providing some of the genetic matter with which he has built his conception of the unfolding of human rights futures, his TREMF thesis, and his theory of human rights movements and NGOs. In retrieving Marxism for his human rights project, Baxi has not, like far too many, thrown out the baby of Marxian insight with the bathwater of communist practice.[112] Baxi's germinal work in *The Future of Human Rights* speaks volumes of the value-added that Marxian insight has contributed to the human rights project.

However, analysis of this one Baxian book does not, of course, offer a complete picture of the extent to which Baxi's international law scholarship has been impacted by Marxian insight. A passage from his *Hague General Course* is sufficient to illustrate this point. According to Baxi:

> Substantial movement towards global justice in conflicts jurisprudence lies in the direction that seeks to convert it into an arena of global justice through human rights informed and animating will. Any realistic prospect of innovation in this direction becomes possible when conflicts theory takes human suffering *seriously* as a way of taking human rights seriously ... For this to happen, as Karl Marx said in 1850, two conditions need to be fulfilled: the suffering humanity needs to acquire the power to think, and the thinking humanity the capacity to suffer.[113]

As indelibly as it has been marked by Marxian insight, the main idea expressed in the above passage sums up the sense and sensibilities of Baxi's powerful contribution to international (human rights) legal thought.

---

[112] See Roth, 'Marxian insights'.
[113] See U. Baxi, 'Mass Torts, Multinational Enterprise Liability and Private International Law' (1999) 276 *Recueil des Cours* 297 at 423.

But it is impossible fully to understand Baxi's human rights praxis without factoring in the fact that he is, first and foremost, a TWAIL scholar. That is one of the reasons why the Marxian insights that have exerted such a significant influence on Baxi's scholarship must be more properly viewed as intellectual resources that have aided the development of Baxi's ground-breaking TWAIL work and animated his germinal contributions to international (human rights) theory more generally.

9

Exploitation as an international legal concept

SUSAN MARKS

In critical commentary on South Africa's Truth and Reconciliation Commission, Mahmood Mamdani advanced an argument that became known as the 'beneficiary thesis'. At stake was the question of whom the truth and reconciliation process should engage. The Commission's work rested on the idea that 'key to the injustice of apartheid [was] the relationship between perpetrators and victims'.[1] According to Mamdani, however, the pivotal relationship should rather have been that between those who benefited and those who suffered from the system itself. For the perpetrators were a relatively small group, when compared to apartheid's many beneficiaries, and so too were the perpetrators' victims when compared to the vast majority of the population victimised by the system's indignities, hardships and oppressions on a daily basis. 'To what extent', Mamdani wondered, 'does a process that ignores the aspirations of the vast majority of victims risk turning disappointment into frustration and outrage...?'[2] Since apartheid was fundamentally a 'program for massive redistribution', post-apartheid justice had to be 'social justice ... systemic justice' and, accordingly, what was called for was systemic change.[3]

In effect, though he does not use the term, Mamdani is speaking here of exploitation. He is saying that the TRC failed to grapple with the extent to which, and the ways in which, one section of society had prospered at the expense of another. It failed to grapple with apartheid as a system for using some people as a means for securing the advantage of others. And, if its diagnosis was inadequate, then inevitably its prescription also fell short. Of course, Mamdani does not suggest that South African history is unique in this respect. Exploitation is by no means a feature only of apartheid, and the TRC is by no means alone in choosing not to see it.

---

[1] M. Mamdani, 'Reconciliation Without Justice' in H, De Vries and S. Weber (eds.), *Religion and Media* (Stanford: Stanford University Press, 2001), p. 377 at p. 385.
[2] Ibid.   [3] Ibid., p. 387.

From a Marxist perspective, exploitation is indeed a structural feature of capitalism. Capital accumulation depends on labour exploitation, in turn made possible by the inequalities of bargaining power that arise from class divisions. In other accounts, the focus is on forms of exploitation that are linked to other social divisions, such as those based on gender, race and ethnicity. Exploitation is also, of course, a key preoccupation in histories of imperialism, and in analyses of the global distribution of power and wealth in the contemporary world.

In this chapter, I want to consider international law from the standpoint of an interest in exploitation. In doing so, what is most immediately striking is that, as in the case of the TRC, this is a phenomenon that goes to a large extent unremarked. There is much discussion of discrimination, injustice, exclusion, violence, indignity and abuse. There is a great deal of talk about victims, vulnerable groups, marginalised communities, disempowered populations and less developed countries. But there is very little mention of those on the other side of the equation, those advantaged in these processes and relations. The beneficiaries seem to pass largely unnoticed, or at any rate without comment. To be sure, exploitation is not entirely absent from the vocabulary of international law. The exploitation of children is prominent on the international legal agenda, as is the sexual exploitation of women and, more generally, human trafficking. There is also a long history of international law-making with regard to slavery, forced labour and child labour, while sweatshop working conditions are addressed in international legal instruments that stretch back to the early activity of the International Labour Organization.

Clearly those are all important and very serious forms of exploitation. However, it is equally clear to many of us, I think, that exploitation goes considerably further and deeper than them. In what follows I want to explore something of how much further and deeper it goes. What are the character and proportions of exploitation as a problem in the world today? That is obviously a very big question, which could be investigated in a number of different registers. My investigation will be theoretical, and my guide will be a literature that begins with Marx's analysis of the workings of capitalism, and includes some of the many and varied treatments of the topic by later scholars building on his insights. Against this background, I want to re-focus on international law. What ideas about exploitation inform its engagement in this sphere? What limitations and further potentials are associated with those ideas? The thrust of my discussion will be that there is both the need for, and the possibility of, a new kind of international legal engagement with exploitation, more adequate to the realities of our rapacious world. But, since exploitation is not only an analytical concept but also a term of everyday speech, I should start by reviewing some of its many connotations.

1. Exploitation

What is it to exploit someone? Dictionaries commonly distinguish between a positive or neutral meaning and a pejorative meaning. To exploit in the positive or neutral sense is to make use of, or derive benefit from, resources, assets, skills or opportunities. So, for example, I may exploit a patent, an oil field, or indeed my own talents. To exploit in the pejorative sense is to take wrongful advantage of another person for one's own ends, to pursue one's own gain at another's unfair expense. This, of course, is the sense in which I have been using the term so far. On closer inspection, however, the distinction between these two meanings may not be so stable. Concerns about the impact of intellectual property protection for control over essential medicines, food seeds and indigenous knowledge, and about the social costs of natural resources extraction, both for immediately affected communities and for the planet as a whole, remind us that exploitation in the positive or neutral sense may not always be positive or neutral. It too may involve the pursuit of one person's or collectivity's gain at another's unfair expense.

The term 'exploitation' is a relatively recent addition to the English language. Etymologically it is obviously linked with the word 'exploit', which itself goes back a very long way. The *Oxford English Dictionary* includes citations from the fifteenth and even late fourteenth centuries. As a noun, exploit was initially synonymous with success, progress or, in some usages, command. By the sixteenth century, however, an exploit had come to denote, as it still does, a feat, a marvellous deed, or an achievement displaying exceptional bravery and skill. The word derives from the Latin *explicitum* (that which is unfolded), alluding presumably to the unfolding of events or perhaps (as the related verb 'explicate' may suggest) to the unfolding – in the sense of narrating and interpreting – of adventures. As a verb, exploit had a broadly corresponding meaning. From the fifteenth century to the early nineteenth century, to exploit meant to accomplish, succeed, achieve or act with effect. It was only during the mid- and later nineteenth century that the modern meanings, and particularly the pejorative modern meaning, began to develop, in tandem with the 'process' noun exploitation.

Exploitation, then, entered the English language during the epoch which Eric Hobsbawm has dubbed the 'age of capital'.[4] These were the years when the expansion of the bourgeois economic mode accelerated dramatically and began to seem boundless and unstoppable. And if industrial capitalism shifted into a new gear at this time, so too did reflection on it. For this was also the time when the term 'capitalism' came into currency.[5] The concept of exploitation thus emerged in English concurrently with the emergence of capitalism as a concept and problematic. According to the *Oxford English Dictionary*, the use of the verb 'exploit' in its pejorative inflection was initially heard as a Gallicism. It seems likely, however, that alongside French, German (*ausbeuten*: to exploit) was an important influence, since it was above all in the debates and writings which culminated in the publication of Karl Marx's *Das Kapital* in 1867 that the new concept took off. Maybe there was still some trace, too, of the word's etymological affinities with 'explicate'. Exploitation, perhaps, is a form of unfairness or oppression that requires to be unfolded, told about, and scrutinised for its significance and implications. That, at any rate, is the understanding which Marx and his translators helped to foster.[6]

1.1. Marx's analysis

Marx's account of exploitation appears in the first volume of *Capital*, in the context of his discussion of how capital produces and is produced. Having considered market relations, the sphere of exchange, Marx announces that he will now take his readers down into the gloomier, less edifying domain of production. He had earlier explained how in the market the worker and capitalist meet as equals. The one sells productive capacity – 'labour-power' – and the other buys it, on the basis of a freely concluded contract in which equivalent is exchanged for equivalent. Money is paid for labour-power provided, and everyone seems to 'work together, to their mutual advantage, for the common weal, and in the common interest'.[7] As we descend into the sphere of production, however, things immediately begin to change. As Marx famously describes it, the capitalist now 'strides out in front ... smirk[ing] self-importantly and ... intent on business', while the

---

[4] See E. Hobsbawm, *The Age of Capital* (London: Abacus, 1975).
[5] On this, see *ibid.*, at p. 13.
[6] The first English translation of *Das Kapital*, by Samuel Moore and Edward Aveling, appeared in 1887. It was based on the third German edition of volume 1, and was edited by Friedrich Engels.
[7] K. Marx, *Capital, Vol. 1*, B. Fowkes (trans.) (London: Penguin, 1976), p. 280.

worker 'is timid and holds back, like someone who has brought his own hide to market and now has nothing else to expect but – a tanning'.[8] For it is in the production process that the secret of capitalist accumulation is to be found: the extraction of profit out of labour.

How is profit produced? Marx's explanation rests on a distinction between necessary labour and surplus labour. Necessary labour is that which is needed for the worker's own subsistence. Surplus labour is that which goes beyond what is needed for the worker's own subsistence. Marx imagines the worker's day being divided into two. In the first part the worker undertakes necessary labour. During this time, she is working, in effect, for herself. She is covering her own costs, quantified in her wages, that is to say, in the price which the capitalist has had to pay for her labour-power. In the remaining part of the day, the worker undertakes surplus labour. During this time, she is no longer working for herself, but for the capitalist. What she produces belongs to her boss. In the production process, Marx considers that all labour is geared to the creation of 'value'. But while necessary labour reproduces its own value, surplus labour generates profit, or what he calls in this context 'surplus-value'. The proportion of necessary labour to surplus labour determines what he terms the 'rate of surplus-value'. In Marx's analysis, exploitation is the extraction – or, as he also puts it, the 'extortion' – of surplus labour. And the degree of exploitation in any given situation is expressed in the rate of surplus-value.[9]

In his celebrated discussion of the limits of the working day, Marx draws out some of the implications of this analysis. In the first place, capital accumulates by absorbing surplus-value, that is to say, in his terms by exploiting labour. With this in mind, Marx proposes that there is something uncanny about capital, something we intuitively feel is not right. In his memorable image, capital has a vampiric quality, and exhibits a strange kind of living death: '[c]apital is dead labour [i.e. accumulated surplus-value reaped from labour in the past] which, vampire-like, lives only by sucking living labour, and lives the more, the more labour it sucks.'[10] Further, as the last part of this passage suggests, the logic of capital accumulation is that it is always in the interests of the capitalist to exploit workers more, so as to raise the rate of surplus-value. The higher the rate of surplus-value, the more capital can be accumulated. One aspect of this concerns the length of the working day: the longer the working day, the more the rate of surplus-value will rise. But just as

---

[8] *Ibid.*, p. 280.   [9] See *ibid.*, pp. 320 *et seq.*   [10] *Ibid.*, p. 342.

the capitalist is driven to push for the addition of more hours, so too the worker will want to resist that. Faced with the prospect of having her labour not simply used, but abused or 'despoiled', the worker will want to demand fair limits to the working day.[11]

Marx considers that exploitation is a feature of all modes of production based around a social division of classes. Thus, under capitalism, it is the fact that the ruling class owns the means of production, while the working class owns nothing but its own labour-power, that enables the ruling class to extract surplus-value. Workers are induced to undertake surplus labour for their employers because they know that if they don't, there are others waiting on the sidelines – the 'reserve army' of the unemployed – who will. What, for Marx, is distinctive about capitalism compared to other class-based modes of production, such as slavery and feudalism, is that in the capitalist mode of production exploitation is masked. As economist Anwar Shaikh explains, the 'historical specificity of capitalism arises from the fact that its relations of exploitation are almost completely hidden behind the surface of its relations of exchange'.[12] Whereas in slave-owning and feudal societies the exploitation of labour is readily apparent, in capitalist society labour is paid for and regulated according to a contract negotiated between two seemingly free and equal parties. It is only when we look behind, or beneath, that contract at the relations of production that we find 'a world of hierarchy and inequality, of orders and obedience, of bosses and subordinates'.[13] We find a world in which the working class works to support the ruling class, and hence 'to reproduce the very conditions of their [the former's] own subordination'.[14]

The account of exploitation I have just described obviously aims at explaining the exploitation of labour as an aspect of capitalism. Some scholars have drawn a distinction between this 'technical' sense of exploitation and the 'general' or everyday sense of exploitation which I sketched out at the beginning of this discussion. The point is commonly made that, in his various writings, Marx used the term in both of these senses. On the other hand, one may equally argue that, even when he was using the term in its technical sense, Marx was referring to the general idea that the gain of some is being pursued at the unfair expense of others. In his chapter on the working day, Marx imagines what a worker protesting the excessive lengthening of the working day might say to his

[11] Ibid., p. 343 ('Using my labour and despoiling it are quite different things').
[12] A. Shaikh, 'Exploitation', in K. Nielsen and R. Ware (eds.), Exploitation (Atlantic Highlands, NJ: Humanities Press, 1997), p. 70 at p. 73.
[13] Ibid.   [14] Ibid., p. 71 (emphasis omitted).

employer: 'the thing you represent when you come face to face with me [i.e. capital] has no heart in its breast. What seems to throb there is my own heartbeat.'[15] Exploitation in Marx's account is expressed in this conceit. Capitalism is an exploitative system because the ruling class *lives off* the working class; it draws its life (or rather its strange, undead existence) from the working class. And the more the ruling class flourishes, the more the working class is debilitated. As Marx put it in an earlier work, 'in the same relations in which wealth is produced, poverty is produced also'.[16]

1.2. Exploitation today

Marx wrote in the milieu of nineteenth-century Europe and, specifically, in the case of *Capital*, of Victorian England. This affects the way he writes. His terminology draws on intellectual traditions that were once part of the general public culture and, as such, familiar to all educated readers, but that is no longer the case. At the same time, we no longer speak of people getting their hides tanned, and much of his humour seems quaint to us now. More importantly, Marx's historical context also affects what he writes, his description and analysis. Of course, the smirking capitalist and cowering worker were always caricatures, but a caricature only exaggerates realities; it does not invent them. Nearly 150 years later, brutal, abusive labour conditions and arrogant, pitiless bosses certainly still exist, but in most legal systems, as well as under international law, workers have rights. More than that, today's capitalists are commonly employers of a caring, sharing sort. Since Victorian times, the organisation of work has gone through many transformations, and social theorists now speak of productive processes in terms of post-Fordism. In their book, *The New Spirit of Capitalism*, Luc Boltanski and Ève Chiapello describe how in France, for example, approaches to management altered in the mid-1970s, abandoning the hierarchical Fordist model and developing a new network-based form of organisation, founded on employee initiative, issue ownership, and relative work autonomy.[17] Chastened by the criticisms of the 1960s and early 1970s, capitalism took on a new spirit, more sensitive than in earlier times to the dangers of alienation, commodification, disempowerment and unfreedom.

---

[15] *Capital*, Vol. 1, p. 343.
[16] *Ibid.*, p. 799, n. 23. Marx quotes here from his own earlier work, *Poverty of Philosophy*.
[17] L. Boltanski and E. Chiapello, *The New Spirit of Capitalism*, G. Elliott (trans.) (London and New York: Verso, 2005).

Boltanski and Chiapello do not suggest that this meant that exploitation disappeared; rather, it took on new forms. Shaping these new forms is another great change affecting productive processes in our own time: globalisation. Of the many accounts that have been written of this, one of the most vivid is Naomi Klein's *No Logo*.[18] Klein describes there how the focus of commercial activity in many countries of the global North shifted during the second half of the twentieth century from production to distribution. Instead of making things themselves, companies increasingly preferred to concentrate on marketing. In today's world, clothes, shoes, computers and other manufactured goods are 'sourced', just like natural resources. And just like natural resources, they are mostly sourced from countries of the global South. As Klein points out, the change is not just about where goods are produced. It is also about how they are produced. Manufacturing has become an affair of 'orders', placed with contractors, and through them often a long chain of subcontractors, who must continually compete to fulfil specifications while offering the cheapest possible prices. In this context, exploitation has all the complexity of globalisation itself. On the one hand, and to a greater extent than previously, relations are involved between people in different countries, often separated by many intermediaries. This makes exploitation all the more difficult to grasp. On the other hand, as indicated, it takes on new forms within countries. One contemporary form of exploitation to which Boltanski and Chiapello call particular attention is what they refer to as the exploitation of mobility. As they explain, 'some people's immobility is necessary for other people's mobility', and in today's world the capacity to move about, network and multiply the settings in which one acts and interacts, is a key element in the accumulation of social (and actual) capital.[19]

Just as these changes affecting productive processes have not put an end to exploitation (and may even have exacerbated it in some respects), neither has the fact that workers today have rights. This is not only because those rights are not always protected and respected. It is also because workplace rights do not overcome the structural embeddedness of exploitation, the logics that constantly push for rates of surplus-value to be raised and capital accumulated. These logics are reflected in pressures faced by managers to maximise profits for their shareholders, and by

---

[18] N. Klein, *No Logo* (London: Flamingo, 2001).
[19] Boltanski and Chiapello, *The New Spirit of Capitalism*, p. 362 (emphasis omitted).

governments in capital-importing states to create conditions favourable to foreign investment. Workplace rights have come under particular strain in countries where governments have vied to attract foreign investment by reducing social protections (the so-called 'race to the bottom'). As many have argued, the conditions of the Victorian factory have been not so much overcome as displaced elsewhere. Despite, then, the very different context in which we study capitalism today, Marx's account of exploitation still remains relevant. Of course, this is not to say that it is universally accepted, nor that it is accepted without qualification by those whom it broadly persuades. In particular, the 'labour theory of value' which underpins the explanation of profit is today widely doubted. This is the idea that the value of a commodity depends on the normal or 'socially necessary' amount of labour time needed to produce it. For G. A. Cohen, the basis for the charge that capitalism is an exploitative system is not that labour creates value, but that only labour creates what has value.[20] Beyond this, three aspects have figured in recent debates: the relation between exploitation and class, the extent to which exploitation involves coercion, and the identification of exploitation with injustice. Let us look briefly at each of these aspects in turn.

In Marx's analysis, exploitation is linked to the inequalities that arise from class divisions. What of other social divisions, such as those based on gender, race, ethnicity and location in the global economy? Relations of exploitation indexed to these kinds of asymmetries were not investigated by Marx, or not to any very significant degree, and (except where raised through the critique of imperialism) had little prominence in classical Marxist thought. In recent decades, however, feminist scholars have thrown light on some of the many ways in which relations between men and women involve exploitation.[21] Likewise, analysts of global political economy have shown how relations between, on the one hand, governments and big corporations and, on the other, peasant farmers in Third World countries also involve exploitation.[22] How are we to situate these

[20] G. A. Cohen, 'The Labor Theory of Value and the Concept of Exploitation', in K. Nielsen and R. Ware (eds.), *Exploitation* (Atlantic Highlands, NJ: Humanities Press, 1997), p. 94.

[21] See, e.g., M. Mies, *Patriarchy and Accumulation on a World Scale* (London: Zed Books, 1986).

[22] See, e.g., S. Amin, *Maldevelopment: Anatomy of a Global Failure*, M. Wolfers (trans.) (London: Zed Books, 1990). See also G. Omvedt, 'Capitalism, Nature, Peasants, and Women: Contemporary Problems of Marxism', in Nielsen and Ware (eds.), *Exploitation*, p. 294.

spheres of exploitation with respect to the sphere of exploitation described by Marx? Is class simply another social division, to be set alongside gender, ethnicity and so on, or does it possess some degree of pre-eminence in a theory of exploitation? Putting the case that class relations do indeed possess some degree of pre-eminence, Shaikh writes:

> This does not mean that these other relations lack a history and logic of their own. It only means that within any given mode of production, they are bound to the system by the force field of this central relation, and characteristically shaped by its ever-present gravitational pull.[23]

The claim here is not, then, that class exploitation is more serious or worrying than other sorts of exploitation – clearly it is not. Rather, the claim is that, for example, 'capitalist patriarchy is distinct from feudal patriarchy precisely because capitalist relations of production are characteristically different from feudal ones'.[24]

Does exploitation involve coercion? Marx writes of workers being 'compelled' to sell their labour-power, and depicts surplus labour as an instance of forced unremunerated labour.[25] His later interpreters have attached differing weight to this aspect. However, most are clear that what is at issue is less the action of particular individuals than the impact of general constraints and influences. It is the force of circumstances within the capitalist order that makes people consent to take part in exploitative arrangements.[26] In the case of wage-labourers, this is a matter, as Marx observes, of labour market pressures and the demands of physical survival. But Boltanski and Chiapello emphasise that it is not only a matter of those material constraints; ideology also plays an important part. I will return to this point in later discussion. For the moment, it is enough to observe that, through the operations of ideology, engagement in an exploitative system is made to seem justified and legitimate. Above all, it is made to seem necessary for the common good. The outcome of these processes is what Boltanski and Chiapello understand by the 'spirit' of capitalism – a term that refers in their account not so much to a particular ethos (as it did for Max Weber), as to an analytical category, the name for whatever

---

[23] Shaikh, 'Exploitation', p. 74.   [24] *Ibid*, p. 75.
[25] See further, J. Reiman, 'Exploitation, Force, and the Moral Assessment of Capitalism: Thoughts on Roemer and Cohen' in Nielsen and Ware (eds.), *Exploitation*, p. 154.
[26] See further, A. Wood, *Karl Marx*, 2nd edn, (London and New York: Routledge, 2004), p. 253.

ideological resources are used to mobilise engagement with the capitalist order in a specific time and place.[27]

The ideological legitimation of exploitation obviously has social effects. Confronted with the claim that exploitation is a structural feature of contemporary socio-economic life, many people do not accept that this is the case. Others, while accepting that the accumulation of capital does or may involve exploitation, do not consider that this is an undesirable state of affairs. Most of these people presumably regret that some are prospering at others' expense, but believe that exploitation ultimately benefits everyone, including those exploited. Or they believe that there is no better alternative than our current, exploitative arrangements. For yet others, and certainly for Marx, exploitation is unambiguously undesirable. However, should it be characterised as unjust? Some Marxists have argued that it should not, inasmuch as concepts of justice are themselves rooted in specific historical circumstances.[28] Marx makes this point about the historicity of justice in his text published under the title *Critique of the Gotha Programme*.[29] Challenging the idea that socialists should denounce capitalism for its failure to achieve a just distribution of the social product, he asks: 'What is a "just" distribution? Don't the bourgeoisie claim that the present distribution is "just"? And on the basis of the present mode of production, isn't it in fact the only "just" distribution?'[30] From this perspective, exploitation is 'just' in capitalist conditions. However, those conditions are contingent and hence alterable, and exploitation is at the same time unjust from the standpoint of how the world could be.

1.3. Key features

Let me try now to draw together some of the threads of my discussion so far. As Iris Marion Young reminds us, exploitation is one of a number of different 'faces of oppression'.[31] What then is its distinctiveness? Based on

---

[27] See Boltanski and Chiapello, *The New Spirit of Capitalism*, p. 8; cf. M. Weber, *The Protestant Ethic and the Spirit of Capitalism* (London: Routledge, 2001).
[28] See, e.g., Wood, *Karl Marx*, 2nd edn, ch. 9.
[29] *Marx: Later Political Writings*, T. Carver (ed.) (Cambridge: Cambridge University Press), p. 208.
[30] *Ibid.*, p. 211.
[31] I. M. Young, *Justice and the Politics of Difference* (Princeton, NJ: Princeton University Press, 1990), pp. 48 ff.

the foregoing, seven key features can be highlighted. First, the core meaning of exploitation is concerned with pursuing one's own gain at another's unfair expense. To exploit a person is to use that person as the instrument of one's own ends.[32] Second, in the study of capitalism, exploitation refers to the extraction of profit out of labour. Workers are exploited insofar as they are used to produce and expand capital for others. Systemic imperatives to accumulate more and more capital translate into organisational pressures for more and more exploitation. Third, the extent to which capitalism involves exploitation is not immediately visible. Exploitative relations are disavowed by law, and masked by an ideology that represents participants in the labour market as free and equal. If exploitation is to be challenged or even analysed, it therefore requires exposure; the claims that constitute the surface-level reality must be penetrated to reveal the different truth beneath. This is always difficult, but globalisation has added greatly to the difficulty, insofar as relations of exploitation involve chains of interaction spanning the globe.

Fourth, exploitation is linked to the inequalities that arise from the division of classes. In recent decades, exploitation has been rethought in connection with inequalities arising from other social divisions, such as those based on gender, race, ethnicity and location in the global economy. Marxist scholars argue that, while these latter divisions have their own history and dynamics, class relations mediate them, so that exploitation always remains impressed with the stamp of the capitalist mode of production. Fifth, exploitation may involve abusive working conditions and inhumane, bullying bosses, but it need not. Mostly, the coercion that induces wage-labourers to allow themselves to be exploited comes from the limited options open to those concerned. Ideology also has a key role in legitimating exploitation. Sixth, exploitation is a distributive issue. As Marx's discussion of the limits of the working day reminds us, capitalism is a conflictual system. The appropriate extent of the working day is not just a question of management or economics; it has distributive, and hence political, significance. To contest exploitative relations is to engage in redistributive social struggle. Seventh and finally, informing that struggle is an awareness that, while exploitation may be just by the

---

[32] This, of course, is often associated with Kant's formulation of the Categorical Imperative: 'To exploit someone is to treat that person purely as a means to your own ends, and not as an "end in themself".' See I. Kant, 'Groundwork for a Metaphysic of Morals' in *The Moral Law*, H. Paton (ed.) (London: Hutchinson, 1948), pp. 90–1. On the relation between this and the Marxian conception of exploitation, see J. Wolff, 'Marx and Exploitation' (1999) 3 *Journal of Ethics* 105, esp. at 112 ff.

standards which contemporary society sets for itself, those standards are themselves unjust when assessed against the possibility of transformative change. This points to the need to consider exploitation as simultaneously contingent and necessary – contingent, in the sense that things do not have to be as they are, but also necessary, in the sense that exploitative relations are not simply arbitrary or accidental, but belong with the logic of a system which must itself be brought within the frame.

2. Exploitation and international law

My focus to this point has been on exploitation in general. Turning now to take up the question of exploitation as an international legal issue, I need to become more concrete. When activists invoke international law to challenge exploitation, when lawyers advise on rights and duties regarding exploitation under international law, and when academics discuss the theme of exploitation in international legal writing, what is it that they have in mind? What do such people talk about when they talk about exploitation? In order to explore this, we will need to move for a while into a different key from the one in which we have proceeded so far. We will need to tune in to the work of international organisations and activists, and to pay attention to the details of treaties and other standard-setting documents, themselves resonant of a variety of epochs, institutions and debates. Later on, we will take stock of this survey of international legal materials, and as we try to develop a picture of how exploitation looks when viewed from the perspective of international law, our discussion will return again to exploitation theory.

2.1. *International legal perspectives*

Much of the time, reference to exploitation in international legal materials is to exploitation in the positive or neutral sense indicated earlier: the exploitation of oil and gas, the exploitation of fish stocks and forests, the exploitation of patents, trade marks and copyright, and so on. As I noted then, the distinction between the positive or neutral sense and the pejorative sense of the term 'exploitation' may not in fact be as stable as at first appears. Certainly, concerns about the negative impacts of mining, fisheries, forestry and intellectual property rights are reflected in international law, and in writing about it. Such concerns are, of course, the stuff of international environmental law, and have a considerable history within the law of the sea. Today they are also very much on the agenda of international trade law, international human rights law, and the international law of indigenous peoples' rights. What is important for present purposes, however, is that the issue in these arenas is almost never exploitation (in the pejorative sense) as such. Rather, it is non-sustainability, environmental degradation, expropriation of indigenous property, unfair trade, or the abuse of human rights. Thus, for instance, the TRIPs agreement has been subjected to sustained criticism for its impact on access to drugs needed to treat HIV-AIDS. But while the point is undoubtedly in the background that the shareholders of pharmaceutical companies are being enabled to prosper at the expense of – quite literally, to drain life from – people infected with this disease, this point remains in the background. Front and centre are instead questions to do with the human rights of those infected and the measures that may be taken by governments in poor countries (compulsory licensing, etc.) to make the drugs available. Those who have benefited from patent revenues remain comfortably out of view.

Beyond this engagement with exploitation in the 'positive or neutral' sense, there are also some contexts in which exploitation is used in international legal materials to name a problem, i.e. in a pejorative sense, as part of an effort to secure the redress of something considered bad. The earliest treaty in which this occurs relates to prostitution. In 1949 the United Nations General Assembly approved the text of the Convention for the Suppression of the Traffic in Persons and of the Exploitation of the Prostitution of Others. The Convention was designed to supplement earlier treaties dealing with what had been successively termed the 'white slave trade' and 'traffic in women', and was now called 'exploitation of prostitution'. Under Article 1 states parties agree to:

> punish any person who, to gratify the passions of another:
> 1. Procures, entices or leads away, for the purposes of prostitution, another person, even with the consent of that person;
> 2. Exploits the prostitution of another person, even with the consent of that person.

States parties further agree to punish any person who keeps, finances or knowingly rents a building for a brothel. In the years since 1949 sex has remained a key aspect of what is in issue in international legal activity addressed to exploitation. Under Article 6 of the Convention on the Elimination of All Forms of Discrimination against Women (1979), states parties are obliged to:

take all appropriate measures, including legislation, to suppress all forms of traffic in women and exploitation of prostitution of women.

More recently, concerns about the heightened prevalence and scale of human trafficking led to the elaboration of the Protocol to Prevent, Suppress and Punish Trafficking in Persons, Especially Women and Children, Supplementing the United Nations Convention against Transnational Organized Crime (the 'Palermo Protocol', opened for signature in 2000). The Protocol contains the first definition of exploitation in any treaty.

The Protocol deals with trafficking in persons ('paying particular attention to women and children')[33] where pursued transnationally, as part of organised criminal activity. Obligations are imposed on states parties to criminalise human trafficking, take preventive measures, and provide protection for victims. The Protocol proceeds from a notion of human trafficking as non-consensual recruitment or transfer for the purpose of exploitation. Accordingly, the definition of exploitation is part of the definition of trafficking in persons:

> 'Trafficking in persons' shall mean the recruitment, transportation, transfer, harbouring or receipt of persons, by means of the threat or use of force or other forms of coercion, of abduction, of fraud, of deception, of the abuse of power or of a position of vulnerability or of the giving or receiving of payments or benefits to achieve the consent of a person having control over another person, for the purpose of exploitation. Exploitation shall include, at a minimum, the exploitation of the prostitution of others or other forms of sexual exploitation, forced labour or services, slavery or practices similar to slavery, servitude or the removal of organs.[34]

As in the earlier treaties, then, exploitation is understood as sexual exploitation; at the same time, reference is also included to forced labour and other slave-like practices, the removal of organs, and (since the definition is non-exhaustive) other possible practices. This obviously encompasses forced domestic labour – a major element in concerns about human trafficking in many countries today. In 2005 a further anti-trafficking treaty was adopted within the framework of the Council of Europe: the European Convention on Action against Trafficking in Human Beings.[35]

---

[33] Article 2(a).
[34] Article 3(a). The Convention goes on to provide that the consent of the victim is irrelevant where coercion, fraud and the like have been used, and that, where the victim is a child, even coercion, fraud and the like are irrelevant; it is enough that the child has been recruited, transported etc. for the purpose of exploitation. See Articles 3(b) and 3(c) respectively.
[35] At the time of writing, the Convention had not yet entered into force.

The Convention uses the same concept of human trafficking (and hence exploitation) as the Palermo Protocol, but is somewhat broader in scope, inasmuch as it aims not only at transnational trafficking, but also at trafficking within a single country, and not only at organised criminal activity, but also at trafficking by individuals without ties to criminal organisations. The Convention is part of a wider campaign against human trafficking in the Council of Europe, promoted under the slogan 'Human being – not for sale'.

Alongside these treaties, exploitation features most prominently in international legal provisions concerning children. In a brief reference which appears in an article dealing also with rights relating to marriage and maternity, the International Covenant on Economic, Social and Cultural Rights (1966) declares that '[c]hildren and young persons should be protected from economic and social exploitation'.[36] The Convention on the Rights of the Child (1989) has a more elaborate provision:

> States Parties shall take all appropriate legislative, administrative, social and educational measures to protect the child from all forms of physical or mental violence, injury or abuse, neglect or negligent treatment, maltreatment or exploitation, including sexual abuse, while in the care of parent(s), legal guardian(s) or any other person who has the care of the child.[37]

Here then the focus is again on exploitation as a phenomenon that includes sexual abuse, while also going beyond it. Commercial sexual exploitation of children is addressed in the Optional Protocol to the Convention on the Rights of the Child on the Sale of Children, Child Prostitution and Child Pornography, opened for signature in 2000. In preambular paragraphs it is recalled that girl children are especially vulnerable in this regard. The Optional Protocol obliges states parties to criminalise a range of acts, among them 'offering, delivering or accepting, by whatever means, a child for the purpose of (*inter alia*) sexual exploitation of the child'.[38] Overall, a very considerable proportion of current writing and activism on the theme of exploitation pertains to the exploitation of children, whether that takes the form of commercial sexual exploitation, non-commercial sexual exploitation, or non-sex-based child labour. In recent years, reports have surfaced of the sexual exploitation of refugee and displaced children, and of other children in conflict or 'post-conflict' zones – mostly girls – by members of peacekeeping forces, officials of humanitarian agencies, and

---

[36] Article 10(3). [37] Article 19(1). [38] Article 3(1).

aid workers. The abuses also involve adult women, and exploitation of this kind is today a preoccupation within international refugee law and policy, the international protection of human rights, and the legal regulation of peacekeeping operations, among other domains.

With regard to child labour, the various treaties concluded on that subject within the framework of the International Labour Organization, though they do not use the term 'exploitation', are further legal reference points in debates about the exploitation of children. So too is the ILO's 1998 Declaration on Fundamental Principles and Rights at Work, designating the abolition of child labour a universal norm applicable even in the absence of treaty ratification. The earliest ILO instrument in which the term 'exploitation' does actually appear is concerned with indigenous peoples. In the Organization's Indigenous and Tribal Populations Recommendation, adopted in 1957, it is advised that ILO member states should take administrative measures to 'prevent the exploitation of workers belonging to the populations concerned on account of their unfamiliarity with the industrial environment to which they are introduced'.[39] A 1983 Recommendation relates the problem of labour exploitation to disability: the need is highlighted for member states to lend support to initiatives designed to 'eliminate the potential for exploitation [of people with disabilities] within the framework of vocational training and sheltered employment'.[40] A further Recommendation in the following year extends the concern to migrant workers: member states in the position of both countries of employment and countries of origin are enjoined to take measures to 'prevent the exploitation of migrant workers'.[41] The International Convention on the Protection of the Rights of All Migrant Workers and Members of their Families, opened for signature within the framework of the UN in 1990 and in force since 2003, sets out the rights of migrant workers across a wider range of spheres than those touched

---

[39] Indigenous and Tribal Populations Recommendation, 1957, ILO Recommendation No. 104, para. 36(g). The later Convention on Indigenous and Tribal Peoples in Independent Countries, 1989 (ILO Convention No. 169) is more demanding with respect to the guarantee of fair working conditions for indigenous employees. However, it does not use the term 'exploitation'. See Article 20.

[40] Vocational Rehabilitation and Employment (Disabled Persons) Recommendation, 1983, ILO Recommendation No. 168, para. 11(m).

[41] Employment Policy (Supplementary Provisions) Recommendation, 1984, ILO Recommendation No. 169, para. 43(b). Exploitation of workers in the maritime sector is also touched on in the ILO Maritime Labour Convention, 2006: see Guideline 1.4.1, para. 2(d) and (e).

on in the ILO Recommendation. In that treaty, however, the only reference to exploitation is to exploitation in the sphere of housing. Certain categories of migrant workers are said to have the right to equality of treatment with nationals of the state of employment with respect to (*inter alia*) 'access to housing, including social housing schemes, and protection against exploitation in respect of rents'.[42]

A final category of international norms and standards which is widely understood to touch on issues of exploitation, even if (as with child labour) the term is not actually used, has to do with slavery, forced labour and pay and conditions at work. Slavery is a longstanding topic within international law, and the prohibition of forced labour and other similar practices is well established within international human rights and labour law. Beyond this, the Universal Declaration of Human Rights proclaims the right of everyone to 'just and favourable conditions of work', 'equal pay for equal work', and 'just and favourable remuneration ensuring for himself and his family an existence worthy of human dignity'.[43] The Declaration also proclaims the right of everyone to 'form and to join trade unions' and to 'rest and leisure, including reasonable limitation of working hours and periodic holidays with pay'.[44] State obligations with regard to these matters are specified further in provisions of the International Covenant on Economic, Social and Cultural Rights (1966) and other human rights treaties, where protection is given as well to the right to safe and healthy working conditions.[45] State obligations are also specified in the many treaties and other non-binding instruments that have been adopted within the framework of the ILO, on topics ranging from the eight-hour day and forty-eight-hour week (the ILO's first convention, adopted in 1919) to the rights and protection at work of seafarers (the Maritime Labour Convention, adopted in 2006).[46] It is notable, however, that the online 'ILO Thesaurus' – 'a compilation of more than 4,000 terms relating to the world of work ... in English, French, and Spanish ... [which] covers labour and employment policy, human resources planning, labour standards, labour administration and labour relations, vocational training, economic and social development, social security, working conditions, wages, occupational safety and health and enterprise promotion' – does not include the word 'exploitation'.[47]

---

[42] Article 43(1)(d).   [43] Article 23(1), (2) and (3).   [44] Articles 23(4) and 24.
[45] E.g., International Covenant on Economic, Social and Cultural Rights, Article 7(b).
[46] See Hours of Work (Industry) Convention, 1919, ILO Convention No. 1, and Maritime Labour Convention, 2006.
[47] See www.ilo.org/public/libdoc/ILO-Thesaurus/english/.

2.2. False contingency

We now have some elements towards an answer to the question: what do people engaged with international law talk about when they talk about exploitation? Of course, the materials I have reviewed are only indicative, not conclusive, and ultimately no available meaning is foreclosed. With that caveat, a few points emerge. It is clear that what is in question is very often sexual exploitation, affecting primarily women and girls. Here exploitation is a form of violence against women or child abuse. Where trafficking is involved, it is also a large and lucrative domain of transnational crime. The focus of international legal initiatives is accordingly on the creation of an adequate regime of crime control, and on the implications for human rights, the rights of refugees, the legal regulation of peacekeeping, and so on. A further point is that these initiatives are linked through the concept of exploitation to a history of international law-making that goes back to the moral panics about prostitution and 'white slavery' of the first half of the twentieth century in parts of Europe and the United States. To note this link is not to suggest that contemporary concerns about human trafficking are merely moral panics. It is, however, to contemplate the possibility that there remain traces of the earlier thinking within the international legal imagination, and that one aspect of these traces may be to place morality at the centre of what is at stake. I will return to this point in a moment.

Additionally, and alongside these concerns, exploitation is associated in international law with slavery, forced labour and other slave-like conditions. More generally, it is associated with the denial of decent working conditions and of fair pay. On the other hand, the fact that the word 'exploitation' is not normally part of the 'official', formal discourse of the ILO and other organisations on these matters may suggest a perception that the concept of exploitation does not belong in the sphere of labour regulation, perhaps because it is too political, or too divisive, or simply too embarrassing. A final observation relates to the exceptional contexts in which the word 'exploitation' has been used. Labour standards in these contexts are hard to detach from the long history of paternalism towards indigenous peoples, people with disabilities, and other groups represented by the authorities as incapable, helpless, and touchingly innocent of the ways of the world. Needless to say, this is a posture more conducive to justifying exploitation than to curbing it. The ILO's 1957 Indigenous and Tribal Populations Recommendation illustrates something of the problem when it manifests concern that indigenous workers may be exploited 'on account of their unfamiliarity with the industrial environment to which they are introduced' – but not concern that, through this industrial environment, the individuals in question have been left with no means of subsistence other than exploitative wage-labour. As with sexual exploitation, so too in the sphere of labour exploitation, the supercession of this earlier phase of international legal activity may not be complete.

If we compare all this with the account of exploitation which I outlined earlier, and resolved eventually into seven key features, it is obvious that there are some commonalities, but also some important differences. To begin with the commonalities, all the international legal materials we have reviewed exhibit the first feature of exploitation in my list. Whatever the specific concern, exploitation is always understood as a matter of pursuing gain at another's unfair expense. While greater emphasis is placed in some contexts than in others on taking wrongful advantage of another person's vulnerability, the core idea of treating someone as the instrument of one's own ends is invariably there. The differences start to appear as soon as we come to the question of what that entails. The second feature of exploitation I highlighted concerns the extraction of profit out of labour. Systemic imperatives within capitalism generate organisational pressures for more and more exploitation. Marx illustrates this point with reference to the struggle in Victorian England over the length of the working day. In our own time, the most striking illustrations come perhaps from the world of the 'export processing zone', where order-driven manufacturing has fostered employment that in some places again involves unconscionably long hours, intermittent pay, poor health and safety standards, and only the barest rest and leisure.[48] As we have seen, international law insists that workers have rights to fair pay and decent conditions. In doing so, however, its implicit message is that exploitation is work gone wrong. Exploitative employment appears as a kind of pathology of the labour contract. What the Marxian analysis brings out is that, on the contrary, exploitation belongs with the normal functioning of a system in which capital accumulation depends on labour exploitation. In Marx's language, capital is dead labour reanimated by sucking living labour 'and lives the more, the more labour it sucks'.[49] There is a systemic impetus, a momentum and an orientation, towards practices and relations that are more and more exploitative.

[48] See, e.g., Oxfam, *Trading Away Our Rights: Women in the Global Supply Chain* (Oxford: Oxfam, 2004).
[49] *Capital*, Vol. 1, p. 342.

I pass over my third key feature of exploitation and return to it later. As for the fourth, regarding the link between exploitation and social inequalities, international legal engagement with human trafficking and child exploitation has made vivid the relation between exploitation and inequalities in the sphere of gender. It has also highlighted the important point that these inequalities affect not only the extent, but also the forms of exploitation. Most obviously, women and girls are disproportionately exposed to exploitation for sex and domestic work. But which women and girls are disproportionately exposed? While the question of the 'root causes' of human trafficking is part of the debate, it cannot dispose of the much larger question of the socio-economic conditions in which this activity becomes possible and develops – not just as a category of transnational crime, but also, of course, as a branch of business. The fifth key feature to which I called attention relates to the issue of coercion. Some forms of exploitation are manifestly based on duress. More commonly, however, what is involved is voluntary employment. 'Human being – not for sale' is a good slogan for an anti-trafficking campaign, but from another perspective, the sale of people compelled through the force of circumstances to alienate their own energy, time, and hence life – their 'labour-power' – is the quintessential capitalist transaction. To be sure, the system depends on their not giving up all of this at once: as Marx explains, for labour-power to remain a saleable commodity, its owner must retain ultimate ownership over it. He must give it up only 'for a definite period of time, temporarily'.[50] On the other hand, for the capitalist to find labour-power in the market, the worker, 'instead of being able to sell [things produced with his labour], must rather be compelled to offer for sale as a commodity that very labour-power which exists only in his living body'.[51] The point here is not that wage-labour is indistinguishable from forced or trafficked labour, still less that the degree and nature of labour exploitation remain always the same, and always objectionable in the same measure. The point is simply that account must be taken of the compulsion that comes not from violence, threats or deceit, but from the limitation of options and the denial of opportunities.

At stake in the sixth feature I enumerated is the character of exploitation as a distributive and hence inescapably political issue. In exploitative relations, a redistribution occurs, such that the advantage of some is bought at the cost of the disadvantage of others. Some gain, while others lose. Thus, for Marx, the exhaustion of the worker corresponds to the enrichment of

[50] Ibid., p. 271. [51] Ibid., p. 272.

the capitalist. More generally, privilege is linked to deprivation. It follows that challenge to exploitation is itself a redistributive demand, a demand for a new allocation of what is collectively available – in effect, a new political settlement. In the international legal materials we have surveyed, relatively little is evident of this 'political' aspect. The problem and its solution seem to lie in the domain of morality, culture, expertise, administration, or law. Anti-trafficking initiatives aim at the implementation and enforcement of criminal sanctions, along with preventive measures and victim protection. Likewise, the focus of efforts concerning child labour, forced labour and unfair employment is on regulatory action, backed up by public education. Antedating the current campaign against human trafficking, we have seen, is an earlier episode of international law-making pursued under the signature of moral rectitude and patriarchal power. Whatever the place of morality and patriarchy in contemporary debates, the impression is of exploitation as a local dysfunction, and something which we may look to the state and civil society to correct. This brings me to the final feature of exploitation in my list, the insight that exploitation is contingent, but also, at another level, necessary. That exploitative arrangements should, and could, be different is an important theme of critical international legal scholarship.[52] This is also, of course, the premise from which activism for global justice proceeds. What is less frequently observed is the Marxian point that these arrangements are not simply random facts, but coherent elements within the dynamic totality of the world as a whole. While assuredly unjust from the standpoint of transformative change, exploitation must be recognised as functional to – and hence, in another sense, just within – current conditions. Against the false contingency that leaves us to think of injustice as arbitrary or accidental, exploitation theory invites us to see that there are instead systemic logics at work. The silence of international law's interlocutors about these systemic logics is their silence about capitalism.

2.3. The ideology of mutuality

If exploitation as an international legal issue maps only inadequately onto the much more pervasive reality described by Marx and later analysts, why is this so? How are we to account for such a disjuncture between

---

[52] Perhaps more than any other international legal scholar, David Kennedy has thematised this issue of winners and losers. See, e.g., D. Kennedy, *Dark Sides of Virtue* (Princeton, NJ: Princeton University Press, 2004).

international law and material reality? Quite obviously the explanation is to be sought in the play and interplay of many different phenomena. Of these I am interested now in just one: ideology. I use the term 'ideology' to refer to the rhetorical and other symbolic processes that help to sustain prevailing privilege by making it seem justified and legitimate. These processes can work in a wide – indeed infinite – variety of ways, but in broad terms we may note two principal patterns. On the one hand, privilege may be rationalised or 'spun'. For example, it may be made to seem desirable, natural, essential or inevitable. On the other hand, privilege may be masked. That is to say, it may be concealed behind something more acceptable. While ideology is often associated with the notion of false consciousness, neither of these patterns involves falsehood insofar as both partly constitute the truth of the privilege at stake. In earlier discussion I recalled something of the legitimating ideology of capitalism. What is distinctive about capitalism compared to other class-based modes of production, I recalled, is that in the capitalist mode exploitation is masked. (This was the third in my enumeration of key features of exploitation, put to one side earlier on.) Whereas in slave-owning and feudal societies exploitation is entirely patent, in capitalist society it gets concealed behind the formal freedom and equality of the labour market. Hence Marx's spatial image of surface and depths. On the surface is a 'very Eden of the innate rights of man . . . [in which the capitalist and the worker] contract as free persons, who are equal before the law'.[53] It is only when we move from the glare of exchange down into the depths of production that a different picture of wage-labour begins to emerge.

This analysis remains pertinent, but in reflecting on the engagement of international law with exploitation, I want additionally to consider another aspect of what legitimates privilege in the contemporary world. This aspect might be called the ideology of 'mutuality'. Marx in fact touches on it in a passage I have already cited, but which is worth repeating here. In the 'very Eden' that is the surface-level in capitalist society, not only are the parties to the labour contract free and equal; they also 'work together to their mutual advantage, for the common weal, and in the common interest'.[54] If this idea could serve as ideology in Marx's day, it has become absolutely central to legitimation processes in the twenty-first century, when the *Zeitgeist* is surely all about mutual advantage. Our talk is of 'win-win', 'good for the planet, good for you', and 'a rising tide lifts all boats'. We study techniques of 'principled negotiation', 'mutual gains

[53] *Capital*, Vol. 1, p. 280. [54] *Ibid*.

bargaining', and 'creative collaboration'. Synergies, interdependence, and teamwork are our abiding preoccupations, and when someone claims to discern a 'zero-sum' game, we say: try harder, there is always some angle from which everyone can be shown to be better off. In many ways we are actually quite aware of inequalities today. To a much greater extent than in Marx's time, we confront discrimination (albeit, of course, still very partially and inadequately) – even its subtle forms, like institutional racism. What we seem to find much more difficult to contemplate is exploitation. Fortunately, when the going gets tough, there are always economists, policy analysts and even philosophers on hand, ready to allay our fears by explaining that those who lose actually also win. What exploitation theory reminds us is that this is ideology. Concealed behind the veneer of mutuality is a reality in which (to speak again with Marx) 'in the same relations in which wealth is produced, poverty is produced also'.[55]

I referred earlier to the account of the 'new spirit of capitalism' put forward by Boltanski and Chiapello. I explained that, for them, capitalism's 'spirit' is comprised of the ideological resources used to mobilise engagement with it in specific circumstances. Ideological resources dialectically generate critical resources – more concretely, they generate critiques. At one level, the history of modernity can be told as a story of episodic moves to disarm these critiques, followed by their re-arming in connection with the renewal of ideology. Boltanski's and Chiapello's story about post-Fordism in France is an instance of this.[56] The new network-based form of organisation disarmed the earlier critiques of alienation, commodification, disempowerment and unfreedom. In doing so, however, it brought with it fresh ideology, and hence the necessity, and ground, for fresh critique. It is here that the ideology of mutuality assumes importance – not, as indicated, because it is novel, but because within expert discourses, everyday talk and indeed unspoken 'common sense' it has acquired new significance and new centrality. And if mutuality has become central to the legitimating ideology of capitalism today, then equally, exploitation must become central to the critique of that ideology. Against the ideology that asserts that 'a rising tide lifts all boats' etc. must be counterposed the critique of a distribution of advantages and disadvantages which is systematically asymmetrical. It bears some emphasis that the claim here is not that ideology involves falsehood. Perhaps a rising tide does actually

---

[55] See n. 16 above.
[56] On the 'disarming' and 're-arming' of critiques, see Boltanski and Chiapello, *The New Spirit of Capitalism*, pp. 27 ff., pp. 483 ff., and *passim*.

lift all boats. I am not sure that I fully understand the implications of this phrase as it is used by economists and others, but I am willing to accept that it may be true. Rather, the claim is that ideology masks, conceals, or screens off other important aspects of reality; in effect, it takes up too much space and prevents us from seeing oppression. To return to the ideological phenomena with which Marx was concerned, the parties to the labour contract really do contract as formally free agents, and they really are equal before the law. But just as the freedom and equality of the labour market masks the unfreedom and inequality that prevails in productive relations, so too mutuality (however real) masks exploitation.

3. Conclusion

Let me briefly recapitulate before concluding. I began by observing that the problem of exploitation goes largely unremarked in international law. Insofar as this problem is remarked, I have argued that international legal discussions do scant justice to the much richer concept explicated by Marx and later analysts. I have suggested that this may have something to do with what I have called the ideology of mutuality, inasmuch as that tends to obscure the extent to which enhancements of the life-chances of some are linked to limitations of the life-chances of others. The thrust of my analysis is that international law needs to develop a new kind of engagement with the problem of exploitation. In drawing this chapter to a close, I will outline in a moment some possible aspects of this. But first, the question arises, *could* this occur? On one view, international law is enmeshed at a fundamental structural level with the exploitative logics of capitalism in a way that removes all emancipatory potential.[57] However valid the premises of such an argument, to my mind the conclusion does not follow. It fails to take sufficient account of the contradictoriness that defines our world, and of the immanence of counter-logics, obscured through ideology, but nonetheless available for reactivation in the service of emancipation through critique.[58]

What then would this new engagement with the problem of exploitation entail? It would place at the centre of international law the question of beneficiaries. International law has long been preoccupied with

[57] This view has received eloquent expression in the work of China Miéville. See C. Miéville, 'The commodity-form theory of international law', Chapter 3 in this volume, and *Between Equal Rights* (Leiden and Boston: Brill, 2005).
[58] I elaborate on this in 'International Judicial Activism and the Commodity-Form Theory of International Law', (2007) 18 *European Journal of International Law* 199.

victims – victims of human rights abuse, victims of discrimination, victims of war crimes. In recent years, with developments in the sphere of international criminal law, it has also become much preoccupied with perpetrators. But, as Mahmood Mamdani observes in comments recalled at the beginning of this chapter, beyond victims and perpetrators there are also beneficiaries. We should not be simplistic about this. If perpetrators are often also in some sense victims (not least, as in the case of apartheid, victims of a brutalising, militarist, hypermasculine culture), and if victims are apt themselves to become perpetrators (as Mamdani himself showed in later work on Rwanda),[59] so too beneficiaries may be advantaged in some contexts, while being disadvantaged in others. The category of 'beneficiary' refers less to a particular group of people than to a particular facet of human experience. To place the question of this facet of experience at the centre of international law is to move onto the international legal agenda issues that include, but also go far beyond, those currently subsumed under the topic of exploitation.

At the same time, a more adequate engagement with the problem of exploitation would also bring out the connections between these issues, and orient international law to a vision of the world as a structured totality. Quite obviously, exploitation is only one of many critical concepts that can be deployed to throw light on the asymmetrical distribution of advantage within countries and across the globe. Social exclusion and human rights are two alternative concepts that have particular currency today. Social exclusion is useful in pointing to the forms which deprivation can take – its phenomenology and at least some aspects of its sociology. But, as Boltanski and Chiapello observe, since no one seems to profit from social exclusion, 'no one can be deemed responsible . . . unless out of negligence or error'; the focus is on easing personal misfortune.[60] Human rights do fix responsibility: the state has the obligation to respect and ensure rights. But the obligations of the state are largely exhausted by regulatory measures. Since, once again, no one seems to profit, no need appears to arise for systemic change; the focus is on remedying official misconduct or inadvertence. What is distinctive about the concept of exploitation is that it re-specifies deprivation, not just as a matter of personal misfortune, and not just as an instance of official misconduct or inadvertence,

---

[59] M. Mamdani, *When Victims Become Killers* (Princeton, NJ: Princeton University Press, 2002).
[60] Boltanski and Chiapello, *The New Spirit of Capitalism*, p. 354.

but as a relational, redistributive, and ultimately systemic, problem, with necessarily systemic solutions.

Of course, simply grasping exploitation can itself be hard. This is especially the case in our own time, when what is in question is so often, and perhaps to a greater extent than ever before, less a matter of face-to-face relations than of long and complex chains of interaction. Exploitation today frequently involves people at distant locations, acting in ignorance of one another and through many intermediaries. How is one to 'relate the activity of a dealer in a trading room in London to the poverty of street-children in the shantytown of an African city'?[61] Boltanski and Chiapello call attention here to the difficulty, yet, in doing so, exemplify its evasion: the dealer is in London, while the street-children are somewhere in 'Africa'. Finally, then, a more adequate kind of engagement with the problem of exploitation would point up the enormity and complexity, but also the irreducible specificity, of this facet of contemporary life.

[61] *Ibid.*, p. 373.

Index

abyssal thinking, 203–4, 205
activism, 272
Adorno, Theodor, 2, 9, 14
Afghanistan, 137, 189, 193
African National Congress, 162
agency, structure and, 174, 192
Akehurst, Michael, 117
al Qaeda, 50
Alcantara, Oscar, 93n8, 95, 97
alchemy, 168
Algeria, 167
alienation, 4, 5, 14, 35, 287, 304
Allott, Philip, 30n2
Althusser, Louis, 8n26
Amnesty International, 173
Anand, R.P., 260
Anderson, Benedict, 122
Anderson, Elizabeth, 247n76
Anghie, Antony, 123n143, 259
Angola, 163, 167, 184
anti-capitalist movements, 1
apartheid, 281
Aquinas, Thomas, 27
arbitration, international commercial arbitration, 80–1
Aristotle, 246
Armenians, 145
Arrighi, Giovanni, 180, 182–3, 183, 188–9, 195, 196
Arthur, Chris, 106, 146, 150
atomisation, 14
Australia, 206
Austro-Hungarian Empire, 138, 143, 156, 158
Avineri, Shlomo, 226n19

Bauer, Bruno, 35
Bauer, Otto, 138, 140–1
Baxi, Upendra, 25–6, 77
   departure from Marx, 275–8
   historical materialism, 262–4
   human rights and NGOs, 270–5
   human rights scholar, 255–5
   Marxism, 252–4, 260–80

   new proletariat, 260–2
   TREMF theory, 264–70
   TWAIL scholar, 253, 254, 257–60, 269–70, 278
BBC, 27, 28
Bedjaoui, Mohammed, 260
Bellifore, Ricardo, 265
beneficiary thesis, 281, 282, 306
Benjamin, Walter, 2, 44
Bennett, Oliver, 171–3
Benvenisti, Eyal, 67n45
Berlin, Isaiah, 233–4
Bewes, Timothy, 6–7
Bhopal disaster, 78, 82
Blanquists, 227, 230
Blishchenko, Igor, 144–5, 158, 166
Bolsheviks, 137–43, 228, 307
Boltanski, Luc, 287–8, 290, 304, 306
Bottomore, Tom, 90
Bowring, Bill, 21–2, 133–68
Bracking, Sarah, 276
Brazil, 49–50, 187, 197
Brecht, Bertolt, 13, 231n36
Brezhnev doctrine, 137
Brilmayer, Lea, 67
Brownlie, Ian, 89
Bukhara, 145
Bukharin, Nikolai, 126, 146
Bull, Hedley, 97
Burma, 159
Bush, George W., 49–50
Butler, William, 135, 164

Cain, Maureen, 100
Callinicos, Alex, 129
Canning, George, 126
capital adequacy standards, 179
capital flows, 178–9, 185
capital logic, 111
capitalism
   accumulation by dispossession, 186–7, 189–90, 191–2
   age of capital, 284

capitalism (*cont.*)
  discourse, 191–2
  exploitation and, 264–5, 269, 282–3, 284–7
  global capitalism, 170–8
  imperialism and, 120, 187
  late capitalism, 180–7, 200–1
  law and, 187
  Marxist legacy, 4–7
  masking, 303–5
  new spirit of capitalism, 287–8, 304
  patriarchy, 290
  post-structural analysis, 170–8
  spirit of capitalism, 287, 290–1
  trade law and empire of capital, 205–10
Carty, Anthony, 22–3, 169–98
Cassese, Antonio, 159
Caucasus, 141
CEE states, EU recognition, 58–9
certification mechanisms, 76
Ceylon, 159
Chai, Winberg, 271–2
Charlesworth, H., 73
Chiapello, Eve, 287–8, 290, 304, 306, 307
children
  abuse, 299
  exploitation, 296–7
  labour, 26, 282, 296–7, 301
  rights, 296
Chile, 184, 239
Chimni, B.S., 18–19, 25, 26, 53–91, 92, 101, 104–5, 133–4, 254n10, 276
China
  alliances, 195
  capitalism, 189–90
  Chinese diaspora, 183
  colonialism, 13
  economic growth, 195
  Opium Wars, 183
  revolutionary potential, 195
  state immunity, 75n74
  United States and, 187, 188, 193, 194, 195, 197
Chinkin, Christine, 73
choice of law, 76, 80
citizenship, individual and, 37, 243
civil society
  bourgeois civil society, 37
  dissent, 63
  Hegel, 33, 34
  Marxist analysis, 222, 224
  NGOs and human rights, 270–5
  state-civil society dichotomy, 37–40, 47–9
  universalism and, 47–9
civilizing mission, 102, 144, 258
clash of civilisations, 43
class

class law, 126–7
division, 292
exploitation, 289–90
ideology, 7
interests, 56, 65, 239
international law and, 104
interpretation of treaties and, 69
Marxist legacy, 4–5, 98
new proletariat, 260–2
struggle, 25, 49, 104, 131
transnational capitalist class, 61–2, 64, 65, 75, 80, 81–2
treaties and, 67–8
Clinton, Bill, 178
Cohen, G.A., 289
Cohen, Jean, 49
Cold War, 43, 44, 87, 165, 172, 184
collective rights, 83, 269
Colletti, Lucio, 243
Colombia, 189
colonialism, *see* imperialism
commodification
  commodity-form theory of international law, 19–21, 105–20, 131, 148–51
  fetishising services, 24, 210–15, 219
  fetishism of commodities, 5–6, 7, 14, 24, 28, 49, 211, 236n44
  GATS and commodity-form theory, 210–15, 219
  human genetic material, 268
  Marxist legacy, 4–7, 14, 28, 210–11, 289
common heritage of mankind, 75–6
comparative advantage, 203
competition, 11
Congo (DRC), 189
consent, 45, 67, 68
consumerism, 81, 172, 180–1, 185
cosmopolitanism, 35, 123, 127–9
Council of Europe, Human Trafficking Convention, 295–6
Cox, Robert, 16
Craven, Matthew, 256–7
Crawford, James, 85
crime, *see* transnational crime
Critical Legal Studies, 92–3, 95, 96–7, 148
critical theory, 93, 278
Cruickshank, Albert, 190
cultural pessimism, 173
customary international law, 69, 70–2, 89, 136
Cutler, Claire, 23–4, 100, 199–219
Czechoslovakia, 137, 144, 164, 181

Dahl, Robert, 240n51
Damrosch, Lori, 135
Darwin, Charles, 27
databases, 268

INDEX

Davis, Mike, 12–13
De Gaulle, Charles, 191
decolonisation, 103, 122–4, 157, 158–60, 167
deconstruction, 18, 39–42, 191
deliberative democracy, 56, 67, 68–9, 72–3
democracy
  Bolsheviks, 141–2
  bourgeois democracy, 223
  cosmopolitan democracy, 128
  European Union and, 59
  Marxist critique, 26, 240–5
  meanings, 59
  pretext, 60
  social democracy, 170, 174, 186, 234, 238
  subaltern classes and, 265
depoliticisation, 27–9, 173, 176–7
derivatives, 171
Derrida, Jacques, 27–8, 93
Descartes, René, 27
determinism, 3, 57, 97
developing countries
  capital, 179
  democracy, 244
  environment, 81
  exploitation, 288, 289
  famines, 12–13
  GATS and, 212, 214
  plunder, 183–4
  resentment, 172
  toxic waste dumping, 268
  trade-related market-friendly rights and, 267
  under-development, 12–13
dialectics, 18, 38–47, 60, 97, 167–8, 202
disability, 297, 299
dispute resolution, private justice, 75
domestic laws, integration of international law, 73–4
Dominican Republic, 184
Dostoyevsky, Fyodor, 38
Drake, William, 214–15, 218n75
dualism, 73, 74
Dumbarton Oaks proposals, 159
Durkheim, Émile, 48
Dutt, R. Palme, 89
Dworkin, Ronald, 38n25, 232

Eagleton, Terry, 9, 27–8
East Asian crisis (1997), 80, 186
economic rights, 83
Einstein, Albert, 27
El Niño, 12, 13
Ellul, Jacques, 46
Engels, Friedrich, 3, 7, 8, 9, 13, 14, 31, 97, 226n18, 227, 230–2

Enron, 187
environment, 77, 81–2
epistemic communities, 214–15
equality
  egalitarian liberalism, 232, 234
  human rights and, 234
  juridical equality, 109, 117, 123n144, 127, 148–9, 211
  legal equality and force, 20, 61, 117, 121
  poverty and political equality, 244
  sovereign equality, 61, 85, 136, 182, 188
erga omnes obligations, 41
Estonia, 145, 156
European Union, 58–9, 195–6, 198
Evans, Tony, 82–3
exclusion, social exclusion, 306
exploitation
  beneficiary thesis, 281, 282, 306
  capitalism and, 264–5, 269, 282–3, 284–7
  colonial resources, 81, 183–4
  contemporary exploitation, 287–91
  etymology, 283
  globalisation, 169
  international law and, 26–7, 293–305
  key features, 291–3
  legitimation, 26
  Marx's analysis, 4, 284–7
  meanings, 283–4, 292, 293–4, 300
  seabed, 76
export processing zone, 300

Factory Acts, 130–1
false consciousness, 8
false contingency, 15–16, 299–302
false necessity, 15–16
family, 33, 34
Fanon, Frantz, 10
feminism, 90
fetishism of commodities, 5–6, 7, 14, 24, 28, 49, 211
feudalism, 286, 290
Feuerbach, Ludwig, 17, 33, 34, 47
Fine, Bob, 150–1
Finland, 50, 145, 156
Fischer, Ernst, 262, 263, 270–1
forced labour, 282, 290, 298–9, 301
Fordism, 287, 304
foreign direct investment, 62, 78–9, 213
forum non conveniens, 77–8
forum shopping, 80
Foucault, Michel, 93, 171, 173–4
France
  1871 Paris Commune, 226, 227, 230
  advanced capitalism, 190
  alliances, 195
  anti-Americanism, 191

France (cont.)
  Blanquists, 227, 230
  Declaration of the Rights of Man, 149, 224–5, 227
  empire, 143, 167
  May 68, 170
  political economy, 197
  Revolution, 33, 166, 228
France, Anatole, 238
Francis of Assisi, Saint, 177–8
Frankfurt School, 9, 278
free capital flows, 178–9
freedom of expression, 37
freedom of high seas, 208
Freeman, Alwyn, 136, 137, 165–6
Fuller, Lon, 235n42
functionalism, 68
futures, 171

G8, 50
Garcia Amador, F.V., 84
Garlan, Edwin, 147
Gathii, James, 259
GATS, 78, 210–15, 217, 218, 219
GATT, 79, 176, 177–8, 212–14
gender, 73, 301
Geneva protests, 50
genocide, 173
Germany, 48, 182, 183, 195, 197, 231n36
Ghandi, Mahatma, 278
Gibney, Mark, 86
Giddens, Anthony, 188
Global Compact, 84, 268
global governance, 128
globalisation
  complexity, 14
  contemporary exploitation, 288
  cosmopolitanism, 35
  debate, 100
  decentred law-making, 80
  global capitalism, 170–8
  imperialism, 60, 77, 87–8
  informal globalisation, 30, 48
  post-Marxist critique, 169
  post-structuralism and, 170–8
  power and, 59
  trade-related market-friendly rights and, 266
Golan, Galia, 162–3
Gowan, Peter, 128
Gramsci, Antonio, 2, 216–17, 271
Greece, 85
Grotius, Hugo, 96, 208, 209
Grushkin, Dimitrii, 160
Guatemala, 184, 239
Gupta, Bhabani Sen, 163

Habermas, Jürgen, 30n1
Hardt, Michael, 14, 15, 22–3, 169, 171, 174–8, 181, 192
Harrison, Graham, 276
Hart, H.L.A., 97
Harvey, David, 181, 183–4, 186–7, 189–90, 191–2, 194–5, 195, 196, 197, 200
Hazard, John, 146–7, 152, 155
Head, Michael, 146, 152
Hegel, Georg, 1, 7, 18, 33, 34, 36, 224n11
Held, David, 128
high seas, 208
Hilferding, Rudolf, 186
historical materialism, 2–4, 57, 97, 201–2, 216, 262–4
Hitler, Adolf, 155, 156
HIV-AIDS, 294
Hobsbawm, Eric, 157, 284
Hong Kong, 183
Horkheimer, Max, 2, 9
human rights
  abuse of discourse, 256
  activism, 272
  Baxi scholarship, 255–5
  bourgeois state and, 37, 82–3
  collective rights, 83, 269
  European Union and, 59
  form and substance, 233–45
  individuality and, 37, 82, 225
  international law, 82–4
  limitations, 25
  Marxism and, 24–5, 232–51
  natural rights, 221n2
  negative rights, 238
  NGOs and, 270–5
  poverty and, 233–4, 238
  realism, 272
  right-good distinction, 245–50
  secular theology, 17–18, 32, 36, 38, 49
  state responsibility, 306
  Third World and, 257–60
  trade-related market-friendly rights, 26, 255, 264–70
  universality, 25, 36, 47–9, 82
  Western view, 102
human trafficking, 26, 282, 294–7, 299, 301, 302
humanism, liberal humanism, 35–8
humanitarian intervention, 35, 88–9, 121n132, 128–9
Hungary, Soviet invasion, 137, 164
Hutchinson, John, 140
Hutton, Will, 185, 186, 195, 196, 197

idealism, 3, 43, 44, 95, 103, 148
ideology

concept, 7–8, 303
critique of, 9–10, 290, 303
ideology of mutuality, 26–7, 303–5
law as ideology, 102–4, 103–4
imperialism
 Baxi, 257–60, 276
 biopolitical empire, 171
 bourgeois imperial international law, 60, 61–2, 64, 73, 77
 capitalism and, 120, 187
 civilizing mission, 102, 144, 258
 colonial state, 58
 colonialism and environment, 81
 colonialism as terrorism, 258
 decolonisation, 103, 122–4, 157, 158–60, 167
 international law and, 61, 120–6, 131
 international trade law, 205–10
 Marx and colonialism, 276
 Marxist legacy, 10–13, 187–98
 neo-colonialism, 124–6
 new imperialism, 209
 post-structuralism, 170–8
 racism, 206, 258
 sovereignty empire, 22
 Soviet Union, 144–5
 state jurisdiction and colonialism, 74–5
 state responsibility and, 84–6
 universal jurisdiction, 78
 use of force, 87–9
India, 13, 159, 183, 187, 197
indigenous peoples, 297, 299–300
individualism, 37, 82, 172, 225, 232, 243
intellectual property rights, 79, 82, 283, 293–4
interdependence, 13–14, 15, 166
International Chamber of Commerce, 80
International Court of Justice, 66, 88
International Covenant on Civil and Political Rights, 160, 238, 296
International Covenant on Economic, Social and Cultural Rights, 83, 160, 298
international economic law
 See also trade
 arbitration, 80–1
 commercial jurisdiction, 75
 developments, 78–81
 foreign investment, 78–9
 lex mercatoria, 80–1
 monetary law, 79–80, 170, 181
 nation-state and, 177
 reform, 178–80
international financial institutions, 62, 83–4, 177, 184, 258, 267
international humanitarian law, 88
International Labour Organisation, 282, 297–8, 298, 299–300

international law
 agenda shaping, 187–98
 alternative text, 53–7
 capitalism and, 4
 commodity-form theory, 19–20, 105–20, 131, 148
 contemporary character, 60–5
 crisis, 30–1, 50
 critical Marxist course, 18–19, 53–91
 deconstruction, 40–2
 domestic laws and, 73–4
 dualism, 73, 74
 environment, 81–2
 epistemology, 53
 exploitation and, 26–7, 293–305
 history, 209
 human rights, 82–4
 imperialism and, 61, 120–6, 131, 205–10
 indeterminacy, 19, 38–47, 56–7, 94–5
 legal form, 97–8
 liberal project, 209
 mainstream scholarship, 53–5, 133–4
 Marxism and, 16–27
 Marxist-Leninist theory, 135–7
 Marxist lessons, 17–18, 30–52
 monist view, 73–4
 outsiders, 57
 overarching authority, 114–15
 phases, 60n24
 reification, 6
 rule of law. *See* rule of law
 self-determination, 161–2
 sources, 65–73, 136
 Soviet contradictions, 20–1, 133–68
 state-civil society dichotomy, 39–40
 subaltern classes and, 19, 53–91
 totality concept, 15
 transnational law and, 199–201
International Law Commission, 84–6
International Monetary Fund, 83, 84, 177, 178, 179, 184, 185, 258, 267
international relations, 42–4, 181–7
investment, foreign investment, 62, 78–9, 213
Iran, 189, 194
Iraq War, 18, 30, 49–52, 88, 166–7, 189, 194
Ireland, 143
Israel, 167
Israeli-Palestinian conflict, 193–4
Italy, city states, 43

Jackson, Robert, 123n144
Jamaica, 239
Jameson, Frederic, 2, 14
Japan, 180, 181, 182, 183, 187, 193, 197, 198
Jessop, Bob, 111–12
Jessup, Philip, 201

Jewish Bund, 138–9
Johnston, Douglas M., 68
Jones, Branwen, 276
jurisdiction
  commercial jurisdiction, 75
  geographical extension, 75–6
  justice jurisdiction, 77–8
  multilateral extraterritoriality, 77
  states, 74–8
  territorial, 74–5
  unilateral extraterritorial jurisdiction, 76–7
  universal jurisdiction, 78
jus cogens, 41
jus gentium, 206
justice
  consent and, 45
  distributive justice, 72–3, 128
  global justice, 279
  impossibility of international justice, 256
  Iraq War and, 50–2
  justice jurisdiction, 77–8
  liberal society, 41
  Marx and, 31
  private justice, 75, 80–1
  social justice, 281
  subaltern classes, 53

Kanet, Roger, 163
Kant, Immanuel, 27, 31, 35
Kautsky, Karl, 138, 139, 190, 194, 196
Kelsey, Jane, 213, 217
Kendall, Wilmoore, 250
Kennedy, John F., 165
Kenya, 167
Keynes, John Maynard, 170
Khorezm, 145
Khrushchev, Nikita, 165
Kissinger, Henry, 195
Klein, Naomi, 288
Klein, Pierre, 67n41
Korean War, 181
Korovin, E.A., 66, 133, 147, 153, 155
Koskenniemi, Martti, 17–18, 30–52, 93, 94, 95, 96, 101, 125, 126, 133, 170–1, 173, 205n17, 252
Krisch, Nico, 76
Krygier, Martin, 222, 223, 224n11, 229
Kubalkova, Vendulka, 190
Kymlicka, Will, 232, 242n58

labour
  See also exploitation
  child labour, 26, 282, 301
  contemporary conditions, 287–91
  ILO Conventions, 297–8
  Maritime Labour Convention, 298
  mobility, 171, 213, 288
  power, 301
  theory of value, 180, 285, 289
  working conditions, 287, 298, 299
Lachs, Manfred, 130
Laclau, Ernesto, 45
Laski, Harold, 87, 89
Latvia, 136n19, 145, 156
law
  as ideology, 102–4, 103–4
  capitalism and, 187
  club law, 117
  coercion, 112–18, 126–7, 169–70
  commodity-form theory, 19–21, 105–20, 131, 148–51
  dialectical nature, 24
  equality, 20, 61, 109, 117, 121, 123n144, 127, 148–9, 211
  general Marxist theory, 105–10
  legal form, 97–8
  legal positivism. *See* positivism
  Pashukanis theory, 105–20, 126–8, 146–58
  pluralism, 200
  praxis concept of law, 202, 215–19
  self-help, 115–18
  sociological theory, 104–5
League of Nations, 155, 156, 160, 196
Lenin, V. I., 11–12, 47, 118–19, 126, 137–45, 156, 157, 158–9, 186, 194, 197, 222–3, 229, 230, 243, 276
lex mercatoria, 80–1
liberalism
  egalitarian liberalism, 232, 234
  individualism and, 232
  international law and, 209
  liberal cosmopolitanism, 128
  liberal humanism, 35–8
  Marxist critique, 96–7, 223–5
  modernity, 34
  neutralist ethos, 245–6
  normalising existing order, 251
  trade, 203
  universalism, 30–1
Liberia, 189
Lithuania, 141, 145, 156
Locke, John, 208–9
Lockley, Joseph, 120–1
Loomis, Charles, 270
Lowe, Vaughan, 70n55
Lukács, Georg, 2, 6, 14
Lukes, Steven, 24
Luxemburg, Rosa, 10–11, 13, 47, 142, 175, 186, 228, 229, 240, 271

INDEX

McBride, Sean, 173
McDougal, Myres, 94
Mackinder, Halford, 194
McLean, Janet, 207
Malaysia, 77, 167
Malik, Charles Habib, 159
Malthus, Thomas, 1
Mamdani, Mahmood, 281, 306
managerialism, 92–3
Marcuse, Herbert, 219
Maritime Labour Convention, 298
market economy, 170, 184
market ideology, 218
Marks, Susan, 26–7, 103, 244n61, 281–307
Marx, Karl
   See also Marxism; specific Marxist concepts
   1843, 32–3, 34
   colonialism and, 276
   critical project, 32–3
   equality and force, 20, 61, 117, 121
   Factory Acts, 130–1
   on history, 199, 215, 271
   influences, 1
   Ireland, 143
   rights of man, 149
   winner of BBC competitions, 27, 28
Marxism
   See also specific Marxist concepts
   alternative Marxisms, 100–1
   Baxi and, 252–4, 260–80
   Bolsheviks v Austro-Marxism, 137–40
   depoliticisation, 27–9
   eclecticism, 253
   human rights and, 24–5, 232–51
   international law critique, 53–91
   international law lessons, 17–18, 30–52
   legacy, 2–16
   Marxist-Leninist theory of international law, 135–7
   necessity of Marxist theory, 92–8
   official theories, 99, 151–5
   post-structuralism and, 169–78
   re-examination, 16–27
   rule of law and, 129–32, 148, 222–32, 234–8, 277–8
   specificity, 98
   survival, 1–2
masking of capitalism, 303–5
massification, 271, 272
materialism
   historical materialism, 2–4, 57, 97, 201–2, 216, 262–4
   Marxist legacy, 2–4, 98, 104
   Pashukanis, 146, 167
M'Baye, Keba, 260
mentalism, 191

mercantilism, 109–10
Mickelson, Karen, 81
Miéville, China, 19–21, 24, 92–132, 134, 148–51, 157–8, 166–7, 205, 255–6
MIGA, 78
migration, 197
Migration Convention, 297–8
Mill, John Stuart, 221n2
Miller, Lyn, 123–4
migrant workers, 297–8
mobility, 171, 213, 288
Molotov-Ribbentrop Pact (1939), 155
monetarism, 79–80, 170
monism, 73–4
Monsanto, 268
Montevideo Convention on Rights and Duties of States, 57
More, Thomas, 208n34
Morsink, Johannes, 158–9
Mozambique, 163, 167
Müllerson, Rein, 135
Munck, Ronaldo, 271
Muravchik, Joshua, 252
Mutua, Makau, 257
mutuality, 27, 302–5
myths, 51, 95

national interest, 56, 67
national liberation movements, 134, 137, 158, 162–3
nationality, definition, 139, 140
NATO, 88
natural rights, 221n2
Negri, Antonio, 22–3, 169, 171, 174–8, 181, 192
neo-colonialism, 124–6
neo-Keynesianism, 184
neo-liberalism, 80, 83, 84, 170, 197
Nepal, 85
Nesiah, Vasuki, 259
Netherlands, 143, 180, 182, 183, 188, 208
Neufeld, Mark, 271
New Approaches to International Law, 90
New Haven School, 54–5, 56
New International Economic Order, 125, 167–8
New Stream, 92–3, 95, 98, 103, 148
Newton, Isaac, 27
NGOs, 63, 270–5
Nicaragua, 88, 239
Nicolaidis, Kalypso, 214–15, 218n75
Nixon, Richard, 176
non-state actors, 60, 63
North Korea, 189
nuclear threat, 172
Nussbaum, Martha, 232, 245–6

OECD, Multilateral Agreement on Investment, 212–13
Okafor, Obiora, 25–6
opinio juris, 72
Orford, Anne, 102
Ottoman Empire, 143, 156, 158
outsiders, 57
outsourcing, 288

Pakistan, 159
Palermo Protocol, 295
Palestine Liberation Organisation, 162
Palestinian-Israeli conflict, 193–4
Pan African Congress, 162
Panama, 121n132
Pashukanis, E. B., 20–1, 98, 134
   bourgeois state and international law, 58
   commodity-from theory of law, 103–10
   death, 146, 152
   definition of treaty, 66, 133
   'lawness' of international law, 114–15
   legacy, 152
   limitations, 149–51
   materialism, 167
   official trajectory, 151–5
   self-determination and, 156–8
   on Soviet international law, 164
   state derivation, 110–3
   superordinate authority, 114–15
   theory of law, 103–20, 126–8, 131, 145–58
paternalism, 299
patriarchy, 290
peasantry, 226
pharmaceuticals, 294
Philippines, 143
Picciotto, Sol, 100
Plasseraud, Yves, 138
Plekhanov, Georgy, 104, 231n35
Poland, 141
Polany, Karl, 214
politicide, 173
Portugal, 122, 143, 163, 167, 205, 208
positivism, 21–2, 53–4, 104, 105, 134, 136, 146, 166, 187, 206, 215
post-Fordism, 287, 304
post-structuralism, 169–78, 191
postmodernism, 169, 200
Poulantzas, N., 58, 59
poverty, 233–4, 238, 244, 307
power
   biopolitical power, 171, 174
   customary international law and, 71
   democracy and, 242
   dictatorship of proletariat, 222, 226, 230–1
   equal rights and, 20, 61, 117, 121
   Foucault, 171, 173–4

GATS and, 215
human rights and, 238–9
international law and, 54, 56, 59–60, 61–2
interpretation of treaties, 69
labour power, 301
political economy of power, 118–20
politics, 126–7
rule of law and, 128, 129–30
treaties and coercion, 67, 69
universalising national laws, 76
praxis, concept of law, 202, 215–19
privatisations, 80, 212
progress narrative, 54
property theory, 208–9, 210, 224
prostitution, 294–7, 299
Proudhon, Joseph, 39n28
Prussia, 35, 227–8
Puerto Rico, 143, 167
Purvis, N., 93, 94, 95, 97
Putin, Vladimir, 197

Quaye, Christopher, 162

racism, 206, 258
Radek, Karl, 143
Rajagopal, Balakrishnan, 259
rational choice, 203
Rawls, John, 38n25, 232
Reagan, Ronald, 182, 185
realism, 43, 44, 215, 272
refugees, 296–7
reification, 6, 14, 28
Renner, Karl, 90, 138, 140
reprisals, 94
resistance movements, 60
Ricardo, David, 1, 7
Robespierre, Maximilien, 37
Roman law, 206
Romania, 136n19
Romulo, Carlos Po, 159
Roosevelt, Franklin, 181, 188, 191
Roth, Brad, 24–5, 220–51, 252, 261, 265, 277, 278
Rousseau, Jean-Jacques, 242, 243
rule of law
   advanced capitalism and, 190
   class interests and, 65
   international rule of law, 127–32, 148
   Marxism and, 129–32, 148, 222–32, 234–8, 277–8
   new cosmopolitanism, 127–9
   recognition of CEE countries and, 59
   Soviet theories, 135
Rupert, Mark, 202
Russia, 158, 193, 195, 197
   See also Soviet Union

Rwanda, 306
Rytina, Joan, 270

San Francisco Conference (1945), 158, 159
Santos, Boaventura de Sousa, 203–4, 205
Saussure, Ferdinand de, 191
Schmitt, Carl, 32, 237
Scobbie, Iain, 135, 137
Scott, Shirley, 103, 104
sea, law of, 75
seabed, 76
secularism, 33, 34, 35, 36, 41
self-consciousness, 271, 272
self-determination
  international law, 123, 127, 161–2
  Marxist contradictions, 47
  Pashukanis and, 156–8
  post-war drive, 124
  Soviet contradictions, 134, 166–7
  Soviet positivism and, 21–2, 133–68
  Soviet practice, 144–5
  Soviet principle, 137–43
  United Nations and, 158, 159, 160, 161–2
  Wilsonian concept, 143
Serge, Victor, 229
services, fetishising, 24, 210–15, 219
services, trade in, 78, 210–15, 217, 218, 219
Shaikh, Anwar, 286
Sharlet, Robert, 152
Shrimps dispute, 77
Sierra Leone, 189
Silva, Luiz Inácio da, 49
Silver, Beverly, 180, 182–3, 183, 188–9, 195, 196
Singapore, 183
slavery, 282, 286, 295, 298, 299, 303
Smith, Adam, 1, 7
Smith, Anthony D., 140
Smith, Hazel, 202
social breakdown, 172
social contract, 243
social exclusion, 306
social impact assessments, 69
social movements, 90, 174
soft law, 72–3
solidarity, 48
Sorel, Georges, 51
sources of international law, 65–73, 136
South Africa, 167
South African Truth and Reconciliation Commission, 281–2
South Korea, 186
sovereignty
  economic reform and, 178–80
  humanitarian interventions and, 128–9
  international law structure, 164, 188
  post-structural analysis, 175
  reconfiguration, 22–3
  reprisals and, 95
  sovereign equality, 61, 85, 136, 182, 188
  US hegemony and, 189
  value, 125
  Westphalian order, 43, 170, 182, 187, 188, 196
Soviet Union
  1st Five-Year Plan, 151
  anti-imperialism, 165–6
  bilateral treaties, 156
  Bolsheviks v Austro-Marxism, 137–40
  collapse of communism, 170
  Decree on Peace, 156
  empire, 144–5
  German invasion (1941), 155
  international law contradictions, 133–68
  invasion of Czechoslovakia, 137, 144, 164
  invasion of Hungary, 137, 164
  League of Nations membership, 155, 156
  national liberation movements and, 134, 137, 158, 162–3
  New Economic Policy, 150
  October Revolution, 229
  official Marxism, 99, 151–5
  Pashukanis theory of international law, 105–20, 126–8, 145–58
  perestroika, 166
  practice of self-determination, 144–5, 158–63, 167–8
  self-determination principle, 21–2, 134, 137–43, 166–7
  theory of international law, 133, 135–7
  United States and, 188
Spain, 125–6, 143, 205
Speed, R., 165
Springer, Rudolf, 141
Stalin, Joseph, 136n19, 137, 140–1, 151, 152, 155, 157, 159, 229
state derivation, 110–13
state responsibility, 68, 71, 84–6
state socialism, 27
states
  bourgeois state, 33–5, 37, 49, 58, 59, 82–3, 111–12
  civil society and, 37–40
  colonial state, 58, 61–2
  definition, 57–8
  human rights obligations, 306
  international law and, 57–60
  jurisdiction, 74–8
  market-states, 170, 184
  mercantilist consolidation, 109–10
  positivism, 187
  redistributive role, 267–8, 269

states (*cont.*)
  secular theology, 18, 32, 37–8
  sovereignty. *See* sovereignty
  totalitarian state, 37–8
  US empire and nation-states, 176, 177–8
Stiglitz, Joseph, 178–80, 181, 185
structural adjustment programmes, 83
structural constraints, 54, 56
structuralism, 191
structure, agency and, 174, 192
Stuchka, Piotr, 104, 146, 154
subaltern classes
  Baxi and, 26, 254, 255, 257, 258, 260, 261, 268
  international law and, 19, 53–91
  Marx and, 262, 265
sustainable development, 82
SWAPO, 162
sweatshops, 282
Switzerland, 85
Sypnowich, Christine, 152
Syria, 159, 189

Taiwan, 183
Taylor, Nicola, 265
terra nullius, 206
territory, nationality and, 139, 140–1
terrorism, 172–3, 197, 258
theology, political theology, 36–7, 43, 44, 47
Third World Approaches to International Law (TWAIL), 25–6, 253, 254, 257–60, 269–70, 278
Thompson, E.P., 64–5, 223, 235, 277–8
Thucydides, 43
Todd, Emmanuel, 183, 190, 191, 192–4, 195, 196, 197
Tordesillas Treaty (1494), 205
torture, 173
totality, 13–16, 98, 174
toxic waste dumping, 268
trade
  See also WTO
  18th century expansion, 109
  capital imperialism, 205–10
  environment and, 77
  historical materialism and, 201–2
  liberal theory, 203
  trade-related market-friendly rights, 26, 255, 264–70
  transnational v international, 199–201
trade unions, 298
trafficking, 26, 197, 282, 294–7, 299, 301–2
transfer of technology, 82
transnational capitalist class, 61–2, 64, 65, 75, 80, 81–2

transnational companies, 78–9, 82, 174, 176, 268
transnational crime, 295–6, 299, 301
transnational law, 199–201
treaties
  African tribes and, 206
  definitions, 66, 133–4
  implementation, 69–70
  negotiations, 62–3, 67–8
  social impact assessments, 69
  Soviet approach to, 136–7, 153, 155
TRIMS, 78
TRIPS, 78, 82, 294
Trotsky, Leon, 137, 146, 229, 231n35
Tunkin, G., 21, 99, 135–6, 159, 162–5, 167
Turkey, 145, 194

Udechuku, E., 124
Ukraine, 141, 145
Umozurike, U., 124–5
Unger, Roberto, 15n57, 32
Union Carbide, 82
United Kingdom
  19th century hegemony, 182
  capitalist imperialism, 208
  empire, 143, 167, 180, 183
  Marx and Victorian England, 287, 300
  post-war decline, 188, 196
  reprisals in Yemen, 94
  Spanish ex-colonies and, 126
  Tudor enclosures, 190
  United States and, 189, 196
  Victorian working conditions, 287, 300
United Nations
  Commission on Human Rights, 83–4
  Decolonisation Declaration (1960), 157
  Friendly Relations Declaration (1970), 88
  neo-liberalism, 84
  reprisals, 94–5
  self-determination, 158, 159, 160, 161–2
  use of force, 87, 88, 94
United States
  1970s economic decisions, 176–7
  Anti-Dumping Agreement and, 74
  Bhopal disaster and, 78
  capitalism and, 175–6
  choice of law, 76
  Cold War, 165
  confrontational strategy, 194–5
  Constitution, 175
  credit-led economy, 180–1, 183, 185, 186
  currency dominance, 185–6
  customary international law and, 73n65
  developing world and, 183–6
  economic dependence, 190–1, 194
  elite intentions, 194–5

hegemony, 167, 169, 174–6, 177, 182–3, 186, 194–5, 196
imperialism, 22–3, 50, 87–8, 143, 167
international human rights law and, 83
international law agenda, 187–98
labour stagnation, 171
Middle East policy, 193–4, 197
military power, 182–3
military protectorates, 189, 196
New Deal, 181, 196
Nicaragua and, 88
pan-Americanism, 121
Panama invasion, 121n132
project, 187–98
secularism, 36
unilateral extraterritorial jurisdiction, 76–7
unilateralism, 185, 193–4, 196
Vietnam War, 165–6
war economy, 181–3, 186
WTO disputes, 77
Universal Declaration on Human Rights, 159, 162, 266–7, 298
universalism, 7, 8, 16–17, 18, 25, 30, 35, 36, 47–9, 76, 82, 157
Unocal, 268
use of force, 65, 87–9
Utrecht, Peace of (1713), 43

Vattel, Emmerich de, 209
Venezuela, 239
Venice, 208
Vienna Convention on the Law of Treaties (1969), 66, 67, 68–9
Vietnam, 167, 184
Vietnam War, 165–6
Von Arx, Susan, 103–4
Vyshinksy, Andrey, 20, 99n27, 136–7, 154, 167

Waldron, Jeremy, 232
Walker, Geoffrey, 129n169
Warrington, Ronnie, 152
Washington consensus, 50

Weber, Max, 183, 290
Weeks, Kathi, 14, 15
Weeramantry, Christopher, 260
West, civilizing mission, 102
Williams, Patricia, 168
Williams, Raymond, 3, 4, 17
Wilson, Heather, 161
Wilson, Woodrow, 143, 188
Wittgenstein, Ludwig, 191, 192
Wolff, Robert, 264–5
women
 exploitation, 282, 297, 301
 trafficking, 282, 294–6, 299, 301–2
 violence against women, 299
 Women's Convention, 294–5
Wood, Ellen Meiksins, 207–10
World Bank, 35, 83, 84, 177, 184, 258, 267
world society, 94, 172
World Trade Organisation
 Anti-Dumping Agreement, 74
 class power, 62
 cosmopolitanism and, 35
 Doha Round, 79
 establishment, 79
 GATS, 78, 210–15, 217, 218, 219
 GATT, 79, 176, 177–8, 212–14
 multilateral extraterritorial jurisdiction, 77
 nation state and, 177
 national deference principle, 69, 74
 neo-liberalism, 83
 rule of law and, 65
 scope, 79, 200
 TRIMS, 78
 TRIPS, 78, 82, 294

Yemen, 94
Young, Iris Marion, 291
Yugoslavia, 189

Zhdanov, Andrei, 159
Zionism, 139
Žižek, Slavoj, 9–10, 29

For EU product safety concerns, contact us at Calle de José Abascal, 56–1°, 28003 Madrid, Spain or eugpsr@cambridge.org.

www.ingramcontent.com/pod-product-compliance
Ingram Content Group UK Ltd.
Pitfield, Milton Keynes, MK11 3LW, UK
UKHW011655080825
461487UK00024B/307